OECD Institutional Investors Statistics 2017

OECD

BETTER POLICIES FOR BETTER LIVES

This work is published under the responsibility of the Secretary-General of the OECD. The opinions expressed and arguments employed herein do not necessarily reflect the official views of OECD member countries.

This document, as well as any data and any map included herein, are without prejudice to the status of or sovereignty over any territory, to the delimitation of international frontiers and boundaries and to the name of any territory, city or area.

Please cite this publication as:
OECD (2017), *OECD Institutional Investors Statistics 2017*, OECD Publishing, Paris.
http://dx.doi.org/10.1787/instinv-2017-en

ISBN 978-92-64-28227-8 (print)

Annual: OECD Institutional Investors Statistics
ISSN 2225-2061 (print)
ISSN 2225-207X (online)

The statistical data for Israel are supplied by and under the responsibility of the relevant Israeli authorities. The use of such data by the OECD is without prejudice to the status of the Golan Heights, East Jerusalem and Israeli settlements in the West Bank under the terms of international law.

Corrigenda to OECD publications may be found on line at: *www.oecd.org/publishing/corrigenda*.

Table of contents

Conventional signs and abbreviations

Signs and abbreviations

.. Not available

. Decimal point

0 Nil or negligible

Concepts and definitions

Metadata (data):

http://stats.oecd.org/OECDStat_Metadata/ShowMetadata.ashx?Dataset=7IA_A_Q

Metadata (indicators):

http://stats.oecd.org/OECDStat_Metadata/ShowMetadata.ashx?Dataset=7II_INDIC

On-line database

OECD Institutional Investors Statistics (*http://dx.doi.org/10.1787/instinv-data-en*).

System of National Accounts

Commission of the European Communities, International Monetary Fund, Organisation for Economic Co-operation and Development, United Nations, World Bank, Brussels/Luxembourg, New York, Paris, Washington, DC., 1993, *System of National Accounts 1993*, *http://unstats.un.org/unsd/nationalaccount/docs/1993sna.pdf*.

European Commission, International Monetary Fund, Organisation for Economic Co-operation and Development, United Nations, World Bank, New York, 2009, *System of National Accounts 2008*, *http://unstats.un.org/unsd/nationalaccount/docs/SNA2008.pdf*.

Methodology

Annual data refer to Q4. Quarterly data are available in the database.

ISO currency abbreviations

Abbreviation	Country	Currency
AUD	Australia	dollar
EUR	Austria	euro
EUR	Belgium	euro
CAD	Canada	dollar
CLP	Chile	peso
CZK	Czech Republic	koruna
DKK	Denmark	krone
EUR	Estonia	euro
EUR	Finland	euro
EUR	France	euro
EUR	Germany	euro
EUR	Greece	euro
HUF	Hungary	forint
ISK	Iceland	krona
EUR	Ireland	euro
ILS	Israel	new shekel
EUR	Italy	euro
JPY	Japan	yen
KRW	Korea	won
EUR	Latvia	euro
EUR	Luxembourg	euro
MXN	Mexico	peso
EUR	Netherlands	euro
NOK	Norway	krone
PLN	Poland	zloty
EUR	Portugal	euro
EUR	Slovak Republic	euro
EUR	Slovenia	euro
EUR	Spain	euro
SEK	Sweden	krona
CHF	Switzerland	franc
TRY	Turkey	new lira
GBP	United Kingdom	pound
USD	United States	dollar
EUR	Lithuania	euro
RUB	Russian Federation	ruble

International comparisons

Table 1. Financial assets and liabilities of investment funds, as a percentage of GDP

Per cent

	2009	2010	2011	2012	2013	2014	2015	2016
Financial assets								
Austria	50.0	51.1	44.6	46.5	46.1	48.9	48.9	49.0
Belgium	27.7	26.3	22.0	22.5	26.7	31.2	36.1	35.6
Canada	54.6	57.9	56.3	62.0	71.6	80.3	89.2	97.8
Chile	..	..	..	..	..	20.2	22.6	25.0
Czech Republic	3.8	4.2	3.7	4.1	4.6	5.0	5.3	6.7
Denmark	..	..	..	86.5	97.0	105.6	102.0	105.7
Estonia	3.9	4.0	2.7	2.9	3.3	3.1	3.0	3.4
Finland	32.0	35.6	30.6	36.4	40.6	46.0	51.9	55.6
France	77.0	74.0	64.4	67.1	66.2	67.7	70.2	74.2
Germany	39.9	42.2	40.4	45.7	48.4	53.0	55.7	59.1
Greece	3.7	3.0	2.1	2.5	2.8	2.7	2.4	2.3
Hungary	11.5	13.8	11.0	11.5	14.7	16.5	16.3	15.8
Iceland	12.2	17.5	22.6	23.9	24.6	24.9	26.8	27.3
Ireland	..	..	..	..	..	..	..	..
Israel	16.3	17.9	15.2	17.1	21.9	23.7	19.7	17.5
Italy	14.1	13.1	10.4	10.2	11.9	15.0	17.4	18.1
Japan	19.2	19.7	18.4	20.7	26.2	29.4	32.7	34.0
Korea	28.3	26.0	21.5	23.0	23.5	25.7	27.2	29.7
Latvia	1.2	1.5	1.6	1.4	1.3	1.0	..	..
Luxembourg	5 434.6	6 011.7	5 470.1	6 009.6	6 276.5	6 767.1	7 348.0	7 568.7
Netherlands	..	..	..	..	..	..	..	..
Norway	..	..	..	..	..	..	..	..
Poland	..	..	..	..	..	..	..	..
Portugal	..	..	..	..	..	..	..	..
Slovak Republic	..	..	..	..	..	..	..	..
Slovenia	6.2	6.3	4.9	5.1	5.1	5.7	6.0	6.1
Spain	18.5	16.0	14.7	14.4	18.2	22.5	24.1	24.6
Sweden	46.5	50.9	44.9	51.5	62.9	76.6	76.2	81.8
Switzerland	..	..	..	..	..	..	..	..
United Kingdom	..	..	..	..	..	..	..	..
United States	85.8	89.3	86.1	94.4	105.8	108.2	103.0	106.3
Lithuania	0.5	0.6	0.5	0.5	0.7	0.8	0.9	1.3
Russian Federation	1.7	1.5	1.4	1.5	1.6	1.7	1.9	2.1
Financial liabilities								
Austria	50.2	51.5	45.0	47.1	46.7	49.5	49.7	50.0
Belgium	27.9	26.3	22.2	22.6	26.9	31.3	36.2	35.7
Canada	54.6	57.9	56.3	62.0	71.6	80.3	89.2	97.8
Chile	..	..	..	..	..	0.3	0.5	0.4
Czech Republic	3.9	4.2	4.2	5.5	6.1	6.8	7.3	8.2
Denmark	..	..	..	88.5	97.0	105.2	101.9	103.9
Estonia	4.0	4.0	2.7	2.9	3.2	2.9	3.0	3.5
Finland	31.9	35.6	30.4	36.5	40.7	45.8	52.0	55.7
France	78.1	75.2	65.9	68.9	68.2	70.1	73.0	76.7
Germany	43.6	45.8	43.9	49.2	51.9	56.4	59.1	62.6
Greece	3.9	3.7	2.8	3.3	3.6	3.8	3.5	3.4
Hungary	12.1	14.7	12.0	12.6	15.7	17.4	17.2	17.0
Iceland	12.2	17.5	22.8	24.0	24.7	24.9	26.8	27.4
Ireland	..	..	..	..	..	..	..	..
Israel	..	..	..	..	..	..	..	..
Italy	15.4	14.0	11.4	11.4	12.6	15.6	17.4	18.0
Japan	19.2	19.7	18.4	20.7	26.2	29.4	32.7	34.0
Korea	28.8	26.3	21.6	23.1	23.6	25.9	27.4	29.8
Latvia	1.3	1.6	1.7	1.5	1.2	1.0	..	..
Luxembourg	5 453.1	6 040.9	5 488.2	6 027.2	6 293.9	6 788.1	7 366.6	7 586.0
Netherlands	..	..	..	..	..	..	..	..
Norway	..	..	..	..	..	..	..	..
Poland	..	..	..	..	..	..	..	..
Portugal	..	..	..	..	..	..	..	..
Slovak Republic	..	..	..	..	..	..	..	..
Slovenia	6.2	6.3	4.9	5.1	5.1	5.7	6.0	6.1
Spain	19.2	16.7	15.2	14.9	18.8	22.7	24.3	24.8
Sweden	46.5	50.9	44.9	51.5	62.9	76.6	76.2	81.8
Switzerland	..	..	..	..	..	..	..	..
United Kingdom	..	..	..	..	..	..	..	..
United States	87.4	90.8	87.5	95.8	107.4	109.9	104.9	108.1
Lithuania	0.5	0.6	0.5	0.6	0.7	0.8	1.1	1.7
Russian Federation	2.5	2.4	2.3	2.4	2.9	3.1	3.2	3.3

Note: Detailed metadata at:

http://metalinks.oecd.org/instinv/20170920/843b (financial assets)
http://metalinks.oecd.org/instinv/20170920/7af4 (financial liabilities).
Information on data for Israel: http://oe.cd/israel-disclaimer.
Information on data for Luxembourg:
http://metalinks.oecd.org/instinv/20170920/b48b (financial assets)
http://metalinks.oecd.org/instinv/20170920/ba94 (financial liabilities).

Table 2. Financial assets and liabilities of insurance corporations, as a percentage of GDP

Per cent

	2009	2010	2011	2012	2013	2014	2015	2016
Financial assets								
Austria	35.2	35.4	33.7	35.7	35.3	36.3	35.4	34.5
Belgium	67.7	68.1	67.4	73.3	72.7	79.1	77.4	74.0
Canada	37.0	37.9	38.5	39.7	40.4	42.4	43.0	44.9
Chile	..	..	..	..	..	18.3	19.0	19.9
Czech Republic	11.5	11.6	11.5	11.2	11.6	12.1	11.8	11.1
Denmark	..	..	..	98.6	97.4	107.2	105.0	114.5
Estonia	5.7	6.8	5.6	5.6	5.2	5.1	5.3	5.9
Finland	26.5	28.4	26.7	29.2	30.1	33.2	34.3	34.2
France	90.8	94.8	91.0	99.5	103.2	111.7	112.6	120.6
Germany	57.5	57.8	56.5	59.4	60.9	63.7	62.7	63.4
Greece	6.0	6.5	6.7	7.7	8.5	8.7	8.9	8.7
Hungary	8.9	8.9	8.2	8.3	8.1	8.1	7.9	7.9
Iceland	8.1	8.4	8.4	8.3	8.3	8.0	7.6	7.2
Ireland	..	134.3	125.0	125.2	120.8	124.7	98.9	99.6
Israel	30.9	32.4	31.2	33.1	34.5	35.9	36.1	36.5
Italy	33.9	32.0	30.7	32.6	36.0	40.7	45.7	48.5
Japan	76.4	76.9	78.5	82.3	87.3	89.6	87.8	89.8
Korea	44.4	46.2	49.1	55.5	58.4	62.8	64.8	67.9
Latvia	..	..	..	..	..	..	..	..
Luxembourg	273.7	301.2	283.1	303.7	306.4	325.5	336.1	341.9
Netherlands	61.5	64.6	67.3	70.3	66.8	73.5	69.5	69.7
Norway	38.7	39.6	38.9	40.0	42.2	45.3	48.4	51.6
Poland	10.4	10.3	9.5	10.3	10.3	10.6	10.4	9.9
Portugal	..	..	..	..	..	..	..	..
Slovak Republic	..	..	..	11.2	8.1	8.9	8.5	9.3
Slovenia	13.9	14.9	14.9	17.2	17.9	18.7	18.0	18.3
Spain	22.8	22.6	23.7	25.3	26.5	28.5	28.7	27.9
Sweden	29.6	29.7	27.9	29.9	31.0	33.8	32.7	32.6
Switzerland	80.4	80.4	82.7	87.1	83.8	86.7	85.8	..
United Kingdom	..	..	..	..	..	..	..	..
United States	44.7	46.4	46.9	47.5	47.5	48.0	45.8	46.6
Lithuania	3.7	3.1	2.8	3.2	2.7	2.7	2.9	3.1
Russian Federation	2.0	1.7	1.6	1.6	1.7	1.8	1.8	2.1
Financial liabilities								
Austria	36.9	37.8	35.9	36.4	36.2	35.9	34.5	33.1
Belgium	66.9	68.1	67.4	68.4	69.0	70.2	69.9	75.1
Canada	38.8	39.7	40.3	41.3	41.7	43.8	44.0	46.2
Chile	..	..	..	..	..	0.4	0.6	0.4
Czech Republic	11.2	12.0	12.0	12.7	13.0	12.7	11.8	11.5
Denmark	..	..	..	98.6	96.9	106.6	109.9	114.9
Estonia	5.5	6.1	5.4	5.4	4.9	5.0	5.3	5.9
Finland	26.1	26.9	25.2	27.4	28.9	31.3	32.1	33.1
France	90.4	94.1	91.5	93.7	97.1	100.9	102.6	122.3
Germany	59.1	58.5	56.2	59.1	61.1	61.8	63.6	63.7
Greece	6.6	6.9	7.2	8.1	9.0	9.2	9.5	8.8
Hungary	9.2	9.3	8.7	8.4	8.2	8.1	7.9	7.8
Iceland	8.2	8.5	8.5	8.6	8.7	8.3	7.7	7.2
Ireland	..	136.7	127.6	129.1	123.0	129.7	102.8	103.1
Israel	..	..	..	..	..	..	..	..
Italy	34.9	35.3	34.0	35.3	38.5	42.1	45.7	48.6
Japan	72.2	72.0	73.4	76.6	79.0	78.5	77.0	78.1
Korea	44.2	47.4	49.9	55.3	58.8	62.3	64.8	66.7
Latvia	..	..	..	..	..	..	..	..
Luxembourg	272.8	300.8	281.6	301.6	304.6	321.3	336.5	342.4
Netherlands	64.4	65.1	68.0	70.6	67.1	73.9	69.8	70.9
Norway	36.5	37.5	37.2	40.5	43.2	46.4	50.0	53.0
Poland	10.5	10.4	9.7	10.4	10.5	10.8	10.5	10.0
Portugal	..	..	..	..	..	..	..	..
Slovak Republic	..	..	..	8.0	7.7	8.2	8.6	9.0
Slovenia	14.7	15.1	15.0	16.7	17.3	18.2	17.9	18.0
Spain	22.5	22.7	24.2	25.6	27.4	29.5	28.2	28.1
Sweden	26.6	27.7	26.8	25.7	25.0	27.3	25.7	25.4
Switzerland	..	..	..	..	..	..	..	..
United Kingdom	..	..	..	..	..	..	..	..
United States	40.9	41.7	41.0	41.4	42.9	42.7	41.3	42.1
Lithuania	3.7	3.0	3.3	3.4	3.2	3.7	4.0	4.5
Russian Federation	2.1	1.9	1.7	1.6	1.9	2.1	2.0	2.3

Note: Detailed metadata at:

http://metalinks.oecd.org/instinv/20170920/4e07 (financial assets)
http://metalinks.oecd.org/instinv/20170920/8cb6 (financial liabilities).
Information on data for Israel: http://oe.cd/israel-disclaimer.
Information on data for Luxembourg:
http://metalinks.oecd.org/instinv/20170920/6041 (financial assets)
http://metalinks.oecd.org/instinv/20170920/6662 (financial liabilities).

Table 3. Financial assets and liabilities of pension funds, as a percentage of GDP

Per cent

	2009	2010	2011	2012	2013	2014	2015	2016
Financial assets								
Austria	4.8	5.1	4.8	5.2	5.5	5.8	5.9	6.2
Belgium	3.6	3.9	3.8	4.1	5.0	5.5	5.8	5.9
Canada	67.0	71.4	71.1	75.0	78.2	84.0	91.1	91.8
Chile	..	..	..	..	..	67.5	69.0	69.6
Czech Republic	5.4	5.7	6.1	7.3	7.8	7.7	8.1	7.9
Denmark	..	..	..	73.9	66.5	73.9	73.5	76.8
Estonia	7.2	7.9	7.3	8.7	9.9	11.8	13.5	15.4
Finland	2.0	2.3	2.0	1.8	1.5	1.4	1.4	1.7
France	..	..	..	..	..	..	..	..
Germany	13.4	13.7	13.8	15.6	14.8	16.6	17.1	18.2
Greece	..	..	..	..	0.1	0.2	0.2	0.7
Hungary	13.5	15.0	4.0	4.0	4.1	4.2	4.2	4.5
Iceland	115.5	122.2	127.1	136.5	142.0	145.4	147.2	143.8
Ireland	..	44.0	40.7	43.8	49.9	51.8	42.3	42.4
Israel	68.5	70.3	65.7	68.9	71.3	74.8	75.9	77.2
Italy	1.6	1.9	1.9	3.8	4.1	4.9	5.2	5.2
Japan	29.3	28.4	28.9	29.5	29.8	30.8	30.3	29.7
Korea	3.3	3.5	4.3	5.1	6.0	7.7	8.8	9.9
Latvia	6.1	7.5	7.0	7.6	8.4	9.8	10.9	12.6
Luxembourg	2.3	2.2	2.2	2.5	2.5	3.5	3.5	3.5
Netherlands	118.5	125.2	133.5	154.3	155.0	185.4	182.3	193.7
Norway	6.8	7.0	6.6	7.5	8.3	9.2	10.1	10.5
Poland	13.4	15.6	14.6	16.8	18.3	8.8	7.9	8.4
Portugal	..	..	..	..	..	..	..	..
Slovak Republic	..	..	..	4.9	10.5	10.2	10.0	10.2
Slovenia	4.7	5.4	5.5	5.8	5.9	6.2	6.4	6.3
Spain	9.6	9.8	9.7	10.4	10.8	11.5	11.7	12.0
Sweden	68.6	71.4	68.0	73.9	80.5	90.1	89.0	91.9
Switzerland	90.7	92.1	91.3	97.1	102.5	108.5	109.5	..
United Kingdom	..	..	..	..	..	..	..	..
United States	91.4	97.3	96.2	97.6	101.7	101.0	99.0	100.6
Lithuania	3.6	4.1	3.9	4.3	4.6	5.2	5.9	6.7
Russian Federation	1.8	1.8	2.0	2.3	2.8	2.8	3.5	4.0
Financial liabilities								
Austria	4.8	4.8	4.9	5.0	5.3	5.7	5.6	5.8
Belgium	3.9	4.2	4.0	4.6	5.1	5.7	5.9	5.9
Canada	67.0	71.4	71.1	75.0	78.2	84.0	91.1	91.8
Chile	..	..	..	..	..	0.7	0.8	0.7
Czech Republic	5.5	5.9	6.1	6.7	7.1	7.8	8.1	8.4
Denmark	..	..	..	71.6	64.7	71.7	71.3	75.8
Estonia	7.2	7.9	7.3	8.7	9.9	11.8	13.5	15.3
Finland	2.4	2.0	1.8	1.8	1.9	1.8	1.7	1.5
France	..	..	..	..	..	..	..	..
Germany	13.4	13.8	13.9	14.6	15.1	15.8	16.1	16.3
Greece	..	..	..	..	0.1	0.2	0.2	0.7
Hungary	13.4	14.9	4.0	4.2	4.2	4.3	4.3	4.5
Iceland	115.6	122.2	127.3	136.8	142.2	145.6	147.3	143.9
Ireland	..	44.4	41.0	43.9	48.6	51.7	42.2	42.3
Israel	..	..	..	..	..	..	..	..
Italy	3.2	3.5	3.7	4.3	4.8	5.3	5.4	5.7
Japan	29.5	28.6	29.2	29.7	29.6	30.6	30.0	29.4
Korea	3.3	3.5	4.2	5.1	6.1	7.8	8.7	9.9
Latvia	6.1	7.5	7.0	7.6	8.4	9.8	11.0	12.6
Luxembourg	2.3	2.2	2.2	2.5	2.5	3.5	3.5	3.5
Netherlands	112.3	120.0	137.7	153.4	147.1	173.0	176.8	188.4
Norway	7.9	8.1	7.6	7.8	8.5	9.2	10.1	10.7
Poland	13.4	15.6	14.6	16.8	18.3	8.8	7.9	8.4
Portugal	..	..	..	..	..	..	..	..
Slovak Republic	..	..	..	9.3	9.6	10.4	10.0	10.7
Slovenia	4.6	5.4	5.6	5.8	5.9	6.2	6.4	6.4
Spain	9.7	9.8	9.8	10.5	11.3	12.0	12.0	11.8
Sweden	64.7	68.3	71.0	71.9	75.4	84.8	85.4	88.3
Switzerland	101.5	100.6	101.6	104.9	107.5	110.2	112.4	..
United Kingdom	..	..	..	..	..	..	..	..
United States	92.4	98.2	97.1	98.6	102.8	102.1	99.9	101.5
Lithuania	3.6	4.1	3.9	4.3	4.6	5.2	5.9	6.7
Russian Federation	1.8	1.8	2.0	2.3	2.8	2.8	3.5	4.0

Note: Detailed metadata at:

http://metalinks.oecd.org/instinv/20170920/c6d6 (financial assets)
http://metalinks.oecd.org/instinv/20170920/2e8c (financial liabilities).
Information on data for Israel: http://oe.cd/israel-disclaimer.
Information on data for Luxembourg:
http://metalinks.oecd.org/instinv/20170920/7d30 (financial assets)
http://metalinks.oecd.org/instinv/20170920/8dae (financial liabilities).

OECD Institutional Investors Statistics 2017

Country tables

AUSTRIA

Table 1. Financial assets and liabilities of institutional investors, 2016

Million EUR (1999 ATS euro)

	Total	Investment funds			
		Non-money market funds			Money market funds
		Total	Open-end non-money market funds	Closed-end non-money market funds	Total
Financial assets	171 051	170 978	170 978	..	73
Currency and deposits	7 628	7 626	7 626	..	3
Debt securities	83 180	83 110	83 110	..	70
Debt securities, short term	339	338	338	..	0
Debt securities, long term	82 842	82 771	82 771	..	70
Debt securities issued by residents	13 276	13 276	13 276	..	0
Debt securities issued by non-residents	69 904	69 833	69 833	..	70
Loans	14	14	14	..	0
Loans, short-term	1	1	1	..	0
Loans, long-term	12	12	12	..	0
Loans granted to residents	0	0	0	..	0
Loans granted to non-residents	14	14	14	..	0
Equity and investment fund shares/units	80 221	80 221	80 221	..	0
Equity and investment fund shares issued/units by residents	29 954	29 954	29 954	..	0
Equity and investment fund shares/units issued by non residents	50 268	50 268	50 268	..	0
Other accounts receivable	0	0	0	..	0

	Total	Investment funds			
		Non-money market funds			Money market funds
		Total	Open-end non-money market funds	Closed-end non-money market funds	Total
Financial liabilities	174 762	174 688	174 688	..	73
Currency and deposits	0	0	0	..	0
Debt securities	0	0	0	..	0
Debt securities, short term	0	0	0	..	0
Debt securities, long term	0	0	0	..	0
Loans	474	474	474	..	0
Loans, short-term	99	99	99	..	0
Loans, long-term	375	375	375	..	0
Equity and investment fund shares/units	174 272	174 199	174 199	..	73
Insurance pension and standardised guaratees	0	0	0	..	0
Financial derivatives and employee stock options	16	16	16	..	0
Other accounts payable	0	0	0	..	0

	Total	Insurance corporations and pension funds			
		Insurance corporations			Pension funds
		Total	Life insurance corporations	Non-life insurance corporations	Total
Financial assets	141 951	120 399	..	..	21 552
Currency and deposits	4 066	3 165	..	..	901
Debt securities	56 117	55 710	..	..	407
Debt securities, short-term	11	10	..	..	1
Debt securities, long term	56 106	55 700	..	..	405
Debt securities issued by residents	17 917	17 745	..	..	172
Debt securities issued by non-residents	38 199	37 965	..	..	234
Loans	6 469	6 469	..	..	0
Loans, short-term	1 709	1 709	..	..	0
Loans, long-term	4 760	4 760	..	..	0
Loans granted to residents	5 110	5 110	..	..	0
Loans granted to non-residents	1 359	1 359	..	..	0
Equity and investment fund shares/units	69 066	48 852	..	..	20 214
Equity and investment fund shares/units issued by residents	56 584	38 976	..	..	17 608
Equity and investment fund shares/units issued by non residents	12 482	9 876	..	..	2 606
Other accounts receivable	1 575	1 544	..	..	30

	Total	Insurance corporations and pension funds			
		Insurance corporations			Pension funds
		Total	Life insurance corporations	Non-life insurance corporations	Total
Financial liabilities	135 858	115 568	..	..	20 289
Currency and deposits	0	0	..	..	0
Debt securities	3 662	3 662	..	..	0
Debt securities, short term	0	0	..	..	0
Debt securities, long term	3 662	3 662	..	..	0
Loans	3 219	3 206	..	..	13
Loans, short-term	1 962	1 951	..	..	11
Loans, long-term	1 257	1 255	..	..	2
Equity and investment fund shares/units	13 854	13 679	..	..	175
Insurance pension and standardised guaratees	113 748	93 647	..	..	20 101
Financial derivatives and employee stock options	0	0	..	..	0
Other accounts payable	1 376	1 376	..	..	0

Note: Detailed metadata at: http://metalinks.oecd.org/instinv/20170920/75e8

Table 2. Financial assets and liabilities of investment funds

Million EUR

	2009	2010	2011	2012	2013	2014	2015	2016
Investment funds								
Financial net worth	-409	-1 088	-1 274	-1 767	-2 036	-2 027	-2 778	-3 710
Financial assets	143 131	150 643	137 655	147 443	148 711	161 627	166 255	171 051
Currency and deposits	10 336	10 102	9 409	8 083	8 038	8 116	9 302	7 628
Debt securities	78 291	77 731	75 377	81 185	79 164	85 113	83 937	83 180
Loans	0	14	14	15	16	17	13	14
Equity and investment fund shares	54 431	62 576	52 660	57 950	61 455	68 350	72 955	80 221
Equity	16 878	20 168	16 402	19 207	21 330	22 904	23 589	25 587
Investment fund shares	37 553	42 408	36 258	38 744	40 126	45 446	49 365	54 634
Money market fund shares	912	680	1 035	123	135	313	304	309
Non-Money market fund shares	36 641	41 728	35 223	38 621	39 991	45 133	49 062	54 325
Insurance pension and standardised guarantees	0	0	0	0	0	0	0	0
Financial derivatives and employee stock options	73	221	193	209	38	32	49	8
Other accounts receivable	0	0	0	0	0	0	0	0
Financial liabilities	143 541	151 731	138 929	149 210	150 747	163 654	169 033	174 762
Debt securities	0	0	0	0	0	8	8	0
Short-term debt securities	0	0	0	0	0	0	0	0
Long-term debt securities	0	0	0	0	0	8	8	0
Loans	4 892	4 006	1 372	1 399	1 310	946	706	474
Short-term loans	4 625	3 782	1 153	1 210	1 124	786	622	99
Long-term loans	267	224	220	190	185	159	85	375
Equity and investment fund shares	138 649	147 701	137 509	147 805	149 435	162 677	168 314	174 272
Insurance pension and standardised guarantees	0	0	0	0	0	0	0	0
Financial derivatives and employee stock options	0	24	48	6	3	24	4	16
Other accounts payable	0	0	0	0	0	0	0	0
Non-financial assets	1 937	2 268	2 873	3 195	3 377	3 832	4 364	4 969
Money market funds								
Financial net worth	-272	-180	-98	-50	-28	-11	-5	0
Financial assets	2 613	2 400	1 196	400	188	145	80	73
Currency and deposits	0	0	0	0	0	0	8	3
Debt securities	2 526	2 330	1 179	397	188	145	72	70
Loans	0	0	0	0	0	0	0	0
Equity and investment fund shares	87	70	17	3	0	0	0	0
Equity	4	0	0	0	0	0	0	0
Investment fund shares	83	70	17	3	0	0	0	0
Money market fund shares	32	17	6	0	0	0	0	0
Non-Money market fund shares	50	53	11	3	0	0	0	0
Insurance pension and standardised guarantees	0	0	0	0	0	0	0	0
Financial derivatives and employee stock options	0	0	0	0	0	0	0	0
Other accounts receivable	0	0	0	0	0	0	0	0
Financial liabilities	2 885	2 581	1 294	450	216	156	85	73
Debt securities	0	0	0	0	0	0	0	0
Short-term debt securities	0	0	0	0	0	0	0	0
Long-term debt securities	0	0	0	0	0	0	0	0
Loans	0	0	0	0	0	0	0	0
Short-term loans	0	0	0	0	0	0	0	0
Long-term loans	0	0	0	0	0	0	0	0
Equity and investment fund shares	2 885	2 581	1 294	450	216	156	85	73
Insurance pension and standardised guarantees	0	0	0	0	0	0	0	0
Financial derivatives and employee stock options	0	0	0	0	0	0	0	0
Other accounts payable	0	0	0	0	0	0	0	0
Non-financial assets	..	..	..	..	..	..	..	..
Non-money market funds								
Financial net worth	-138	-908	-1 176	-1 717	-2 008	-2 016	-2 773	-3 710
Financial assets	140 518	148 243	136 459	147 043	148 522	161 481	166 175	170 978
Currency and deposits	10 336	10 102	9 409	8 083	8 038	8 116	9 294	7 626
Debt securities	75 765	75 401	74 199	80 788	78 976	84 968	83 865	83 110
Loans	0	14	14	15	16	17	13	14
Equity and investment fund shares	54 344	62 506	52 643	57 948	61 455	68 350	72 955	80 221
Equity	16 874	20 168	16 402	19 207	21 330	22 904	23 589	25 587
Investment fund shares	37 470	42 338	36 241	38 741	40 126	45 446	49 365	54 634
Money market fund shares	879	663	1 028	123	135	313	304	309
Non-Money market fund shares	36 591	41 675	35 213	38 618	39 991	45 133	49 062	54 325
Insurance pension and standardised guarantees	0	0	0	0	0	0	0	0
Financial derivatives and employee stock options	73	221	193	209	38	32	49	8
Other accounts receivable	0	0	0	0	0	0	0	0
Financial liabilities	140 656	149 150	137 635	148 760	150 531	163 498	168 948	174 688
Debt securities	0	0	0	0	0	8	8	0
Short-term debt securities	0	0	0	0	0	0	0	0
Long-term debt securities	0	0	0	0	0	8	8	0
Loans	4 892	4 006	1 372	1 399	1 310	946	706	474
Short-term loans	4 625	3 782	1 153	1 210	1 124	786	622	99
Long-term loans	267	224	220	190	185	159	85	375
Equity and investment fund shares	135 764	145 120	136 215	147 355	149 218	162 520	168 230	174 199
Insurance pension and standardised guarantees	0	0	0	0	0	0	0	0
Financial derivatives and employee stock options	0	24	48	6	3	24	4	16
Other accounts payable	0	0	0	0	0	0	0	0
Non-financial assets	..	..	..	..	..	..	..	..
Open-end non-money market funds								
Financial net worth	-138	-908	-1 176	-1 717	-2 008	-2 016	-2 773	-3 710
Financial assets	140 518	148 243	136 459	147 043	148 522	161 481	166 175	170 978

Table 2. Financial assets and liabilities of investment funds *(cont.)*

Million EUR

	2009	2010	2011	2012	2013	2014	2015	2016
Currency and deposits	10 336	10 102	9 409	8 083	8 038	8 116	9 294	7 626
Debt securities	75 765	75 401	74 199	80 788	78 976	84 968	83 865	83 110
Loans	0	14	14	15	16	17	13	14
Equity and investment fund shares	54 344	62 506	52 643	57 948	61 455	68 350	72 955	80 221
Equity	16 874	20 168	16 402	19 207	21 330	22 904	23 589	25 587
Investment fund shares	37 470	42 338	36 241	38 741	40 126	45 446	49 365	54 634
Money market fund shares	879	663	1 028	123	135	313	304	309
Non-Money market fund shares	36 591	41 675	35 213	38 618	39 991	45 133	49 062	54 325
Insurance pension and standardised guarantees	0	0	0	0	0	0	0	0
Financial derivatives and employee stock options	73	221	193	209	38	32	49	8
Other accounts receivable	0	0	0	0	0	0	0	0
Financial liabilities	140 656	149 150	137 635	148 760	150 531	163 498	168 948	174 688
Debt securities	0	0	0	0	0	8	8	0
Short-term debt securities	0	0	0	0	0	0	0	0
Long-term debt securities	0	0	0	0	0	8	8	0
Loans	4 892	4 006	1 372	1 399	1 310	946	706	474
Short-term loans	4 625	3 782	1 153	1 210	1 124	786	622	99
Long-term loans	267	224	220	190	185	159	85	375
Equity and investment fund shares	135 764	145 120	136 215	147 355	149 218	162 520	168 230	174 199
Insurance pension and standardised guarantees	0	0	0	0	0	0	0	0
Financial derivatives and employee stock options	0	24	48	6	3	24	4	16
Other accounts payable	0	0	0	0	0	0	0	0
Non-financial assets	1 937	2 268	2 873	3 195	3 377	3 832	4 364	4 969
Open-end investment funds								
Financial net worth	-410	-1 088	-1 274	-1 767	-2 036	-2 027	-2 778	-3 710
Financial assets	143 131	150 643	137 655	147 443	148 710	161 626	166 255	171 051
Currency and deposits	10 336	10 102	9 409	8 083	8 038	8 116	9 302	7 629
Debt securities	78 291	77 731	75 378	81 185	79 164	85 113	83 937	83 180
Loans	0	14	14	15	16	17	13	14
Equity and investment fund shares	54 431	62 576	52 660	57 951	61 455	68 350	72 955	80 221
Equity	16 878	20 168	16 402	19 207	21 330	22 904	23 589	25 587
Investment fund shares	37 553	42 408	36 258	38 744	40 126	45 446	49 365	54 634
Money market fund shares	911	680	1 034	123	135	313	304	309
Non-Money market fund shares	36 641	41 728	35 224	38 621	39 991	45 133	49 062	54 325
Insurance pension and standardised guarantees	0	0	0	0	0	0	0	0
Financial derivatives and employee stock options	73	221	193	209	38	32	49	8
Other accounts receivable	0	0	0	0	0	0	0	0
Financial liabilities	143 541	151 731	138 929	149 210	150 747	163 654	169 033	174 761
Debt securities	0	0	0	0	0	8	8	0
Short-term debt securities	0	0	0	0	0	0	0	0
Long-term debt securities	0	0	0	0	0	8	8	0
Loans	4 892	4 006	1 372	1 399	1 310	946	706	474
Short-term loans	4 625	3 782	1 153	1 210	1 124	786	622	99
Long-term loans	267	224	220	190	185	159	85	375
Equity and investment fund shares	138 649	147 701	137 509	147 805	149 434	162 676	168 315	174 272
Insurance pension and standardised guarantees	0	0	0	0	0	0	0	0
Financial derivatives and employee stock options	0	24	48	6	3	24	4	16
Other accounts payable	0	0	0	0	0	0	0	0
Non-financial assets	..	..	..	..	..	..	..	..

Note: Detailed metadata at: http://metalinks.oecd.org/instinv/20170920/75e8

AUSTRIA

Table 3. Financial assets and liabilities of insurance corporations and pension funds

Million EUR

	2009	2010	2011	2012	2013	2014	2015	2016
Insurance corporations and pension funds								
Financial net worth	-5 030	-6 206	-6 810	-2 004	-1 950	2 103	3 940	6 093
Financial assets	114 256	119 266	118 939	129 497	131 705	139 412	140 327	141 951
Currency and deposits	4 077	3 085	4 288	4 264	5 455	4 495	5 421	4 066
Debt securities	40 900	43 456	43 306	47 163	49 162	55 185	53 952	56 117
Loans	7 151	7 256	7 024	7 410	6 142	6 643	6 308	6 469
Equity and investment fund shares	52 939	57 477	56 363	62 213	63 129	65 669	67 456	69 066
Equity	15 185	15 120	14 720	14 695	14 885	14 514	14 953	14 616
Investment fund shares	37 754	42 358	41 642	47 518	48 243	51 155	52 503	54 450
Money market fund shares	250	269	165	76	44	105	240	133
Non-Money market fund shares	37 504	42 089	41 478	47 443	48 200	51 050	52 263	54 318
Insurance pension and standardised guarantees	7 497	6 353	6 610	6 997	6 283	5 683	5 535	4 658
Financial derivatives and employee stock options	39	70	66	48	13	30	24	0
Other accounts receivable	1 654	1 568	1 283	1 402	1 521	1 707	1 633	1 575
Financial liabilities	119 286	125 471	125 748	131 501	133 655	137 309	136 388	135 858
Debt securities	2 178	2 531	2 529	2 510	3 300	3 239	4 039	3 662
Short-term debt securities	0	0	0	0	0	0	0	0
Long-term debt securities	2 178	2 531	2 529	2 510	3 300	3 239	4 039	3 662
Loans	4 711	4 446	4 587	4 701	3 266	2 820	2 918	3 219
Short-term loans	4 312	3 469	3 381	3 688	2 374	1 988	1 809	1 962
Long-term loans	399	978	1 206	1 013	892	831	1 109	1 257
Equity and investment fund shares	14 963	16 306	14 373	16 125	17 645	16 426	14 935	13 854
Insurance pension and standardised guarantees	96 148	100 848	103 104	107 095	108 525	113 167	113 010	113 748
Financial derivatives and employee stock options	0	0	0	0	0	0	0	0
Other accounts payable	1 286	1 340	1 155	1 070	919	1 658	1 484	1 376
Non-financial assets	..	..	..	..	..	..	..	..
Insurance corporations								
Financial net worth	-4 931	-7 052	-6 621	-2 476	-2 625	1 493	3 126	4 830
Financial assets	100 602	104 246	104 124	113 085	114 005	120 089	120 403	120 399
Currency and deposits	3 538	2 663	3 644	3 689	4 205	3 885	4 866	3 165
Debt securities	40 516	43 005	42 854	46 787	48 707	54 735	53 516	55 710
Loans	7 151	7 256	7 024	7 379	6 098	6 643	6 299	6 469
Equity and investment fund shares	40 261	43 407	42 714	46 840	47 222	47 445	48 570	48 852
Equity	15 159	15 097	14 699	14 655	14 825	14 482	14 921	14 575
Investment fund shares	25 102	28 310	28 014	32 185	32 397	32 963	33 649	34 277
Money market fund shares	235	256	142	76	44	105	233	115
Non-Money market fund shares	24 867	28 054	27 872	32 109	32 353	32 858	33 416	34 162
Insurance pension and standardised guarantees	7 497	6 353	6 610	6 997	6 283	5 683	5 535	4 658
Financial derivatives and employee stock options	39	69	66	48	13	30	24	0
Other accounts receivable	1 601	1 492	1 213	1 345	1 476	1 668	1 593	1 544
Financial liabilities	105 533	111 297	110 744	115 561	116 630	118 596	117 276	115 568
Debt securities	2 167	2 520	2 518	2 499	3 289	3 239	4 039	3 662
Short-term debt securities	0	0	0	0	0	0	0	0
Long-term debt securities	2 167	2 520	2 518	2 499	3 289	3 239	4 039	3 662
Loans	4 711	4 446	4 587	4 701	3 266	2 811	2 910	3 206
Short-term loans	4 312	3 469	3 381	3 688	2 374	1 981	1 808	1 951
Long-term loans	399	978	1 206	1 013	892	830	1 102	1 255
Equity and investment fund shares	14 704	16 110	14 177	15 929	17 463	16 243	14 752	13 679
Insurance pension and standardised guarantees	82 665	86 881	88 308	91 362	91 693	94 645	94 091	93 647
Financial derivatives and employee stock options	0	0	0	0	0	0	0	0
Other accounts payable	1 286	1 340	1 155	1 070	919	1 658	1 484	1 376
Non-financial assets	3 725	3 689	3 735	3 792	3 983	4 199	4 260	4 401
Pension funds								
Financial net worth	-99	846	-189	472	675	610	813	1 263
Financial assets	13 654	15 020	14 815	16 412	17 700	19 323	19 924	21 552
Currency and deposits	539	422	644	575	1 250	610	555	901
Debt securities	384	451	452	375	455	450	435	407
Loans	0	0	0	31	44	0	9	0
Equity and investment fund shares	12 678	14 070	13 649	15 373	15 907	18 224	18 886	20 214
Equity	26	23	21	40	60	31	32	41
Investment fund shares	12 652	14 048	13 628	15 333	15 847	18 192	18 854	20 173
Money market fund shares	15	13	23	0	0	0	7	17
Non-Money market fund shares	12 637	14 035	13 605	15 333	15 847	18 192	18 847	20 156
Insurance pension and standardised guarantees	0	0	0	0	0	0	0	0
Financial derivatives and employee stock options	0	1	0	0	0	0	0	0
Other accounts receivable	53	76	70	58	44	39	40	30
Financial liabilities	13 753	14 174	15 004	15 941	17 025	18 713	19 111	20 289
Debt securities	11	11	11	11	11	0	0	0
Short-term debt securities	0	0	0	0	0	0	0	0
Long-term debt securities	11	11	11	11	11	0	0	0
Loans	0	0	0	0	0	8	9	13
Short-term loans	0	0	0	0	0	7	1	11
Long-term loans	0	0	0	0	0	1	7	2
Equity and investment fund shares	259	196	196	196	182	183	183	175
Insurance pension and standardised guarantees	13 483	13 967	14 796	15 733	16 831	18 521	18 920	20 101
Financial derivatives and employee stock options	0	0	0	0	0	0	0	0
Other accounts payable	0	0	0	0	0	0	0	0
Non-financial assets	..	..	..	..	..	..	..	..

Note: Detailed metadata at: http://metalinks.oecd.org/instinv/20170920/75e8

AUSTRIA

Table 4. Portfolio composition by type of investor

As percentage of financial assets and of financial liabilities

Per cent

	2009	2010	2011	2012	2013	2014	2015	2016
Investment funds								
Financial assets	100.0	100.0	100.0	100.0	100.0	100.0	100.0	100.0
Currency and deposits	7.2	6.7	6.8	5.5	5.4	5.0	5.6	4.5
Debt securities	54.7	51.6	54.8	55.1	53.2	52.7	50.5	48.6
Loans	0.0	0.0	0.0	0.0	0.0	0.0	0.0	0.0
Equity and investment fund shares	38.0	41.5	38.3	39.3	41.3	42.3	43.9	46.9
Insurance pension and standardised guarantee schemes	0.0	0.0	0.0	0.0	0.0	0.0	0.0	0.0
Financial derivatives and employee stock options	0.1	0.1	0.1	0.1	0.0	0.0	0.0	0.0
Other accounts receivable	0.0	0.0	0.0	0.0	0.0	0.0	0.0	0.0
Financial liabilities	100.0	100.0	100.0	100.0	100.0	100.0	100.0	100.0
Currency and deposits	0.0	0.0	0.0	0.0	0.0	0.0	0.0	0.0
Debt securities	0.0	0.0	0.0	0.0	0.0	0.0	0.0	0.0
Loans	3.4	2.6	1.0	0.9	0.9	0.6	0.4	0.3
Equity and investment fund shares	96.6	97.3	99.0	99.1	99.1	99.4	99.6	99.7
Insurance pension and standardised guarantee schemes	0.0	0.0	0.0	0.0	0.0	0.0	0.0	0.0
Financial derivatives and employee stock options	0.0	0.0	0.0	0.0	0.0	0.0	0.0	0.0
Other accounts receivable	0.0	0.0	0.0	0.0	0.0	0.0	0.0	0.0
Insurance corporations								
Financial assets	100.0	100.0	100.0	100.0	100.0	100.0	100.0	100.0
Currency and deposits	3.5	2.6	3.5	3.3	3.7	3.2	4.0	2.6
Debt securities	40.3	41.3	41.2	41.4	42.7	45.6	44.4	46.3
Loans	7.1	7.0	6.7	6.5	5.3	5.5	5.2	5.4
Equity and investment fund shares	40.0	41.6	41.0	41.4	41.4	39.5	40.3	40.6
Insurance pension and standardised guarantee schemes	7.5	6.1	6.3	6.2	5.5	4.7	4.6	3.9
Financial derivatives and employee stock options	0.0	0.1	0.1	0.0	0.0	0.0	0.0	0.0
Other accounts receivable	1.6	1.4	1.2	1.2	1.3	1.4	1.3	1.3
Financial liabilities	100.0	100.0	100.0	100.0	100.0	100.0	100.0	100.0
Currency and deposits	0.0	0.0	0.0	0.0	0.0	0.0	0.0	0.0
Debt securities	2.1	2.3	2.3	2.2	2.8	2.7	3.4	3.2
Loans	4.5	4.0	4.1	4.1	2.8	2.4	2.5	2.8
Equity and investment fund shares	13.9	14.5	12.8	13.8	15.0	13.7	12.6	11.8
Insurance pension and standardised guarantee schemes	78.3	78.1	79.7	79.1	78.6	79.8	80.2	81.0
Financial derivatives and employee stock options	0.0	0.0	0.0	0.0	0.0	0.0	0.0	0.0
Other accounts receivable	1.2	1.2	1.0	0.9	0.8	1.4	1.3	1.2
Pension funds								
Financial assets	100.0	100.0	100.0	100.0	100.0	100.0	100.0	100.0
Currency and deposits	3.9	2.8	4.3	3.5	7.1	3.2	2.8	4.2
Debt securities	2.8	3.0	3.1	2.3	2.6	2.3	2.2	1.9
Loans	0.0	0.0	0.0	0.2	0.2	0.0	0.0	0.0
Equity and investment fund shares	92.9	93.7	92.1	93.7	89.9	94.3	94.8	93.8
Insurance pension and standardised guarantee schemes	0.0	0.0	0.0	0.0	0.0	0.0	0.0	0.0
Financial derivatives and employee stock options	0.0	0.0	0.0	0.0	0.0	0.0	0.0	0.0
Other accounts receivable	0.4	0.5	0.5	0.4	0.2	0.2	0.2	0.1
Financial liabilities	100.0	100.0	100.0	100.0	100.0	100.0	100.0	100.0
Currency and deposits	0.0	0.0	0.0	0.0	0.0	0.0	0.0	0.0
Debt securities	0.1	0.1	0.1	0.1	0.1	0.0	0.0	0.0
Loans	0.0	0.0	0.0	0.0	0.0	0.0	0.0	0.1
Equity and investment fund shares	1.9	1.4	1.3	1.2	1.1	1.0	1.0	0.9
Insurance pension and standardised guarantee schemes	98.0	98.5	98.6	98.7	98.9	99.0	99.0	99.1
Financial derivatives and employee stock options	0.0	0.0	0.0	0.0	0.0	0.0	0.0	0.0
Other accounts receivable	0.0	0.0	0.0	0.0	0.0	0.0	0.0	0.0

Note: Detailed metadata at: http://metalinks.oecd.org/instinv/20170920/a49a

BELGIUM

Table 1. Financial assets and liabilities of institutional investors, 2016

Million EUR (1999 BEF euro)

	Total	Investment funds			
		Non-money market funds			Money market funds
		Total	Open-end non-money market funds	Closed-end non-money market funds	Total
Financial assets	150 138	148 165	148 165	..	1 974
Currency and deposits	6 092	5 863	5 863	..	229
Debt securities	31 036	29 291	29 291	..	1 745
Debt securities, short term	2 435	942	942	..	1 493
Debt securities, long term	28 600	28 349	28 349	..	251
Debt securities issued by residents	2 294	1 615	1 615	..	679
Debt securities issued by non-residents	28 741	27 676	27 676	..	1 065
Loans	0	0	0	..	0
Loans, short-term	0	0	0	..	0
Loans, long-term	0	0	0	..	0
Loans granted to residents	0	0	0	..	0
Loans granted to non-residents	0	0	0	..	0
Equity and investment fund shares/units	108 865	108 865	108 865	..	0
Equity and investment fund shares issued/units by residents	20 211	20 211	20 211	..	0
Equity and investment fund shares/units issued by non residents	88 653	88 653	88 653	..	0
Other accounts receivable	3 198	3 198	3 198	..	0

	Total	Investment funds			
		Non-money market funds			Money market funds
		Total	Open-end non-money market funds	Closed-end non-money market funds	Total
Financial liabilities	150 436	148 463	148 463	..	1 974
Currency and deposits	0	0	0	..	0
Debt securities	0	0	0	..	0
Debt securities, short term	0	0	0	..	0
Debt securities, long term	0	0	0	..	0
Loans	132	132	132	..	0
Loans, short-term	1	1	1	..	0
Loans, long-term	131	131	131	..	0
Equity and investment fund shares/units	147 040	145 099	145 099	..	1 940
Insurance pension and standardised guaratees	0	0	0	..	0
Financial derivatives and employee stock options	29	29	29	..	0
Other accounts payable	3 236	3 202	3 202	..	33

	Total	Insurance corporations and pension funds			
		Insurance corporations			Pension funds
		Total	Life insurance corporations	Non-life insurance corporations	Total
Financial assets	336 777	311 898	..	..	24 879
Currency and deposits	11 322	10 425	..	..	897
Debt securities	207 245	204 522	..	..	2 723
Debt securities, short-term	765	765	..	..	0
Debt securities, long term	206 480	203 758	..	..	2 723
Debt securities issued by residents	85 242	84 441	..	..	802
Debt securities issued by non-residents	122 003	120 082	..	..	1 921
Loans	27 866	27 696	..	..	170
Loans, short-term	5 322	5 322	..	..	0
Loans, long-term	22 544	22 373	..	..	170
Loans granted to residents	22 288	22 118	..	..	170
Loans granted to non-residents	5 578	5 578	..	..	0
Equity and investment fund shares/units	74 259	53 966	..	..	20 294
Equity and investment fund shares/units issued by residents	22 090	14 203	..	..	7 887
Equity and investment fund shares/units issued by non residents	52 169	39 763	..	..	12 406
Other accounts receivable	7 617	7 389	..	..	229

	Total	Insurance corporations and pension funds			
		Insurance corporations			Pension funds
		Total	Life insurance corporations	Non-life insurance corporations	Total
Financial liabilities	341 449	316 493	..	..	24 956
Currency and deposits	0	0	..	..	0
Debt securities	4 081	4 081	..	..	0
Debt securities, short term	0	0	..	..	0
Debt securities, long term	4 081	4 081	..	..	0
Loans	13 448	13 448	..	..	0
Loans, short-term	5 460	5 460	..	..	0
Loans, long-term	7 988	7 988	..	..	0
Equity and investment fund shares/units	29 054	29 054	..	..	0
Insurance pension and standardised guarantees	288 122	263 166	..	..	24 956
Financial derivatives and employee stock options	1 072	1 072	..	..	0
Other accounts payable	5 672	5 672	..	..	0

Note: Detailed metadata at: http://metalinks.oecd.org/instinv/20170920/75e8

BELGIUM

Table 2. Financial assets and liabilities of investment funds

Million EUR

	2009	2010	2011	2012	2013	2014	2015	2016
Investment funds								
Financial net worth	-814	33	-604	-575	-646	-343	-298	-298
Financial assets	96 446	96 163	83 424	87 177	104 752	124 934	148 177	150 138
Currency and deposits	15 562	11 621	9 936	7 804	6 786	6 665	9 153	6 092
Debt securities	32 445	31 617	30 112	25 492	25 873	28 318	40 030	31 036
Loans	0	0	0	0	0	0	0	0
Equity and investment fund shares	42 488	47 438	38 711	49 400	67 552	84 484	94 423	108 865
Equity	28 236	28 772	20 412	28 073	34 533	41 579	39 006	49 665
Investment fund shares	14 252	18 666	18 299	21 327	33 020	42 905	55 416	59 200
Money market fund shares	682	504	789	312	284	714	10 717	3 213
Non-Money market fund shares	13 570	18 162	17 510	21 015	32 735	42 191	44 699	55 987
Insurance pension and standardised guarantees	0	0	0	0	0	0	0	0
Financial derivatives and employee stock options	2 399	2 247	1 914	2 057	1 678	1 614	1 059	949
Other accounts receivable	3 551	3 240	2 751	2 424	2 863	3 854	3 512	3 198
Financial liabilities	97 260	96 129	84 028	87 752	105 398	125 277	148 475	150 436
Debt securities	0	0	0	0	0	0	0	0
Short-term debt securities	0	0	0	0	0	0	0	0
Long-term debt securities	0	0	0	0	0	0	0	0
Loans	93	90	78	90	89	150	181	132
Short-term loans	0	0	0	0	0	2	3	1
Long-term loans	93	90	78	90	89	149	178	131
Equity and investment fund shares	94 867	94 258	82 483	86 345	103 240	122 673	145 672	147 040
Insurance pension and standardised guarantees	0	0	0	0	0	0	0	0
Financial derivatives and employee stock options	0	13	53	0	4	14	12	29
Other accounts payable	2 300	1 768	1 415	1 317	2 065	2 440	2 611	3 236
Non-financial assets	..	..	..	..	..	..	..	..
Money market funds								
Financial net worth	0	0	0	0	-22	0	0	0
Financial assets	1 945	1 917	4 373	996	994	800	12 273	1 974
Currency and deposits	287	250	535	147	142	147	2 025	229
Debt securities	1 593	1 627	3 755	829	847	650	10 216	1 745
Loans	0	0	0	0	0	0	0	0
Equity and investment fund shares	29	21	0	5	0	0	0	0
Equity	0	0	0	0	0	0	0	0
Investment fund shares	29	21	0	5	0	0	0	0
Money market fund shares	2	9	0	2	0	0	0	0
Non-Money market fund shares	27	12	0	3	0	0	0	0
Insurance pension and standardised guarantees	0	0	0	0	0	0	0	0
Financial derivatives and employee stock options	0	0	0	0	0	0	0	0
Other accounts receivable	36	19	83	14	5	3	33	0
Financial liabilities	1 945	1 917	4 373	996	1 016	800	12 273	1 974
Debt securities	0	0	0	0	0	0	0	0
Short-term debt securities	0	0	0	0	0	0	0	0
Long-term debt securities	0	0	0	0	0	0	0	0
Loans	0	14	0	0	1	19	0	0
Short-term loans	0	0	0	0	0	0	0	0
Long-term loans	0	14	0	0	1	19	0	0
Equity and investment fund shares	1 926	1 902	4 366	991	1 012	780	12 255	1 940
Insurance pension and standardised guarantees	0	0	0	0	0	0	0	0
Financial derivatives and employee stock options	0	0	0	0	2	0	0	0
Other accounts payable	19	2	6	5	1	0	19	33
Non-financial assets	..	..	..	..	..	..	..	..
Non-money market funds								
Financial net worth	-814	33	-604	-575	-624	-343	-298	-298
Financial assets	94 501	94 245	79 052	86 181	103 759	124 134	135 904	148 165
Currency and deposits	15 275	11 371	9 402	7 656	6 644	6 517	7 129	5 863
Debt securities	30 852	29 990	26 356	24 662	25 026	27 668	29 814	29 291
Loans	0	0	0	0	0	0	0	0
Equity and investment fund shares	42 459	47 417	38 711	49 395	67 552	84 484	94 423	108 865
Equity	28 236	28 772	20 412	28 073	34 533	41 579	39 006	49 665
Investment fund shares	14 222	18 645	18 299	21 322	33 020	42 905	55 416	59 200
Money market fund shares	679	495	789	310	284	714	10 717	3 213
Non-Money market fund shares	13 543	18 150	17 510	21 012	32 735	42 191	44 699	55 987
Insurance pension and standardised guarantees	0	0	0	0	0	0	0	0
Financial derivatives and employee stock options	2 399	2 247	1 914	2 057	1 678	1 614	1 059	949
Other accounts receivable	3 516	3 221	2 669	2 410	2 858	3 851	3 479	3 198
Financial liabilities	95 315	94 212	79 656	86 756	104 382	124 477	136 202	148 463
Debt securities	0	0	0	0	0	0	0	0
Short-term debt securities	0	0	0	0	0	0	0	0
Long-term debt securities	0	0	0	0	0	0	0	0
Loans	93	76	78	90	88	131	181	132
Short-term loans	0	0	0	0	0	2	3	1
Long-term loans	93	76	78	90	88	129	178	131
Equity and investment fund shares	92 940	92 357	78 118	85 354	102 228	121 893	133 417	145 099
Insurance pension and standardised guarantees	0	0	0	0	0	0	0	0
Financial derivatives and employee stock options	0	13	52	0	2	14	12	29
Other accounts payable	2 281	1 767	1 409	1 312	2 064	2 440	2 592	3 202
Non-financial assets	..	..	..	..	..	..	..	..
Open-end non-money market funds								
Financial net worth	-814	33	-604	-575	-624	-343	-298	-298
Financial assets	94 501	94 245	79 052	86 181	103 759	124 134	135 904	148 165

BELGIUM

Table 2. Financial assets and liabilities of investment funds *(cont.)*

Million EUR

	2009	2010	2011	2012	2013	2014	2015	2016
Currency and deposits	15 275	11 371	9 402	7 656	6 644	6 517	7 129	5 863
Debt securities	30 852	29 990	26 356	24 662	25 026	27 668	29 814	29 291
Loans	0	0	0	0	0	0	0	0
Equity and investment fund shares	42 459	47 417	38 711	49 395	67 552	84 484	94 423	108 865
Equity	28 236	28 772	20 412	28 073	34 533	41 579	39 006	49 665
Investment fund shares	14 222	18 645	18 299	21 322	33 020	42 905	55 416	59 200
Money market fund shares	679	495	789	310	284	714	10 717	3 213
Non-Money market fund shares	13 543	18 150	17 510	21 012	32 735	42 191	44 699	55 987
Insurance pension and standardised guarantees	0	0	0	0	0	0	0	0
Financial derivatives and employee stock options	2 399	2 247	1 914	2 057	1 678	1 614	1 059	949
Other accounts receivable	3 516	3 221	2 669	2 410	2 858	3 851	3 479	3 198
Financial liabilities	95 315	94 212	79 656	86 756	104 382	124 477	136 202	148 463
Debt securities	0	0	0	0	0	0	0	0
Short-term debt securities	0	0	0	0	0	0	0	0
Long-term debt securities	0	0	0	0	0	0	0	0
Loans	93	76	78	90	88	131	181	132
Short-term loans	0	0	0	0	0	2	3	1
Long-term loans	93	76	78	90	88	129	178	131
Equity and investment fund shares	92 940	92 357	78 118	85 354	102 228	121 893	133 417	145 099
Insurance pension and standardised guarantees	0	0	0	0	0	0	0	0
Financial derivatives and employee stock options	0	13	52	0	2	14	12	29
Other accounts payable	2 281	1 767	1 409	1 312	2 064	2 440	2 592	3 202
Non-financial assets	..	..	..	..	..	..	..	..
Open-end investment funds								
Financial net worth	-814	33	-604	-575	-646	-343	-298	-298
Financial assets	96 446	96 163	83 424	87 177	104 752	124 934	148 177	150 138
Currency and deposits	15 562	11 621	9 936	7 804	6 786	6 665	9 153	6 092
Debt securities	32 445	31 617	30 112	25 492	25 873	28 318	40 030	31 036
Loans	0	0	0	0	0	0	0	0
Equity and investment fund shares	42 488	47 438	38 711	49 400	67 552	84 484	94 423	108 865
Equity	28 236	28 772	20 412	28 073	34 533	41 579	39 006	49 665
Investment fund shares	14 252	18 666	18 299	21 327	33 020	42 905	55 416	59 200
Money market fund shares	682	504	789	312	284	714	10 717	3 213
Non-Money market fund shares	13 570	18 162	17 510	21 015	32 735	42 191	44 699	55 987
Insurance pension and standardised guarantees	0	0	0	0	0	0	0	0
Financial derivatives and employee stock options	2 399	2 247	1 914	2 057	1 678	1 614	1 059	949
Other accounts receivable	3 551	3 240	2 751	2 424	2 863	3 854	3 512	3 198
Financial liabilities	97 260	96 129	84 028	87 752	105 398	125 277	148 475	150 436
Debt securities	0	0	0	0	0	0	0	0
Short-term debt securities	0	0	0	0	0	0	0	0
Long-term debt securities	0	0	0	0	0	0	0	0
Loans	93	90	78	90	89	150	181	132
Short-term loans	0	0	0	0	0	2	3	1
Long-term loans	93	90	78	90	89	149	178	131
Equity and investment fund shares	94 867	94 258	82 483	86 345	103 240	122 673	145 672	147 040
Insurance pension and standardised guarantees	0	0	0	0	0	0	0	0
Financial derivatives and employee stock options	0	13	53	0	4	14	12	29
Other accounts payable	2 300	1 768	1 415	1 317	2 065	2 440	2 611	3 236
Non-financial assets	..	..	..	..	..	..	..	..

Note: Detailed metadata at: http://metalinks.oecd.org/instinv/20170920/75e8

Table 3. Financial assets and liabilities of insurance corporations and pension funds

Million EUR

	2009	2010	2011	2012	2013	2014	2015	2016
Insurance corporations and pension funds								
Financial net worth	1 750	-1 026	-909	17 084	13 975	35 004	30 144	-4 672
Financial assets	248 806	262 677	269 800	299 788	304 391	339 351	341 074	336 777
Currency and deposits	9 573	8 505	11 191	9 569	8 658	9 899	10 067	11 322
Debt securities	161 973	174 908	182 196	203 027	196 077	217 785	210 821	207 245
Loans	12 755	13 185	13 665	18 025	22 092	26 035	27 974	27 866
Equity and investment fund shares	54 623	55 692	50 442	57 352	66 204	73 954	77 617	74 259
Equity	19 775	20 118	18 760	22 941	27 428	28 736	29 700	20 230
Investment fund shares	34 848	35 574	31 681	34 411	38 776	45 218	47 917	54 029
Money market fund shares	556	611	486	373	482	481	985	3 344
Non-Money market fund shares	34 292	34 963	31 195	34 038	38 295	44 737	46 931	50 685
Insurance pension and standardised guarantees	6 490	6 204	6 823	7 368	6 465	7 241	9 911	7 194
Financial derivatives and employee stock options	189	173	169	242	157	219	190	1 273
Other accounts receivable	3 204	4 011	5 313	4 206	4 738	4 218	4 496	7 617
Financial liabilities	247 057	263 703	270 708	282 705	290 416	304 347	310 930	341 449
Debt securities	2 352	1 971	2 156	2 290	2 551	2 649	3 997	4 081
Short-term debt securities	0	0	0	0	0	0	0	0
Long-term debt securities	2 352	1 971	2 156	2 290	2 551	2 649	3 997	4 081
Loans	11 952	12 645	15 109	13 499	14 418	14 708	17 292	13 448
Short-term loans	6 784	7 235	8 497	7 227	8 648	9 075	9 163	5 460
Long-term loans	5 168	5 410	6 612	6 272	5 770	5 632	8 129	7 988
Equity and investment fund shares	16 361	18 012	15 598	17 347	15 940	17 887	16 372	29 054
Insurance pension and standardised guarantees	211 367	226 555	232 833	244 380	251 603	263 263	267 082	288 122
Financial derivatives and employee stock options	0	0	0	0	0	0	0	1 072
Other accounts payable	5 025	4 520	5 012	5 188	5 904	5 840	6 188	5 672
Non-financial assets	3 426	3 400	3 571	3 776	3 522	3 666	3 636	77
Insurance corporations								
Financial net worth	2 637	71	74	18 901	14 439	35 821	30 773	-4 595
Financial assets	236 140	248 564	255 547	283 940	284 806	317 141	317 482	311 898
Currency and deposits	9 134	7 974	10 845	9 049	8 143	9 274	9 385	10 425
Debt securities	160 842	173 291	180 160	201 043	193 863	215 202	208 174	204 522
Loans	12 609	13 074	13 543	17 903	21 931	25 828	27 718	27 696
Equity and investment fund shares	43 755	43 910	38 950	44 189	50 397	56 010	58 387	53 966
Equity	18 698	18 835	17 373	21 463	25 567	27 160	27 362	17 469
Investment fund shares	25 057	25 075	21 577	22 726	24 829	28 851	31 026	36 496
Money market fund shares	235	235	190	206	233	217	618	2 962
Non-Money market fund shares	24 822	24 840	21 387	22 521	24 596	28 633	30 408	33 534
Insurance pension and standardised guarantees	6 490	6 204	6 823	7 368	6 047	6 646	9 365	6 628
Financial derivatives and employee stock options	189	173	169	242	157	219	190	1 273
Other accounts receivable	3 122	3 937	5 058	4 146	4 269	3 963	4 263	7 389
Financial liabilities	233 503	248 494	255 473	265 039	270 367	281 320	286 709	316 493
Debt securities	2 352	1 971	2 156	2 290	2 551	2 649	3 997	4 081
Short-term debt securities	0	0	0	0	0	0	0	0
Long-term debt securities	2 352	1 971	2 156	2 290	2 551	2 649	3 997	4 081
Loans	11 952	12 645	15 109	13 499	14 418	14 708	17 290	13 448
Short-term loans	6 784	7 235	8 497	7 227	8 648	9 075	9 160	5 460
Long-term loans	5 168	5 410	6 612	6 272	5 770	5 632	8 129	7 988
Equity and investment fund shares	16 361	18 012	15 598	17 347	15 940	17 887	16 372	29 054
Insurance pension and standardised guarantees	197 813	211 345	217 597	226 714	231 554	240 236	242 863	263 166
Financial derivatives and employee stock options	0	0	0	0	0	0	0	1 072
Other accounts payable	5 025	4 520	5 012	5 188	5 904	5 840	6 188	5 672
Non-financial assets	3 362	3 338	3 505	3 715	3 461	3 598	3 559	0
Pension funds								
Financial net worth	-887	-1 097	-983	-1 818	-464	-817	-629	-77
Financial assets	12 667	14 113	14 252	15 848	19 585	22 210	23 592	24 879
Currency and deposits	439	531	347	520	515	625	682	897
Debt securities	1 131	1 617	2 036	1 984	2 214	2 583	2 647	2 723
Loans	147	111	122	122	160	207	255	170
Equity and investment fund shares	10 868	11 782	11 432	13 163	15 808	17 944	19 229	20 294
Equity	1 077	1 283	1 337	1 478	1 861	1 577	2 338	2 761
Investment fund shares	9 792	10 499	10 105	11 685	13 947	16 367	16 891	17 533
Money market fund shares	321	376	296	167	249	263	368	381
Non-Money market fund shares	9 471	10 123	9 808	11 517	13 698	16 104	16 523	17 151
Insurance pension and standardised guarantees	0	0	0	0	419	595	545	566
Financial derivatives and employee stock options	0	0	0	0	0	0	0	0
Other accounts receivable	81	73	255	60	469	255	233	229
Financial liabilities	13 554	15 210	15 235	17 666	20 049	23 027	24 222	24 956
Debt securities	0	0	0	0	0	0	0	0
Short-term debt securities	0	0	0	0	0	0	0	0
Long-term debt securities	0	0	0	0	0	0	0	0
Loans	0	0	0	0	0	0	2	0
Short-term loans	0	0	0	0	0	0	2	0
Long-term loans	0	0	0	0	0	0	0	0
Equity and investment fund shares	0	0	0	0	0	0	0	0
Insurance pension and standardised guarantees	13 554	15 210	15 235	17 666	20 049	23 027	24 219	24 956
Financial derivatives and employee stock options	0	0	0	0	0	0	0	0
Other accounts payable	0	0	0	0	0	0	0	0
Non-financial assets	64	62	66	61	61	68	77	77

Note: Detailed metadata at: http://metalinks.oecd.org/instinv/20170920/75e8

Table 4. Portfolio composition by type of investor

As percentage of financial assets and of financial liabilities

Per cent

	2009	2010	2011	2012	2013	2014	2015	2016
Investment funds								
Financial assets	100.0	100.0	100.0	100.0	100.0	100.0	100.0	100.0
Currency and deposits	16.1	12.1	11.9	9.0	6.5	5.3	6.2	4.1
Debt securities	33.6	32.9	36.1	29.2	24.7	22.7	27.0	20.7
Loans	0.0	0.0	0.0	0.0	0.0	0.0	0.0	0.0
Equity and investment fund shares	44.1	49.3	46.4	56.7	64.5	67.6	63.7	72.5
Insurance pension and standardised guarantee schemes	0.0	0.0	0.0	0.0	0.0	0.0	0.0	0.0
Financial derivatives and employee stock options	2.5	2.3	2.3	2.4	1.6	1.3	0.7	0.6
Other accounts receivable	3.7	3.4	3.3	2.8	2.7	3.1	2.4	2.1
Financial liabilities	100.0	100.0	100.0	100.0	100.0	100.0	100.0	100.0
Currency and deposits	0.0	0.0	0.0	0.0	0.0	0.0	0.0	0.0
Debt securities	0.0	0.0	0.0	0.0	0.0	0.0	0.0	0.0
Loans	0.1	0.1	0.1	0.1	0.1	0.1	0.1	0.1
Equity and investment fund shares	97.5	98.1	98.2	98.4	98.0	97.9	98.1	97.7
Insurance pension and standardised guarantee schemes	0.0	0.0	0.0	0.0	0.0	0.0	0.0	0.0
Financial derivatives and employee stock options	0.0	0.0	0.1	0.0	0.0	0.0	0.0	0.0
Other accounts receivable	2.4	1.8	1.7	1.5	2.0	1.9	1.8	2.2
Insurance corporations								
Financial assets	100.0	100.0	100.0	100.0	100.0	100.0	100.0	100.0
Currency and deposits	3.9	3.2	4.2	3.2	2.9	2.9	3.0	3.3
Debt securities	68.1	69.7	70.5	70.8	68.1	67.9	65.6	65.6
Loans	5.3	5.3	5.3	6.3	7.7	8.1	8.7	8.9
Equity and investment fund shares	18.5	17.7	15.2	15.6	17.7	17.7	18.4	17.3
Insurance pension and standardised guarantee schemes	2.7	2.5	2.7	2.6	2.1	2.1	2.9	2.1
Financial derivatives and employee stock options	0.1	0.1	0.1	0.1	0.1	0.1	0.1	0.4
Other accounts receivable	1.3	1.6	2.0	1.5	1.5	1.2	1.3	2.4
Financial liabilities	100.0	100.0	100.0	100.0	100.0	100.0	100.0	100.0
Currency and deposits	0.0	0.0	0.0	0.0	0.0	0.0	0.0	0.0
Debt securities	1.0	0.8	0.8	0.9	0.9	0.9	1.4	1.3
Loans	5.1	5.1	5.9	5.1	5.3	5.2	6.0	4.2
Equity and investment fund shares	7.0	7.2	6.1	6.5	5.9	6.4	5.7	9.2
Insurance pension and standardised guarantee schemes	84.7	85.1	85.2	85.5	85.6	85.4	84.7	83.2
Financial derivatives and employee stock options	0.0	0.0	0.0	0.0	0.0	0.0	0.0	0.3
Other accounts receivable	2.2	1.8	2.0	2.0	2.2	2.1	2.2	1.8
Pension funds								
Financial assets	100.0	100.0	100.0	100.0	100.0	100.0	100.0	100.0
Currency and deposits	3.5	3.8	2.4	3.3	2.6	2.8	2.9	3.6
Debt securities	8.9	11.5	14.3	12.5	11.3	11.6	11.2	10.9
Loans	1.2	0.8	0.9	0.8	0.8	0.9	1.1	0.7
Equity and investment fund shares	85.8	83.5	80.6	83.1	80.7	80.8	81.5	81.6
Insurance pension and standardised guarantee schemes	0.0	0.0	0.0	0.0	2.1	2.7	2.3	2.3
Financial derivatives and employee stock options	0.0	0.0	0.0	0.0	0.0	0.0	0.0	0.0
Other accounts receivable	0.6	0.5	1.8	0.4	2.4	1.2	1.0	0.9
Financial liabilities	100.0	100.0	100.0	100.0	100.0	100.0	100.0	100.0
Currency and deposits	0.0	0.0	0.0	0.0	0.0	0.0	0.0	0.0
Debt securities	0.0	0.0	0.0	0.0	0.0	0.0	0.0	0.0
Loans	0.0	0.0	0.0	0.0	0.0	0.0	0.0	0.0
Equity and investment fund shares	0.0	0.0	0.0	0.0	0.0	0.0	0.0	0.0
Insurance pension and standardised guarantee schemes	100.0	100.0	100.0	100.0	100.0	100.0	100.0	100.0
Financial derivatives and employee stock options	0.0	0.0	0.0	0.0	0.0	0.0	0.0	0.0
Other accounts receivable	0.0	0.0	0.0	0.0	0.0	0.0	0.0	0.0

Note: Detailed metadata at: http://metalinks.oecd.org/instinv/20170920/a49a

CANADA

Table 1. Financial assets and liabilities of institutional investors, 2016

Million CAD

	Investment funds				
	Total	Non-money market funds			Money market funds
		Total	Open-end non-money market funds	Closed-end non-money market funds	Total
Financial assets	1 983 822	1 954 394	..	..	29 428
Currency and deposits	13 774	12 786	..	..	988
Debt securities	452 376	427 369	..	..	25 007
Debt securities, short term	43 595	24 365	..	..	19 230
Debt securities, long term	408 781	403 004	..	..	5 777
Debt securities issued by residents	337 262	313 061	..	..	24 201
Debt securities issued by non-residents	115 114	114 308	..	..	806
Loans	5 102	5 102	..	..	0
Loans, short-term	..	..	..	..	..
Loans, long-term	..	..	..	..	..
Loans granted to residents	..	..	..	..	..
Loans granted to non-residents	..	..	..	..	..
Equity and investment fund shares/units	1 344 784	1 344 451	..	..	333
Equity and investment fund shares issued/units by residents	890 730	890 397	..	..	333
Equity and investment fund shares/units issued by non residents	454 054	454 054	..	..	0
Other accounts receivable	167 786	164 686	..	..	3 100

	Investment funds				
	Total	Non-money market funds			Money market funds
		Total	Open-end non-money market funds	Closed-end non-money market funds	Total
Financial liabilities	1 983 822	1 954 394	..	..	29 428
Currency and deposits	..	..	..	..	..
Debt securities	..	..	..	..	..
Debt securities, short term	..	..	..	..	..
Debt securities, long term	..	..	..	..	..
Loans	0	0	..	..	0
Loans, short-term	..	..	..	..	..
Loans, long-term	..	..	..	..	..
Equity and investment fund shares/units	1 969 285	1 940 032	..	..	29 253
Insurance pension and standardised guaratees	..	..	..	..	..
Financial derivatives and employee stock options	..	..	..	..	..
Other accounts payable	14 537	14 362	..	..	175

	Insurance corporations and pension funds				
	Total	Insurance corporations			Pension funds
		Total	Life insurance corporations	Non-life insurance corporations	Total
Financial assets	2 771 314	910 115	753 778	156 337	1 861 199
Currency and deposits	44 228	8 832	4 817	4 015	35 396
Debt securities	1 049 360	392 056	297 851	94 205	657 304
Debt securities, short-term	57 698	16 298	14 686	1 612	41 400
Debt securities, long term	991 662	375 758	283 165	92 593	615 904
Debt securities issued by residents	940 577	374 241	282 304	91 937	566 336
Debt securities issued by non-residents	108 783	17 815	15 547	2 268	90 968
Loans	133 188	69 210	68 074	1 136	63 978
Loans, short-term	..	..	..	..	..
Loans, long-term	..	..	..	..	..
Loans granted to residents	..	..	..	..	..
Loans granted to non-residents	..	..	..	..	..
Equity and investment fund shares/units	1 263 363	342 510	315 547	26 963	920 853
Equity and investment fund shares/units issued by residents	792 686	320 773	296 590	24 183	471 913
Equity and investment fund shares/units issued by non residents	470 677	21 737	18 957	2 780	448 940
Other accounts receivable	145 380	97 507	67 489	30 018	47 873

	Insurance corporations and pension funds				
	Total	Insurance corporations			Pension funds
		Total	Life insurance corporations	Non-life insurance corporations	Total
Financial liabilities	2 797 610	936 411	759 708	176 703	1 861 199
Currency and deposits	..	..	..	..	..
Debt securities	12 084	12 084	12 084	..	..
Debt securities, short term	..	..	..	..	..
Debt securities, long term	12 084	12 084	12 084	..	..
Loans	18 472	15 921	13 639	2 282	2 551
Loans, short-term	..	..	..	..	..
Loans, long-term	..	..	..	..	..
Equity and investment fund shares/units	302 121	302 121	230 777	71 344	..
Insurance pension and standardised guarantees	2 183 024	468 093	468 093	..	1 714 931
Financial derivatives and employee stock options	..	..	..	..	..
Other accounts payable	281 909	138 192	35 115	103 077	143 717

Note: Detailed metadata at: http://metalinks.oecd.org/instinv/20170920/75e8

CANADA

Table 2. Financial assets and liabilities of investment funds

Million CAD

	2009	2010	2011	2012	2013	2014	2015	2016
Investment funds								
Financial net worth	0	0	0	0	0	0	0	0
Financial assets	855 592	962 804	997 350	1 130 261	1 358 462	1 591 784	1 772 508	1 983 822
Currency and deposits	6 080	4 565	7 286	10 025	9 646	10 906	10 387	13 774
Debt securities	243 973	260 333	301 290	337 161	355 880	406 477	425 610	452 376
Loans	4 622	5 380	5 407	5 275	5 114	5 553	5 045	5 102
Equity and investment fund shares	572 426	666 146	649 595	734 187	917 937	1 084 425	1 210 045	1 344 784
Equity	443 519	503 196	465 043	510 588	617 291	717 366	760 707	843 752
Investment fund shares	128 907	162 950	184 552	223 599	300 646	367 059	449 338	501 032
Money market fund shares	..	..	..	..	..	..	..	..
Non-Money market fund shares	..	..	..	..	..	..	..	..
Insurance pension and standardised guarantees	..	..	..	..	..	..	..	..
Financial derivatives and employee stock options	..	..	..	..	..	..	..	..
Other accounts receivable	28 491	26 380	33 772	43 613	69 885	84 423	121 421	167 786
Financial liabilities	855 592	962 804	997 350	1 130 261	1 358 462	1 591 784	1 772 508	1 983 822
Debt securities	..	..	..	..	..	..	..	..
Short-term debt securities	..	..	..	..	..	..	..	..
Long-term debt securities	..	..	..	..	..	..	..	..
Loans	0	0	0	0	0	0	0	0
Short-term loans	..	..	..	..	..	..	..	..
Long-term loans	..	..	..	..	..	..	..	..
Equity and investment fund shares	852 184	959 108	991 637	1 122 100	1 348 995	1 580 288	1 759 837	1 969 285
Insurance pension and standardised guarantees	..	..	..	..	..	..	..	..
Financial derivatives and employee stock options	..	..	..	..	..	..	..	..
Other accounts payable	3 408	3 696	5 713	8 161	9 467	11 496	12 671	14 537
Non-financial assets	0	0	0	0	0	0	0	0
Money market funds								
Financial net worth	0	0	0	0	0	0	0	0
Financial assets	61 423	42 242	39 590	33 331	30 532	27 936	29 494	29 428
Currency and deposits	1 223	617	842	189	197	186	372	988
Debt securities	59 442	40 529	37 855	31 799	29 768	26 688	28 081	25 007
Loans	0	0	0	0	0	0	0	0
Equity and investment fund shares	585	398	332	383	295	346	412	333
Equity	282	199	111	144	53	0	0	5
Investment fund shares	303	199	221	239	242	346	412	328
Money market fund shares	..	..	..	..	..	..	..	..
Non-Money market fund shares	..	..	..	..	..	..	..	..
Insurance pension and standardised guarantees	..	..	..	..	..	..	..	..
Financial derivatives and employee stock options	..	..	..	..	..	..	..	..
Other accounts receivable	173	698	561	960	272	716	629	3 100
Financial liabilities	61 423	42 242	39 590	33 331	30 532	27 936	29 494	29 428
Debt securities	..	..	..	..	..	..	..	..
Short-term debt securities	..	..	..	..	..	..	..	..
Long-term debt securities	..	..	..	..	..	..	..	..
Loans	0	0	0	0	0	0	0	0
Short-term loans	..	..	..	..	..	..	..	..
Long-term loans	..	..	..	..	..	..	..	..
Equity and investment fund shares	61 192	41 974	39 372	33 124	30 346	27 762	29 313	29 253
Insurance pension and standardised guarantees	..	..	..	..	..	..	..	..
Financial derivatives and employee stock options	..	..	..	..	..	..	..	..
Other accounts payable	231	268	218	207	186	174	181	175
Non-financial assets	0	0	0	0	0	0	0	0
Non-money market funds								
Financial net worth	0	0	0	0	0	0	0	0
Financial assets	794 169	920 562	957 760	1 096 930	1 327 930	1 563 848	1 743 014	1 954 394
Currency and deposits	4 857	3 948	6 444	9 836	9 449	10 720	10 015	12 786
Debt securities	184 531	219 804	263 435	305 362	326 112	379 789	397 529	427 369
Loans	4 622	5 380	5 407	5 275	5 114	5 553	5 045	5 102
Equity and investment fund shares	571 841	665 748	649 263	733 804	917 642	1 084 079	1 209 633	1 344 451
Equity	443 237	502 997	464 932	510 444	617 238	717 366	760 707	843 747
Investment fund shares	128 604	162 751	184 331	223 360	300 404	366 713	448 926	500 704
Money market fund shares	..	..	..	..	..	..	..	..
Non-Money market fund shares	..	..	..	..	..	..	..	..
Insurance pension and standardised guarantees	..	..	..	..	..	..	..	..
Financial derivatives and employee stock options	..	..	..	..	..	..	..	..
Other accounts receivable	28 318	25 682	33 211	42 653	69 613	83 707	120 792	164 686
Financial liabilities	794 169	920 562	957 760	1 096 930	1 327 930	1 563 848	1 743 014	1 954 394
Debt securities	..	..	..	..	..	..	..	..
Short-term debt securities	..	..	..	..	..	..	..	..
Long-term debt securities	..	..	..	..	..	..	..	..
Loans	0	0	0	0	0	0	0	0
Short-term loans	..	..	..	..	..	..	..	..
Long-term loans	..	..	..	..	..	..	..	..
Equity and investment fund shares	790 992	917 134	952 265	1 088 976	1 318 649	1 552 526	1 730 524	1 940 032
Insurance pension and standardised guarantees	..	..	..	..	..	..	..	..
Financial derivatives and employee stock options	..	..	..	..	..	..	..	..
Other accounts payable	3 177	3 428	5 495	7 954	9 281	11 322	12 490	14 362
Non-financial assets	0	0	0	0	0	0	0	0
Open-end non-money market funds								
Financial net worth	..	..	..	..	..	..	..	..
Financial assets	..	..	..	..	..	..	..	..

Table 2. Financial assets and liabilities of investment funds *(cont.)*

Million CAD

	2009	2010	2011	2012	2013	2014	2015	2016
Currency and deposits	..	..	..	..	..	..	..	..
Debt securities	..	..	..	..	..	..	..	..
Loans	..	..	..	..	..	..	..	..
Equity and investment fund shares	..	..	..	..	..	..	..	..
Equity	..	..	..	..	..	..	..	..
Investment fund shares	..	..	..	..	..	..	..	..
Money market fund shares	..	..	..	..	..	..	..	..
Non-Money market fund shares	..	..	..	..	..	..	..	..
Insurance pension and standardised guarantees	..	..	..	..	..	..	..	..
Financial derivatives and employee stock options	..	..	..	..	..	..	..	..
Other accounts receivable	..	..	..	..	..	..	..	..
Financial liabilities	..	..	..	..	..	..	..	..
Debt securities	..	..	..	..	..	..	..	..
Short-term debt securities	..	..	..	..	..	..	..	..
Long-term debt securities	..	..	..	..	..	..	..	..
Loans	..	..	..	..	..	..	..	..
Short-term loans	..	..	..	..	..	..	..	..
Long-term loans	..	..	..	..	..	..	..	..
Equity and investment fund shares	..	..	..	..	..	..	..	..
Insurance pension and standardised guarantees	..	..	..	..	..	..	..	..
Financial derivatives and employee stock options	..	..	..	..	..	..	..	..
Other accounts payable	..	..	..	..	..	..	..	..
Non-financial assets	..	..	..	..	..	..	..	..
Open-end investment funds								
Financial net worth	..	..	..	..	..	..	..	..
Financial assets	..	..	..	..	..	..	..	..
Currency and deposits	..	..	..	..	..	..	..	..
Debt securities	..	..	..	..	..	..	..	..
Loans	..	..	..	..	..	..	..	..
Equity and investment fund shares	..	..	..	..	..	..	..	..
Equity	..	..	..	..	..	..	..	..
Investment fund shares	..	..	..	..	..	..	..	..
Money market fund shares	..	..	..	..	..	..	..	..
Non-Money market fund shares	..	..	..	..	..	..	..	..
Insurance pension and standardised guarantees	..	..	..	..	..	..	..	..
Financial derivatives and employee stock options	..	..	..	..	..	..	..	..
Other accounts receivable	..	..	..	..	..	..	..	..
Financial liabilities	..	..	..	..	..	..	..	..
Debt securities	..	..	..	..	..	..	..	..
Short-term debt securities	..	..	..	..	..	..	..	..
Long-term debt securities	..	..	..	..	..	..	..	..
Loans	..	..	..	..	..	..	..	..
Short-term loans	..	..	..	..	..	..	..	..
Long-term loans	..	..	..	..	..	..	..	..
Equity and investment fund shares	..	..	..	..	..	..	..	..
Insurance pension and standardised guarantees	..	..	..	..	..	..	..	..
Financial derivatives and employee stock options	..	..	..	..	..	..	..	..
Other accounts payable	..	..	..	..	..	..	..	..
Non-financial assets	..	..	..	..	..	..	..	..

Note: Detailed metadata at: http://metalinks.oecd.org/instinv/20170920/75e8

CANADA

Table 3. Financial assets and liabilities of insurance corporations and pension funds

Million CAD

	2009	2010	2011	2012	2013	2014	2015	2016
Insurance corporations and pension funds								
Financial net worth	-28 061	-31 105	-33 005	-30 467	-25 045	-28 927	-19 673	-26 296
Financial assets	1 630 081	1 816 590	1 940 085	2 089 545	2 250 175	2 505 780	2 664 821	2 771 314
Currency and deposits	14 462	18 373	24 123	27 429	32 455	38 928	45 818	44 228
Debt securities	670 083	711 117	799 616	846 025	855 960	960 943	1 009 969	1 049 360
Loans	98 466	102 127	102 133	103 921	106 274	114 099	124 933	133 188
Equity and investment fund shares	653 620	752 944	742 381	829 760	986 656	1 119 315	1 180 663	1 263 363
Equity	546 690	626 533	613 218	688 599	820 591	929 592	981 152	1 045 145
Investment fund shares	106 930	126 411	129 163	141 161	166 065	189 723	199 511	218 218
Money market fund shares	..	..	..	..	..	..	..	..
Non-Money market fund shares	..	..	..	..	..	..	..	..
Insurance pension and standardised guarantees	..	..	..	..	..	..	..	..
Financial derivatives and employee stock options	..	..	..	..	..	..	..	..
Other accounts receivable	56 677	88 083	100 581	109 255	121 533	124 397	142 859	145 380
Financial liabilities	1 658 142	1 847 695	1 973 090	2 120 012	2 275 220	2 534 707	2 684 494	2 797 610
Debt securities	7 144	7 071	7 561	7 662	8 008	9 225	10 945	12 084
Short-term debt securities	..	..	..	..	..	..	..	..
Long-term debt securities	7 144	7 071	7 561	7 662	8 008	9 225	10 945	12 084
Loans	19 049	21 796	20 239	20 754	16 098	19 471	15 588	18 472
Short-term loans	..	..	..	..	..	..	..	..
Long-term loans	..	..	..	..	..	..	..	..
Equity and investment fund shares	214 566	235 614	220 915	238 979	253 787	280 569	248 036	302 121
Insurance pension and standardised guarantees	1 262 178	1 395 833	1 527 809	1 654 645	1 786 279	1 985 289	2 125 935	2 183 024
Financial derivatives and employee stock options	..	..	..	..	..	..	..	..
Other accounts payable	155 205	187 381	196 566	197 972	211 048	240 153	283 990	281 909
Non-financial assets	6 764	6 991	7 401	7 924	8 026	8 150	8 173	8 112
Insurance corporations								
Financial net worth	-28 061	-31 105	-33 005	-30 467	-25 045	-28 927	-19 673	-26 296
Financial assets	579 323	629 539	680 990	723 118	767 135	840 036	854 955	910 115
Currency and deposits	7 390	7 285	7 795	9 478	7 889	10 076	11 171	8 832
Debt securities	283 365	299 569	311 260	340 470	340 703	372 663	376 135	392 056
Loans	67 797	70 348	72 718	71 993	68 205	73 986	70 361	69 210
Equity and investment fund shares	192 635	219 569	218 176	242 225	280 157	305 251	309 215	342 510
Equity	85 705	93 158	89 013	101 064	114 092	115 528	109 704	124 292
Investment fund shares	106 930	126 411	129 163	141 161	166 065	189 723	199 511	218 218
Money market fund shares	..	..	..	..	..	..	..	..
Non-Money market fund shares	..	..	..	..	..	..	..	..
Insurance pension and standardised guarantees	..	..	..	..	..	..	..	..
Financial derivatives and employee stock options	..	..	..	..	..	..	..	..
Other accounts receivable	28 136	32 768	71 041	58 952	70 181	78 060	88 073	97 507
Financial liabilities	607 384	660 644	713 995	753 585	792 180	868 963	874 628	936 411
Debt securities	7 144	7 071	7 561	7 662	8 008	9 225	10 945	12 084
Short-term debt securities	..	..	..	..	..	..	..	..
Long-term debt securities	7 144	7 071	7 561	7 662	8 008	9 225	10 945	12 084
Loans	18 871	21 685	20 157	20 667	16 065	18 604	14 633	15 921
Short-term loans	..	..	..	..	..	..	..	..
Long-term loans	..	..	..	..	..	..	..	..
Equity and investment fund shares	214 566	235 614	220 915	238 979	253 787	280 569	248 036	302 121
Insurance pension and standardised guarantees	268 562	294 064	359 326	378 422	399 383	438 221	468 630	468 093
Financial derivatives and employee stock options	..	..	..	..	..	..	..	..
Other accounts payable	98 241	102 210	106 036	107 855	114 937	122 344	132 384	138 192
Non-financial assets	6 764	6 991	7 401	7 924	8 026	8 150	8 173	8 112
Pension funds								
Financial net worth	0	0	0	0	0	0	0	0
Financial assets	1 050 758	1 187 051	1 259 095	1 366 427	1 483 040	1 665 744	1 809 866	1 861 199
Currency and deposits	7 072	11 088	16 328	17 951	24 566	28 852	34 647	35 396
Debt securities	386 718	411 548	488 356	505 555	515 257	588 280	633 834	657 304
Loans	30 669	31 779	29 415	31 928	38 069	40 113	54 572	63 978
Equity and investment fund shares	460 985	533 375	524 205	587 535	706 499	814 064	871 448	920 853
Equity	460 985	533 375	524 205	587 535	706 499	814 064	871 448	920 853
Investment fund shares	..	..	..	..	..	..	..	..
Money market fund shares	..	..	..	..	..	..	..	..
Non-Money market fund shares	..	..	..	..	..	..	..	..
Insurance pension and standardised guarantees	..	..	..	..	..	..	..	..
Financial derivatives and employee stock options	..	..	..	..	..	..	..	..
Other accounts receivable	28 541	55 315	29 540	50 303	51 352	46 337	54 786	47 873
Financial liabilities	1 050 758	1 187 051	1 259 095	1 366 427	1 483 040	1 665 744	1 809 866	1 861 199
Debt securities	..	..	..	..	..	..	..	..
Short-term debt securities	..	..	..	..	..	..	..	..
Long-term debt securities	..	..	..	..	..	..	..	..
Loans	178	111	82	87	33	867	955	2 551
Short-term loans	..	..	..	..	..	..	..	..
Long-term loans	..	..	..	..	..	..	..	..
Equity and investment fund shares	0	0	0	0	..	..	..	..
Insurance pension and standardised guarantees	993 616	1 101 769	1 168 483	1 276 223	1 386 896	1 547 068	1 657 305	1 714 931
Financial derivatives and employee stock options	..	..	..	..	..	..	..	..
Other accounts payable	56 964	85 171	90 530	90 117	96 111	117 809	151 606	143 717
Non-financial assets	0	0	0	0	0	0	0	0

Note: Detailed metadata at: http://metalinks.oecd.org/instinv/20170920/75e8

Table 4. Portfolio composition by type of investor

As percentage of financial assets and of financial liabilities

Per cent

	2009	2010	2011	2012	2013	2014	2015	2016
Investment funds								
Financial assets	100.0	100.0	100.0	100.0	100.0	100.0	100.0	100.0
Currency and deposits	0.7	0.5	0.7	0.9	0.7	0.7	0.6	0.7
Debt securities	28.5	27.0	30.2	29.8	26.2	25.5	24.0	22.8
Loans	0.5	0.6	0.5	0.5	0.4	0.3	0.3	0.3
Equity and investment fund shares	66.9	69.2	65.1	65.0	67.6	68.1	68.3	67.8
Insurance pension and standardised guarantee schemes	0.0	0.0	0.0	0.0	0.0	0.0	0.0	0.0
Financial derivatives and employee stock options	0.0	0.0	0.0	0.0	0.0	0.0	0.0	0.0
Other accounts receivable	3.3	2.7	3.4	3.9	5.1	5.3	6.9	8.5
Financial liabilities	100.0	100.0	100.0	100.0	100.0	100.0	100.0	100.0
Currency and deposits	0.0	0.0	0.0	0.0	0.0	0.0	0.0	0.0
Debt securities	0.0	0.0	0.0	0.0	0.0	0.0	0.0	0.0
Loans	0.0	0.0	0.0	0.0	0.0	0.0	0.0	0.0
Equity and investment fund shares	99.6	99.6	99.4	99.3	99.3	99.3	99.3	99.3
Insurance pension and standardised guarantee schemes	0.0	0.0	0.0	0.0	0.0	0.0	0.0	0.0
Financial derivatives and employee stock options	0.0	0.0	0.0	0.0	0.0	0.0	0.0	0.0
Other accounts receivable	0.4	0.4	0.6	0.7	0.7	0.7	0.7	0.7
Insurance corporations								
Financial assets	100.0	100.0	100.0	100.0	100.0	100.0	100.0	100.0
Currency and deposits	1.3	1.2	1.1	1.3	1.0	1.2	1.3	1.0
Debt securities	48.9	47.6	45.7	47.1	44.4	44.4	44.0	43.1
Loans	11.7	11.2	10.7	10.0	8.9	8.8	8.2	7.6
Equity and investment fund shares	33.3	34.9	32.0	33.5	36.5	36.3	36.2	37.6
Insurance pension and standardised guarantee schemes	0.0	0.0	0.0	0.0	0.0	0.0	0.0	0.0
Financial derivatives and employee stock options	0.0	0.0	0.0	0.0	0.0	0.0	0.0	0.0
Other accounts receivable	4.9	5.2	10.4	8.2	9.1	9.3	10.3	10.7
Financial liabilities	100.0	100.0	100.0	100.0	100.0	100.0	100.0	100.0
Currency and deposits	0.0	0.0	0.0	0.0	0.0	0.0	0.0	0.0
Debt securities	1.2	1.1	1.1	1.0	1.0	1.1	1.3	1.3
Loans	3.1	3.3	2.8	2.7	2.0	2.1	1.7	1.7
Equity and investment fund shares	35.3	35.7	30.9	31.7	32.0	32.3	28.4	32.3
Insurance pension and standardised guarantee schemes	44.2	44.5	50.3	50.2	50.4	50.4	53.6	50.0
Financial derivatives and employee stock options	0.0	0.0	0.0	0.0	0.0	0.0	0.0	0.0
Other accounts receivable	16.2	15.5	14.9	14.3	14.5	14.1	15.1	14.8
Pension funds								
Financial assets	100.0	100.0	100.0	100.0	100.0	100.0	100.0	100.0
Currency and deposits	0.7	0.9	1.3	1.3	1.7	1.7	1.9	1.9
Debt securities	36.8	34.7	38.8	37.0	34.7	35.3	35.0	35.3
Loans	2.9	2.7	2.3	2.3	2.6	2.4	3.0	3.4
Equity and investment fund shares	43.9	44.9	41.6	43.0	47.6	48.9	48.1	49.5
Insurance pension and standardised guarantee schemes	..	..	..	..	..	..	..	..
Financial derivatives and employee stock options	..	..	..	..	..	..	..	..
Other accounts receivable	2.7	4.7	2.3	3.7	3.5	2.8	3.0	2.6
Financial liabilities	100.0	100.0	100.0	100.0	100.0	100.0	100.0	100.0
Currency and deposits	0.0	0.0	0.0	0.0	0.0	0.0	0.0	0.0
Debt securities	0.0	0.0	0.0	0.0	0.0	0.0	0.0	0.0
Loans	0.0	0.0	0.0	0.0	0.0	0.1	0.1	0.1
Equity and investment fund shares	0.0	0.0	0.0	0.0	0.0	0.0	0.0	0.0
Insurance pension and standardised guarantee schemes	94.6	92.8	92.8	93.4	93.5	92.9	91.6	92.1
Financial derivatives and employee stock options	0.0	0.0	0.0	0.0	0.0	0.0	0.0	0.0
Other accounts receivable	5.4	7.2	7.2	6.6	6.5	7.1	8.4	7.7

Note: Detailed metadata at: http://metalinks.oecd.org/instinv/20170920/a49a

Table 1. Financial assets and liabilities of institutional investors, 2016

Million CLP

	Investment funds				
	Total	Non-money market funds			Money market funds
		Total	Open-end non-money market funds	Closed-end non-money market funds	Total
Financial assets	41 833 227	28 652 662	17 693 316	10 959 346	13 180 565
Currency and deposits	..	..	124 345	..	124 345
Debt securities	..	..	14 279 311	..	13 056 220
Debt securities, short term	..	..	3 243 951	..	12 749 884
Debt securities, long term	..	..	11 035 360	..	306 336
Debt securities issued by residents	..	..	13 786 086	..	13 012 164
Debt securities issued by non-residents	..	..	493 225	..	44 056
Loans	..	..	..	..	..
Loans, short-term	..	..	..	..	..
Loans, long-term	..	..	..	..	..
Loans granted to residents	..	..	..	..	..
Loans granted to non-residents	..	..	..	..	..
Equity and investment fund shares/units	..	..	3 289 660	..	..
Equity and investment fund shares issued/units by residents	..	..	1 040 920	..	..
Equity and investment fund shares/units issued by non residents	..	..	2 248 740	..	..
Other accounts receivable	..	..	..	..	..

	Investment funds				
	Total	Non-money market funds			Money market funds
		Total	Open-end non-money market funds	Closed-end non-money market funds	Total
Financial liabilities	664 957	664 930	3 857	661 072	27
Currency and deposits	..	..	..	..	..
Debt securities	..	..	..	..	..
Debt securities, short term	..	..	..	..	..
Debt securities, long term	..	..	..	..	..
Loans	..	..	..	..	..
Loans, short-term	..	..	..	..	..
Loans, long-term	..	..	..	..	..
Equity and investment fund shares/units	..	..	..	..	..
Insurance pension and standardised guaratees	..	..	..	..	..
Financial derivatives and employee stock options	..	..	..	..	..
Other accounts payable	..	..	..	..	..

	Insurance corporations and pension funds				
	Total	Insurance corporations			Pension funds
		Total	Life insurance corporations	Non-life insurance corporations	Total
Financial assets	149 722 473	33 293 844	31 976 133	1 317 711	116 428 629
Currency and deposits	7 571 956	354 607	206 067	148 540	7 217 349
Debt securities	78 879 795	23 337 925	22 319 001	1 018 924	55 541 871
Debt securities, short-term	..	..	..	..	1 739 872
Debt securities, long term	..	..	..	..	53 801 999
Debt securities issued by residents	71 978 307	19 707 263	18 691 367	1 015 896	52 271 043
Debt securities issued by non-residents	6 901 489	3 630 662	3 627 634	3 027	3 270 827
Loans	4 064 950	3 574 454	3 572 425	2 029	490 496
Loans, short-term	477 128	455 145	455 145	0	21 983
Loans, long-term	3 587 822	3 119 309	3 117 280	2 029	468 513
Loans granted to residents	..	..	..	..	490 496
Loans granted to non-residents	..	..	..	..	..
Equity and investment fund shares/units	56 770 438	3 730 615	3 675 276	55 339	53 039 823
Equity and investment fund shares/units issued by residents	17 669 007	3 168 198	3 114 321	53 877	14 500 809
Equity and investment fund shares/units issued by non residents	39 101 430	562 417	560 955	1 462	38 539 014
Other accounts receivable	..	2 349 170	2 256 587	92 583	..

	Insurance corporations and pension funds				
	Total	Insurance corporations			Pension funds
		Total	Life insurance corporations	Non-life insurance corporations	Total
Financial liabilities	1 870 432	618 665	615 786	2 880	1 251 767
Currency and deposits	..	..	..	..	..
Debt securities	..	..	..	..	..
Debt securities, short term	..	..	..	..	..
Debt securities, long term	..	..	..	..	..
Loans	..	..	..	..	..
Loans, short-term	..	..	..	..	..
Loans, long-term	..	..	..	..	..
Equity and investment fund shares/units	..	..	..	..	..
Insurance pension and standardised guaratees	..	..	..	..	..
Financial derivatives and employee stock options	..	..	..	..	..
Other accounts payable	..	..	..	..	1 251 767

Note: Detailed metadata at: http://metalinks.oecd.org/instinv/20170920/e6c2

CHILE

Table 2. Financial assets and liabilities of investment funds

Million CLP

	2009	2010	2011	2012	2013	2014	2015	2016
Investment funds								
Financial net worth	..	..	..	..	..	29 671 577	35 162 158	41 168 270
Financial assets	..	..	..	..	..	30 061 688	35 914 898	41 833 227
Currency and deposits	..	..	..	..	..	..	..	..
Debt securities	..	..	..	..	..	..	..	..
Loans	..	..	..	..	..	..	..	..
Equity and investment fund shares	..	..	..	..	..	..	..	..
Equity	..	..	..	..	..	..	..	..
Investment fund shares	..	..	..	..	..	..	..	..
Money market fund shares	..	..	..	..	..	..	..	..
Non-Money market fund shares	..	..	..	..	..	..	..	..
Insurance pension and standardised guarantees	..	..	..	..	..	..	..	..
Financial derivatives and employee stock options	..	..	..	..	..	..	..	..
Other accounts receivable	..	..	..	..	..	..	..	..
Financial liabilities	..	..	..	..	..	390 112	752 740	664 957
Debt securities	..	..	..	..	..	..	..	..
Short-term debt securities	..	..	..	..	..	..	..	..
Long-term debt securities	..	..	..	..	..	..	..	..
Loans	..	..	..	..	..	..	..	..
Short-term loans	..	..	..	..	..	..	..	..
Long-term loans	..	..	..	..	..	..	..	..
Equity and investment fund shares	..	..	..	..	..	..	..	..
Insurance pension and standardised guarantees	..	..	..	..	..	..	..	..
Financial derivatives and employee stock options	..	..	..	..	..	..	..	..
Other accounts payable	..	..	..	..	..	..	..	..
Non-financial assets	..	..	..	..	..	727 934	932 960	964 306
Money market funds								
Financial net worth	..	..	..	..	..	11 926 154	12 426 624	13 180 537
Financial assets	..	..	..	..	..	11 979 017	12 426 677	13 180 565
Currency and deposits	..	..	..	..	..	43 760	171 319	124 345
Debt securities	..	..	..	..	..	11 935 257	12 255 358	13 056 220
Loans	..	..	..	..	..	..	..	..
Equity and investment fund shares	..	..	..	..	..	..	..	..
Equity	..	..	..	..	..	..	..	..
Investment fund shares	..	..	..	..	..	..	..	..
Money market fund shares	..	..	..	..	..	..	..	..
Non-Money market fund shares	..	..	..	..	..	..	..	..
Insurance pension and standardised guarantees	..	..	..	..	..	..	..	..
Financial derivatives and employee stock options	..	..	..	..	..	..	..	..
Other accounts receivable	..	..	..	..	..	..	..	..
Financial liabilities	..	..	..	..	..	52 863	53	27
Debt securities	..	..	..	..	..	..	..	..
Short-term debt securities	..	..	..	..	..	..	..	..
Long-term debt securities	..	..	..	..	..	..	..	..
Loans	..	..	..	..	..	..	..	..
Short-term loans	..	..	..	..	..	..	..	..
Long-term loans	..	..	..	..	..	..	..	..
Equity and investment fund shares	..	..	..	..	..	..	..	..
Insurance pension and standardised guarantees	..	..	..	..	..	..	..	..
Financial derivatives and employee stock options	..	..	..	..	..	..	..	..
Other accounts payable	..	..	..	..	..	..	..	..
Non-financial assets	..	..	..	..	..	32 431	46 075	66 109
Non-money market funds								
Financial net worth	..	..	..	..	..	17 745 423	22 735 534	27 987 732
Financial assets	..	..	..	..	..	18 082 672	23 488 221	28 652 662
Currency and deposits	..	..	..	..	..	..	..	..
Debt securities	..	..	..	..	..	..	..	..
Loans	..	..	..	..	..	..	..	..
Equity and investment fund shares	..	..	..	..	..	..	..	..
Equity	..	..	..	..	..	..	..	..
Investment fund shares	..	..	..	..	..	..	..	..
Money market fund shares	..	..	..	..	..	..	..	..
Non-Money market fund shares	..	..	..	..	..	..	..	..
Insurance pension and standardised guarantees	..	..	..	..	..	..	..	..
Financial derivatives and employee stock options	..	..	..	..	..	..	..	..
Other accounts receivable	..	..	..	..	..	..	..	..
Financial liabilities	..	..	..	..	..	337 249	752 687	664 930
Debt securities	..	..	..	..	..	..	..	..
Short-term debt securities	..	..	..	..	..	..	..	..
Long-term debt securities	..	..	..	..	..	..	..	..
Loans	..	..	..	..	..	..	..	..
Short-term loans	..	..	..	..	..	..	..	..
Long-term loans	..	..	..	..	..	..	..	..
Equity and investment fund shares	..	..	..	..	..	..	..	..
Insurance pension and standardised guarantees	..	..	..	..	..	..	..	..
Financial derivatives and employee stock options	..	..	..	..	..	..	..	..
Other accounts payable	..	..	..	..	..	..	..	..
Non-financial assets	..	..	..	..	..	695 502	886 886	898 197
Open-end non-money market funds								
Financial net worth	..	..	..	..	..	14 734 438	15 871 049	17 689 459
Financial assets	..	..	..	..	..	14 740 401	15 879 662	17 693 316

Table 2. Financial assets and liabilities of investment funds *(cont.)*

Million CLP

	2009	2010	2011	2012	2013	2014	2015	2016
Currency and deposits	..	..	..	..	..	110 999	144 523	124 345
Debt securities	..	..	..	..	..	11 457 419	11 676 251	14 279 311
Loans	..	..	..	..	..	..	..	..
Equity and investment fund shares	..	..	..	..	..	3 171 984	4 058 888	3 289 660
Equity	..	..	..	..	..	883 211	821 190	892 043
Investment fund shares	..	..	..	..	..	2 288 773	3 237 698	2 397 618
Money market fund shares	..	..	..	..	..	..	..	..
Non-Money market fund shares	..	..	..	..	..	..	..	..
Insurance pension and standardised guarantees	..	..	..	..	..	..	..	..
Financial derivatives and employee stock options	..	..	..	..	..	..	..	..
Other accounts receivable	..	..	..	..	..	..	..	..
Financial liabilities	..	..	..	..	..	5 963	8 613	3 857
Debt securities	..	..	..	..	..	..	..	..
Short-term debt securities	..	..	..	..	..	..	..	..
Long-term debt securities	..	..	..	..	..	..	..	..
Loans	..	..	..	..	..	..	..	..
Short-term loans	..	..	..	..	..	..	..	..
Long-term loans	..	..	..	..	..	..	..	..
Equity and investment fund shares	..	..	..	..	..	..	..	..
Insurance pension and standardised guarantees	..	..	..	..	..	..	..	..
Financial derivatives and employee stock options	..	..	..	..	..	..	..	..
Other accounts payable	..	..	..	..	..	..	..	..
Non-financial assets	..	..	..	..	..	20 826	52 731	46 863
Open-end investment funds								
Financial net worth	..	..	..	..	..	26 660 592	28 297 673	30 869 996
Financial assets	..	..	..	..	..	26 719 418	28 306 339	30 873 881
Currency and deposits	..	..	..	..	..	154 759	315 842	248 689
Debt securities	..	..	..	..	..	23 392 675	23 931 609	27 335 531
Loans	..	..	..	..	..	..	..	..
Equity and investment fund shares	..	..	..	..	..	..	..	3 289 660
Equity	..	..	..	..	..	..	..	892 043
Investment fund shares	..	..	..	..	..	..	..	2 397 618
Money market fund shares	..	..	..	..	..	..	..	..
Non-Money market fund shares	..	..	..	..	..	..	..	..
Insurance pension and standardised guarantees	..	..	..	..	..	..	..	..
Financial derivatives and employee stock options	..	..	..	..	..	..	..	..
Other accounts receivable	..	..	..	..	..	..	..	..
Financial liabilities	..	..	..	..	..	58 826	8 666	3 884
Debt securities	..	..	..	..	..	..	..	..
Short-term debt securities	..	..	..	..	..	..	..	..
Long-term debt securities	..	..	..	..	..	..	..	..
Loans	..	..	..	..	..	..	..	..
Short-term loans	..	..	..	..	..	..	..	..
Long-term loans	..	..	..	..	..	..	..	..
Equity and investment fund shares	..	..	..	..	..	..	..	..
Insurance pension and standardised guarantees	..	..	..	..	..	..	..	..
Financial derivatives and employee stock options	..	..	..	..	..	..	..	..
Other accounts payable	..	..	..	..	..	..	..	..
Non-financial assets	..	..	..	..	..	53 257	98 805	112 972

Note: Detailed metadata at: http://metalinks.oecd.org/instinv/20170920/e6c2

CHILE

Table 3. Financial assets and liabilities of insurance corporations and pension funds

Million CLP

	2009	2010	2011	2012	2013	2014	2015	2016
Insurance corporations and pension funds								
Financial net worth	..	..	..	..	..	125 953 303	137 263 750	147 852 040
Financial assets	..	..	..	..	..	127 702 283	139 498 064	149 722 473
Currency and deposits	..	..	..	..	..	7 423 782	8 668 098	7 571 956
Debt securities	..	..	..	..	..	58 422 149	66 300 575	78 879 795
Loans	..	..	..	..	..	3 622 921	3 718 752	4 064 950
Equity and investment fund shares	..	..	..	..	..	56 235 414	59 196 576	56 770 438
Equity	..	..	..	..	..	8 954 179	8 399 011	9 694 054
Investment fund shares	..	..	..	..	..	47 281 235	50 797 565	47 076 383
Money market fund shares	..	..	..	..	..	..	..	..
Non-Money market fund shares	..	..	..	..	..	..	..	..
Insurance pension and standardised guarantees	..	..	..	..	..	..	..	..
Financial derivatives and employee stock options	..	..	..	..	..	-195 142	-407 146	86 163
Other accounts receivable	..	..	..	..	..	..	..	..
Financial liabilities	..	..	..	..	..	1 743 980	2 234 314	1 870 432
Debt securities	..	..	..	..	..	..	..	..
Short-term debt securities	..	..	..	..	..	..	..	..
Long-term debt securities	..	..	..	..	..	..	..	..
Loans	..	..	..	..	..	..	..	..
Short-term loans	..	..	..	..	..	..	..	..
Long-term loans	..	..	..	..	..	..	..	..
Equity and investment fund shares	..	..	..	..	..	..	..	..
Insurance pension and standardised guarantees	..	..	..	..	..	..	..	..
Financial derivatives and employee stock options	..	..	..	..	..	..	..	..
Other accounts payable	..	..	..	..	..	..	..	..
Non-financial assets	..	..	..	..	..	..	3 791 125	..
Insurance corporations								
Financial net worth	..	..	..	..	..	26 554 708	29 060 184	32 675 179
Financial assets	..	..	..	..	..	27 222 468	30 064 643	33 293 844
Currency and deposits	..	..	..	..	..	457 706	401 273	354 607
Debt securities	..	..	..	..	..	18 966 501	21 727 444	23 337 925
Loans	..	..	..	..	..	2 946 519	3 139 873	3 574 454
Equity and investment fund shares	..	..	..	..	..	2 849 529	3 261 873	3 730 615
Equity	..	..	..	..	..	433 578	367 160	414 182
Investment fund shares	..	..	..	..	..	2 415 952	2 894 713	3 316 432
Money market fund shares	..	..	..	..	..	..	..	..
Non-Money market fund shares	..	..	..	..	..	..	..	..
Insurance pension and standardised guarantees	..	..	..	..	..	..	0	0
Financial derivatives and employee stock options	..	..	..	..	..	-190 947	-487 029	-52 927
Other accounts receivable	..	..	..	..	..	2 193 159	2 021 209	2 349 170
Financial liabilities	..	..	..	..	..	667 760	1 004 459	618 665
Debt securities	..	..	..	..	..	..	..	..
Short-term debt securities	..	..	..	..	..	..	..	..
Long-term debt securities	..	..	..	..	..	..	..	..
Loans	..	..	..	..	..	..	..	..
Short-term loans	..	..	..	..	..	..	..	..
Long-term loans	..	..	..	..	..	..	..	..
Equity and investment fund shares	..	..	..	..	..	..	..	..
Insurance pension and standardised guarantees	..	..	..	..	..	..	..	..
Financial derivatives and employee stock options	..	..	..	..	..	..	..	..
Other accounts payable	..	..	..	..	..	..	..	..
Non-financial assets	..	..	..	..	..	3 297 155	3 791 125	4 103 190
Pension funds								
Financial net worth	..	..	..	..	..	99 398 595	108 203 566	115 176 862
Financial assets	..	..	..	..	..	100 479 815	109 433 421	116 428 629
Currency and deposits	..	..	..	..	..	6 966 076	8 266 825	7 217 349
Debt securities	..	..	..	..	..	39 455 648	44 573 132	55 541 871
Loans	..	..	..	..	..	676 402	578 879	490 496
Equity and investment fund shares	..	..	..	..	..	53 385 385	55 934 703	53 039 823
Equity	..	..	..	..	..	8 520 602	8 031 851	9 279 872
Investment fund shares	..	..	..	..	..	44 865 284	47 902 852	43 759 951
Money market fund shares	..	..	..	..	..	..	..	..
Non-Money market fund shares	..	..	..	..	..	..	..	..
Insurance pension and standardised guarantees	..	..	..	..	..	..	..	..
Financial derivatives and employee stock options	..	..	..	..	..	-4 196	79 882	139 090
Other accounts receivable	..	..	..	..	..	..	..	..
Financial liabilities	..	..	..	..	..	1 081 220	1 229 855	1 251 767
Debt securities	..	..	..	..	..	..	..	..
Short-term debt securities	..	..	..	..	..	..	..	..
Long-term debt securities	..	..	..	..	..	..	..	..
Loans	..	..	..	..	..	..	..	..
Short-term loans	..	..	..	..	..	..	..	..
Long-term loans	..	..	..	..	..	..	..	..
Equity and investment fund shares	..	..	..	..	..	..	..	..
Insurance pension and standardised guarantees	..	..	..	..	..	..	..	..
Financial derivatives and employee stock options	..	..	..	..	..	..	..	..
Other accounts payable	..	..	..	..	..	1 081 220	1 229 855	1 251 767
Non-financial assets	..	..	..	..	..	..	..	..

Note: Detailed metadata at: http://metalinks.oecd.org/instinv/20170920/e6c2

Table 4. Portfolio composition by type of investor

As percentage of financial assets and of financial liabilities

Per cent

	2009	2010	2011	2012	2013	2014	2015	2016
Investment funds								
Financial assets	..	..	..	..	..	100.0	100.0	100.0
Currency and deposits	..	..	..	..	..	..	..	..
Debt securities	..	..	..	..	..	..	..	..
Loans	..	..	..	..	..	..	..	..
Equity and investment fund shares	..	..	..	..	..	..	..	..
Insurance pension and standardised guarantee schemes	..	..	..	..	..	..	..	..
Financial derivatives and employee stock options	..	..	..	..	..	..	..	..
Other accounts receivable	..	..	..	..	..	..	..	..
Financial liabilities	..	..	..	..	..	100.0	100.0	100.0
Currency and deposits	..	..	..	..	..	..	..	..
Debt securities	..	..	..	..	..	..	..	..
Loans	..	..	..	..	..	..	..	..
Equity and investment fund shares	..	..	..	..	..	..	..	..
Insurance pension and standardised guarantee schemes	..	..	..	..	..	..	..	..
Financial derivatives and employee stock options	..	..	..	..	..	..	..	..
Other accounts receivable	..	..	..	..	..	..	..	..
Insurance corporations								
Financial assets	..	..	..	..	..	100.0	100.0	100.0
Currency and deposits	..	..	..	..	..	1.7	1.3	1.1
Debt securities	..	..	..	..	..	69.7	72.3	70.1
Loans	..	..	..	..	..	10.8	10.4	10.7
Equity and investment fund shares	..	..	..	..	..	10.5	10.8	11.2
Insurance pension and standardised guarantee schemes	..	..	..	..	..	0.0	0.0	0.0
Financial derivatives and employee stock options	..	..	..	..	..	-0.7	-1.6	-0.2
Other accounts receivable	..	..	..	..	..	8.1	6.7	7.1
Financial liabilities	..	..	..	..	..	100.0	100.0	100.0
Currency and deposits	..	..	..	..	..	..	..	..
Debt securities	..	..	..	..	..	..	..	..
Loans	..	..	..	..	..	..	..	..
Equity and investment fund shares	..	..	..	..	..	..	..	..
Insurance pension and standardised guarantee schemes	..	..	..	..	..	..	..	..
Financial derivatives and employee stock options	..	..	..	..	..	..	..	..
Other accounts receivable	..	..	..	..	..	..	..	..
Pension funds								
Financial assets	..	..	..	..	..	100.0	100.0	100.0
Currency and deposits	..	..	..	..	..	6.9	7.6	6.2
Debt securities	..	..	..	..	..	39.3	40.7	47.7
Loans	..	..	..	..	..	0.7	0.5	0.4
Equity and investment fund shares	..	..	..	..	..	53.1	51.1	45.6
Insurance pension and standardised guarantee schemes	..	..	..	..	..	0.0	0.0	0.0
Financial derivatives and employee stock options	..	..	..	..	..	0.0	0.1	0.1
Other accounts receivable	..	..	..	..	..	0.0	0.0	0.0
Financial liabilities	..	..	..	..	..	100.0	100.0	100.0
Currency and deposits	..	..	..	..	..	0.0	0.0	0.0
Debt securities	..	..	..	..	..	0.0	0.0	0.0
Loans	..	..	..	..	..	0.0	0.0	0.0
Equity and investment fund shares	..	..	..	..	..	0.0	0.0	0.0
Insurance pension and standardised guarantee schemes	..	..	..	..	..	0.0	0.0	0.0
Financial derivatives and employee stock options	..	..	..	..	..	0.0	0.0	0.0
Other accounts receivable	..	..	..	..	..	100.0	100.0	100.0

Note: Detailed metadata at: http://metalinks.oecd.org/instinv/20170920/a49a

CZECH REPUBLIC

Table 1. Financial assets and liabilities of institutional investors, 2016

Million CZK

	Investment funds				
		Non-money market funds			Money market funds
	Total	Total	Open-end non-money market funds	Closed-end non-money market funds	Total
Financial assets	317 608	316 961	316 961	..	647
Currency and deposits	36 542	36 218	36 218	..	324
Debt securities	109 623	109 339	109 339	..	284
Debt securities, short term	1 073	1 064	1 064	..	9
Debt securities, long term	108 550	108 275	108 275	..	275
Debt securities issued by residents	56 812	56 580	56 580	..	232
Debt securities issued by non-residents	52 811	52 759	52 759	..	52
Loans	30 754	30 754	30 754	..	0
Loans, short-term	2 960	2 960	2 960	..	0
Loans, long-term	27 794	27 794	27 794	..	0
Loans granted to residents	23 066	23 066	23 066	..	0
Loans granted to non-residents	7 688	7 688	7 688	..	0
Equity and investment fund shares/units	135 949	135 911	135 911	..	38
Equity and investment fund shares issued/units by residents	19 178	19 178	19 178	..	0
Equity and investment fund shares/units issued by non residents	116 771	116 733	116 733	..	38
Other accounts receivable	4 570	4 570	4 570	..	0

	Investment funds				
		Non-money market funds			Money market funds
	Total	Total	Open-end non-money market funds	Closed-end non-money market funds	Total
Financial liabilities	391 424	390 217	390 217	..	1 207
Currency and deposits	0	0	0	..	0
Debt securities	213	213	213	..	0
Debt securities, short term	0	0	0	..	0
Debt securities, long term	213	213	213	..	0
Loans	11 003	10 845	10 845	..	158
Loans, short-term	603	597	597	..	6
Loans, long-term	10 400	10 248	10 248	..	152
Equity and investment fund shares/units	355 828	354 779	354 779	..	1 049
Insurance pension and standardised guaratees	0	0	0	..	0
Financial derivatives and employee stock options	1 268	1 268	1 268	..	0
Other accounts payable	23 112	23 112	23 112	..	0

	Insurance corporations and pension funds				
		Insurance corporations			Pension funds
	Total	Total	Life insurance corporations	Non-life insurance corporations	Total
Financial assets	906 757	531 009	..	..	375 748
Currency and deposits	58 755	36 832	..	..	21 923
Debt securities	624 656	281 946	..	..	342 710
Debt securities, short-term	1 196	84	..	..	1 112
Debt securities, long term	623 460	281 862	..	..	341 598
Debt securities issued by residents	490 538	206 286	..	..	284 252
Debt securities issued by non-residents	134 118	75 660	..	..	58 458
Loans	1 540	1 514	..	..	26
Loans, short-term	0	0	..	..	0
Loans, long-term	1 540	1 514	..	..	26
Loans granted to residents	1 529	1 503	..	..	26
Loans granted to non-residents	11	11	..	..	0
Equity and investment fund shares/units	118 157	107 725	..	..	10 432
Equity and investment fund shares/units issued by residents	50 216	49 236	..	..	980
Equity and investment fund shares/units issued by non residents	67 941	58 489	..	..	9 452
Other accounts receivable	64 650	64 173	..	..	477

	Insurance corporations and pension funds				
		Insurance corporations			Pension funds
	Total	Total	Life insurance corporations	Non-life insurance corporations	Total
Financial liabilities	948 937	546 817	..	..	402 120
Currency and deposits	0	0	..	..	0
Debt securities	653	653	..	..	0
Debt securities, short term	0	0	..	..	0
Debt securities, long term	653	653	..	..	0
Loans	1 582	1 582	..	..	0
Loans, short-term	1 556	1 556	..	..	0
Loans, long-term	26	26	..	..	0
Equity and investment fund shares/units	101 420	85 793	..	..	15 627
Insurance pension and standardised guarantees	792 355	410 671	..	..	381 684
Financial derivatives and employee stock options	7 212	4 009	..	..	3 203
Other accounts payable	45 715	44 109	..	..	1 606

Note: Detailed metadata at: http://metalinks.oecd.org/instinv/20170920/75e8

CZECH REPUBLIC

Table 2. Financial assets and liabilities of investment funds

Million CZK

	2009	2010	2011	2012	2013	2014	2015	2016
Investment funds								
Financial net worth	-807	-3 630	-19 802	-58 881	-60 679	-77 595	-88 597	-73 816
Financial assets	150 872	164 771	150 453	164 431	187 843	215 862	245 739	317 608
Currency and deposits	24 381	23 806	26 539	32 135	32 867	25 835	24 122	36 542
Debt securities	80 648	87 755	74 728	73 416	82 644	86 384	86 582	109 623
Loans	915	1 888	3 848	7 667	11 335	17 097	21 001	30 754
Equity and investment fund shares	40 147	49 014	41 725	45 337	56 293	80 967	107 258	135 949
Equity	23 916	29 562	24 396	26 537	27 063	31 029	39 403	48 163
Investment fund shares	16 231	19 452	17 329	18 800	29 230	49 938	67 855	87 786
Money market fund shares	5 164	4 150	2 775	362	594	791	246	921
Non-Money market fund shares	11 067	15 302	14 554	18 438	28 636	49 147	67 609	86 865
Insurance pension and standardised guarantees	13	12	15	14	17	20	16	7
Financial derivatives and employee stock options	573	575	189	513	387	101	496	163
Other accounts receivable	4 195	1 721	3 409	5 349	4 300	5 458	6 264	4 570
Financial liabilities	151 679	168 401	170 255	223 312	248 522	293 457	334 336	391 424
Debt securities	0	0	0	205	68	0	237	213
Short-term debt securities	0	0	0	0	0	0	0	0
Long-term debt securities	0	0	0	205	68	0	237	213
Loans	358	1 672	4 217	25 359	13 918	15 594	9 210	11 003
Short-term loans	358	0	0	5 448	0	1 137	587	603
Long-term loans	0	1 672	4 217	19 911	13 918	14 457	8 623	10 400
Equity and investment fund shares	142 408	160 194	158 057	183 146	220 804	261 751	307 698	355 828
Insurance pension and standardised guarantees	0	0	0	0	0	0	0	0
Financial derivatives and employee stock options	1 139	620	1 497	414	1 041	1 275	528	1 268
Other accounts payable	7 774	5 915	6 484	14 188	12 691	14 837	16 663	23 112
Non-financial assets	..	..	..	..	..	..	..	..
Money market funds								
Financial net worth	2 403	818	594	-1 398	-1 368	-153	596	-560
Financial assets	49 397	44 381	14 840	1 948	1 121	1 176	1 416	647
Currency and deposits	13 005	13 716	3 801	1 566	875	495	455	324
Debt securities	36 035	30 247	11 038	234	244	680	960	284
Loans	0	0	0	146	0	0	0	0
Equity and investment fund shares	315	313	0	0	0	0	0	38
Equity	0	0	0	0	0	0	0	0
Investment fund shares	315	313	0	0	0	0	0	38
Money market fund shares	110	68	0	0	0	0	0	38
Non-Money market fund shares	205	245	0	0	0	0	0	0
Insurance pension and standardised guarantees	1	1	1	1	1	1	1	1
Financial derivatives and employee stock options	41	104	0	1	1	0	0	0
Other accounts receivable	0	0	0	0	0	0	0	0
Financial liabilities	46 994	43 563	14 246	3 346	2 489	1 329	820	1 207
Debt securities	0	0	0	196	56	0	0	0
Short-term debt securities	0	0	0	0	0	0	0	0
Long-term debt securities	0	0	0	196	56	0	0	0
Loans	0	0	0	0	0	44	121	158
Short-term loans	0	0	0	0	0	31	2	6
Long-term loans	0	0	0	0	0	13	119	152
Equity and investment fund shares	46 707	43 232	14 219	3 148	2 423	1 283	699	1 049
Insurance pension and standardised guarantees	0	0	0	0	0	0	0	0
Financial derivatives and employee stock options	287	331	27	2	10	1	0	0
Other accounts payable	0	0	0	0	0	1	0	0
Non-financial assets	..	..	..	..	..	..	..	..
Non-money market funds								
Financial net worth	-3 210	-4 448	-20 396	-57 483	-59 311	-77 442	-89 193	-73 256
Financial assets	101 475	120 390	135 613	162 483	186 722	214 686	244 323	316 961
Currency and deposits	11 376	10 090	22 738	30 569	31 992	25 340	23 667	36 218
Debt securities	44 613	57 508	63 690	73 182	82 400	85 704	85 622	109 339
Loans	915	1 888	3 848	7 521	11 335	17 097	21 001	30 754
Equity and investment fund shares	39 832	48 701	41 725	45 337	56 293	80 967	107 258	135 911
Equity	23 916	29 562	24 396	26 537	27 063	31 029	39 403	48 163
Investment fund shares	15 916	19 139	17 329	18 800	29 230	49 938	67 855	87 748
Money market fund shares	5 054	4 082	2 775	362	594	791	246	883
Non-Money market fund shares	10 862	15 057	14 554	18 438	28 636	49 147	67 609	86 865
Insurance pension and standardised guarantees	12	11	14	13	16	19	15	6
Financial derivatives and employee stock options	532	471	189	512	386	101	496	163
Other accounts receivable	4 195	1 721	3 409	5 349	4 300	5 458	6 264	4 570
Financial liabilities	104 685	124 838	156 009	219 966	246 033	292 128	333 516	390 217
Debt securities	0	0	0	9	12	0	237	213
Short-term debt securities	0	0	0	0	0	0	0	0
Long-term debt securities	0	0	0	9	12	0	237	213
Loans	358	1 672	4 217	25 359	13 918	15 550	9 089	10 845
Short-term loans	358	0	0	5 448	0	1 106	585	597
Long-term loans	0	1 672	4 217	19 911	13 918	14 444	8 504	10 248
Equity and investment fund shares	95 701	116 962	143 838	179 998	218 381	260 468	306 999	354 779
Insurance pension and standardised guarantees	0	0	0	0	0	0	0	0
Financial derivatives and employee stock options	852	289	1 470	412	1 031	1 274	528	1 268
Other accounts payable	7 774	5 915	6 484	14 188	12 691	14 836	16 663	23 112
Non-financial assets	..	..	..	..	..	..	..	..
Open-end non-money market funds								
Financial net worth	-3 210	-4 448	-20 396	-57 483	-59 311	-77 442	-89 193	-73 256
Financial assets	101 475	120 390	135 613	162 483	186 722	214 686	244 323	316 961

Table 2. Financial assets and liabilities of investment funds *(cont.)*

Million CZK

	2009	2010	2011	2012	2013	2014	2015	2016
Currency and deposits	11 376	10 090	22 738	30 569	31 992	25 340	23 667	36 218
Debt securities	44 613	57 508	63 690	73 182	82 400	85 704	85 622	109 339
Loans	915	1 888	3 848	7 521	11 335	17 097	21 001	30 754
Equity and investment fund shares	39 832	48 701	41 725	45 337	56 293	80 967	107 258	135 911
Equity	23 916	29 562	24 396	26 537	27 063	31 029	39 403	48 163
Investment fund shares	15 916	19 139	17 329	18 800	29 230	49 938	67 855	87 748
Money market fund shares	5 054	4 082	2 775	362	594	791	246	883
Non-Money market fund shares	10 862	15 057	14 554	18 438	28 636	49 147	67 609	86 865
Insurance pension and standardised guarantees	12	11	14	13	16	19	15	6
Financial derivatives and employee stock options	532	471	189	512	386	101	496	163
Other accounts receivable	4 195	1 721	3 409	5 349	4 300	5 458	6 264	4 570
Financial liabilities	104 685	124 838	156 009	219 966	246 033	292 128	333 516	390 217
Debt securities	0	0	0	9	12	0	237	213
Short-term debt securities	0	0	0	0	0	0	0	0
Long-term debt securities	0	0	0	9	12	0	237	213
Loans	358	1 672	4 217	25 359	13 918	15 550	9 089	10 845
Short-term loans	358	0	0	5 448	0	1 106	585	597
Long-term loans	0	1 672	4 217	19 911	13 918	14 444	8 504	10 248
Equity and investment fund shares	95 701	116 962	143 838	179 998	218 381	260 468	306 999	354 779
Insurance pension and standardised guarantees	0	0	0	0	0	0	0	0
Financial derivatives and employee stock options	852	289	1 470	412	1 031	1 274	528	1 268
Other accounts payable	7 774	5 915	6 484	14 188	12 691	14 836	16 663	23 112
Non-financial assets	..	..	..	..	..	..	..	..
Open-end investment funds								
Financial net worth	-807	-3 630	-19 802	-58 881	-60 679	-77 595	-88 597	-73 816
Financial assets	150 872	164 771	150 453	164 431	187 843	215 862	245 739	317 608
Currency and deposits	24 381	23 806	26 539	32 135	32 867	25 835	24 122	36 542
Debt securities	80 648	87 755	74 728	73 416	82 644	86 384	86 582	109 623
Loans	915	1 888	3 848	7 667	11 335	17 097	21 001	30 754
Equity and investment fund shares	40 147	49 014	41 725	45 337	56 293	80 967	107 258	135 949
Equity	23 916	29 562	24 396	26 537	27 063	31 029	39 403	48 163
Investment fund shares	16 231	19 452	17 329	18 800	29 230	49 938	67 855	87 786
Money market fund shares	5 164	4 150	2 775	362	594	791	246	921
Non-Money market fund shares	11 067	15 302	14 554	18 438	28 636	49 147	67 609	86 865
Insurance pension and standardised guarantees	13	12	15	14	17	20	16	7
Financial derivatives and employee stock options	573	575	189	513	387	101	496	163
Other accounts receivable	4 195	1 721	3 409	5 349	4 300	5 458	6 264	4 570
Financial liabilities	151 679	168 401	170 255	223 312	248 522	293 457	334 336	391 424
Debt securities	0	0	0	205	68	0	237	213
Short-term debt securities	0	0	0	0	0	0	0	0
Long-term debt securities	0	0	0	205	68	0	237	213
Loans	358	1 672	4 217	25 359	13 918	15 594	9 210	11 003
Short-term loans	358	0	0	5 448	0	1 137	587	603
Long-term loans	0	1 672	4 217	19 911	13 918	14 457	8 623	10 400
Equity and investment fund shares	142 408	160 194	158 057	183 146	220 804	261 751	307 698	355 828
Insurance pension and standardised guarantees	0	0	0	0	0	0	0	0
Financial derivatives and employee stock options	1 139	620	1 497	414	1 041	1 275	528	1 268
Other accounts payable	7 774	5 915	6 484	14 188	12 691	14 837	16 663	23 112
Non-financial assets	..	..	..	..	..	..	..	..

Note: Detailed metadata at: http://metalinks.oecd.org/instinv/20170920/75e8

CZECH REPUBLIC

Table 3. Financial assets and liabilities of insurance corporations and pension funds

Million CZK

	2009	2010	2011	2012	2013	2014	2015	2016
Insurance corporations and pension funds								
Financial net worth	6 875	-20 615	-23 539	-38 068	-26 933	-29 417	-368	-42 180
Financial assets	662 692	685 952	706 705	752 759	798 759	856 215	915 226	906 757
Currency and deposits	57 701	50 542	48 750	60 860	67 832	54 507	55 120	58 755
Debt securities	462 373	468 043	494 623	523 698	550 041	611 360	673 391	624 656
Loans	2 624	2 707	828	763	644	5 916	1 398	1 540
Equity and investment fund shares	71 496	87 012	87 910	98 590	105 483	107 927	110 508	118 157
Equity	24 793	26 080	23 313	22 139	19 219	23 385	19 132	23 732
Investment fund shares	46 703	60 932	64 597	76 451	86 264	84 542	91 376	94 425
Money market fund shares	14 062	12 145	1 406	1 545	1 126	645	694	452
Non-Money market fund shares	32 641	48 787	63 191	74 906	85 138	83 897	90 682	93 973
Insurance pension and standardised guarantees	32 106	36 861	35 948	32 037	36 797	37 853	38 928	38 507
Financial derivatives and employee stock options	677	936	447	754	636	394	717	492
Other accounts receivable	35 715	39 851	38 199	36 057	37 326	38 258	35 164	64 650
Financial liabilities	655 817	706 567	730 244	790 827	825 692	885 632	915 594	948 937
Debt securities	493	521	511	466	479	505	502	653
Short-term debt securities	0	0	0	0	0	0	0	0
Long-term debt securities	493	521	511	466	479	505	502	653
Loans	890	143	119	107	1 280	575	576	1 582
Short-term loans	801	89	79	78	972	1	1	1 556
Long-term loans	89	54	40	29	308	574	575	26
Equity and investment fund shares	90 175	99 339	90 950	111 490	89 743	101 058	105 128	101 420
Insurance pension and standardised guarantees	532 890	576 781	605 323	641 036	689 110	733 547	760 091	792 355
Financial derivatives and employee stock options	1 725	1 519	4 243	3 086	3 195	8 128	6 488	7 212
Other accounts payable	29 644	28 264	29 098	34 642	41 885	41 819	42 809	45 715
Non-financial assets	..	..	..	..	..	..	..	..
Insurance corporations								
Financial net worth	11 675	-15 823	-19 998	-62 831	-56 798	-24 515	1 138	-15 808
Financial assets	451 621	458 228	462 621	454 744	477 104	523 199	543 663	531 009
Currency and deposits	33 965	32 814	29 375	34 198	33 234	31 098	31 237	36 832
Debt securities	288 633	271 733	280 312	259 510	272 306	309 375	334 282	281 946
Loans	2 624	2 707	828	763	644	5 916	1 373	1 514
Equity and investment fund shares	61 835	77 151	81 349	95 311	101 060	102 085	103 238	107 725
Equity	21 778	24 206	22 308	21 552	18 237	22 168	17 737	21 462
Investment fund shares	40 057	52 945	59 041	73 759	82 823	79 917	85 501	86 263
Money market fund shares	12 287	11 160	1 406	1 545	1 126	640	692	452
Non-Money market fund shares	27 770	41 785	57 635	72 214	81 697	79 277	84 809	85 811
Insurance pension and standardised guarantees	32 104	36 859	35 946	32 035	36 795	37 850	38 925	38 504
Financial derivatives and employee stock options	627	697	353	541	358	327	565	315
Other accounts receivable	31 833	36 267	34 458	32 386	32 707	36 548	34 043	64 173
Financial liabilities	439 946	474 051	482 619	517 575	533 902	547 714	542 525	546 817
Debt securities	493	521	511	466	479	505	502	653
Short-term debt securities	0	0	0	0	0	0	0	0
Long-term debt securities	493	521	511	466	479	505	502	653
Loans	890	143	119	107	1 280	575	576	1 582
Short-term loans	801	89	79	78	972	1	1	1 556
Long-term loans	89	54	40	29	308	574	575	26
Equity and investment fund shares	76 686	84 871	78 306	88 468	86 142	85 739	87 251	85 793
Insurance pension and standardised guarantees	332 059	360 556	373 152	394 298	405 867	415 501	408 993	410 671
Financial derivatives and employee stock options	1 048	620	2 233	1 929	1 546	5 149	3 906	4 009
Other accounts payable	28 770	27 340	28 298	32 307	38 588	40 245	41 297	44 109
Non-financial assets	..	..	..	..	..	..	..	..
Pension funds								
Financial net worth	-4 800	-4 792	-3 541	24 763	29 865	-4 902	-1 506	-26 372
Financial assets	211 071	227 724	244 084	298 015	321 655	333 016	371 563	375 748
Currency and deposits	23 736	17 728	19 375	26 662	34 598	23 409	23 883	21 923
Debt securities	173 740	196 310	214 311	264 188	277 735	301 985	339 109	342 710
Loans	0	0	0	0	0	0	25	26
Equity and investment fund shares	9 661	9 861	6 561	3 279	4 423	5 842	7 270	10 432
Equity	3 015	1 874	1 005	587	982	1 217	1 395	2 270
Investment fund shares	6 646	7 987	5 556	2 692	3 441	4 625	5 875	8 162
Money market fund shares	1 775	985	0	0	0	5	2	0
Non-Money market fund shares	4 871	7 002	5 556	2 692	3 441	4 620	5 873	8 162
Insurance pension and standardised guarantees	2	2	2	2	2	3	3	3
Financial derivatives and employee stock options	50	239	94	213	278	67	152	177
Other accounts receivable	3 882	3 584	3 741	3 671	4 619	1 710	1 121	477
Financial liabilities	215 871	232 516	247 625	273 252	291 790	337 918	373 069	402 120
Debt securities	0	0	0	0	0	0	0	0
Short-term debt securities	0	0	0	0	0	0	0	0
Long-term debt securities	0	0	0	0	0	0	0	0
Loans	0	0	0	0	0	0	0	0
Short-term loans	0	0	0	0	0	0	0	0
Long-term loans	0	0	0	0	0	0	0	0
Equity and investment fund shares	13 489	14 468	12 644	23 022	3 601	15 319	17 877	15 627
Insurance pension and standardised guarantees	200 831	216 225	232 171	246 738	283 243	318 046	351 098	381 684
Financial derivatives and employee stock options	677	899	2 010	1 157	1 649	2 979	2 582	3 203
Other accounts payable	874	924	800	2 335	3 297	1 574	1 512	1 606
Non-financial assets	..	..	..	..	..	..	..	..

Note: Detailed metadata at: http://metalinks.oecd.org/instinv/20170920/75e8

Table 4. Portfolio composition by type of investor

As percentage of financial assets and of financial liabilities

Per cent

	2009	2010	2011	2012	2013	2014	2015	2016
Investment funds								
Financial assets	100.0	100.0	100.0	100.0	100.0	100.0	100.0	100.0
Currency and deposits	16.2	14.4	17.6	19.5	17.5	12.0	9.8	11.5
Debt securities	53.5	53.3	49.7	44.6	44.0	40.0	35.2	34.5
Loans	0.6	1.1	2.6	4.7	6.0	7.9	8.5	9.7
Equity and investment fund shares	26.6	29.7	27.7	27.6	30.0	37.5	43.6	42.8
Insurance pension and standardised guarantee schemes	0.0	0.0	0.0	0.0	0.0	0.0	0.0	0.0
Financial derivatives and employee stock options	0.4	0.3	0.1	0.3	0.2	0.0	0.2	0.1
Other accounts receivable	2.8	1.0	2.3	3.3	2.3	2.5	2.5	1.4
Financial liabilities	100.0	100.0	100.0	100.0	100.0	100.0	100.0	100.0
Currency and deposits	0.0	0.0	0.0	0.0	0.0	0.0	0.0	0.0
Debt securities	0.0	0.0	0.0	0.1	0.0	0.0	0.1	0.1
Loans	0.2	1.0	2.5	11.4	5.6	5.3	2.8	2.8
Equity and investment fund shares	93.9	95.1	92.8	82.0	88.8	89.2	92.0	90.9
Insurance pension and standardised guarantee schemes	0.0	0.0	0.0	0.0	0.0	0.0	0.0	0.0
Financial derivatives and employee stock options	0.8	0.4	0.9	0.2	0.4	0.4	0.2	0.3
Other accounts receivable	5.1	3.5	3.8	6.4	5.1	5.1	5.0	5.9
Insurance corporations								
Financial assets	100.0	100.0	100.0	100.0	100.0	100.0	100.0	100.0
Currency and deposits	7.5	7.2	6.3	7.5	7.0	5.9	5.7	6.9
Debt securities	63.9	59.3	60.6	57.1	57.1	59.1	61.5	53.1
Loans	0.6	0.6	0.2	0.2	0.1	1.1	0.3	0.3
Equity and investment fund shares	13.7	16.8	17.6	21.0	21.2	19.5	19.0	20.3
Insurance pension and standardised guarantee schemes	7.1	8.0	7.8	7.0	7.7	7.2	7.2	7.3
Financial derivatives and employee stock options	0.1	0.2	0.1	0.1	0.1	0.1	0.1	0.1
Other accounts receivable	7.0	7.9	7.4	7.1	6.9	7.0	6.3	12.1
Financial liabilities	100.0	100.0	100.0	100.0	100.0	100.0	100.0	100.0
Currency and deposits	0.0	0.0	0.0	0.0	0.0	0.0	0.0	0.0
Debt securities	0.1	0.1	0.1	0.1	0.1	0.1	0.1	0.1
Loans	0.2	0.0	0.0	0.0	0.2	0.1	0.1	0.3
Equity and investment fund shares	17.4	17.9	16.2	17.1	16.1	15.7	16.1	15.7
Insurance pension and standardised guarantee schemes	75.5	76.1	77.3	76.2	76.0	75.9	75.4	75.1
Financial derivatives and employee stock options	0.2	0.1	0.5	0.4	0.3	0.9	0.7	0.7
Other accounts receivable	6.5	5.8	5.9	6.2	7.2	7.3	7.6	8.1
Pension funds								
Financial assets	100.0	100.0	100.0	100.0	100.0	100.0	100.0	100.0
Currency and deposits	11.2	7.8	7.9	8.9	10.8	7.0	6.4	5.8
Debt securities	82.3	86.2	87.8	88.6	86.3	90.7	91.3	91.2
Loans	0.0	0.0	0.0	0.0	0.0	0.0	0.0	0.0
Equity and investment fund shares	4.6	4.3	2.7	1.1	1.4	1.8	2.0	2.8
Insurance pension and standardised guarantee schemes	0.0	0.0	0.0	0.0	0.0	0.0	0.0	0.0
Financial derivatives and employee stock options	0.0	0.1	0.0	0.1	0.1	0.0	0.0	0.0
Other accounts receivable	1.8	1.6	1.5	1.2	1.4	0.5	0.3	0.1
Financial liabilities	100.0	100.0	100.0	100.0	100.0	100.0	100.0	100.0
Currency and deposits	0.0	0.0	0.0	0.0	0.0	0.0	0.0	0.0
Debt securities	0.0	0.0	0.0	0.0	0.0	0.0	0.0	0.0
Loans	0.0	0.0	0.0	0.0	0.0	0.0	0.0	0.0
Equity and investment fund shares	6.2	6.2	5.1	8.4	1.2	4.5	4.8	3.9
Insurance pension and standardised guarantee schemes	93.0	93.0	93.8	90.3	97.1	94.1	94.1	94.9
Financial derivatives and employee stock options	0.3	0.4	0.8	0.4	0.6	0.9	0.7	0.8
Other accounts receivable	0.4	0.4	0.3	0.9	1.1	0.5	0.4	0.4

Note: Detailed metadata at: http://metalinks.oecd.org/instinv/20170920/a49a

DENMARK

Table 1. Financial assets and liabilities of institutional investors, 2016

Million DKK

	Total	Investment funds			
		Non-money market funds			Money market funds
		Total	Open-end non-money market funds	Closed-end non-money market funds	Total
Financial assets	2 182 680	2 182 680	2 182 680	..	..
Currency and deposits	49 942	49 942	49 942	..	..
Debt securities	1 123 181	1 123 181	1 123 181	..	..
Debt securities, short term	462	462	462	..	..
Debt securities, long term	1 122 719	1 122 719	1 122 719	..	..
Debt securities issued by residents	593 227	593 227	593 227	..	..
Debt securities issued by non-residents	529 954	529 954	529 954	..	..
Loans	38	38	38	..	..
Loans, short-term	30	30	30	..	..
Loans, long-term	8	8	8	..	..
Loans granted to residents	0	0	0	..	..
Loans granted to non-residents	38	38	38	..	..
Equity and investment fund shares/units	1 002 224	1 002 224	1 002 224	..	..
Equity and investment fund shares issued/units by residents	238 489	238 489	238 489	..	..
Equity and investment fund shares/units issued by non residents	763 735	763 735	763 735	..	..
Other accounts receivable	..	..	..	..	..

	Total	Investment funds			
		Non-money market funds			Money market funds
		Total	Open-end non-money market funds	Closed-end non-money market funds	Total
Financial liabilities	2 145 855	2 145 855	2 145 855	..	..
Currency and deposits	..	..	..	..	..
Debt securities	..	..	..	..	..
Debt securities, short term	..	..	..	..	..
Debt securities, long term	..	..	..	..	..
Loans	94 111	94 111	94 111	..	..
Loans, short-term	93 076	93 076	93 076	..	..
Loans, long-term	1 035	1 035	1 035	..	..
Equity and investment fund shares/units	2 040 284	2 040 284	2 040 284	..	..
Insurance pension and standardised guaratees	..	..	..	..	..
Financial derivatives and employee stock options	11 460	11 460	11 460	..	..
Other accounts payable	..	..	..	..	..

	Total	Insurance corporations and pension funds			
		Insurance corporations			Pension funds
		Total	Life insurance corporations	Non-life insurance corporations	Total
Financial assets	3 948 271	2 363 359	..	..	1 584 912
Currency and deposits	91 910	29 104	..	..	62 806
Debt securities	1 568 402	820 959	..	..	747 443
Debt securities, short-term	19 056	8 198	..	..	10 858
Debt securities, long term	1 549 346	812 761	..	..	736 585
Debt securities issued by residents	1 029 762	571 802	..	..	457 960
Debt securities issued by non-residents	538 640	249 157	..	..	289 483
Loans	41 621	22 708	..	..	18 913
Loans, short-term	24 238	5 743	..	..	18 495
Loans, long-term	17 383	16 965	..	..	418
Loans granted to residents	25 632	20 256	..	..	5 376
Loans granted to non-residents	15 989	2 452	..	..	13 537
Equity and investment fund shares/units	2 003 350	1 341 919	..	..	661 431
Equity and investment fund shares/units issued by residents	1 383 401	889 615	..	..	493 786
Equity and investment fund shares/units issued by non residents	619 949	452 304	..	..	167 645
Other accounts receivable	75 276	52 281	..	..	22 995

	Total	Insurance corporations and pension funds			
		Insurance corporations			Pension funds
		Total	Life insurance corporations	Non-life insurance corporations	Total
Financial liabilities	3 936 267	2 371 636	..	..	1 564 631
Currency and deposits	..	..	..	..	..
Debt securities	6 832	6 904	..	..	-72
Debt securities, short term	..	..	..	..	..
Debt securities, long term	6 832	6 904	..	..	-72
Loans	207 639	173 241	..	..	34 398
Loans, short-term	195 809	161 495	..	..	34 314
Loans, long-term	11 830	11 746	..	..	84
Equity and investment fund shares/units	283 913	177 460	..	..	106 453
Insurance pension and standardised guarantees	3 232 132	1 886 822	..	..	1 345 310
Financial derivatives and employee stock options	91 778	42 568	..	..	49 210
Other accounts payable	113 973	84 641	..	..	29 332

Note: Detailed metadata at: http://metalinks.oecd.org/instinv/20170920/75e8

DENMARK

Table 2. Financial assets and liabilities of investment funds

Million DKK

	2009	2010	2011	2012	2013	2014	2015	2016
Investment funds								
Financial net worth	..	..	..	-38 247	713	7 077	2 093	36 825
Financial assets	..	..	..	1 638 793	1 872 524	2 087 626	2 066 818	2 182 680
Currency and deposits	..	..	..	22 930	34 273	41 649	42 075	49 942
Debt securities	..	..	..	905 026	1 036 270	1 110 216	1 045 483	1 123 181
Loans	..	..	..	362	590	727	483	38
Equity and investment fund shares	..	..	..	705 778	790 863	917 741	966 843	1 002 224
Equity	..	..	..	564 017	632 065	740 630	775 557	817 812
Investment fund shares	..	..	..	141 761	158 798	177 111	191 286	184 412
Money market fund shares	..	..	..	..	..	..	..	..
Non-Money market fund shares	..	..	..	141 761	158 798	177 111	191 286	184 412
Insurance pension and standardised guarantees	..	..	..	..	..	..	..	..
Financial derivatives and employee stock options	..	..	..	4 697	10 528	17 293	11 934	7 295
Other accounts receivable	..	..	..	..	..	..	..	..
Financial liabilities	..	..	..	1 677 040	1 871 811	2 080 549	2 064 725	2 145 855
Debt securities	..	..	..	..	..	..	..	..
Short-term debt securities	..	..	..	..	..	..	..	..
Long-term debt securities	..	..	..	..	..	..	..	..
Loans	..	..	..	107 393	127 339	135 986	124 240	94 111
Short-term loans	..	..	..	106 941	126 773	134 697	123 170	93 076
Long-term loans	..	..	..	452	566	1 289	1 070	1 035
Equity and investment fund shares	..	..	..	1 565 455	1 738 051	1 918 770	1 927 242	2 040 284
Insurance pension and standardised guarantees	..	..	..	..	..	..	..	..
Financial derivatives and employee stock options	..	..	..	4 192	6 421	25 793	13 243	11 460
Other accounts payable	..	..	..	..	..	..	..	..
Non-financial assets	..	..	..	0	0	0	0	0
Money market funds								
Financial net worth	..	..	..	..	..	..	..	..
Financial assets	..	..	..	..	..	..	..	..
Currency and deposits	..	..	..	..	..	..	..	..
Debt securities	..	..	..	..	..	..	..	..
Loans	..	..	..	..	..	..	..	..
Equity and investment fund shares	..	..	..	..	..	..	..	..
Equity	..	..	..	..	..	..	..	..
Investment fund shares	..	..	..	..	..	..	..	..
Money market fund shares	..	..	..	..	..	..	..	..
Non-Money market fund shares	..	..	..	..	..	..	..	..
Insurance pension and standardised guarantees	..	..	..	..	..	..	..	..
Financial derivatives and employee stock options	..	..	..	..	..	..	..	..
Other accounts receivable	..	..	..	..	..	..	..	..
Financial liabilities	..	..	..	..	..	..	..	..
Debt securities	..	..	..	..	..	..	..	..
Short-term debt securities	..	..	..	..	..	..	..	..
Long-term debt securities	..	..	..	..	..	..	..	..
Loans	..	..	..	..	..	..	..	..
Short-term loans	..	..	..	..	..	..	..	..
Long-term loans	..	..	..	..	..	..	..	..
Equity and investment fund shares	..	..	..	..	..	..	..	..
Insurance pension and standardised guarantees	..	..	..	..	..	..	..	..
Financial derivatives and employee stock options	..	..	..	..	..	..	..	..
Other accounts payable	..	..	..	..	..	..	..	..
Non-financial assets	..	..	..	..	..	..	..	..
Non-money market funds								
Financial net worth	..	..	..	-38 247	713	7 077	2 093	36 825
Financial assets	..	..	..	1 638 793	1 872 524	2 087 626	2 066 818	2 182 680
Currency and deposits	..	..	..	22 930	34 273	41 649	42 075	49 942
Debt securities	..	..	..	905 026	1 036 270	1 110 216	1 045 483	1 123 181
Loans	..	..	..	362	590	727	483	38
Equity and investment fund shares	..	..	..	705 778	790 863	917 741	966 843	1 002 224
Equity	..	..	..	564 017	632 065	740 630	775 557	817 812
Investment fund shares	..	..	..	141 761	158 798	177 111	191 286	184 412
Money market fund shares	..	..	..	..	..	..	..	..
Non-Money market fund shares	..	..	..	141 761	158 798	177 111	191 286	184 412
Insurance pension and standardised guarantees	..	..	..	..	..	..	..	..
Financial derivatives and employee stock options	..	..	..	4 697	10 528	17 293	11 934	7 295
Other accounts receivable	..	..	..	..	..	..	..	..
Financial liabilities	..	..	..	1 677 040	1 871 811	2 080 549	2 064 725	2 145 855
Debt securities	..	..	..	..	..	..	..	..
Short-term debt securities	..	..	..	..	..	..	..	..
Long-term debt securities	..	..	..	..	..	..	..	..
Loans	..	..	..	107 393	127 339	135 986	124 240	94 111
Short-term loans	..	..	..	106 941	126 773	134 697	123 170	93 076
Long-term loans	..	..	..	452	566	1 289	1 070	1 035
Equity and investment fund shares	..	..	..	1 565 455	1 738 051	1 918 770	1 927 242	2 040 284
Insurance pension and standardised guarantees	..	..	..	..	..	..	..	..
Financial derivatives and employee stock options	..	..	..	4 192	6 421	25 793	13 243	11 460
Other accounts payable	..	..	..	..	..	..	..	..
Non-financial assets	..	..	..	0	0	0	0	0
Open-end non-money market funds								
Financial net worth	..	..	..	-38 247	713	7 077	2 093	36 825
Financial assets	..	..	..	1 638 793	1 872 524	2 087 626	2 066 818	2 182 680

Table 2. Financial assets and liabilities of investment funds *(cont.)*

Million DKK

	2009	2010	2011	2012	2013	2014	2015	2016
Currency and deposits	..	..	..	22 930	34 273	41 649	42 075	49 942
Debt securities	..	..	..	905 026	1 036 270	1 110 216	1 045 483	1 123 181
Loans	..	..	..	362	590	727	483	38
Equity and investment fund shares	..	..	..	705 778	790 863	917 741	966 843	1 002 224
Equity	..	..	..	564 017	632 065	740 630	775 557	817 812
Investment fund shares	..	..	..	141 761	158 798	177 111	191 286	184 412
Money market fund shares	..	..	..	..	..	..	..	..
Non-Money market fund shares	..	..	..	141 761	158 798	177 111	191 286	184 412
Insurance pension and standardised guarantees	..	..	..	..	..	..	..	..
Financial derivatives and employee stock options	..	..	..	4 697	10 528	17 293	11 934	7 295
Other accounts receivable	..	..	..	..	..	..	..	..
Financial liabilities	..	..	..	1 677 040	1 871 811	2 080 549	2 064 725	2 145 855
Debt securities	..	..	..	..	..	..	..	..
Short-term debt securities	..	..	..	..	..	..	..	..
Long-term debt securities	..	..	..	..	..	..	..	..
Loans	..	..	..	107 393	127 339	135 986	124 240	94 111
Short-term loans	..	..	..	106 941	126 773	134 697	123 170	93 076
Long-term loans	..	..	..	452	566	1 289	1 070	1 035
Equity and investment fund shares	..	..	..	1 565 455	1 738 051	1 918 770	1 927 242	2 040 284
Insurance pension and standardised guarantees	..	..	..	..	..	..	..	..
Financial derivatives and employee stock options	..	..	..	4 192	6 421	25 793	13 243	11 460
Other accounts payable	..	..	..	..	..	..	..	..
Non-financial assets	..	..	..	0	0	0	0	0
Open-end investment funds								
Financial net worth	..	..	..	-38 247	713	7 077	2 093	36 825
Financial assets	..	..	..	1 638 793	1 872 524	2 087 626	2 066 818	2 182 680
Currency and deposits	..	..	..	22 930	34 273	41 649	42 075	49 942
Debt securities	..	..	..	905 026	1 036 270	1 110 216	1 045 483	1 123 181
Loans	..	..	..	362	590	727	483	38
Equity and investment fund shares	..	..	..	705 778	790 863	917 741	966 843	1 002 224
Equity	..	..	..	564 017	632 065	740 630	775 557	817 812
Investment fund shares	..	..	..	141 761	158 798	177 111	191 286	184 412
Money market fund shares	..	..	..	..	..	..	..	..
Non-Money market fund shares	..	..	..	141 761	158 798	177 111	191 286	184 412
Insurance pension and standardised guarantees	..	..	..	..	..	..	..	..
Financial derivatives and employee stock options	..	..	..	4 697	10 528	17 293	11 934	7 295
Other accounts receivable	..	..	..	..	..	..	..	..
Financial liabilities	..	..	..	1 677 040	1 871 811	2 080 549	2 064 725	2 145 855
Debt securities	..	..	..	..	..	..	..	..
Short-term debt securities	..	..	..	..	..	..	..	..
Long-term debt securities	..	..	..	..	..	..	..	..
Loans	..	..	..	107 393	127 339	135 986	124 240	94 111
Short-term loans	..	..	..	106 941	126 773	134 697	123 170	93 076
Long-term loans	..	..	..	452	566	1 289	1 070	1 035
Equity and investment fund shares	..	..	..	1 565 455	1 738 051	1 918 770	1 927 242	2 040 284
Insurance pension and standardised guarantees	..	..	..	..	..	..	..	..
Financial derivatives and employee stock options	..	..	..	4 192	6 421	25 793	13 243	11 460
Other accounts payable	..	..	..	..	..	..	..	..
Non-financial assets	..	..	..	0	0	0	0	0

Note: Detailed metadata at: http://metalinks.oecd.org/instinv/20170920/75e8

DENMARK

Table 3. Financial assets and liabilities of insurance corporations and pension funds

Million DKK

	2009	2010	2011	2012	2013	2014	2015	2016
Insurance corporations and pension funds								
Financial net worth	..	..	..	42 448	44 394	57 633	-54 525	12 004
Financial assets	..	..	..	3 267 838	3 163 058	3 581 842	3 618 939	3 948 271
Currency and deposits	..	..	..	93 246	82 199	95 547	72 344	91 910
Debt securities	..	..	..	1 432 204	1 296 804	1 422 096	1 516 181	1 568 402
Loans	..	..	..	33 964	31 148	49 428	53 415	41 621
Equity and investment fund shares	..	..	..	1 589 070	1 632 510	1 731 417	1 765 627	2 003 350
Equity	..	..	..	670 938	602 528	582 031	708 937	838 441
Investment fund shares	..	..	..	917 557	1 029 982	1 149 386	1 056 690	1 164 909
Money market fund shares	..	..	..	..	..	..	..	..
Non-Money market fund shares	..	..	..	917 557	1 029 982	1 149 386	1 056 690	1 164 909
Insurance pension and standardised guarantees	..	..	..	11 533	13 821	7 958	8 762	7 209
Financial derivatives and employee stock options	..	..	..	52 566	36 318	208 162	141 070	160 503
Other accounts receivable	..	..	..	55 255	70 258	67 234	61 540	75 276
Financial liabilities	..	..	..	3 225 390	3 118 664	3 524 209	3 673 464	3 936 267
Debt securities	..	..	..	-25	-34	2 253	5 939	6 832
Short-term debt securities	..	..	..	..	..	..	..	..
Long-term debt securities	..	..	..	-25	-34	2 253	5 939	6 832
Loans	..	..	..	182 053	130 917	160 502	210 786	207 639
Short-term loans	..	..	..	162 701	114 802	137 986	191 226	195 809
Long-term loans	..	..	..	19 352	16 115	22 516	19 560	11 830
Equity and investment fund shares	..	..	..	216 031	219 094	206 619	287 902	283 913
Insurance pension and standardised guarantees	..	..	..	2 641 560	2 616 361	2 959 236	3 035 943	3 232 132
Financial derivatives and employee stock options	..	..	..	32 554	24 167	84 390	67 655	91 778
Other accounts payable	..	..	..	153 217	128 159	111 209	65 239	113 973
Non-financial assets	..	..	..	0	0	0	0	0
Insurance corporations								
Financial net worth	..	..	..	-838	9 784	13 089	-98 843	-8 277
Financial assets	..	..	..	1 867 615	1 879 816	2 119 934	2 128 965	2 363 359
Currency and deposits	..	..	..	38 520	37 419	33 408	28 292	29 104
Debt securities	..	..	..	645 801	633 653	686 828	790 180	820 959
Loans	..	..	..	23 689	20 074	22 648	21 605	22 708
Equity and investment fund shares	..	..	..	1 066 074	1 107 305	1 187 082	1 165 735	1 341 919
Equity	..	..	..	423 876	366 841	352 264	429 284	572 956
Investment fund shares	..	..	..	641 623	740 464	834 818	736 451	768 963
Money market fund shares	..	..	..	..	..	..	..	..
Non-Money market fund shares	..	..	..	641 623	740 464	834 818	736 451	768 963
Insurance pension and standardised guarantees	..	..	..	11 247	13 535	7 960	8 764	7 211
Financial derivatives and employee stock options	..	..	..	48 041	33 097	142 346	78 086	89 177
Other accounts receivable	..	..	..	34 243	34 733	39 662	36 303	52 281
Financial liabilities	..	..	..	1 868 453	1 870 032	2 106 845	2 227 808	2 371 636
Debt securities	..	..	..	47	38	2 325	6 011	6 904
Short-term debt securities	..	..	..	..	..	..	..	..
Long-term debt securities	..	..	..	47	38	2 325	6 011	6 904
Loans	..	..	..	74 351	94 067	123 777	182 676	173 241
Short-term loans	..	..	..	57 368	79 728	109 630	165 048	161 495
Long-term loans	..	..	..	16 983	14 339	14 147	17 628	11 746
Equity and investment fund shares	..	..	..	136 747	137 208	126 074	203 596	177 460
Insurance pension and standardised guarantees	..	..	..	1 534 037	1 537 852	1 703 826	1 763 031	1 886 822
Financial derivatives and employee stock options	..	..	..	29 301	21 833	66 440	27 343	42 568
Other accounts payable	..	..	..	93 970	79 034	84 403	45 151	84 641
Non-financial assets	..	..	..	0	0	0	0	0
Pension funds								
Financial net worth	..	..	..	43 286	34 610	44 544	44 318	20 281
Financial assets	..	..	..	1 400 223	1 283 242	1 461 908	1 489 974	1 584 912
Currency and deposits	..	..	..	54 726	44 780	62 139	44 052	62 806
Debt securities	..	..	..	786 403	663 151	735 268	726 001	747 443
Loans	..	..	..	10 275	11 074	26 780	31 810	18 913
Equity and investment fund shares	..	..	..	522 996	525 205	544 335	599 892	661 431
Equity	..	..	..	247 062	235 687	229 767	279 653	265 485
Investment fund shares	..	..	..	275 934	289 518	314 568	320 239	395 946
Money market fund shares	..	..	..	..	..	..	..	..
Non-Money market fund shares	..	..	..	275 934	289 518	314 568	320 239	395 946
Insurance pension and standardised guarantees	..	..	..	286	286	-2	-2	-2
Financial derivatives and employee stock options	..	..	..	4 525	3 221	65 816	62 984	71 326
Other accounts receivable	..	..	..	21 012	35 525	27 572	25 237	22 995
Financial liabilities	..	..	..	1 356 937	1 248 632	1 417 364	1 445 656	1 564 631
Debt securities	..	..	..	-72	-72	-72	-72	-72
Short-term debt securities	..	..	..	..	..	..	..	..
Long-term debt securities	..	..	..	-72	-72	-72	-72	-72
Loans	..	..	..	107 702	36 850	36 725	28 110	34 398
Short-term loans	..	..	..	105 333	35 074	28 356	26 178	34 314
Long-term loans	..	..	..	2 369	1 776	8 369	1 932	84
Equity and investment fund shares	..	..	..	79 284	81 886	80 545	84 306	106 453
Insurance pension and standardised guarantees	..	..	..	1 107 523	1 078 509	1 255 410	1 272 912	1 345 310
Financial derivatives and employee stock options	..	..	..	3 253	2 334	17 950	40 312	49 210
Other accounts payable	..	..	..	59 247	49 125	26 806	20 088	29 332
Non-financial assets	..	..	..	0	0	0	0	0

Note: Detailed metadata at: http://metalinks.oecd.org/instinv/20170920/75e8

Table 4. Portfolio composition by type of investor

As percentage of financial assets and of financial liabilities

Per cent

	2009	2010	2011	2012	2013	2014	2015	2016
Investment funds								
Financial assets	..	..	..	100.0	100.0	100.0	100.0	100.0
Currency and deposits	..	..	..	1.4	1.8	2.0	2.0	2.3
Debt securities	..	..	..	55.2	55.3	53.2	50.6	51.5
Loans	..	..	..	0.0	0.0	0.0	0.0	0.0
Equity and investment fund shares	..	..	..	43.1	42.2	44.0	46.8	45.9
Insurance pension and standardised guarantee schemes	..	..	..	0.0	0.0	0.0	0.0	0.0
Financial derivatives and employee stock options	..	..	..	0.3	0.6	0.8	0.6	0.3
Other accounts receivable	..	..	..	0.0	0.0	0.0	0.0	0.0
Financial liabilities	..	..	..	100.0	100.0	100.0	100.0	100.0
Currency and deposits	..	..	..	0.0	0.0	0.0	0.0	0.0
Debt securities	..	..	..	0.0	0.0	0.0	0.0	0.0
Loans	..	..	..	6.4	6.8	6.5	6.0	4.4
Equity and investment fund shares	..	..	..	93.3	92.9	92.2	93.3	95.1
Insurance pension and standardised guarantee schemes	..	..	..	0.0	0.0	0.0	0.0	0.0
Financial derivatives and employee stock options	..	..	..	0.2	0.3	1.2	0.6	0.5
Other accounts receivable	..	..	..	0.0	0.0	0.0	0.0	0.0
Insurance corporations								
Financial assets	..	..	..	100.0	100.0	100.0	100.0	100.0
Currency and deposits	..	..	..	2.1	2.0	1.6	1.3	1.2
Debt securities	..	..	..	34.6	33.7	32.4	37.1	34.7
Loans	..	..	..	1.3	1.1	1.1	1.0	1.0
Equity and investment fund shares	..	..	..	57.1	58.9	56.0	54.8	56.8
Insurance pension and standardised guarantee schemes	..	..	..	0.6	0.7	0.4	0.4	0.3
Financial derivatives and employee stock options	..	..	..	2.6	1.8	6.7	3.7	3.8
Other accounts receivable	..	..	..	1.8	1.8	1.9	1.7	2.2
Financial liabilities	..	..	..	100.0	100.0	100.0	100.0	100.0
Currency and deposits	..	..	..	0.0	0.0	0.0	0.0	0.0
Debt securities	..	..	..	0.0	0.0	0.1	0.3	0.3
Loans	..	..	..	4.0	5.0	5.9	8.2	7.3
Equity and investment fund shares	..	..	..	7.3	7.3	6.0	9.1	7.5
Insurance pension and standardised guarantee schemes	..	..	..	82.1	82.2	80.9	79.1	79.6
Financial derivatives and employee stock options	..	..	..	1.6	1.2	3.2	1.2	1.8
Other accounts receivable	..	..	..	5.0	4.2	4.0	2.0	3.6
Pension funds								
Financial assets	..	..	..	100.0	100.0	100.0	100.0	100.0
Currency and deposits	..	..	..	3.9	3.5	4.3	3.0	4.0
Debt securities	..	..	..	56.2	51.7	50.3	48.7	47.2
Loans	..	..	..	0.7	0.9	1.8	2.1	1.2
Equity and investment fund shares	..	..	..	37.4	40.9	37.2	40.3	41.7
Insurance pension and standardised guarantee schemes	..	..	..	0.0	0.0	0.0	0.0	0.0
Financial derivatives and employee stock options	..	..	..	0.3	0.3	4.5	4.2	4.5
Other accounts receivable	..	..	..	1.5	2.8	1.9	1.7	1.5
Financial liabilities	..	..	..	100.0	100.0	100.0	100.0	100.0
Currency and deposits	..	..	..	0.0	0.0	0.0	0.0	0.0
Debt securities	..	..	..	0.0	0.0	0.0	0.0	0.0
Loans	..	..	..	7.9	3.0	2.6	1.9	2.2
Equity and investment fund shares	..	..	..	5.8	6.6	5.7	5.8	6.8
Insurance pension and standardised guarantee schemes	..	..	..	81.6	86.4	88.6	88.1	86.0
Financial derivatives and employee stock options	..	..	..	0.2	0.2	1.3	2.8	3.1
Other accounts receivable	..	..	..	4.4	3.9	1.9	1.4	1.9

Note: Detailed metadata at: http://metalinks.oecd.org/instinv/20170920/a49a

ESTONIA

Table 1. Financial assets and liabilities of institutional investors, 2016

Million EUR (2011 EEK euro)

	Investment funds				
		Non-money market funds			Money market funds
	Total	Total	Open-end non-money market funds	Closed-end non-money market funds	Total
Financial assets	728	728	336	392	0
Currency and deposits	66	66	33	33	0
Debt securities	17	17	9	8	0
Debt securities, short term	0	0	0	0	0
Debt securities, long term	17	17	9	8	0
Debt securities issued by residents	9	9	1	7	0
Debt securities issued by non-residents	8	8	8	0	0
Loans	69	69	0	69	0
Loans, short-term	3	3	0	3	0
Loans, long-term	65	65	0	65	0
Loans granted to residents	44	44	0	44	0
Loans granted to non-residents	25	25	0	25	0
Equity and investment fund shares/units	573	573	292	281	0
Equity and investment fund shares issued/units by residents	162	162	6	155	0
Equity and investment fund shares/units issued by non residents	412	412	285	126	0
Other accounts receivable	3	3	2	1	0

	Investment funds				
		Non-money market funds			Money market funds
	Total	Total	Open-end non-money market funds	Closed-end non-money market funds	Total
Financial liabilities	743	743	336	407	0
Currency and deposits	0	0	0	0	0
Debt securities	0	0	0	0	0
Debt securities, short term	0	0	..	..	0
Debt securities, long term	0	0	..	..	0
Loans	21	21	0	21	0
Loans, short-term	8	8	..	..	0
Loans, long-term	13	13	..	..	0
Equity and investment fund shares/units	715	715	331	384	0
Insurance pension and standardised guaratees	0	0	0	0	0
Financial derivatives and employee stock options	0	0	0	0	0
Other accounts payable	7	7	5	2	0

	Insurance corporations and pension funds				
		Insurance corporations			Pension funds
	Total	Total	Life insurance corporations	Non-life insurance corporations	Total
Financial assets	4 485	1 244	..	..	3 241
Currency and deposits	900	162	..	..	738
Debt securities	1 114	532	..	..	582
Debt securities, short-term	0	0	..	..	0
Debt securities, long term	1 114	532	..	..	582
Debt securities issued by residents	54	12	..	..	42
Debt securities issued by non-residents	1 061	520	..	..	541
Loans	0	0	..	..	0
Loans, short-term	0	0	..	..	0
Loans, long-term	0	0	..	..	0
Loans granted to residents	0	0	..	..	0
Loans granted to non-residents	0	0	..	..	0
Equity and investment fund shares/units	2 408	493	..	..	1 915
Equity and investment fund shares/units issued by residents	198	61	..	..	137
Equity and investment fund shares/units issued by non residents	2 210	432	..	..	1 778
Other accounts receivable	40	35	..	..	5

	Insurance corporations and pension funds				
		Insurance corporations			Pension funds
	Total	Total	Life insurance corporations	Non-life insurance corporations	Total
Financial liabilities	4 483	1 244	..	..	3 238
Currency and deposits	0	0	..	..	0
Debt securities	0	0	..	..	0
Debt securities, short term	0	0	..	..	0
Debt securities, long term	0	0	..	..	0
Loans	24	24	..	..	0
Loans, short-term	0	0	..	..	0
Loans, long-term	24	24	..	..	0
Equity and investment fund shares/units	408	408	..	..	0
Insurance pension and standardised guarantees	3 873	638	..	..	3 235
Financial derivatives and employee stock options	0	0	..	..	0
Other accounts payable	178	175	..	..	3

Note: Detailed metadata at: http://metalinks.oecd.org/instinv/20170920/a2d2

Table 2. Financial assets and liabilities of investment funds

Million EUR

	2009	2010	2011	2012	2013	2014	2015	2016
Investment funds								
Financial net worth	-11	-6	-10	-1	19	29	2	-15
Financial assets	552	585	447	514	631	603	607	728
Currency and deposits	63	27	22	48	56	53	46	66
Debt securities	79	67	67	75	70	70	62	17
Loans	36	20	18	14	32	27	33	69
Equity and investment fund shares	366	462	337	369	460	435	464	573
Equity	247	315	207	224	314	287	323	443
Investment fund shares	118	147	130	144	147	148	140	130
Money market fund shares	..	..	..	..	..	..	..	..
Non-Money market fund shares	..	..	..	..	..	..	..	..
Insurance pension and standardised guarantees	0	0	0	0	0	0	0	0
Financial derivatives and employee stock options	0	4	0	1	4	6	0	0
Other accounts receivable	8	5	2	6	10	11	2	3
Financial liabilities	562	592	457	514	612	574	605	743
Debt securities	22	19	12	0	0	0	0	0
Short-term debt securities	0	0	0	0	0	0	0	0
Long-term debt securities	22	19	12	0	0	0	0	0
Loans	10	4	13	26	24	27	21	21
Short-term loans	1	1	1	1	0	27	8	8
Long-term loans	9	3	12	25	24	0	14	13
Equity and investment fund shares	520	564	429	485	583	538	580	715
Insurance pension and standardised guarantees	0	0	0	0	0	0	0	0
Financial derivatives and employee stock options	0	0	0	0	0	1	0	0
Other accounts payable	10	5	3	3	5	7	3	7
Non-financial assets	12	12	13	14	0	0	0	0
Money market funds								
Financial net worth	0	0	0	0	0	0	0	0
Financial assets	0	0	0	0	0	0	0	0
Currency and deposits	0	0	0	0	0	0	0	0
Debt securities	0	0	0	0	0	0	0	0
Loans	0	0	0	0	0	0	0	0
Equity and investment fund shares	0	0	0	0	0	0	0	0
Equity	0	0	0	0	0	0	0	0
Investment fund shares	0	0	0	0	0	0	0	0
Money market fund shares	..	..	..	..	..	..	..	..
Non-Money market fund shares	..	..	..	..	..	..	..	..
Insurance pension and standardised guarantees	0	0	0	0	0	0	0	0
Financial derivatives and employee stock options	0	0	0	0	0	0	0	0
Other accounts receivable	0	0	0	0	0	0	0	0
Financial liabilities	0	0	0	0	0	0	0	0
Debt securities	0	0	0	0	0	0	0	0
Short-term debt securities	0	0	0	0	0	0	0	0
Long-term debt securities	0	0	0	0	0	0	0	0
Loans	0	0	0	0	0	0	0	0
Short-term loans	0	0	0	0	0	0	0	0
Long-term loans	0	0	0	0	0	0	0	0
Equity and investment fund shares	0	0	0	0	0	0	0	0
Insurance pension and standardised guarantees	0	0	0	0	0	0	0	0
Financial derivatives and employee stock options	0	0	0	0	0	0	0	0
Other accounts payable	0	0	0	0	0	0	0	0
Non-financial assets	0	0	0	0	0	0	0	0
Non-money market funds								
Financial net worth	-11	-6	-10	-1	19	29	2	-15
Financial assets	552	585	447	514	631	603	607	728
Currency and deposits	63	27	22	48	56	53	46	66
Debt securities	79	67	67	75	70	70	62	17
Loans	36	20	18	14	32	27	33	69
Equity and investment fund shares	366	462	337	369	460	435	464	573
Equity	247	315	207	224	314	287	323	443
Investment fund shares	118	147	130	144	147	148	140	130
Money market fund shares	0	0	0	0	0	0	0	0
Non-Money market fund shares	118	147	130	144	147	148	140	130
Insurance pension and standardised guarantees	0	0	0	0	0	0	0	0
Financial derivatives and employee stock options	0	4	0	1	4	6	0	0
Other accounts receivable	8	5	2	6	10	11	2	3
Financial liabilities	562	592	457	514	612	574	605	743
Debt securities	22	19	12	0	0	0	0	0
Short-term debt securities	0	0	0	0	0	0	0	0
Long-term debt securities	22	19	12	0	0	0	0	0
Loans	10	4	13	26	24	27	21	21
Short-term loans	1	1	1	1	0	27	8	8
Long-term loans	9	3	12	25	24	0	14	13
Equity and investment fund shares	520	564	429	485	583	538	580	715
Insurance pension and standardised guarantees	0	0	0	0	0	0	0	0
Financial derivatives and employee stock options	0	0	0	0	0	1	0	0
Other accounts payable	10	5	3	3	5	7	3	7
Non-financial assets	12	12	13	14	0	0	0	0
Open-end non-money market funds								
Financial net worth	0	0	0	-1	-1	0	0	0
Financial assets	437	506	362	384	438	389	341	336

ESTONIA

Table 2. Financial assets and liabilities of investment funds *(cont.)*

Million EUR

	2009	2010	2011	2012	2013	2014	2015	2016
Currency and deposits	49	19	13	12	21	32	24	33
Debt securities	50	58	59	72	68	64	54	9
Loans	0	0	0	0	0	0	0	0
Equity and investment fund shares	334	424	288	297	344	288	263	292
Equity	216	277	159	159	206	151	131	176
Investment fund shares	118	147	129	137	138	138	131	116
Money market fund shares	..	..	..	..	..	..	..	..
Non-Money market fund shares	..	..	..	..	..	..	..	..
Insurance pension and standardised guarantees	0	0	0	0	0	0	0	0
Financial derivatives and employee stock options	0	2	0	1	4	4	0	0
Other accounts receivable	4	3	2	1	1	1	0	2
Financial liabilities	437	506	362	384	439	389	341	336
Debt securities	0	0	0	0	0	0	0	0
Short-term debt securities	..	..	..	..	..	..	..	..
Long-term debt securities	..	..	..	..	..	..	..	..
Loans	0	0	0	0	0	0	0	0
Short-term loans	..	..	..	..	..	..	..	..
Long-term loans	..	..	..	..	..	..	..	..
Equity and investment fund shares	427	501	360	383	435	383	339	331
Insurance pension and standardised guarantees	0	0	0	0	0	0	0	0
Financial derivatives and employee stock options	0	0	0	0	0	0	0	0
Other accounts payable	10	4	2	1	4	6	2	5
Non-financial assets	0	0	0	0	0	0	0	0
Open-end investment funds								
Financial net worth	0	0	0	-1	-1	0	0	0
Financial assets	437	506	362	384	438	389	341	336
Currency and deposits	49	19	13	12	21	32	24	33
Debt securities	50	58	59	72	68	64	54	9
Loans	0	0	0	0	0	0	0	0
Equity and investment fund shares	334	424	288	297	344	288	263	292
Equity	216	277	159	159	206	151	131	176
Investment fund shares	118	147	129	137	138	138	131	116
Money market fund shares	..	..	..	..	..	..	..	..
Non-Money market fund shares	..	..	..	..	..	..	..	..
Insurance pension and standardised guarantees	0	0	0	0	0	0	0	0
Financial derivatives and employee stock options	0	2	0	1	4	4	0	0
Other accounts receivable	4	3	2	1	1	1	0	2
Financial liabilities	437	506	362	384	439	389	341	336
Debt securities	0	0	0	0	0	0	0	0
Short-term debt securities	..	..	..	..	..	..	..	..
Long-term debt securities	..	..	..	..	..	..	..	..
Loans	0	0	0	0	0	0	0	0
Short-term loans	..	..	..	..	..	..	..	..
Long-term loans	..	..	..	..	..	..	..	..
Equity and investment fund shares	427	501	360	383	435	383	339	331
Insurance pension and standardised guarantees	0	0	0	0	0	0	0	0
Financial derivatives and employee stock options	0	0	0	0	0	0	0	0
Other accounts payable	10	4	2	1	4	6	2	5
Non-financial assets	0	0	0	0	0	0	0	0

Note: Detailed metadata at: http://metalinks.oecd.org/instinv/20170920/a2d2

Table 3. Financial assets and liabilities of insurance corporations and pension funds

Million EUR

	2009	2010	2011	2012	2013	2014	2015	2016
Insurance corporations and pension funds								
Financial net worth	24	103	22	31	60	20	0	3
Financial assets	1 821	2 158	2 148	2 564	2 855	3 336	3 814	4 485
Currency and deposits	328	285	347	420	475	498	651	900
Debt securities	637	532	631	689	688	890	1 031	1 114
Loans	8	1	17	1	4	2	3	0
Equity and investment fund shares	774	1 224	1 091	1 407	1 628	1 894	2 072	2 408
Equity	192	214	241	325	314	300	286	290
Investment fund shares	582	1 009	850	1 082	1 314	1 594	1 786	2 117
Money market fund shares	0	0	0	0	0	0	0	0
Non-Money market fund shares	582	1 009	850	1 082	1 314	1 594	1 786	2 117
Insurance pension and standardised guarantees	31	26	23	16	14	16	20	22
Financial derivatives and employee stock options	2	1	0	0	1	0	1	1
Other accounts receivable	41	88	39	30	46	35	36	40
Financial liabilities	1 797	2 055	2 126	2 533	2 796	3 316	3 814	4 483
Debt securities	0	0	0	0	0	0	0	0
Short-term debt securities	0	0	0	0	0	0	0	0
Long-term debt securities	0	0	0	0	0	0	0	0
Loans	4	4	4	16	13	4	4	24
Short-term loans	0	0	0	0	0	0	0	0
Long-term loans	4	4	4	16	13	4	4	24
Equity and investment fund shares	276	342	370	374	296	312	360	408
Insurance pension and standardised guarantees	1 465	1 653	1 711	2 089	2 436	2 937	3 403	3 873
Financial derivatives and employee stock options	1	0	1	0	0	1	0	0
Other accounts payable	50	55	40	54	51	62	47	178
Non-financial assets	17	19	18	19	19	13	13	7
Insurance corporations								
Financial net worth	28	105	21	33	61	19	1	0
Financial assets	799	999	927	1 002	981	1 012	1 075	1 244
Currency and deposits	176	179	153	178	158	114	102	162
Debt securities	287	336	327	296	302	391	433	532
Loans	8	1	17	1	4	2	3	0
Equity and investment fund shares	263	411	375	481	458	456	483	493
Equity	150	170	184	250	193	178	192	193
Investment fund shares	113	241	191	231	265	278	291	300
Money market fund shares	0	0	0	0	0	0	0	0
Non-Money market fund shares	113	241	191	231	265	278	291	300
Insurance pension and standardised guarantees	31	26	23	16	14	16	20	22
Financial derivatives and employee stock options	0	0	0	0	0	0	0	0
Other accounts receivable	34	46	31	30	45	33	35	35
Financial liabilities	772	894	906	968	920	993	1 074	1 244
Debt securities	0	0	0	0	0	0	0	0
Short-term debt securities	0	0	0	0	0	0	0	0
Long-term debt securities	0	0	0	0	0	0	0	0
Loans	4	4	4	16	13	4	4	24
Short-term loans	0	0	0	0	0	0	0	0
Long-term loans	4	4	4	16	13	4	4	24
Equity and investment fund shares	276	342	370	374	296	312	360	408
Insurance pension and standardised guarantees	467	519	496	527	562	624	666	638
Financial derivatives and employee stock options	1	0	0	0	0	0	0	0
Other accounts payable	23	29	36	51	48	54	44	175
Non-financial assets	15	18	18	19	19	13	13	7
Pension funds								
Financial net worth	-3	-2	1	-2	-2	1	-1	3
Financial assets	1 022	1 159	1 220	1 562	1 875	2 324	2 739	3 241
Currency and deposits	152	106	193	242	317	384	549	738
Debt securities	350	197	303	393	386	499	599	582
Loans	0	0	0	0	0	0	0	0
Equity and investment fund shares	511	813	716	927	1 170	1 438	1 590	1 915
Equity	41	45	57	75	121	122	95	97
Investment fund shares	469	768	659	852	1 049	1 317	1 495	1 818
Money market fund shares	0	0	0	0	0	0	0	0
Non-Money market fund shares	469	768	659	852	1 049	1 317	1 495	1 818
Insurance pension and standardised guarantees	0	0	0	0	0	0	0	0
Financial derivatives and employee stock options	1	1	0	0	1	0	1	1
Other accounts receivable	8	41	8	0	1	3	2	5
Financial liabilities	1 025	1 161	1 219	1 564	1 876	2 323	2 740	3 238
Debt securities	0	0	0	0	0	0	0	0
Short-term debt securities	0	0	0	0	0	0	0	0
Long-term debt securities	0	0	0	0	0	0	0	0
Loans	0	0	0	0	0	0	0	0
Short-term loans	0	0	0	0	0	0	0	0
Long-term loans	0	0	0	0	0	0	0	0
Equity and investment fund shares	0	0	0	0	0	0	0	0
Insurance pension and standardised guarantees	998	1 134	1 215	1 562	1 873	2 314	2 737	3 235
Financial derivatives and employee stock options	0	0	1	0	0	1	0	0
Other accounts payable	27	26	4	2	3	9	3	3
Non-financial assets	2	1	0	0	0	0	0	0

Note: Detailed metadata at: http://metalinks.oecd.org/instinv/20170920/a2d2

Table 4. Portfolio composition by type of investor

As percentage of financial assets and of financial liabilities

Per cent

	2009	2010	2011	2012	2013	2014	2015	2016
Investment funds								
Financial assets	100.0	100.0	100.0	100.0	100.0	100.0	100.0	100.0
Currency and deposits	11.4	4.7	5.0	9.4	8.8	8.8	7.6	9.0
Debt securities	14.4	11.5	15.0	14.7	11.1	11.7	10.2	2.3
Loans	6.4	3.5	4.1	2.7	5.0	4.5	5.4	9.4
Equity and investment fund shares	66.3	78.9	75.4	71.8	72.9	72.2	76.4	78.8
Insurance pension and standardised guarantee schemes	0.0	0.0	0.0	0.0	0.0	0.0	0.0	0.0
Financial derivatives and employee stock options	0.0	0.6	0.0	0.2	0.6	1.0	0.0	0.0
Other accounts receivable	1.5	0.8	0.5	1.2	1.5	1.9	0.3	0.4
Financial liabilities	100.0	100.0	100.0	100.0	100.0	100.0	100.0	100.0
Currency and deposits	0.0	0.0	0.0	0.0	0.0	0.0	0.0	0.0
Debt securities	3.9	3.1	2.7	0.0	0.0	0.0	0.0	0.0
Loans	1.8	0.7	2.9	5.1	3.9	4.7	3.5	2.8
Equity and investment fund shares	92.5	95.4	93.8	94.4	95.3	93.8	95.9	96.2
Insurance pension and standardised guarantee schemes	0.0	0.0	0.0	0.0	0.0	0.0	0.0	0.0
Financial derivatives and employee stock options	0.0	0.0	0.0	0.0	0.0	0.2	0.0	0.0
Other accounts receivable	1.8	0.8	0.6	0.5	0.8	1.2	0.5	0.9
Insurance corporations								
Financial assets	100.0	100.0	100.0	100.0	100.0	100.0	100.0	100.0
Currency and deposits	22.0	17.9	16.5	17.8	16.1	11.3	9.5	13.0
Debt securities	35.8	33.6	35.3	29.6	30.8	38.7	40.2	42.8
Loans	1.0	0.1	1.9	0.1	0.4	0.2	0.3	0.0
Equity and investment fund shares	32.9	41.1	40.5	48.0	46.7	45.0	44.9	39.6
Insurance pension and standardised guarantee schemes	3.9	2.6	2.4	1.6	1.4	1.6	1.9	1.8
Financial derivatives and employee stock options	0.0	0.0	0.0	0.0	0.0	0.0	0.0	0.0
Other accounts receivable	4.2	4.6	3.4	3.0	4.6	3.2	3.2	2.8
Financial liabilities	100.0	100.0	100.0	100.0	100.0	100.0	100.0	100.0
Currency and deposits	0.0	0.0	0.0	0.0	0.0	0.0	0.0	0.0
Debt securities	0.0	0.0	0.0	0.0	0.0	0.0	0.0	0.0
Loans	0.5	0.4	0.4	1.7	1.5	0.4	0.3	1.9
Equity and investment fund shares	35.8	38.3	40.9	38.6	32.1	31.4	33.5	32.8
Insurance pension and standardised guarantee schemes	60.5	58.0	54.8	54.4	61.1	62.8	62.0	51.2
Financial derivatives and employee stock options	0.1	0.0	0.0	0.0	0.0	0.0	0.0	0.0
Other accounts receivable	3.0	3.2	3.9	5.3	5.3	5.4	4.1	14.0
Pension funds								
Financial assets	100.0	100.0	100.0	100.0	100.0	100.0	100.0	100.0
Currency and deposits	14.8	9.2	15.8	15.5	16.9	16.5	20.0	22.8
Debt securities	34.3	17.0	24.8	25.2	20.6	21.5	21.9	18.0
Loans	0.0	0.0	0.0	0.0	0.0	0.0	0.0	0.0
Equity and investment fund shares	50.0	70.2	58.7	59.3	62.4	61.9	58.0	59.1
Insurance pension and standardised guarantee schemes	0.0	0.0	0.0	0.0	0.0	0.0	0.0	0.0
Financial derivatives and employee stock options	0.1	0.1	0.0	0.0	0.0	0.0	0.0	0.0
Other accounts receivable	0.7	3.6	0.6	0.0	0.1	0.1	0.1	0.1
Financial liabilities	100.0	100.0	100.0	100.0	100.0	100.0	100.0	100.0
Currency and deposits	0.0	0.0	0.0	0.0	0.0	0.0	0.0	0.0
Debt securities	0.0	0.0	0.0	0.0	0.0	0.0	0.0	0.0
Loans	0.0	0.0	0.0	0.0	0.0	0.0	0.0	0.0
Equity and investment fund shares	0.0	0.0	0.0	0.0	0.0	0.0	0.0	0.0
Insurance pension and standardised guarantee schemes	97.4	97.7	99.6	99.9	99.9	99.6	99.9	99.9
Financial derivatives and employee stock options	0.0	0.0	0.0	0.0	0.0	0.0	0.0	0.0
Other accounts receivable	2.6	2.3	0.3	0.1	0.1	0.4	0.1	0.1

Note: Detailed metadata at: http://metalinks.oecd.org/instinv/20170920/a49a

FINLAND

Table 1. Financial assets and liabilities of institutional investors, 2016

Million EUR (1999 FIM euro)

	Investment funds				
	Total	Non-money market funds			Money market funds
		Total	Open-end non-money market funds	Closed-end non-money market funds	Total
Financial assets	119 880	116 300	..	..	3 580
Currency and deposits	5 050	4 596	..	..	454
Debt securities	37 731	34 611	..	..	3 120
Debt securities, short term	2 249	1 737	..	..	512
Debt securities, long term	35 482	32 874	..	..	2 608
Debt securities issued by residents	6 025	5 412	..	..	613
Debt securities issued by non-residents	31 706	29 199	..	..	2 507
Loans	1 277	1 277	..	..	0
Loans, short-term	36	36	..	..	0
Loans, long-term	1 241	1 241	..	..	0
Loans granted to residents	1 086	1 086	..	..	0
Loans granted to non-residents	191	191	..	..	0
Equity and investment fund shares/units	72 577	72 577	..	..	0
Equity and investment fund shares issued/units by residents	30 202	30 202	..	..	0
Equity and investment fund shares/units issued by non residents	42 375	42 375	..	..	0
Other accounts receivable	790	784	..	..	6

	Investment funds				
	Total	Non-money market funds			Money market funds
		Total	Open-end non-money market funds	Closed-end non-money market funds	Total
Financial liabilities	120 135	116 523	..	..	3 612
Currency and deposits	..	..	..	..	..
Debt securities	0	0	..	..	0
Debt securities, short term	0	0	..	..	..
Debt securities, long term	0	0	..	..	0
Loans	2 497	2 497	..	..	0
Loans, short-term	46	46	..	..	0
Loans, long-term	2 451	2 451	..	..	0
Equity and investment fund shares/units	114 308	110 747	..	..	3 561
Insurance pension and standardised guarantees	..	..	..	..	..
Financial derivatives and employee stock options	2 358	2 358	..	..	0
Other accounts payable	972	921	..	..	51

	Insurance corporations and pension funds				
	Total	Insurance corporations			Pension funds
		Total	Life insurance corporations	Non-life insurance corporations	Total
Financial assets	77 497	73 848	..	..	3 649
Currency and deposits	3 142	3 066	..	..	76
Debt securities	23 066	22 296	..	..	770
Debt securities, short-term	948	940	..	..	8
Debt securities, long term	22 118	21 356	..	..	762
Debt securities issued by residents	5 922	5 410	..	..	512
Debt securities issued by non-residents	17 144	16 886	..	..	258
Loans	2 289	2 106	..	..	183
Loans, short-term	13	13	..	..	0
Loans, long-term	2 276	2 093	..	..	183
Loans granted to residents	1 823	1 640	..	..	183
Loans granted to non-residents	466	466	..	..	0
Equity and investment fund shares/units	45 417	42 835	..	..	2 582
Equity and investment fund shares/units issued by residents	33 011	31 470	..	..	1 541
Equity and investment fund shares/units issued by non residents	12 406	11 365	..	..	1 041
Other accounts receivable	3 119	3 081	..	..	38

	Insurance corporations and pension funds				
	Total	Insurance corporations			Pension funds
		Total	Life insurance corporations	Non-life insurance corporations	Total
Financial liabilities	74 567	71 283	..	..	3 284
Currency and deposits	0	0	..	..	..
Debt securities	509	509	..	..	0
Debt securities, short term	17	17	..	..	0
Debt securities, long term	492	492	..	..	0
Loans	110	110	..	..	0
Loans, short-term	19	19	..	..	0
Loans, long-term	91	91	..	..	0
Equity and investment fund shares/units	5 880	5 880	..	..	..
Insurance pension and standardised guarantees	66 791	63 526	..	..	3 265
Financial derivatives and employee stock options	62	62	..	..	0
Other accounts payable	1 215	1 196	..	..	19

Note: Detailed metadata at: http://metalinks.oecd.org/instinv/20170920/75e8

FINLAND

Table 2. Financial assets and liabilities of investment funds

Million EUR

	2009	2010	2011	2012	2013	2014	2015	2016
Investment funds								
Financial net worth	199	35	369	-81	-273	278	-7	-255
Financial assets	57 892	66 600	60 223	72 745	82 503	94 435	108 876	119 880
Currency and deposits	2 047	2 154	2 430	2 905	4 544	4 003	4 135	5 050
Debt securities	26 138	25 281	25 684	28 865	30 822	34 447	35 811	37 731
Loans	1 352	1 250	1 356	1 403	1 385	1 643	1 045	1 277
Equity and investment fund shares	28 167	36 679	29 569	37 988	43 956	51 962	64 623	72 577
Equity	18 287	23 773	17 884	21 864	27 083	32 155	38 499	43 512
Investment fund shares	9 880	12 906	11 685	16 124	16 873	19 807	26 124	29 065
Money market fund shares	1 277	1 092	1 147	577	834	772	657	583
Non-Money market fund shares	8 603	11 814	10 538	15 547	16 039	19 035	25 467	28 482
Insurance pension and standardised guarantees	..	..	..	..	..	..	..	..
Financial derivatives and employee stock options	1	387	713	1 048	1 256	1 704	2 353	2 455
Other accounts receivable	187	849	471	536	540	676	909	790
Financial liabilities	57 693	66 565	59 854	72 826	82 776	94 157	108 883	120 135
Debt securities	0	0	0	0	0	0	0	0
Short-term debt securities	0	0	0	0	0	0	0	0
Long-term debt securities	0	0	0	0	0	0	0	0
Loans	3	3	8	6	1 921	1 331	2 012	2 497
Short-term loans	0	0	0	0	0	16	42	46
Long-term loans	3	3	8	6	1 921	1 315	1 970	2 451
Equity and investment fund shares	57 249	64 973	58 475	70 447	79 022	90 284	104 251	114 308
Insurance pension and standardised guarantees	..	..	..	..	..	..	..	..
Financial derivatives and employee stock options	74	615	885	1 793	1 228	1 968	2 154	2 358
Other accounts payable	367	974	486	580	605	574	466	972
Non-financial assets	..	..	..	..	..	..	..	..
Money market funds								
Financial net worth	186	180	0	-250	-564	-39	-21	-32
Financial assets	11 953	10 480	11 418	3 244	3 546	3 450	3 458	3 580
Currency and deposits	296	331	401	293	335	412	353	454
Debt securities	11 433	9 942	10 849	2 844	3 105	3 020	3 089	3 120
Loans	0	0	0	0	0	0	0	0
Equity and investment fund shares	209	178	14	12	2	2	0	0
Equity	0	0	0	0	0	0	0	0
Investment fund shares	209	178	14	12	2	2	0	0
Money market fund shares	32	0	14	12	2	2	0	0
Non-Money market fund shares	177	178	0	0	0	0	0	0
Insurance pension and standardised guarantees	..	..	..	..	..	..	..	..
Financial derivatives and employee stock options	0	0	0	25	0	0	0	0
Other accounts receivable	15	29	154	70	104	16	16	6
Financial liabilities	11 767	10 300	11 418	3 494	4 110	3 489	3 479	3 612
Debt securities	0	0	0	0	0	0	0	0
Short-term debt securities	..	..	..	..	..	..	..	..
Long-term debt securities	0	0	0	0	0	0	0	0
Loans	0	0	0	0	136	0	0	0
Short-term loans	0	0	0	0	0	0	0	0
Long-term loans	0	0	0	0	136	0	0	0
Equity and investment fund shares	11 722	10 222	11 347	3 494	3 974	3 398	3 446	3 561
Insurance pension and standardised guarantees	..	..	..	..	..	..	..	..
Financial derivatives and employee stock options	0	0	0	0	0	0	0	0
Other accounts payable	45	78	71	0	0	91	33	51
Non-financial assets	0	0	0	0	0	0	0	0
Non-money market funds								
Financial net worth	13	-145	369	169	291	317	14	-223
Financial assets	45 939	56 120	48 305	69 501	78 957	90 985	105 418	116 300
Currency and deposits	1 751	1 823	2 029	2 612	4 209	3 591	3 782	4 596
Debt securities	14 705	15 339	14 835	26 021	27 717	31 427	32 722	34 611
Loans	1 352	1 250	1 356	1 403	1 385	1 643	1 045	1 277
Equity and investment fund shares	27 958	36 501	29 555	37 976	43 954	51 960	64 623	72 577
Equity	18 287	23 773	17 884	21 864	27 083	32 155	38 499	43 512
Investment fund shares	9 671	12 728	11 671	16 112	16 871	19 805	26 124	29 065
Money market fund shares	1 245	1 092	1 133	565	832	770	657	583
Non-Money market fund shares	8 426	11 636	10 538	15 547	16 039	19 035	25 467	28 482
Insurance pension and standardised guarantees	..	..	..	..	..	..	..	..
Financial derivatives and employee stock options	1	387	713	1 023	1 256	1 704	2 353	2 455
Other accounts receivable	172	820	317	466	436	660	893	784
Financial liabilities	45 926	56 265	48 436	69 332	78 666	90 668	105 404	116 523
Debt securities	0	0	0	0	..	0	0	0
Short-term debt securities	0	0	0	0	..	0	0	0
Long-term debt securities	0	0	0	0	..	..	..	0
Loans	3	3	8	6	1 785	1 331	2 012	2 497
Short-term loans	0	0	0	0	0	16	42	46
Long-term loans	3	3	8	6	1 785	1 315	1 970	2 451
Equity and investment fund shares	45 527	54 751	47 128	66 953	75 048	86 886	100 805	110 747
Insurance pension and standardised guarantees	..	..	..	..	..	..	..	..
Financial derivatives and employee stock options	74	615	885	1 793	1 228	1 968	2 154	2 358
Other accounts payable	322	896	415	580	605	483	433	921
Non-financial assets	0	0	0	0	0	0	0	0
Open-end non-money market funds								
Financial net worth	..	..	..	..	..	..	..	..
Financial assets	..	..	..	..	..	..	..	..

Table 2. Financial assets and liabilities of investment funds *(cont.)*

Million EUR

	2009	2010	2011	2012	2013	2014	2015	2016
Currency and deposits	..	..	..	..	..	..	..	..
Debt securities	..	..	..	..	..	..	..	..
Loans	..	..	..	..	..	..	..	..
Equity and investment fund shares	..	..	..	..	..	..	..	..
Equity	..	..	..	..	..	..	..	..
Investment fund shares	..	..	..	..	..	..	..	..
Money market fund shares	..	..	..	..	..	..	..	..
Non-Money market fund shares	..	..	..	..	..	..	..	..
Insurance pension and standardised guarantees	..	..	..	..	..	..	..	..
Financial derivatives and employee stock options	..	..	..	..	..	..	..	..
Other accounts receivable	..	..	..	..	..	..	..	..
Financial liabilities	..	..	..	..	..	..	..	..
Debt securities	..	..	..	..	..	..	..	..
Short-term debt securities	..	..	..	..	..	..	..	..
Long-term debt securities	..	..	..	..	..	..	..	..
Loans	..	..	..	..	..	..	..	..
Short-term loans	..	..	..	..	..	..	..	..
Long-term loans	..	..	..	..	..	..	..	..
Equity and investment fund shares	..	..	..	..	..	..	..	..
Insurance pension and standardised guarantees	..	..	..	..	..	..	..	..
Financial derivatives and employee stock options	..	..	..	..	..	..	..	..
Other accounts payable	..	..	..	..	..	..	..	..
Non-financial assets	..	..	..	..	..	..	..	..
Open-end investment funds								
Financial net worth	..	..	..	..	..	..	..	..
Financial assets	..	..	..	..	..	..	..	..
Currency and deposits	..	..	..	..	..	..	..	..
Debt securities	..	..	..	..	..	..	..	..
Loans	..	..	..	..	..	..	..	..
Equity and investment fund shares	..	..	..	..	..	..	..	..
Equity	..	..	..	..	..	..	..	..
Investment fund shares	..	..	..	..	..	..	..	..
Money market fund shares	..	..	..	..	..	..	..	..
Non-Money market fund shares	..	..	..	..	..	..	..	..
Insurance pension and standardised guarantees	..	..	..	..	..	..	..	..
Financial derivatives and employee stock options	..	..	..	..	..	..	..	..
Other accounts receivable	..	..	..	..	..	..	..	..
Financial liabilities	..	..	..	..	..	..	..	..
Debt securities	..	..	..	..	..	..	..	..
Short-term debt securities	..	..	..	..	..	..	..	..
Long-term debt securities	..	..	..	..	..	..	..	..
Loans	..	..	..	..	..	..	..	..
Short-term loans	..	..	..	..	..	..	..	..
Long-term loans	..	..	..	..	..	..	..	..
Equity and investment fund shares	..	..	..	..	..	..	..	..
Insurance pension and standardised guarantees	..	..	..	..	..	..	..	..
Financial derivatives and employee stock options	..	..	..	..	..	..	..	..
Other accounts payable	..	..	..	..	..	..	..	..
Non-financial assets	..	..	..	..	..	..	..	..

Note: Detailed metadata at: http://metalinks.oecd.org/instinv/20170920/75e8

Table 3. Financial assets and liabilities of insurance corporations and pension funds

Million EUR

	2009	2010	2011	2012	2013	2014	2015	2016
Insurance corporations and pension funds								
Financial net worth	43	3 224	3 160	3 415	1 553	3 148	3 959	2 930
Financial assets	51 590	57 381	56 438	61 770	64 156	71 096	74 849	77 497
Currency and deposits	1 577	2 238	2 108	2 497	2 818	3 498	3 524	3 142
Debt securities	21 367	22 245	21 177	23 505	24 582	24 852	24 530	23 066
Loans	1 735	1 816	1 824	1 680	1 667	1 584	1 941	2 289
Equity and investment fund shares	25 075	29 211	29 524	31 919	33 479	38 641	42 527	45 417
Equity	6 071	5 155	5 027	4 877	4 870	4 945	5 386	6 775
Investment fund shares	19 004	24 056	24 497	27 042	28 609	33 696	37 141	38 642
Money market fund shares	1 558	1 268	2 532	966	1 188	1 511	1 521	926
Non-Money market fund shares	17 446	22 788	21 965	26 076	27 421	32 185	35 620	37 716
Insurance pension and standardised guarantees	0	0	0	0	0	0	0	338
Financial derivatives and employee stock options	0	173	46	310	132	145	80	126
Other accounts receivable	1 836	1 698	1 759	1 859	1 478	2 376	2 247	3 119
Financial liabilities	51 547	54 157	53 278	58 355	62 603	67 948	70 890	74 567
Debt securities	294	315	273	280	210	554	515	509
Short-term debt securities	6	9	17	13	5	24	19	17
Long-term debt securities	288	306	256	267	205	530	496	492
Loans	477	362	452	182	106	286	124	110
Short-term loans	1	1	1	44	23	65	20	19
Long-term loans	476	361	451	138	83	221	104	91
Equity and investment fund shares	4 040	4 640	4 380	5 162	5 447	5 510	5 335	5 880
Insurance pension and standardised guarantees	45 178	47 651	46 957	51 347	55 448	59 665	63 729	66 791
Financial derivatives and employee stock options	10	128	316	66	91	290	138	62
Other accounts payable	1 548	1 061	900	1 318	1 301	1 643	1 049	1 215
Non-financial assets	..	..	..	..	..	..	..	..
Insurance corporations								
Financial net worth	768	2 716	2 903	3 525	2 381	3 960	4 640	2 565
Financial assets	47 947	53 120	52 543	58 247	61 194	68 175	71 889	73 848
Currency and deposits	1 445	2 142	1 893	2 372	2 604	3 439	3 467	3 066
Debt securities	20 325	21 403	20 211	22 707	23 720	23 971	23 800	22 296
Loans	1 251	1 518	1 514	1 428	1 502	1 426	1 769	2 106
Equity and investment fund shares	23 136	26 221	27 178	29 688	31 799	36 853	40 558	42 835
Equity	5 469	4 232	4 144	4 332	4 360	4 262	4 798	5 674
Investment fund shares	17 667	21 989	23 034	25 356	27 439	32 591	35 760	37 161
Money market fund shares	1 400	1 207	2 439	864	1 066	1 435	1 415	791
Non-Money market fund shares	16 267	20 782	20 595	24 492	26 373	31 156	34 345	36 370
Insurance pension and standardised guarantees	0	0	0	0	0	0	0	338
Financial derivatives and employee stock options	0	173	46	308	130	145	80	126
Other accounts receivable	1 790	1 663	1 701	1 744	1 439	2 341	2 215	3 081
Financial liabilities	47 179	50 404	49 640	54 722	58 813	64 215	67 249	71 283
Debt securities	294	315	273	280	210	554	515	509
Short-term debt securities	6	9	17	13	5	24	19	17
Long-term debt securities	288	306	256	267	205	530	496	492
Loans	477	362	426	182	106	286	124	110
Short-term loans	1	1	1	44	23	65	20	19
Long-term loans	476	361	425	138	83	221	104	91
Equity and investment fund shares	4 040	4 640	4 380	5 162	5 447	5 510	5 335	5 880
Insurance pension and standardised guarantees	40 843	43 924	43 370	47 739	51 684	55 980	60 121	63 526
Financial derivatives and employee stock options	10	128	316	66	91	290	138	62
Other accounts payable	1 515	1 035	875	1 293	1 275	1 595	1 016	1 196
Non-financial assets	949	894	877	881	851	836	814	0
Pension funds								
Financial net worth	-725	508	257	-110	-828	-812	-681	365
Financial assets	3 643	4 261	3 895	3 523	2 962	2 921	2 960	3 649
Currency and deposits	132	96	215	125	214	59	57	76
Debt securities	1 042	842	966	798	862	881	730	770
Loans	484	298	310	252	165	158	172	183
Equity and investment fund shares	1 939	2 990	2 346	2 231	1 680	1 788	1 969	2 582
Equity	602	923	883	545	510	683	588	1 101
Investment fund shares	1 337	2 067	1 463	1 686	1 170	1 105	1 381	1 481
Money market fund shares	158	61	93	102	122	76	106	135
Non-Money market fund shares	1 179	2 006	1 370	1 584	1 048	1 029	1 275	1 346
Insurance pension and standardised guarantees	..	..	..	..	..	..	..	..
Financial derivatives and employee stock options	0	0	0	2	2	0	0	0
Other accounts receivable	46	35	58	115	39	35	32	38
Financial liabilities	4 368	3 753	3 638	3 633	3 790	3 733	3 641	3 284
Debt securities	0	0	0	0	0	0	0	0
Short-term debt securities	0	0	0	0	0	0	0	0
Long-term debt securities	0	0	0	0	0	0	0	0
Loans	0	0	26	0	0	0	0	0
Short-term loans	0	0	0	0	0	0	0	0
Long-term loans	0	0	26	0	0	0	0	0
Equity and investment fund shares	..	..	..	..	..	..	..	..
Insurance pension and standardised guarantees	4 335	3 727	3 587	3 608	3 764	3 685	3 608	3 265
Financial derivatives and employee stock options	0	0	0	0	0	0	0	0
Other accounts payable	33	26	25	25	26	48	33	19
Non-financial assets	0	0	0	0	0	0	0	0

Note: Detailed metadata at: http://metalinks.oecd.org/instinv/20170920/75e8

Table 4. Portfolio composition by type of investor

As percentage of financial assets and of financial liabilities

Per cent

	2009	2010	2011	2012	2013	2014	2015	2016
Investment funds								
Financial assets	100.0	100.0	100.0	100.0	100.0	100.0	100.0	100.0
Currency and deposits	3.5	3.2	4.0	4.0	5.5	4.2	3.8	4.2
Debt securities	45.1	38.0	42.6	39.7	37.4	36.5	32.9	31.5
Loans	2.3	1.9	2.3	1.9	1.7	1.7	1.0	1.1
Equity and investment fund shares	48.7	55.1	49.1	52.2	53.3	55.0	59.4	60.5
Insurance pension and standardised guarantee schemes	0.0	0.0	0.0	0.0	0.0	0.0	0.0	0.0
Financial derivatives and employee stock options	0.0	0.6	1.2	1.4	1.5	1.8	2.2	2.0
Other accounts receivable	0.3	1.3	0.8	0.7	0.7	0.7	0.8	0.7
Financial liabilities	100.0	100.0	100.0	100.0	100.0	100.0	100.0	100.0
Currency and deposits	0.0	0.0	0.0	0.0	0.0	0.0	0.0	0.0
Debt securities	0.0	0.0	0.0	0.0	0.0	0.0	0.0	0.0
Loans	0.0	0.0	0.0	0.0	2.3	1.4	1.8	2.1
Equity and investment fund shares	99.2	97.6	97.7	96.7	95.5	95.9	95.7	95.1
Insurance pension and standardised guarantee schemes	0.0	0.0	0.0	0.0	0.0	0.0	0.0	0.0
Financial derivatives and employee stock options	0.1	0.9	1.5	2.5	1.5	2.1	2.0	2.0
Other accounts receivable	0.6	1.5	0.8	0.8	0.7	0.6	0.4	0.8
Insurance corporations								
Financial assets	100.0	100.0	100.0	100.0	100.0	100.0	100.0	100.0
Currency and deposits	3.0	4.0	3.6	4.1	4.3	5.0	4.8	4.2
Debt securities	42.4	40.3	38.5	39.0	38.8	35.2	33.1	30.2
Loans	2.6	2.9	2.9	2.5	2.5	2.1	2.5	2.9
Equity and investment fund shares	48.3	49.4	51.7	51.0	52.0	54.1	56.4	58.0
Insurance pension and standardised guarantee schemes	0.0	0.0	0.0	0.0	0.0	0.0	0.0	0.5
Financial derivatives and employee stock options	0.0	0.3	0.1	0.5	0.2	0.2	0.1	0.2
Other accounts receivable	3.7	3.1	3.2	3.0	2.4	3.4	3.1	4.2
Financial liabilities	100.0	100.0	100.0	100.0	100.0	100.0	100.0	100.0
Currency and deposits	0.0	0.0	0.0	0.0	0.0	0.0	0.0	0.0
Debt securities	0.6	0.6	0.5	0.5	0.4	0.9	0.8	0.7
Loans	1.0	0.7	0.9	0.3	0.2	0.4	0.2	0.2
Equity and investment fund shares	8.6	9.2	8.8	9.4	9.3	8.6	7.9	8.2
Insurance pension and standardised guarantee schemes	86.6	87.1	87.4	87.2	87.9	87.2	89.4	89.1
Financial derivatives and employee stock options	0.0	0.3	0.6	0.1	0.2	0.5	0.2	0.1
Other accounts receivable	3.2	2.1	1.8	2.4	2.2	2.5	1.5	1.7
Pension funds								
Financial assets	100.0	100.0	100.0	100.0	100.0	100.0	100.0	100.0
Currency and deposits	3.6	2.3	5.5	3.5	7.2	2.0	1.9	2.1
Debt securities	28.6	19.8	24.8	22.7	29.1	30.2	24.7	21.1
Loans	13.3	7.0	8.0	7.2	5.6	5.4	5.8	5.0
Equity and investment fund shares	53.2	70.2	60.2	63.3	56.7	61.2	66.5	70.8
Insurance pension and standardised guarantee schemes	0.0	0.0	0.0	0.0	0.0	0.0	0.0	0.0
Financial derivatives and employee stock options	0.0	0.0	0.0	0.1	0.1	0.0	0.0	0.0
Other accounts receivable	1.3	0.8	1.5	3.3	1.3	1.2	1.1	1.0
Financial liabilities	100.0	100.0	100.0	100.0	100.0	100.0	100.0	100.0
Currency and deposits	0.0	0.0	0.0	0.0	0.0	0.0	0.0	0.0
Debt securities	0.0	0.0	0.0	0.0	0.0	0.0	0.0	0.0
Loans	0.0	0.0	0.7	0.0	0.0	0.0	0.0	0.0
Equity and investment fund shares	0.0	0.0	0.0	0.0	0.0	0.0	0.0	0.0
Insurance pension and standardised guarantee schemes	99.2	99.3	98.6	99.3	99.3	98.7	99.1	99.4
Financial derivatives and employee stock options	0.0	0.0	0.0	0.0	0.0	0.0	0.0	0.0
Other accounts receivable	0.8	0.7	0.7	0.7	0.7	1.3	0.9	0.6

Note: Detailed metadata at: http://metalinks.oecd.org/instinv/20170920/a49a

FRANCE

Table 1. Financial assets and liabilities of institutional investors, 2016

Million EUR (1999 FRF euro)

	Investment funds				
		Non-money market funds			Money market funds
	Total	Total	Open-end non-money market funds	Closed-end non-money market funds	Total
Financial assets	1 654 798	1 303 103	1 303 103	0	351 695
Currency and deposits	87 825	43 506	43 506	0	44 319
Debt securities	638 663	373 994	373 994	0	264 669
Debt securities, short term	196 842	25 989	25 989	0	170 853
Debt securities, long term	441 822	348 005	348 005	0	93 816
Debt securities issued by residents	228 614	118 597	118 597	0	110 016
Debt securities issued by non-residents	410 050	255 397	255 397	0	154 653
Loans	4 687	4 104	4 104	0	583
Loans, short-term	4 364	3 785	3 785	0	579
Loans, long-term	323	319	319	0	4
Loans granted to residents	4 348	3 769	3 769	0	579
Loans granted to non-residents	338	334	334	0	4
Equity and investment fund shares/units	760 199	721 835	721 835	0	38 365
Equity and investment fund shares issued/units by residents	451 823	414 114	414 114	0	37 708
Equity and investment fund shares/units issued by non residents	308 377	307 720	307 720	0	656
Other accounts receivable	126 662	124 827	124 827	0	1 836

	Investment funds				
		Non-money market funds			Money market funds
	Total	Total	Open-end non-money market funds	Closed-end non-money market funds	Total
Financial liabilities	1 709 965	1 358 270	1 358 270	0	351 695
Currency and deposits	11 812	11 147	11 147	0	665
Debt securities	0	0	0	0	0
Debt securities, short term	0	0	0	0	0
Debt securities, long term	0	0	0	0	0
Loans	7 784	7 781	7 781	0	3
Loans, short-term	4 844	4 844	4 844	0	0
Loans, long-term	2 940	2 937	2 937	0	3
Equity and investment fund shares/units	1 523 164	1 176 888	1 176 888	0	346 276
Insurance pension and standardised guaratees	0	0	0	0	0
Financial derivatives and employee stock options	41 582	39 535	39 535	0	2 047
Other accounts payable	125 624	122 920	122 920	0	2 704

	Insurance corporations and pension funds				
		Insurance corporations			Pension funds
	Total	Total	Life insurance corporations	Non-life insurance corporations	Total
Financial assets	2 688 061	2 688 061	2 346 686	341 375	..
Currency and deposits	34 746	34 746	24 050	10 696	..
Debt securities	1 574 776	1 574 776	1 457 697	117 079	..
Debt securities, short-term	23 694	23 694	23 111	583	..
Debt securities, long term	1 551 082	1 551 082	1 434 586	116 496	..
Debt securities issued by residents	847 152	847 152	785 095	62 057	..
Debt securities issued by non-residents	727 624	727 624	672 602	55 022	..
Loans	61 795	61 795	39 529	22 266	..
Loans, short-term	35 864	35 864	23 397	12 467	..
Loans, long-term	25 931	25 931	16 132	9 799	..
Loans granted to residents	51 003	51 003	36 837	14 166	..
Loans granted to non-residents	10 792	10 792	2 692	8 100	..
Equity and investment fund shares/units	836 957	836 957	697 648	139 309	..
Equity and investment fund shares/units issued by residents	682 415	682 415	566 605	115 810	..
Equity and investment fund shares/units issued by non residents	154 542	154 542	131 043	23 499	..
Other accounts receivable	77 073	77 073	52 068	25 005	..

	Insurance corporations and pension funds				
		Insurance corporations			Pension funds
	Total	Total	Life insurance corporations	Non-life insurance corporations	Total
Financial liabilities	2 726 776	2 726 776	2 375 749	351 027	..
Currency and deposits	..	..	..	..	..
Debt securities	80 389	80 389	68 672	11 717	..
Debt securities, short term	..	..	..	..	..
Debt securities, long term	..	..	..	..	..
Loans	63 451	63 451	52 194	11 257	..
Loans, short-term	..	..	..	..	..
Loans, long-term	..	..	..	..	..
Equity and investment fund shares/units	274 569	274 569	136 924	137 645	..
Insurance pension and standardised guarantees	2 184 597	2 184 597	2 031 611	152 986	..
Financial derivatives and employee stock options	2 866	2 866	2 764	102	..
Other accounts payable	120 904	120 904	83 584	37 320	..

Note: Detailed metadata at: http://metalinks.oecd.org/instinv/20170920/75e8

FRANCE

Table 2. Financial assets and liabilities of investment funds

Million EUR

	2009	2010	2011	2012	2013	2014	2015	2016
Investment funds								
Financial net worth	-20 857	-23 789	-30 834	-38 900	-43 614	-51 435	-60 968	-55 168
Financial assets	1 493 726	1 479 830	1 326 157	1 399 454	1 399 994	1 454 248	1 539 889	1 654 798
Currency and deposits	91 350	83 360	84 017	86 872	83 589	85 309	87 221	87 825
Debt securities	631 444	595 379	558 349	590 121	552 979	575 387	601 667	638 663
Loans	4 622	5 746	1 600	1 439	2 331	2 362	2 301	4 687
Equity and investment fund shares	638 115	656 077	556 097	595 237	640 391	650 694	701 899	760 199
Equity	350 302	376 584	312 815	332 447	375 711	385 051	413 225	441 745
Investment fund shares	287 813	279 493	243 282	262 789	264 681	265 643	288 674	318 454
Money market fund shares	114 653	97 541	91 967	98 446	87 471	75 992	84 530	100 541
Non-Money market fund shares	173 160	181 952	151 315	164 343	177 210	189 651	204 144	217 914
Insurance pension and standardised guarantees	0	0	0	0	0	0	0	0
Financial derivatives and employee stock options	13 800	13 481	25 137	25 916	26 096	27 903	26 878	36 761
Other accounts receivable	114 394	125 786	100 956	99 870	94 608	112 593	119 923	126 662
Financial liabilities	1 514 582	1 503 620	1 356 990	1 438 354	1 443 608	1 505 683	1 600 857	1 709 965
Debt securities	0	0	0	0	0	0	0	0
Short-term debt securities	0	0	0	0	0	0	0	0
Long-term debt securities	0	0	0	0	0	0	0	0
Loans	554	4 170	588	3 912	3 020	4 050	4 190	7 784
Short-term loans	548	4 167	584	2 300	1 466	2 491	1 930	4 844
Long-term loans	5	3	4	1 612	1 555	1 559	2 260	2 940
Equity and investment fund shares	1 384 469	1 357 039	1 220 785	1 293 864	1 307 054	1 349 244	1 441 675	1 523 164
Insurance pension and standardised guarantees	0	0	0	0	0	0	0	0
Financial derivatives and employee stock options	10 801	8 685	24 275	26 667	28 154	31 214	30 534	41 582
Other accounts payable	110 466	124 820	100 643	101 346	96 127	113 677	118 049	125 624
Non-financial assets	20 859	23 790	30 837	38 903	43 614	51 435	60 970	55 168
Money market funds								
Financial net worth	0	0	0	0	0	0	0	0
Financial assets	501 628	413 885	369 359	370 535	324 945	294 317	318 661	351 695
Currency and deposits	56 673	47 050	41 234	40 832	46 812	43 546	43 930	44 319
Debt securities	347 523	295 112	273 595	277 341	237 529	220 601	239 966	264 669
Loans	2 022	1 048	487	758	795	891	1 041	583
Equity and investment fund shares	72 532	53 389	38 223	48 547	35 595	26 317	28 004	38 365
Equity	2 419	1 942	63	0	0	0	0	0
Investment fund shares	70 113	51 447	38 160	48 547	35 595	26 317	28 004	38 365
Money market fund shares	67 048	48 598	37 055	48 127	35 232	25 949	27 898	38 017
Non-Money market fund shares	3 065	2 849	1 105	420	363	368	106	347
Insurance pension and standardised guarantees	0	0	0	0	0	0	0	0
Financial derivatives and employee stock options	1 172	787	371	729	703	935	2 499	1 923
Other accounts receivable	21 706	16 499	15 449	2 328	3 510	2 027	3 221	1 836
Financial liabilities	501 628	413 885	369 359	370 535	324 945	294 317	318 661	351 695
Debt securities	0	0	0	0	0	0	0	0
Short-term debt securities	0	0	0	0	0	0	0	0
Long-term debt securities	0	0	0	0	0	0	0	0
Loans	16	3	96	140	0	1	0	3
Short-term loans	16	3	96	140	0	1	0	0
Long-term loans	0	0	0	0	0	0	0	3
Equity and investment fund shares	479 225	394 337	351 070	365 755	318 228	288 903	311 674	346 276
Insurance pension and standardised guarantees	0	0	0	0	0	0	0	0
Financial derivatives and employee stock options	1 100	705	461	515	781	992	2 580	2 047
Other accounts payable	20 474	17 279	16 917	3 213	4 897	2 704	3 673	2 704
Non-financial assets	0	0	0	0	0	0	0	0
Non-money market funds								
Financial net worth	-20 857	-23 789	-30 834	-38 900	-43 614	-51 435	-60 968	-55 168
Financial assets	992 098	1 065 945	956 798	1 028 920	1 075 049	1 159 930	1 221 229	1 303 103
Currency and deposits	34 677	36 310	42 783	46 040	36 777	41 764	43 291	43 506
Debt securities	283 921	300 267	284 754	312 780	315 450	354 785	361 702	373 994
Loans	2 600	4 698	1 113	681	1 536	1 471	1 261	4 104
Equity and investment fund shares	565 583	602 688	517 874	546 690	604 796	624 377	673 894	721 835
Equity	347 883	374 643	312 752	332 447	375 711	385 051	413 225	441 745
Investment fund shares	217 700	228 046	205 122	214 243	229 086	239 326	260 670	280 090
Money market fund shares	47 606	48 943	54 912	50 319	52 239	50 043	56 632	62 523
Non-Money market fund shares	170 094	179 103	150 210	163 923	176 846	189 283	204 037	217 566
Insurance pension and standardised guarantees	0	0	0	0	0	0	0	0
Financial derivatives and employee stock options	12 629	12 695	24 766	25 187	25 392	26 968	24 379	34 838
Other accounts receivable	92 688	109 288	85 507	97 542	91 098	110 566	116 702	124 827
Financial liabilities	1 012 954	1 089 735	987 631	1 067 819	1 118 664	1 211 365	1 282 196	1 358 270
Debt securities	0	0	0	0	0	0	0	0
Short-term debt securities	0	0	0	0	0	0	0	0
Long-term debt securities	0	0	0	0	0	0	0	0
Loans	537	4 167	492	3 772	3 020	4 049	4 190	7 781
Short-term loans	532	4 164	488	2 160	1 466	2 490	1 930	4 844
Long-term loans	5	3	4	1 612	1 555	1 559	2 260	2 937
Equity and investment fund shares	905 244	962 702	869 715	928 109	988 826	1 060 342	1 130 001	1 176 888
Insurance pension and standardised guarantees	0	0	0	0	0	0	0	0
Financial derivatives and employee stock options	9 702	7 980	23 814	26 152	27 373	30 222	27 954	39 535
Other accounts payable	89 992	107 541	83 726	98 133	91 230	110 973	114 376	122 920
Non-financial assets	20 859	23 790	30 837	38 903	43 614	51 435	60 970	55 168
Open-end non-money market funds								
Financial net worth	-20 857	-23 789	-30 834	-38 900	-43 614	-51 435	-60 968	-55 168
Financial assets	992 098	1 065 945	956 798	1 028 920	1 075 049	1 159 930	1 221 229	1 303 103

Table 2. Financial assets and liabilities of investment funds *(cont.)*

Million EUR

	2009	2010	2011	2012	2013	2014	2015	2016
Currency and deposits	34 677	36 310	42 783	46 040	36 777	41 764	43 291	43 506
Debt securities	283 921	300 267	284 754	312 780	315 450	354 785	361 702	373 994
Loans	2 600	4 698	1 113	681	1 536	1 471	1 261	4 104
Equity and investment fund shares	565 583	602 688	517 874	546 690	604 796	624 377	673 894	721 835
Equity	347 883	374 643	312 752	332 447	375 711	385 051	413 225	441 745
Investment fund shares	217 700	228 046	205 122	214 243	229 086	239 326	260 670	280 090
Money market fund shares	47 606	48 943	54 912	50 319	52 239	50 043	56 632	62 523
Non-Money market fund shares	170 094	179 103	150 210	163 923	176 846	189 283	204 037	217 566
Insurance pension and standardised guarantees	0	0	0	0	0	0	0	0
Financial derivatives and employee stock options	12 629	12 695	24 766	25 187	25 392	26 968	24 379	34 838
Other accounts receivable	92 688	109 288	85 507	97 542	91 098	110 566	116 702	124 827
Financial liabilities	1 012 954	1 089 735	987 631	1 067 819	1 118 664	1 211 365	1 282 196	1 358 270
Debt securities	0	0	0	0	0	0	0	0
Short-term debt securities	0	0	0	0	0	0	0	0
Long-term debt securities	0	0	0	0	0	0	0	0
Loans	537	4 167	492	3 772	3 020	4 049	4 190	7 781
Short-term loans	532	4 164	488	2 160	1 466	2 490	1 930	4 844
Long-term loans	5	3	4	1 612	1 555	1 559	2 260	2 937
Equity and investment fund shares	905 244	962 702	869 715	928 109	988 826	1 060 342	1 130 001	1 176 888
Insurance pension and standardised guarantees	0	0	0	0	0	0	0	0
Financial derivatives and employee stock options	9 702	7 980	23 814	26 152	27 373	30 222	27 954	39 535
Other accounts payable	89 992	107 541	83 726	98 133	91 230	110 973	114 376	122 920
Non-financial assets	20 859	23 790	30 837	38 903	43 614	51 435	60 970	55 168
Open-end investment funds								
Financial net worth	-20 857	-23 789	-30 834	-38 900	-43 614	-51 435	-60 968	-55 168
Financial assets	1 493 726	1 479 830	1 326 157	1 399 454	1 399 994	1 454 248	1 539 889	1 654 798
Currency and deposits	91 350	83 360	84 017	86 872	83 589	85 309	87 221	87 825
Debt securities	631 444	595 379	558 349	590 121	552 979	575 387	601 667	638 663
Loans	4 622	5 746	1 600	1 439	2 331	2 362	2 301	4 687
Equity and investment fund shares	638 115	656 077	556 097	595 237	640 391	650 694	701 899	760 199
Equity	350 302	376 584	312 815	332 447	375 711	385 051	413 225	441 745
Investment fund shares	287 813	279 493	243 282	262 789	264 681	265 643	288 674	318 454
Money market fund shares	114 653	97 541	91 967	98 446	87 471	75 992	84 530	100 541
Non-Money market fund shares	173 160	181 952	151 315	164 343	177 210	189 651	204 144	217 914
Insurance pension and standardised guarantees	0	0	0	0	0	0	0	0
Financial derivatives and employee stock options	13 800	13 481	25 137	25 916	26 096	27 903	26 878	36 761
Other accounts receivable	114 394	125 786	100 956	99 870	94 608	112 593	119 923	126 662
Financial liabilities	1 514 582	1 503 620	1 356 990	1 438 354	1 443 608	1 505 683	1 600 857	1 709 965
Debt securities	0	0	0	0	0	0	0	0
Short-term debt securities	0	0	0	0	0	0	0	0
Long-term debt securities	0	0	0	0	0	0	0	0
Loans	554	4 170	588	3 912	3 020	4 050	4 190	7 784
Short-term loans	548	4 167	584	2 300	1 466	2 491	1 930	4 844
Long-term loans	5	3	4	1 612	1 555	1 559	2 260	2 940
Equity and investment fund shares	1 384 469	1 357 039	1 220 785	1 293 864	1 307 054	1 349 244	1 441 675	1 523 164
Insurance pension and standardised guarantees	0	0	0	0	0	0	0	0
Financial derivatives and employee stock options	10 801	8 685	24 275	26 667	28 154	31 214	30 534	41 582
Other accounts payable	110 466	124 820	100 643	101 346	96 127	113 677	118 049	125 624
Non-financial assets	20 859	23 790	30 837	38 903	43 614	51 435	60 970	55 168

Note: Detailed metadata at: http://metalinks.oecd.org/instinv/20170920/75e8

FRANCE

Table 3. Financial assets and liabilities of insurance corporations and pension funds

Million EUR

	2009	2010	2011	2012	2013	2014	2015	2016
Insurance corporations and pension funds								
Financial net worth	7 673	14 353	-9 339	120 316	128 281	231 981	218 294	-38 715
Financial assets	1 760 513	1 895 553	1 874 710	2 076 202	2 182 607	2 398 823	2 469 679	2 688 061
Currency and deposits	15 322	17 513	19 010	24 992	29 306	34 039	36 878	34 746
Debt securities	1 018 877	1 147 206	1 139 217	1 275 546	1 319 433	1 461 006	1 464 553	1 574 776
Loans	34 976	35 546	37 501	35 278	36 169	37 266	38 632	61 795
Equity and investment fund shares	612 297	610 397	584 317	642 192	682 792	746 752	806 263	836 957
Equity	209 951	211 909	205 339	208 716	232 519	252 642	281 492	218 248
Investment fund shares	402 346	398 487	378 979	433 476	450 273	494 110	524 771	618 709
Money market fund shares	58 479	50 769	64 562	84 812	61 604	66 067	65 965	73 737
Non-Money market fund shares	343 866	347 719	314 416	348 664	388 669	428 043	458 806	544 972
Insurance pension and standardised guarantees	74 426	80 196	86 621	92 866	111 346	115 443	119 887	97 533
Financial derivatives and employee stock options	4 551	4 642	7 994	5 276	3 507	4 263	3 412	5 181
Other accounts receivable	63	54	51	53	54	54	54	77 073
Financial liabilities	1 752 840	1 881 201	1 884 050	1 955 886	2 054 326	2 166 842	2 251 385	2 726 776
Debt securities	6 827	6 603	8 522	9 335	11 235	15 892	17 338	80 389
Short-term debt securities	866	673	215	237	107	107	123	..
Long-term debt securities	5 961	5 930	8 307	9 098	11 128	15 785	17 215	..
Loans	67 644	76 284	70 690	77 126	88 206	99 616	104 029	63 451
Short-term loans	37 982	45 246	36 843	43 042	53 029	63 907	66 476	..
Long-term loans	29 662	31 038	33 846	34 084	35 177	35 709	37 552	..
Equity and investment fund shares	100 689	107 449	96 243	99 615	109 596	117 869	118 884	274 569
Insurance pension and standardised guarantees	1 542 953	1 655 957	1 680 705	1 735 678	1 811 041	1 897 780	1 976 939	2 184 597
Financial derivatives and employee stock options	466	225	324	138	426	1 895	386	2 866
Other accounts payable	34 261	34 682	27 566	33 995	33 822	33 790	33 809	120 904
Non-financial assets	24 402	25 683	25 225	26 309	27 356	27 785	28 618	38 711
Insurance corporations								
Financial net worth	7 673	14 353	-9 339	120 316	128 281	231 981	218 294	-38 715
Financial assets	1 760 513	1 895 553	1 874 710	2 076 202	2 182 607	2 398 823	2 469 679	2 688 061
Currency and deposits	15 322	17 513	19 010	24 992	29 306	34 039	36 878	34 746
Debt securities	1 018 877	1 147 206	1 139 217	1 275 546	1 319 433	1 461 006	1 464 553	1 574 776
Loans	34 976	35 546	37 501	35 278	36 169	37 266	38 632	61 795
Equity and investment fund shares	612 297	610 397	584 317	642 192	682 792	746 752	806 263	836 957
Equity	209 951	211 909	205 339	208 716	232 519	252 642	281 492	218 248
Investment fund shares	402 346	398 487	378 979	433 476	450 273	494 110	524 771	618 709
Money market fund shares	58 479	50 769	64 562	84 812	61 604	66 067	65 965	73 737
Non-Money market fund shares	343 866	347 719	314 416	348 664	388 669	428 043	458 806	544 972
Insurance pension and standardised guarantees	74 426	80 196	86 621	92 866	111 346	115 443	119 887	97 533
Financial derivatives and employee stock options	4 551	4 642	7 994	5 276	3 507	4 263	3 412	5 181
Other accounts receivable	63	54	51	53	54	54	54	77 073
Financial liabilities	1 752 840	1 881 201	1 884 050	1 955 886	2 054 326	2 166 842	2 251 385	2 726 776
Debt securities	6 827	6 603	8 522	9 335	11 235	15 892	17 338	80 389
Short-term debt securities	866	673	215	237	107	107	123	..
Long-term debt securities	5 961	5 930	8 307	9 098	11 128	15 785	17 215	..
Loans	67 644	76 284	70 690	77 126	88 206	99 616	104 029	63 451
Short-term loans	37 982	45 246	36 843	43 042	53 029	63 907	66 476	..
Long-term loans	29 662	31 038	33 846	34 084	35 177	35 709	37 552	..
Equity and investment fund shares	100 689	107 449	96 243	99 615	109 596	117 869	118 884	274 569
Insurance pension and standardised guarantees	1 542 953	1 655 957	1 680 705	1 735 678	1 811 041	1 897 780	1 976 939	2 184 597
Financial derivatives and employee stock options	466	225	324	138	426	1 895	386	2 866
Other accounts payable	34 261	34 682	27 566	33 995	33 822	33 790	33 809	120 904
Non-financial assets	24 402	25 683	25 225	26 309	27 356	27 785	28 618	38 711
Pension funds								
Financial net worth	..	..	..	..	..	..	..	..
Financial assets	..	..	..	..	..	..	..	..
Currency and deposits	..	..	..	..	..	..	..	..
Debt securities	..	..	..	..	..	..	..	..
Loans	..	..	..	..	..	..	..	..
Equity and investment fund shares	..	..	..	..	..	..	..	..
Equity	..	..	..	..	..	..	..	..
Investment fund shares	..	..	..	..	..	..	..	..
Money market fund shares	..	..	..	..	..	..	..	..
Non-Money market fund shares	..	..	..	..	..	..	..	..
Insurance pension and standardised guarantees	..	..	..	..	..	..	..	..
Financial derivatives and employee stock options	..	..	..	..	..	..	..	..
Other accounts receivable	..	..	..	..	..	..	..	..
Financial liabilities	..	..	..	..	..	..	..	..
Debt securities	..	..	..	..	..	..	..	..
Short-term debt securities	..	..	..	..	..	..	..	..
Long-term debt securities	..	..	..	..	..	..	..	..
Loans	..	..	..	..	..	..	..	..
Short-term loans	..	..	..	..	..	..	..	..
Long-term loans	..	..	..	..	..	..	..	..
Equity and investment fund shares	..	..	..	..	..	..	..	..
Insurance pension and standardised guarantees	..	..	..	..	..	..	..	..
Financial derivatives and employee stock options	..	..	..	..	..	..	..	..
Other accounts payable	..	..	..	..	..	..	..	..
Non-financial assets	..	..	..	..	..	..	..	..

Note: Detailed metadata at: http://metalinks.oecd.org/instinv/20170920/75e8

FRANCE

Table 4. Portfolio composition by type of investor

As percentage of financial assets and of financial liabilities

Per cent

	2009	2010	2011	2012	2013	2014	2015	2016
Investment funds								
Financial assets	100.0	100.0	100.0	100.0	100.0	100.0	100.0	100.0
Currency and deposits	6.1	5.6	6.3	6.2	6.0	5.9	5.7	5.3
Debt securities	42.3	40.2	42.1	42.2	39.5	39.6	39.1	38.6
Loans	0.3	0.4	0.1	0.1	0.2	0.2	0.1	0.3
Equity and investment fund shares	42.7	44.3	41.9	42.5	45.7	44.7	45.6	45.9
Insurance pension and standardised guarantee schemes	0.0	0.0	0.0	0.0	0.0	0.0	0.0	0.0
Financial derivatives and employee stock options	0.9	0.9	1.9	1.9	1.9	1.9	1.7	2.2
Other accounts receivable	7.7	8.5	7.6	7.1	6.8	7.7	7.8	7.7
Financial liabilities	100.0	100.0	100.0	100.0	100.0	100.0	100.0	100.0
Currency and deposits	0.5	0.6	0.8	0.9	0.6	0.5	0.4	0.7
Debt securities	0.0	0.0	0.0	0.0	0.0	0.0	0.0	0.0
Loans	0.0	0.3	0.0	0.3	0.2	0.3	0.3	0.5
Equity and investment fund shares	91.4	90.3	90.0	90.0	90.5	89.6	90.1	89.1
Insurance pension and standardised guarantee schemes	0.0	0.0	0.0	0.0	0.0	0.0	0.0	0.0
Financial derivatives and employee stock options	0.7	0.6	1.8	1.9	2.0	2.1	1.9	2.4
Other accounts receivable	7.3	8.3	7.4	7.0	6.7	7.5	7.4	7.3
Insurance corporations								
Financial assets	100.0	100.0	100.0	100.0	100.0	100.0	100.0	100.0
Currency and deposits	0.9	0.9	1.0	1.2	1.3	1.4	1.5	1.3
Debt securities	57.9	60.5	60.8	61.4	60.5	60.9	59.3	58.6
Loans	2.0	1.9	2.0	1.7	1.7	1.6	1.6	2.3
Equity and investment fund shares	34.8	32.2	31.2	30.9	31.3	31.1	32.6	31.1
Insurance pension and standardised guarantee schemes	4.2	4.2	4.6	4.5	5.1	4.8	4.9	3.6
Financial derivatives and employee stock options	0.3	0.2	0.4	0.3	0.2	0.2	0.1	0.2
Other accounts receivable	0.0	0.0	0.0	0.0	0.0	0.0	0.0	2.9
Financial liabilities	100.0	100.0	100.0	100.0	100.0	100.0	100.0	100.0
Currency and deposits	0.0	0.0	0.0	0.0	0.0	0.0	0.0	0.0
Debt securities	0.4	0.4	0.5	0.5	0.5	0.7	0.8	2.9
Loans	3.9	4.1	3.8	3.9	4.3	4.6	4.6	2.3
Equity and investment fund shares	5.7	5.7	5.1	5.1	5.3	5.4	5.3	10.1
Insurance pension and standardised guarantee schemes	88.0	88.0	89.2	88.7	88.2	87.6	87.8	80.1
Financial derivatives and employee stock options	0.0	0.0	0.0	0.0	0.0	0.1	0.0	0.1
Other accounts receivable	2.0	1.8	1.5	1.7	1.6	1.6	1.5	4.4
Pension funds								
Financial assets	..	..	..	..	..	..	..	..
Currency and deposits	..	..	..	..	..	..	..	..
Debt securities	..	..	..	..	..	..	..	..
Loans	..	..	..	..	..	..	..	..
Equity and investment fund shares	..	..	..	..	..	..	..	..
Insurance pension and standardised guarantee schemes	..	..	..	..	..	..	..	..
Financial derivatives and employee stock options	..	..	..	..	..	..	..	..
Other accounts receivable	..	..	..	..	..	..	..	..
Financial liabilities	..	..	..	..	..	..	..	..
Currency and deposits	..	..	..	..	..	..	..	..
Debt securities	..	..	..	..	..	..	..	..
Loans	..	..	..	..	..	..	..	..
Equity and investment fund shares	..	..	..	..	..	..	..	..
Insurance pension and standardised guarantee schemes	..	..	..	..	..	..	..	..
Financial derivatives and employee stock options	..	..	..	..	..	..	..	..
Other accounts receivable	..	..	..	..	..	..	..	..

Note: Detailed metadata at: http://metalinks.oecd.org/instinv/20170920/a49a

GERMANY

Table 1. Financial assets and liabilities of institutional investors, 2016

Million EUR (1999 DEM euro)

	Total	Investment funds			
		Non-money market funds			Money market funds
		Total	Open-end non-money market funds	Closed-end non-money market funds	Total
Financial assets	1 859 528	1 856 880	..	..	2 648
Currency and deposits	75 557	75 405	..	..	152
Debt securities	914 143	911 733	..	..	2 410
Debt securities, short term	6 920	6 808	..	..	112
Debt securities, long term	907 224	904 926	..	..	2 298
Debt securities issued by residents	141 973	141 384	..	..	589
Debt securities issued by non-residents	772 170	770 349	..	..	1 821
Loans	18 634	18 621	..	..	13
Loans, short-term	13	0	..	..	13
Loans, long-term	18 621	18 621	..	..	0
Loans granted to residents	1 720	1 717	..	..	3
Loans granted to non-residents	16 914	16 904	..	..	10
Equity and investment fund shares/units	799 202	799 141	..	..	61
Equity and investment fund shares issued/units by residents	..	..	..	..	..
Equity and investment fund shares/units issued by non residents	..	..	..	..	..
Other accounts receivable	32 764	32 752	..	..	12

	Total	Investment funds			
		Non-money market funds			Money market funds
		Total	Open-end non-money market funds	Closed-end non-money market funds	Total
Financial liabilities	1 967 505	1 964 857	..	..	2 648
Currency and deposits	..	..	..	..	..
Debt securities	..	0	..	..	..
Debt securities, short term	..	0	..	..	..
Debt securities, long term	..	0	..	..	..
Loans	30 583	30 583	..	..	..
Loans, short-term	0	0	..	..	..
Loans, long-term	30 583	30 583	..	..	..
Equity and investment fund shares/units	1 907 878	1 905 233	..	..	2 645
Insurance pension and standardised guaratees	..	0	..	..	..
Financial derivatives and employee stock options	16 445	16 445	..	..	0
Other accounts payable	12 599	12 596	..	..	3

	Total	Insurance corporations and pension funds			
		Insurance corporations			Pension funds
		Total	Life insurance corporations	Non-life insurance corporations	Total
Financial assets	2 566 057	1 994 424	..	..	571 633
Currency and deposits	459 199	348 231	..	..	110 968
Debt securities	422 769	380 923	..	..	41 846
Debt securities, short-term	2 457	2 381	..	..	76
Debt securities, long term	420 312	378 542	..	..	41 770
Debt securities issued by residents	112 708	104 966	..	..	7 742
Debt securities issued by non-residents	310 061	275 956	..	..	34 105
Loans	330 046	298 563	..	..	31 483
Loans, short-term	63 068	62 332	..	..	736
Loans, long-term	266 978	236 231	..	..	30 747
Loans granted to residents	267 100	237 610	..	..	29 490
Loans granted to non-residents	62 946	60 953	..	..	1 993
Equity and investment fund shares/units	1 202 392	837 739	..	..	364 653
Equity and investment fund shares/units issued by residents	..	..	..	..	..
Equity and investment fund shares/units issued by non residents	..	..	..	..	..
Other accounts receivable	67 900	50 911	..	..	16 989

	Total	Insurance corporations and pension funds			
		Insurance corporations			Pension funds
		Total	Life insurance corporations	Non-life insurance corporations	Total
Financial liabilities	2 513 320	2 002 193	..	..	511 126
Currency and deposits	..	..	..	..	..
Debt securities	20 409	20 384	..	..	25
Debt securities, short term	994	994	..	..	0
Debt securities, long term	19 415	19 390	..	..	25
Loans	83 874	78 323	..	..	5 550
Loans, short-term	48 769	44 503	..	..	4 265
Loans, long-term	35 105	33 820	..	..	1 285
Equity and investment fund shares/units	249 908	249 908	..	..	0
Insurance pension and standardised guarantees	2 050 563	1 549 190	..	..	501 373
Financial derivatives and employee stock options	1 153	1 153	..	..	0
Other accounts payable	107 413	103 235	..	..	4 178

Note: Detailed metadata at: http://metalinks.oecd.org/instinv/20170920/ebe7

GERMANY

Table 2. Financial assets and liabilities of investment funds

Million EUR

	2009	2010	2011	2012	2013	2014	2015	2016
Investment funds								
Financial net worth	-91 714	-94 052	-95 013	-96 695	-97 653	-98 074	-103 253	-107 977
Financial assets	980 597	1 088 601	1 091 094	1 261 524	1 368 048	1 555 369	1 695 238	1 859 528
Currency and deposits	63 164	56 311	74 226	68 417	70 050	70 131	81 075	75 557
Debt securities	558 331	599 292	607 744	693 135	715 174	824 795	845 544	914 143
Loans	8 244	9 813	9 676	11 773	12 082	13 905	15 551	18 634
Equity and investment fund shares	326 191	397 787	372 637	458 299	541 704	606 113	708 259	799 202
Equity	219 063	253 168	222 201	252 402	307 204	329 351	388 457	421 523
Investment fund shares	107 128	144 619	150 436	205 897	234 500	276 762	319 802	377 679
Money market fund shares	88	145	72	2 025	1 671	1 894	3 152	4 837
Non-Money market fund shares	107 040	144 474	150 364	203 872	232 830	274 867	316 650	372 842
Insurance pension and standardised guarantees	0	0	0	0	0	0	0	0
Financial derivatives and employee stock options	7 594	6 727	8 008	10 889	9 256	14 586	15 504	19 228
Other accounts receivable	17 073	18 672	18 802	19 010	19 782	25 839	29 306	32 764
Financial liabilities	1 072 312	1 182 653	1 186 107	1 358 219	1 465 700	1 653 443	1 798 491	1 967 505
Debt securities	..	..	..	..	..	..	..	..
Short-term debt securities	..	..	..	..	..	..	..	..
Long-term debt securities	..	..	..	..	..	..	..	..
Loans	28 132	30 037	29 447	32 143	29 222	30 753	30 197	30 583
Short-term loans	0	0	0	0	0	0	0	0
Long-term loans	28 132	30 037	29 447	32 143	29 222	30 753	30 197	30 583
Equity and investment fund shares	1 027 377	1 136 949	1 138 727	1 309 466	1 421 287	1 597 283	1 743 031	1 907 878
Insurance pension and standardised guarantees	..	..	..	..	..	..	..	..
Financial derivatives and employee stock options	6 501	6 086	8 794	4 647	4 175	12 041	12 469	16 445
Other accounts payable	10 302	9 581	9 139	11 963	11 017	13 367	12 794	12 599
Non-financial assets	..	..	..	..	..	..	..	..
Money market funds								
Financial net worth	0	0	0	0	0	0	0	0
Financial assets	12 260	10 376	6 622	7 824	4 516	3 895	3 836	2 648
Currency and deposits	2 723	2 286	544	322	315	240	355	152
Debt securities	9 367	7 880	5 927	5 414	4 129	3 633	3 462	2 410
Loans	0	0	0	24	10	0	0	13
Equity and investment fund shares	88	145	72	2 025	24	9	7	61
Equity	..	..	..	..	..	..	..	..
Investment fund shares	88	145	72	2 025	24	9	7	61
Money market fund shares	88	145	72	2 025	5	9	7	61
Non-Money market fund shares	0	0	0	0	19	0	0	0
Insurance pension and standardised guarantees	..	..	..	..	..	..	..	..
Financial derivatives and employee stock options	2	0	2	1	0	0	0	0
Other accounts receivable	80	66	76	37	38	13	12	12
Financial liabilities	12 261	10 376	6 622	7 824	4 515	3 895	3 836	2 648
Debt securities	..	..	..	..	..	..	..	..
Short-term debt securities	..	..	..	..	..	..	..	..
Long-term debt securities	..	..	..	..	..	..	..	..
Loans	..	..	..	..	..	..	..	..
Short-term loans	..	..	..	..	..	..	..	..
Long-term loans	..	..	..	..	..	..	..	..
Equity and investment fund shares	11 951	10 274	6 577	7 703	4 510	3 884	3 834	2 645
Insurance pension and standardised guarantees	..	..	..	..	..	..	..	..
Financial derivatives and employee stock options	158	2	1	0	0	0	0	0
Other accounts payable	152	100	44	121	6	12	2	3
Non-financial assets	..	..	..	..	..	..	..	..
Non-money market funds								
Financial net worth	-91 714	-94 052	-95 013	-96 695	-97 653	-98 074	-103 253	-107 977
Financial assets	968 337	1 078 225	1 084 472	1 253 700	1 363 532	1 551 474	1 691 402	1 856 880
Currency and deposits	60 441	54 025	73 682	68 095	69 735	69 891	80 720	75 405
Debt securities	548 964	591 412	601 817	687 721	711 045	821 162	842 082	911 733
Loans	8 244	9 813	9 676	11 749	12 072	13 905	15 551	18 621
Equity and investment fund shares	326 103	397 642	372 565	456 274	541 680	606 104	708 252	799 141
Equity	219 063	253 168	222 201	252 402	307 204	329 351	388 457	421 523
Investment fund shares	107 040	144 474	150 364	203 872	234 476	276 753	319 795	377 618
Money market fund shares	0	0	0	0	1 666	1 885	3 145	4 776
Non-Money market fund shares	107 040	144 474	150 364	203 872	232 811	274 867	316 650	372 842
Insurance pension and standardised guarantees	0	0	0	0	0	0	0	0
Financial derivatives and employee stock options	7 592	6 727	8 006	10 888	9 256	14 586	15 504	19 228
Other accounts receivable	16 993	18 606	18 726	18 973	19 744	25 826	29 294	32 752
Financial liabilities	1 060 051	1 172 277	1 179 485	1 350 395	1 461 185	1 649 548	1 794 655	1 964 857
Debt securities	0	0	0	0	0	0	0	0
Short-term debt securities	0	0	0	0	0	0	0	0
Long-term debt securities	0	0	0	0	0	0	0	0
Loans	28 132	30 037	29 447	32 143	29 222	30 753	30 197	30 583
Short-term loans	0	0	0	0	0	0	0	0
Long-term loans	28 132	30 037	29 447	32 143	29 222	30 753	30 197	30 583
Equity and investment fund shares	1 015 426	1 126 675	1 132 150	1 301 763	1 416 777	1 593 399	1 739 197	1 905 233
Insurance pension and standardised guarantees	0	0	0	0	0	0	0	0
Financial derivatives and employee stock options	6 343	6 084	8 793	4 647	4 175	12 041	12 469	16 445
Other accounts payable	10 150	9 481	9 095	11 842	11 011	13 355	12 792	12 596
Non-financial assets	..	..	..	..	..	..	..	..
Open-end non-money market funds								
Financial net worth	..	..	..	..	..	..	..	..
Financial assets	..	..	..	..	..	..	..	..

Table 2. Financial assets and liabilities of investment funds *(cont.)*

Million EUR

	2009	2010	2011	2012	2013	2014	2015	2016
Currency and deposits	..	..	..	..	..	..	..	..
Debt securities	..	..	..	..	..	..	..	..
Loans	..	..	..	..	..	..	..	..
Equity and investment fund shares	..	..	..	..	..	..	..	..
Equity	..	..	..	..	..	..	..	..
Investment fund shares	..	..	..	..	..	..	..	..
Money market fund shares	..	..	..	..	..	..	..	..
Non-Money market fund shares	..	..	..	..	..	..	..	..
Insurance pension and standardised guarantees	..	..	..	..	..	..	..	..
Financial derivatives and employee stock options	..	..	..	..	..	..	..	..
Other accounts receivable	..	..	..	..	..	..	..	..
Financial liabilities	..	..	..	..	..	..	..	..
Debt securities	..	..	..	..	..	..	..	..
Short-term debt securities	..	..	..	..	..	..	..	..
Long-term debt securities	..	..	..	..	..	..	..	..
Loans	..	..	..	..	..	..	..	..
Short-term loans	..	..	..	..	..	..	..	..
Long-term loans	..	..	..	..	..	..	..	..
Equity and investment fund shares	..	..	..	..	..	..	..	..
Insurance pension and standardised guarantees	..	..	..	..	..	..	..	..
Financial derivatives and employee stock options	..	..	..	..	..	..	..	..
Other accounts payable	..	..	..	..	..	..	..	..
Non-financial assets	..	..	..	..	..	..	..	..
Open-end investment funds								
Financial net worth	..	..	..	..	..	..	..	..
Financial assets	..	..	..	..	..	..	..	..
Currency and deposits	..	..	..	..	..	..	..	..
Debt securities	..	..	..	..	..	..	..	..
Loans	..	..	..	..	..	..	..	..
Equity and investment fund shares	..	..	..	..	..	..	..	..
Equity	..	..	..	..	..	..	..	..
Investment fund shares	..	..	..	..	..	..	..	..
Money market fund shares	..	..	..	..	..	..	..	..
Non-Money market fund shares	..	..	..	..	..	..	..	..
Insurance pension and standardised guarantees	..	..	..	..	..	..	..	..
Financial derivatives and employee stock options	..	..	..	..	..	..	..	..
Other accounts receivable	..	..	..	..	..	..	..	..
Financial liabilities	..	..	..	..	..	..	..	..
Debt securities	..	..	..	..	..	..	..	..
Short-term debt securities	..	..	..	..	..	..	..	..
Long-term debt securities	..	..	..	..	..	..	..	..
Loans	..	..	..	..	..	..	..	..
Short-term loans	..	..	..	..	..	..	..	..
Long-term loans	..	..	..	..	..	..	..	..
Equity and investment fund shares	..	..	..	..	..	..	..	..
Insurance pension and standardised guarantees	..	..	..	..	..	..	..	..
Financial derivatives and employee stock options	..	..	..	..	..	..	..	..
Other accounts payable	..	..	..	..	..	..	..	..
Non-financial assets	..	..	..	..	..	..	..	..

Note: Detailed metadata at: http://metalinks.oecd.org/instinv/20170920/ebe7

Table 3. Financial assets and liabilities of insurance corporations and pension funds

Million EUR

	2009	2010	2011	2012	2013	2014	2015	2016
Insurance corporations and pension funds								
Financial net worth	-38 111	-20 078	5 842	35 412	-13 706	80 818	1 473	52 737
Financial assets	1 745 556	1 845 571	1 899 067	2 068 570	2 139 327	2 354 495	2 428 430	2 566 057
Currency and deposits	588 867	570 834	576 218	560 467	541 268	523 691	489 446	459 199
Debt securities	180 238	203 255	218 696	281 003	303 382	372 741	382 622	422 769
Loans	266 258	276 338	282 144	288 668	294 355	310 488	322 616	330 046
Equity and investment fund shares	587 614	668 535	694 381	808 638	870 968	1 007 538	1 086 988	1 202 392
Equity	192 208	202 594	197 270	205 400	196 041	201 679	213 276	234 944
Investment fund shares	395 406	465 941	497 111	603 238	674 927	805 859	873 712	967 448
Money market fund shares	7	8	8	1 986	614	702	1 443	1 796
Non-Money market fund shares	395 399	465 933	497 103	601 252	674 313	805 158	872 269	965 652
Insurance pension and standardised guarantees	58 550	59 930	62 247	63 082	64 175	66 801	76 989	79 379
Financial derivatives and employee stock options	4 728	4 936	5 366	6 138	5 979	6 417	4 520	4 372
Other accounts receivable	59 301	61 743	60 015	60 574	59 200	64 819	65 249	67 900
Financial liabilities	1 783 667	1 865 649	1 893 225	2 033 158	2 153 033	2 273 677	2 426 957	2 513 320
Debt securities	17 254	18 771	19 527	24 361	17 635	18 511	20 138	20 409
Short-term debt securities	1 337	1 894	767	1 404	598	686	1 558	994
Long-term debt securities	15 917	16 877	13 760	22 957	17 037	17 825	18 580	19 415
Loans	67 377	66 081	64 289	67 923	66 031	71 138	80 945	83 874
Short-term loans	36 486	40 599	33 384	40 862	36 487	40 047	47 884	48 769
Long-term loans	30 891	25 482	25 905	27 061	29 544	31 091	33 061	35 105
Equity and investment fund shares	136 216	137 616	111 799	158 942	197 652	202 695	255 480	249 908
Insurance pension and standardised guarantees	1 472 570	1 552 555	1 605 347	1 688 032	1 772 406	1 878 720	1 964 992	2 050 563
Financial derivatives and employee stock options	1 154	1 073	1 045	789	924	1 110	1 142	1 153
Other accounts payable	89 096	89 553	91 218	93 111	98 385	101 503	104 260	107 413
Non-financial assets	..	..	..	..	..	..	..	..
Insurance corporations								
Financial net worth	-38 917	-18 410	8 619	7 013	-5 154	57 483	-29 344	-7 769
Financial assets	1 414 901	1 491 692	1 526 640	1 637 864	1 721 787	1 868 962	1 907 442	1 994 424
Currency and deposits	447 988	431 593	437 875	427 202	407 563	405 802	371 512	348 231
Debt securities	152 182	173 816	185 244	238 228	280 251	340 530	346 726	380 923
Loans	243 383	252 735	256 599	262 728	266 264	280 648	291 899	298 563
Equity and investment fund shares	459 767	518 705	532 244	593 685	652 551	723 016	772 133	837 739
Equity	182 858	190 431	185 358	191 386	186 376	189 863	198 704	218 296
Investment fund shares	276 909	328 274	346 886	402 299	466 175	533 153	573 429	619 443
Money market fund shares	0	0	0	0	543	601	1 327	1 636
Non-Money market fund shares	276 909	328 274	346 886	402 299	465 632	532 552	572 102	617 807
Insurance pension and standardised guarantees	55 552	56 473	58 424	58 984	59 802	63 942	71 582	73 685
Financial derivatives and employee stock options	4 728	4 936	5 366	6 138	5 979	6 417	4 520	4 372
Other accounts receivable	51 301	53 434	50 888	50 899	49 377	48 607	49 070	50 911
Financial liabilities	1 453 818	1 510 102	1 518 021	1 630 851	1 726 941	1 811 479	1 936 786	2 002 193
Debt securities	17 254	18 771	19 527	24 361	17 635	18 490	20 116	20 384
Short-term debt securities	1 337	1 894	767	1 404	598	686	1 558	994
Long-term debt securities	15 917	16 877	18 760	22 957	17 037	17 804	18 558	19 390
Loans	63 936	62 322	60 261	63 682	61 605	66 289	75 721	78 323
Short-term loans	34 002	37 755	35 308	37 602	33 029	36 221	43 858	44 503
Long-term loans	29 934	24 567	24 954	26 080	28 576	30 068	31 863	33 820
Equity and investment fund shares	136 216	137 616	111 799	158 942	197 652	202 695	255 480	249 908
Insurance pension and standardised guarantees	1 147 262	1 201 983	1 235 238	1 291 113	1 351 920	1 422 747	1 484 187	1 549 190
Financial derivatives and employee stock options	1 154	1 073	1 045	789	924	1 110	1 142	1 153
Other accounts payable	87 996	88 337	90 151	91 964	97 205	100 148	100 140	103 235
Non-financial assets	..	..	..	..	..	..	..	..
Pension funds								
Financial net worth	806	-1 668	-2 774	28 399	-8 553	23 335	30 819	60 507
Financial assets	330 656	353 879	372 428	430 706	417 540	485 534	520 989	571 633
Currency and deposits	140 879	139 241	138 344	133 265	133 704	117 889	117 934	110 968
Debt securities	28 056	29 439	33 452	42 775	23 131	32 211	35 896	41 846
Loans	22 875	23 603	25 545	25 940	28 091	29 840	30 717	31 483
Equity and investment fund shares	127 847	149 830	162 137	214 953	218 417	284 523	314 855	364 653
Equity	9 350	12 163	11 912	14 014	9 665	11 816	14 572	16 648
Investment fund shares	118 497	137 667	150 225	200 939	208 752	272 707	300 283	348 005
Money market fund shares	7	8	8	1 986	71	100	115	161
Non-Money market fund shares	118 490	137 659	150 217	198 953	208 681	272 606	300 167	347 845
Insurance pension and standardised guarantees	2 999	3 457	3 823	4 098	4 374	4 859	5 407	5 694
Financial derivatives and employee stock options	0	0	0	0	0	0	0	0
Other accounts receivable	8 000	8 309	9 127	9 675	9 823	16 212	16 180	16 989
Financial liabilities	329 850	355 547	375 202	402 307	426 093	462 199	490 170	511 126
Debt securities	0	0	0	0	0	21	22	25
Short-term debt securities	0	0	0	0	0	0	0	0
Long-term debt securities	0	0	0	0	0	21	22	25
Loans	3 442	3 759	4 026	4 241	4 427	4 850	5 224	5 550
Short-term loans	2 484	2 844	3 076	3 260	3 459	3 827	4 026	4 265
Long-term loans	958	915	950	981	968	1 023	1 198	1 285
Equity and investment fund shares	0	0	0	0	0	0	0	0
Insurance pension and standardised guarantees	325 308	350 572	370 109	396 919	420 486	455 973	480 805	501 373
Financial derivatives and employee stock options	0	0	0	0	0	0	0	0
Other accounts payable	1 100	1 216	1 067	1 147	1 180	1 355	4 119	4 178
Non-financial assets	..	..	..	..	..	..	..	..

Note: Detailed metadata at: http://metalinks.oecd.org/instinv/20170920/ebe7

GERMANY

Table 4. Portfolio composition by type of investor

As percentage of financial assets and of financial liabilities

Per cent

	2009	2010	2011	2012	2013	2014	2015	2016
Investment funds								
Financial assets	100.0	100.0	100.0	100.0	100.0	100.0	100.0	100.0
Currency and deposits	6.4	5.2	6.8	5.4	5.1	4.5	4.8	4.1
Debt securities	56.9	55.1	55.7	54.9	52.3	53.0	49.9	49.2
Loans	0.8	0.9	0.9	0.9	0.9	0.9	0.9	1.0
Equity and investment fund shares	33.3	36.5	34.2	36.3	39.6	39.0	41.8	43.0
Insurance pension and standardised guarantee schemes	0.0	0.0	0.0	0.0	0.0	0.0	0.0	0.0
Financial derivatives and employee stock options	0.8	0.6	0.7	0.9	0.7	0.9	0.9	1.0
Other accounts receivable	1.7	1.7	1.7	1.5	1.4	1.7	1.7	1.8
Financial liabilities	100.0	100.0	100.0	100.0	100.0	100.0	100.0	100.0
Currency and deposits	0.0	0.0	0.0	0.0	0.0	0.0	0.0	0.0
Debt securities	0.0	0.0	0.0	0.0	0.0	0.0	0.0	0.0
Loans	2.6	2.5	2.5	2.4	2.0	1.9	1.7	1.6
Equity and investment fund shares	95.8	96.1	96.0	96.4	97.0	96.6	96.9	97.0
Insurance pension and standardised guarantee schemes	0.0	0.0	0.0	0.0	0.0	0.0	0.0	0.0
Financial derivatives and employee stock options	0.6	0.5	0.7	0.3	0.3	0.7	0.7	0.8
Other accounts receivable	1.0	0.8	0.8	0.9	0.8	0.8	0.7	0.6
Insurance corporations								
Financial assets	100.0	100.0	100.0	100.0	100.0	100.0	100.0	100.0
Currency and deposits	31.7	28.9	28.7	26.1	23.7	21.7	19.5	17.5
Debt securities	10.8	11.7	12.1	14.5	16.3	18.2	18.2	19.1
Loans	17.2	16.9	16.8	16.0	15.5	15.0	15.3	15.0
Equity and investment fund shares	32.5	34.8	34.9	36.2	37.9	38.7	40.5	42.0
Insurance pension and standardised guarantee schemes	3.9	3.8	3.8	3.6	3.5	3.4	3.8	3.7
Financial derivatives and employee stock options	0.3	0.3	0.4	0.4	0.3	0.3	0.2	0.2
Other accounts receivable	3.6	3.6	3.3	3.1	2.9	2.6	2.6	2.6
Financial liabilities	100.0	100.0	100.0	100.0	100.0	100.0	100.0	100.0
Currency and deposits	0.0	0.0	0.0	0.0	0.0	0.0	0.0	0.0
Debt securities	1.2	1.2	1.3	1.5	1.0	1.0	1.0	1.0
Loans	4.4	4.1	4.0	3.9	3.6	3.7	3.9	3.9
Equity and investment fund shares	9.4	9.1	7.4	9.7	11.4	11.2	13.2	12.5
Insurance pension and standardised guarantee schemes	78.9	79.6	81.4	79.2	78.3	78.5	76.6	77.4
Financial derivatives and employee stock options	0.1	0.1	0.1	0.0	0.1	0.1	0.1	0.1
Other accounts receivable	6.1	5.8	5.9	5.6	5.6	5.5	5.2	5.2
Pension funds								
Financial assets	100.0	100.0	100.0	100.0	100.0	100.0	100.0	100.0
Currency and deposits	42.6	39.3	37.1	30.9	32.0	24.3	22.6	19.4
Debt securities	8.5	8.3	9.0	9.9	5.5	6.6	6.9	7.3
Loans	6.9	6.7	6.9	6.0	6.7	6.1	5.9	5.5
Equity and investment fund shares	38.7	42.3	43.5	49.9	52.3	58.6	60.4	63.8
Insurance pension and standardised guarantee schemes	0.9	1.0	1.0	1.0	1.0	1.0	1.0	1.0
Financial derivatives and employee stock options	0.0	0.0	0.0	0.0	0.0	0.0	0.0	0.0
Other accounts receivable	2.4	2.3	2.5	2.2	2.4	3.3	3.1	3.0
Financial liabilities	100.0	100.0	100.0	100.0	100.0	100.0	100.0	100.0
Currency and deposits	0.0	0.0	0.0	0.0	0.0	0.0	0.0	0.0
Debt securities	0.0	0.0	0.0	0.0	0.0	0.0	0.0	0.0
Loans	1.0	1.1	1.1	1.1	1.0	1.0	1.1	1.1
Equity and investment fund shares	0.0	0.0	0.0	0.0	0.0	0.0	0.0	0.0
Insurance pension and standardised guarantee schemes	98.6	98.6	98.6	98.7	98.7	98.7	98.1	98.1
Financial derivatives and employee stock options	0.0	0.0	0.0	0.0	0.0	0.0	0.0	0.0
Other accounts receivable	0.3	0.3	0.3	0.3	0.3	0.3	0.8	0.8

Note: Detailed metadata at: http://metalinks.oecd.org/instinv/20170920/a49a

GREECE

Table 1. Financial assets and liabilities of institutional investors, 2016

Million EUR (2001 GRD euro)

		Investment funds			
	Total	Non-money market funds			Money market funds
		Total	Open-end non-money market funds	Closed-end non-money market funds	Total
Financial assets	3 978	3 435	2 931	504	543
Currency and deposits	443	324	187	137	119
Debt securities	1 750	1 327	1 323	4	423
Debt securities, short term	577	182	182	0	395
Debt securities, long term	1 173	1 145	1 141	4	28
Debt securities issued by residents	1 103	695	691	4	408
Debt securities issued by non-residents	647	632	632	0	15
Loans	..	..	..	..	..
Loans, short-term	..	..	..	..	..
Loans, long-term	..	..	..	..	..
Loans granted to residents	..	..	..	..	..
Loans granted to non-residents	..	..	..	..	..
Equity and investment fund shares/units	1 641	1 641	1 375	266	0
Equity and investment fund shares issued/units by residents	738	738	682	56	0
Equity and investment fund shares/units issued by non residents	904	904	695	209	0
Other accounts receivable	..	..	..	..	1

		Investment funds			
	Total	Non-money market funds			Money market funds
		Total	Open-end non-money market funds	Closed-end non-money market funds	Total
Financial liabilities	6 036	5 495	2 933	2 562	541
Currency and deposits	..	..	..	..	..
Debt securities	..	..	..	..	..
Debt securities, short term	..	..	..	..	..
Debt securities, long term	..	..	..	..	..
Loans	346	346	0	346	..
Loans, short-term	2	2	0	2	..
Loans, long-term	344	344	0	344	..
Equity and investment fund shares/units	5 620	5 080	2 909	2 171	540
Insurance pension and standardised guaratees	..	..	..	..	..
Financial derivatives and employee stock options	..	..	..	..	0
Other accounts payable	..	..	..	..	1

		Insurance corporations and pension funds			
	Total	Insurance corporations			Pension funds
		Total	Life insurance corporations	Non-life insurance corporations	Total
Financial assets	16 507	15 333	12 550	2 783	1 173
Currency and deposits	1 647	1 591	1 302	289	56
Debt securities	9 838	9 095	7 444	1 651	743
Debt securities, short-term	1 490	1 396	1 142	253	94
Debt securities, long term	8 348	7 699	6 302	1 397	649
Debt securities issued by residents	3 117	2 846	2 329	517	271
Debt securities issued by non-residents	6 720	6 249	5 115	1 134	471
Loans	149	146	119	26	4
Loans, short-term	14	10	8	2	4
Loans, long-term	136	136	111	25	0
Loans granted to residents	144	140	115	25	4
Loans granted to non-residents	5	5	4	1	0
Equity and investment fund shares/units	3 384	3 071	2 514	557	313
Equity and investment fund shares/units issued by residents	1 247	1 172	960	213	75
Equity and investment fund shares/units issued by non residents	2 137	1 899	1 554	345	238
Other accounts receivable	1 190	1 132	927	206	58

		Insurance corporations and pension funds			
	Total	Insurance corporations			Pension funds
		Total	Life insurance corporations	Non-life insurance corporations	Total
Financial liabilities	16 723	15 534	12 715	2 819	1 189
Currency and deposits	..	..	..	..	..
Debt securities	..	2	1	0	..
Debt securities, short term	..	0	0	0	..
Debt securities, long term	..	2	[illegible]	0	..
Loans	..	240	196	43	..
Loans, short-term	..	51	42	9	..
Loans, long-term	..	189	154	34	..
Equity and investment fund shares/units	..	2 421	1 982	439	..
Insurance pension and standardised guarantees	13 035	11 913	9 751	2 162	1 123
Financial derivatives and employee stock options	0	0	0	0	..
Other accounts payable	1 025	959	785	174	66

Note: Detailed metadata at: http://metalinks.oecd.org/instinv/20170920/dee5

GREECE

Table 2. Financial assets and liabilities of investment funds

Million EUR

	2009	2010	2011	2012	2013	2014	2015	2016
Investment funds								
Financial net worth	-677	-1 535	-1 466	-1 399	-1 325	-1 849	-1 908	-2 058
Financial assets	8 680	6 879	4 380	4 866	5 129	4 868	4 235	3 978
Currency and deposits	2 401	1 706	1 304	1 534	1 099	1 332	595	443
Debt securities	2 758	2 279	1 471	1 465	1 768	1 382	1 671	1 750
Loans	..	..	..	..	..	..	..	..
Equity and investment fund shares	3 168	2 468	1 435	1 695	2 097	1 827	1 821	1 641
Equity	2 622	1 882	1 037	1 322	1 748	1 328	1 288	1 129
Investment fund shares	546	586	398	373	349	499	533	512
Money market fund shares	16	3	9	21	16	15	10	13
Non-Money market fund shares	530	583	389	352	333	484	523	499
Insurance pension and standardised guarantees	..	..	..	..	..	..	..	..
Financial derivatives and employee stock options	..	..	..	..	..	..	..	..
Other accounts receivable	..	..	..	..	..	..	..	..
Financial liabilities	9 357	8 414	5 846	6 265	6 454	6 717	6 143	6 036
Debt securities	..	..	..	..	..	..	..	..
Short-term debt securities	..	..	..	..	..	..	..	..
Long-term debt securities	..	..	..	..	..	..	..	..
Loans	9	16	59	86	81	312	301	346
Short-term loans	0	0	0	0	0	2	2	2
Long-term loans	9	16	59	86	81	310	299	344
Equity and investment fund shares	8 878	7 760	5 133	5 641	6 234	6 261	5 765	5 620
Insurance pension and standardised guarantees	..	..	..	..	..	..	..	..
Financial derivatives and employee stock options	..	..	..	..	..	..	..	..
Other accounts payable	..	..	..	..	..	..	..	..
Non-financial assets	676	1 536	1 462	1 397	1 322	1 845	1 905	2 057
Money market funds								
Financial net worth	-2	-2	-1	0	0	-1	-1	2
Financial assets	1 777	1 183	744	840	719	773	512	543
Currency and deposits	1 610	1 013	627	772	365	539	161	119
Debt securities	162	167	108	61	346	228	351	423
Loans	..	..	..	..	..	..	..	..
Equity and investment fund shares	0	0	5	2	2	2	0	0
Equity	0	0	0	0	0	0	0	0
Investment fund shares	0	0	5	2	2	2	0	0
Money market fund shares	0	0	5	2	2	2	0	0
Non-Money market fund shares	0	0	0	0	0	0	0	0
Insurance pension and standardised guarantees	..	..	..	..	..	..	..	..
Financial derivatives and employee stock options	0	0	0	0	0	0	0	0
Other accounts receivable	5	3	4	5	6	4	0	1
Financial liabilities	1 779	1 185	745	840	719	774	513	541
Debt securities	..	..	..	..	..	..	..	..
Short-term debt securities	..	..	..	..	..	..	..	..
Long-term debt securities	..	..	..	..	..	..	..	..
Loans	..	..	..	..	..	..	..	..
Short-term loans	..	..	..	..	..	..	..	..
Long-term loans	..	..	..	..	..	..	..	..
Equity and investment fund shares	1 775	1 182	739	835	711	762	513	540
Insurance pension and standardised guarantees	..	..	..	..	..	..	..	..
Financial derivatives and employee stock options	0	0	0	0	0	0	0	0
Other accounts payable	4	3	6	5	8	12	0	1
Non-financial assets	..	..	..	..	..	..	..	..
Non-money market funds								
Financial net worth	-675	-1 533	-1 465	-1 399	-1 325	-1 848	-1 907	-2 060
Financial assets	6 903	5 696	3 636	4 026	4 410	4 095	3 723	3 435
Currency and deposits	791	693	677	762	734	793	434	324
Debt securities	2 596	2 112	1 363	1 404	1 422	1 154	1 320	1 327
Loans	..	..	..	..	..	..	..	..
Equity and investment fund shares	3 168	2 468	1 430	1 693	2 095	1 825	1 821	1 641
Equity	2 622	1 882	1 037	1 322	1 748	1 328	1 288	1 129
Investment fund shares	546	586	393	371	347	497	533	512
Money market fund shares	16	3	4	19	14	13	10	13
Non-Money market fund shares	530	583	389	352	333	484	523	499
Insurance pension and standardised guarantees	..	..	..	..	..	..	..	..
Financial derivatives and employee stock options	..	..	..	..	..	..	..	..
Other accounts receivable	..	..	..	..	..	..	..	..
Financial liabilities	7 578	7 229	5 101	5 425	5 735	5 943	5 630	5 495
Debt securities	..	..	..	..	..	..	..	..
Short-term debt securities	..	..	..	..	..	..	..	..
Long-term debt securities	..	..	..	..	..	..	..	..
Loans	9	16	59	86	81	312	301	346
Short-term loans	0	0	0	0	0	2	2	2
Long-term loans	9	16	59	86	81	310	299	344
Equity and investment fund shares	7 103	6 578	4 394	4 806	5 523	5 499	5 252	5 080
Insurance pension and standardised guarantees	..	..	..	..	..	..	..	..
Financial derivatives and employee stock options	..	..	..	..	..	..	..	..
Other accounts payable	..	..	..	..	..	..	..	..
Non-financial assets	676	1 536	1 462	1 397	1 322	1 845	1 905	2 057
Open-end non-money market funds								
Financial net worth	0	2	-2	-2	-2	-2	-1	-2
Financial assets	6 453	5 190	3 262	3 572	3 797	3 344	3 138	2 931

Table 2. Financial assets and liabilities of investment funds *(cont.)*

Million EUR

	2009	2010	2011	2012	2013	2014	2015	2016
Currency and deposits	573	478	392	405	363	580	254	187
Debt securities	2 596	2 112	1 363	1 404	1 420	1 151	1 319	1 323
Loans	..	..	..	..	..	..	..	..
Equity and investment fund shares	3 041	2 355	1 372	1 635	1 890	1 499	1 486	1 375
Equity	2 495	1 769	979	1 264	1 544	1 083	1 033	944
Investment fund shares	546	586	393	371	346	416	453	431
Money market fund shares	16	3	4	19	14	13	10	13
Non-Money market fund shares	530	583	389	352	332	403	443	418
Insurance pension and standardised guarantees	..	..	..	..	..	..	..	..
Financial derivatives and employee stock options	..	..	..	..	..	..	..	..
Other accounts receivable	..	..	..	..	..	..	..	..
Financial liabilities	6 453	5 188	3 264	3 574	3 799	3 346	3 139	2 933
Debt securities	..	..	..	..	..	..	..	..
Short-term debt securities	..	..	..	..	..	..	..	..
Long-term debt securities	..	..	..	..	..	..	..	..
Loans	0	0	0	0	0	0	0	0
Short-term loans	0	0	0	0	0	0	0	0
Long-term loans	0	0	0	0	0	0	0	0
Equity and investment fund shares	6 296	5 008	3 161	3 467	3 696	3 254	3 089	2 909
Insurance pension and standardised guarantees	..	..	..	..	..	..	..	..
Financial derivatives and employee stock options	..	..	..	..	..	..	..	..
Other accounts payable	..	..	..	..	..	..	..	..
Non-financial assets	0	0	0	0	0	0	0	0
Open-end investment funds								
Financial net worth	-2	0	-3	-2	-2	-3	-2	0
Financial assets	8 230	6 373	4 006	4 412	4 516	4 117	3 650	3 474
Currency and deposits	2 183	1 491	1 019	1 177	728	1 119	415	306
Debt securities	2 758	2 279	1 471	1 465	1 766	1 379	1 670	1 746
Loans	..	..	..	..	..	..	..	..
Equity and investment fund shares	3 041	2 355	1 377	1 637	1 892	1 501	1 486	1 375
Equity	2 495	1 769	979	1 264	1 544	1 083	1 033	944
Investment fund shares	546	586	398	373	348	418	453	431
Money market fund shares	16	3	9	21	16	15	10	13
Non-Money market fund shares	530	583	389	352	332	403	443	418
Insurance pension and standardised guarantees	..	..	..	..	..	..	..	..
Financial derivatives and employee stock options	..	..	..	..	..	..	..	..
Other accounts receivable	..	..	..	..	..	..	..	..
Financial liabilities	8 232	6 373	4 009	4 414	4 518	4 120	3 652	3 474
Debt securities	..	..	..	..	..	..	..	..
Short-term debt securities	..	..	..	..	..	..	..	..
Long-term debt securities	..	..	..	..	..	..	..	..
Loans	0	0	0	0	0	0	0	0
Short-term loans	0	0	0	0	0	0	0	0
Long-term loans	0	0	0	0	0	0	0	0
Equity and investment fund shares	8 071	6 190	3 900	4 302	4 407	4 016	3 602	3 449
Insurance pension and standardised guarantees	..	..	..	..	..	..	..	..
Financial derivatives and employee stock options	..	..	..	..	..	..	..	..
Other accounts payable	..	..	..	..	..	..	..	..
Non-financial assets	0	0	0	0	0	0	0	0

Note: Detailed metadata at: http://metalinks.oecd.org/instinv/20170920/dee5

Table 3. Financial assets and liabilities of insurance corporations and pension funds

Million EUR

	2009	2010	2011	2012	2013	2014	2015	2016
Insurance corporations and pension funds								
Financial net worth	..	..	..	..	-921	-879	-1 002	-217
Financial assets	..	..	..	..	15 509	15 893	15 969	16 507
Currency and deposits	..	..	..	..	3 772	2 575	1 943	1 647
Debt securities	..	..	..	..	6 713	8 243	8 323	9 838
Loans	..	..	..	..	132	140	160	149
Equity and investment fund shares	..	..	..	..	2 628	2 880	3 321	3 384
Equity	..	..	..	..	365	404	545	464
Investment fund shares	..	..	..	..	2 264	2 476	2 776	2 920
Money market fund shares	..	..	..	..	367	416	509	626
Non-Money market fund shares	..	..	..	..	1 896	2 060	2 267	2 294
Insurance pension and standardised guarantees	..	..	..	..	390	375	471	296
Financial derivatives and employee stock options	..	..	..	..	8	4	4	2
Other accounts receivable	..	..	..	..	1 866	1 676	1 747	1 190
Financial liabilities	..	..	..	..	16 430	16 772	16 971	16 723
Debt securities	..	..	..	..	..	..	..	..
Short-term debt securities	..	..	..	..	..	..	..	..
Long-term debt securities	..	..	..	..	..	..	..	..
Loans	..	..	..	..	..	..	..	..
Short-term loans	..	..	..	..	..	..	..	..
Long-term loans	..	..	..	..	..	..	..	..
Equity and investment fund shares	..	..	..	..	..	..	..	..
Insurance pension and standardised guarantees	..	..	..	..	12 146	12 213	12 523	13 035
Financial derivatives and employee stock options	..	..	..	..	0	0	0	0
Other accounts payable	..	..	..	..	977	1 198	802	1 025
Non-financial assets	..	..	..	..	921	879	1 002	217
Insurance corporations								
Financial net worth	-1 236	-1 041	-987	-865	-921	-879	-1 002	-201
Financial assets	14 344	14 662	13 906	14 689	15 284	15 453	15 647	15 333
Currency and deposits	1 988	2 837	2 771	2 800	3 547	2 439	1 836	1 591
Debt securities	6 587	6 605	6 256	6 589	6 713	7 985	8 176	9 095
Loans	102	101	97	145	132	132	154	146
Equity and investment fund shares	2 809	2 331	2 150	2 632	2 628	2 842	3 260	3 071
Equity	508	352	284	341	365	399	532	432
Investment fund shares	2 300	1 979	1 865	2 291	2 264	2 444	2 728	2 640
Money market fund shares	114	108	174	468	367	416	509	528
Non-Money market fund shares	2 186	1 871	1 692	1 823	1 896	2 028	2 218	2 112
Insurance pension and standardised guarantees	372	419	404	426	390	375	471	296
Financial derivatives and employee stock options	3	0	0	6	8	4	4	2
Other accounts receivable	2 484	2 369	2 228	2 091	1 866	1 675	1 746	1 132
Financial liabilities	15 580	15 703	14 893	15 554	16 205	16 332	16 649	15 534
Debt securities	37	16	15	15	29	29	29	2
Short-term debt securities	0	0	0	0	0	0	0	0
Long-term debt securities	37	16	15	15	29	29	29	2
Loans	247	1 033	673	332	482	127	165	240
Short-term loans	83	837	469	275	435	65	57	51
Long-term loans	165	196	204	57	47	62	109	189
Equity and investment fund shares	1 904	1 092	878	1 956	2 796	3 206	3 451	2 421
Insurance pension and standardised guarantees	12 289	12 522	12 319	12 256	11 921	11 773	12 202	11 913
Financial derivatives and employee stock options	6	2	1	1	0	0	0	0
Other accounts payable	1 097	1 038	1 007	995	977	1 198	802	959
Non-financial assets	1 236	1 041	987	865	921	879	1 002	201
Pension funds								
Financial net worth	..	..	..	..	0	0	0	-16
Financial assets	..	..	..	..	225	440	322	1 173
Currency and deposits	..	..	..	..	225	136	107	56
Debt securities	..	..	..	..	0	258	146	743
Loans	..	..	..	..	0	8	6	4
Equity and investment fund shares	..	..	..	..	0	38	61	313
Equity	..	..	..	..	0	6	12	32
Investment fund shares	..	..	..	..	0	32	49	280
Money market fund shares	..	..	..	..	0	0	0	99
Non-Money market fund shares	..	..	..	..	0	32	49	182
Insurance pension and standardised guarantees	..	..	..	..	0	0	0	0
Financial derivatives and employee stock options	..	..	..	..	0	0	0	0
Other accounts receivable	..	..	..	..	0	1	1	58
Financial liabilities	..	..	..	..	225	440	322	1 189
Debt securities	..	..	..	..	..	..	..	..
Short-term debt securities	..	..	..	..	..	..	..	..
Long-term debt securities	..	..	..	..	..	..	..	..
Loans	..	..	..	..	..	..	..	..
Short-term loans	..	..	..	..	..	..	..	..
Long-term loans	..	..	..	..	..	..	..	..
Equity and investment fund shares	..	..	..	..	..	..	..	..
Insurance pension and standardised guarantees	..	..	..	..	225	440	322	1 123
Financial derivatives and employee stock options	..	..	..	..	..	..	..	..
Other accounts payable	..	..	..	..	..	..	..	66
Non-financial assets	..	..	..	..	0	0	0	16

Note: Detailed metadata at: http://metalinks.oecd.org/instinv/20170920/dee5

Table 4. Portfolio composition by type of investor

As percentage of financial assets and of financial liabilities

Per cent

	2009	2010	2011	2012	2013	2014	2015	2016
Investment funds								
Financial assets	100.0	100.0	100.0	100.0	100.0	100.0	100.0	100.0
Currency and deposits	27.7	24.8	29.8	31.5	21.4	27.4	14.0	11.1
Debt securities	31.8	33.1	33.6	30.1	34.5	28.4	39.5	44.0
Loans	..	..	..	..	..	..	..	..
Equity and investment fund shares	36.5	35.9	32.8	34.8	40.9	37.5	43.0	41.3
Insurance pension and standardised guarantee schemes	..	..	..	..	..	..	..	..
Financial derivatives and employee stock options	..	..	..	..	..	..	..	..
Other accounts receivable	..	..	..	..	..	..	..	..
Financial liabilities	100.0	100.0	100.0	100.0	100.0	100.0	100.0	100.0
Currency and deposits	..	..	..	..	..	..	..	..
Debt securities	..	..	..	..	..	..	..	..
Loans	0.1	0.2	1.0	1.4	1.3	4.6	4.9	5.7
Equity and investment fund shares	94.9	92.2	87.8	90.0	96.6	93.2	93.8	93.1
Insurance pension and standardised guarantee schemes	..	..	..	..	..	..	..	..
Financial derivatives and employee stock options	..	..	..	..	..	..	..	..
Other accounts receivable	..	..	..	..	..	..	..	..
Insurance corporations								
Financial assets	100.0	100.0	100.0	100.0	100.0	100.0	100.0	100.0
Currency and deposits	13.9	19.3	19.9	19.1	23.2	15.8	11.7	10.4
Debt securities	45.9	45.1	45.0	44.9	43.9	51.7	52.3	59.3
Loans	0.7	0.7	0.7	1.0	0.9	0.9	1.0	0.9
Equity and investment fund shares	19.6	15.9	15.5	17.9	17.2	18.4	20.8	20.0
Insurance pension and standardised guarantee schemes	2.6	2.9	2.9	2.9	2.6	2.4	3.0	1.9
Financial derivatives and employee stock options	0.0	0.0	0.0	0.0	0.1	0.0	0.0	0.0
Other accounts receivable	17.3	16.2	16.0	14.2	12.2	10.8	11.2	7.4
Financial liabilities	100.0	100.0	100.0	100.0	100.0	100.0	100.0	100.0
Currency and deposits	0.0	0.0	0.0	0.0	0.0	0.0	0.0	0.0
Debt securities	0.2	0.1	0.1	0.1	0.2	0.2	0.2	0.0
Loans	1.6	6.6	4.5	2.1	3.0	0.8	1.0	1.5
Equity and investment fund shares	12.2	7.0	5.9	12.6	17.3	19.6	20.7	15.6
Insurance pension and standardised guarantee schemes	78.9	79.7	82.7	78.8	73.6	72.1	73.3	76.7
Financial derivatives and employee stock options	0.0	0.0	0.0	0.0	0.0	0.0	0.0	0.0
Other accounts receivable	7.0	6.6	6.8	6.4	6.0	7.3	4.8	6.2
Pension funds								
Financial assets	..	..	..	..	100.0	100.0	100.0	100.0
Currency and deposits	..	..	..	..	100.0	30.8	33.4	4.8
Debt securities	..	..	..	..	0.0	58.5	45.5	63.3
Loans	..	..	..	..	0.0	1.7	2.0	0.3
Equity and investment fund shares	..	..	..	..	0.0	8.6	19.0	26.7
Insurance pension and standardised guarantee schemes	..	..	..	..	0.0	0.0	0.0	0.0
Financial derivatives and employee stock options	..	..	..	..	0.0	0.0	0.0	0.0
Other accounts receivable	..	..	..	..	0.0	0.3	0.2	4.9
Financial liabilities	..	..	..	..	100.0	100.0	100.0	100.0
Currency and deposits	..	..	..	..	0.0	0.0	0.0	0.0
Debt securities	..	..	..	..	0.0	0.0	0.0	0.0
Loans	..	..	..	..	0.0	0.0	0.0	0.0
Equity and investment fund shares	..	..	..	..	0.0	0.0	0.0	0.0
Insurance pension and standardised guarantee schemes	..	..	..	..	100.0	100.0	100.0	94.4
Financial derivatives and employee stock options	..	..	..	..	0.0	0.0	0.0	0.0
Other accounts receivable	..	..	..	..	0.0	0.0	0.0	5.6

Note: Detailed metadata at: http://metalinks.oecd.org/instinv/20170920/a49a

HUNGARY

Table 1. Financial assets and liabilities of institutional investors, 2016

Million HUF

	Investment funds				
		Non-money market funds			Money market funds
	Total	Total	Open-end non-money market funds	Closed-end non-money market funds	Total
Financial assets	5 534 911	4 740 060	..	..	794 851
Currency and deposits	2 107 121	1 460 691	..	..	646 430
Debt securities	1 954 598	1 820 081	..	..	134 517
Debt securities, short term	295 489	211 964	..	..	83 525
Debt securities, long term	1 659 109	1 608 117	..	..	50 992
Debt securities issued by residents	1 633 611	1 499 873	..	..	133 738
Debt securities issued by non-residents	320 987	320 208	..	..	779
Loans	0	0	..	..	0
Loans, short-term	0	0	..	..	0
Loans, long-term	0	0	..	..	0
Loans granted to residents	0	0	..	..	0
Loans granted to non-residents	0	0	..	..	0
Equity and investment fund shares/units	1 341 383	1 339 908	..	..	1 475
Equity and investment fund shares issued/units by residents	663 824	662 349	..	..	1 475
Equity and investment fund shares/units issued by non residents	677 559	677 559	..	..	0
Other accounts receivable	98 015	85 986	..	..	12 029

	Investment funds				
		Non-money market funds			Money market funds
	Total	Total	Open-end non-money market funds	Closed-end non-money market funds	Total
Financial liabilities	5 938 584	5 144 174	..	..	794 410
Currency and deposits	0	0	..	..	0
Debt securities	0	0	..	..	0
Debt securities, short term	0	0	..	..	0
Debt securities, long term	0	0	..	..	0
Loans	84 543	84 464	..	..	79
Loans, short-term	53 345	53 266	..	..	79
Loans, long-term	31 198	31 198	..	..	0
Equity and investment fund shares/units	5 838 543	5 044 856	..	..	793 687
Insurance pension and standardised guaratees	0	0	..	..	0
Financial derivatives and employee stock options	13 785	13 595	..	..	190
Other accounts payable	1 713	1 259	..	..	454

	Insurance corporations and pension funds				
		Insurance corporations			Pension funds
	Total	Total	Life insurance corporations	Non-life insurance corporations	Total
Financial assets	4 337 496	2 779 506	..	..	1 557 990
Currency and deposits	199 574	125 537	..	..	74 037
Debt securities	2 495 597	1 505 111	..	..	990 486
Debt securities, short-term	200 711	78 771	..	..	121 940
Debt securities, long term	2 294 886	1 426 340	..	..	868 546
Debt securities issued by residents	2 403 102	1 429 237	..	..	973 865
Debt securities issued by non-residents	92 495	75 874	..	..	16 621
Loans	8 063	6 446	..	..	1 617
Loans, short-term	3 047	3 047	..	..	0
Loans, long-term	5 016	3 399	..	..	1 617
Loans granted to residents	4 842	3 225	..	..	1 617
Loans granted to non-residents	3 221	3 221	..	..	0
Equity and investment fund shares/units	1 471 001	979 717	..	..	491 284
Equity and investment fund shares/units issued by residents	708 273	417 609	..	..	290 664
Equity and investment fund shares/units issued by non residents	762 728	562 108	..	..	200 620
Other accounts receivable	57 253	57 075	..	..	178

	Insurance corporations and pension funds				
		Insurance corporations			Pension funds
	Total	Total	Life insurance corporations	Non-life insurance corporations	Total
Financial liabilities	4 332 117	2 745 402	..	..	1 586 715
Currency and deposits	0	0	..	..	0
Debt securities	0	0	..	..	0
Debt securities, short term	0	0	..	..	0
Debt securities, long term	0	0	..	..	0
Loans	5 381	5 377	..	..	4
Loans, short-term	130	126	..	..	4
Loans, long-term	5 251	5 251	..	..	0
Equity and investment fund shares/units	303 872	282 304	..	..	21 568
Insurance pension and standardised guarantees	3 945 758	2 382 520	..	..	1 563 238
Financial derivatives and employee stock options	2 282	1 032	..	..	1 250
Other accounts payable	74 824	74 169	..	..	655

Note: Detailed metadata at: http://metalinks.oecd.org/instinv/20170920/75e8

HUNGARY

Table 2. Financial assets and liabilities of investment funds

Million HUF

	2009	2010	2011	2012	2013	2014	2015	2016
Investment funds								
Financial net worth	-147 569	-237 433	-284 097	-319 083	-322 019	-312 020	-305 122	-403 673
Financial assets	3 028 570	3 732 362	3 109 859	3 283 329	4 415 435	5 334 967	5 539 867	5 534 911
Currency and deposits	1 358 597	1 416 054	1 594 876	1 745 945	2 008 519	2 352 275	2 269 890	2 107 121
Debt securities	772 975	1 060 369	745 223	823 020	1 438 362	1 754 128	1 919 808	1 954 598
Loans	0	0	0	0	0	0	0	0
Equity and investment fund shares	851 263	1 180 774	681 357	612 122	772 543	1 103 523	1 238 349	1 341 383
Equity	319 629	472 378	180 100	197 861	165 187	210 271	254 708	322 341
Investment fund shares	531 634	708 396	501 257	414 261	607 356	893 252	983 641	1 019 042
Money market fund shares	42 399	45 855	41 749	27 455	47 197	59 753	130 626	36 576
Non-Money market fund shares	489 235	662 541	459 508	386 806	560 159	833 499	853 015	982 466
Insurance pension and standardised guarantees	0	0	0	0	0	0	0	0
Financial derivatives and employee stock options	45 725	49 155	27 389	41 238	55 009	45 041	31 810	33 794
Other accounts receivable	10	26 010	61 014	61 004	141 002	80 000	80 010	98 015
Financial liabilities	3 176 139	3 969 795	3 393 956	3 602 412	4 737 454	5 646 987	5 844 989	5 938 584
Debt securities	0	0	0	0	0	0	0	0
Short-term debt securities	0	0	0	0	0	0	0	0
Long-term debt securities	0	0	0	0	0	0	0	0
Loans	71 890	68 096	77 994	71 011	66 700	81 145	50 867	84 543
Short-term loans	17 635	24 495	27 991	25 836	23 824	45 686	33 031	53 345
Long-term loans	54 255	43 601	50 003	45 175	42 876	35 459	17 836	31 198
Equity and investment fund shares	3 098 940	3 895 195	3 302 829	3 463 811	4 662 549	5 526 624	5 778 120	5 838 543
Insurance pension and standardised guarantees	0	0	0	0	0	0	0	0
Financial derivatives and employee stock options	3 867	6 142	8 604	9 006	3 269	33 897	10 961	13 785
Other accounts payable	1 442	362	4 529	58 584	4 936	3 321	5 041	1 713
Non-financial assets	..	..	..	..	..	..	..	..
Money market funds								
Financial net worth	-31 343	-17 659	1 262	43 912	20 044	-21 629	5 738	441
Financial assets	1 121 760	1 359 714	1 360 019	1 270 751	1 455 722	1 224 273	1 173 427	794 851
Currency and deposits	832 161	852 059	1 014 210	1 004 275	1 037 929	981 956	982 384	646 430
Debt securities	285 112	477 397	284 129	201 169	353 790	241 201	187 867	134 517
Loans	0	0	0	0	0	0	0	0
Equity and investment fund shares	4 477	4 248	666	4 303	3 001	1 116	3 166	1 475
Equity	0	0	0	0	0	0	0	0
Investment fund shares	4 477	4 248	666	4 303	3 001	1 116	3 166	1 475
Money market fund shares	4 477	4 248	666	4 303	3 001	1 116	3 166	1 475
Non-Money market fund shares	0	0	0	0	0	0	0	0
Insurance pension and standardised guarantees	0	0	0	0	0	0	0	0
Financial derivatives and employee stock options	0	0	0	0	0	0	0	400
Other accounts receivable	10	26 010	61 014	61 004	61 002	0	10	12 029
Financial liabilities	1 153 103	1 377 373	1 353 757	1 226 839	1 435 678	1 245 902	1 167 689	794 410
Debt securities	0	0	0	0	0	0	0	0
Short-term debt securities	0	0	0	0	0	0	0	0
Long-term debt securities	0	0	0	0	0	0	0	0
Loans	72	9	14	33	42	59	67	79
Short-term loans	72	9	14	33	42	59	67	79
Long-term loans	0	0	0	0	0	0	0	0
Equity and investment fund shares	1 152 781	1 377 347	1 353 175	1 226 331	1 435 555	1 245 738	1 167 563	793 687
Insurance pension and standardised guarantees	0	0	0	0	0	0	0	0
Financial derivatives and employee stock options	0	0	0	0	0	0	0	190
Other accounts payable	250	17	568	475	81	105	59	454
Non-financial assets	..	..	..	..	..	..	..	..
Non-money market funds								
Financial net worth	-116 226	-219 774	-285 359	-362 995	-342 063	-290 391	-310 860	-404 114
Financial assets	1 906 810	2 372 648	1 749 840	2 012 578	2 959 713	4 110 694	4 366 440	4 740 060
Currency and deposits	526 436	563 995	580 666	741 670	970 590	1 370 319	1 287 506	1 460 691
Debt securities	487 863	582 972	461 094	621 851	1 084 572	1 512 927	1 731 941	1 820 081
Loans	0	0	0	0	0	0	0	0
Equity and investment fund shares	846 786	1 176 526	680 691	607 819	769 542	1 102 407	1 235 183	1 339 908
Equity	319 629	472 378	180 100	197 861	165 187	210 271	254 708	322 341
Investment fund shares	527 157	704 148	500 591	409 958	604 355	892 136	980 475	1 017 567
Money market fund shares	37 922	41 607	41 083	23 152	44 196	58 637	127 460	35 101
Non-Money market fund shares	489 235	662 541	459 508	386 806	560 159	833 499	853 015	982 466
Insurance pension and standardised guarantees	0	0	0	0	0	0	0	0
Financial derivatives and employee stock options	45 725	49 155	27 389	41 238	55 009	45 041	31 810	33 394
Other accounts receivable	0	0	0	0	80 000	80 000	80 000	85 986
Financial liabilities	2 023 036	2 592 422	2 035 199	2 375 573	3 301 776	4 401 085	4 677 300	5 144 174
Debt securities	0	0	0	0	0	0	0	0
Short-term debt securities	0	0	0	0	0	0	0	0
Long-term debt securities	0	0	0	0	0	0	0	0
Loans	71 818	68 087	77 980	70 978	66 658	81 086	50 800	84 464
Short-term loans	17 563	24 486	27 977	25 803	23 782	45 627	32 964	53 266
Long-term loans	54 255	43 601	50 003	45 175	42 876	35 459	17 836	31 198
Equity and investment fund shares	1 946 159	2 517 848	1 944 654	2 237 480	3 226 994	4 282 886	4 610 557	5 044 856
Insurance pension and standardised guarantees	0	0	0	0	0	0	0	0
Financial derivatives and employee stock options	3 867	6 142	8 604	9 006	3 269	33 897	10 961	13 595
Other accounts payable	1 192	345	3 961	58 109	4 855	3 216	4 982	1 259
Non-financial assets	..	..	..	..	..	..	..	..
Open-end non-money market funds								
Financial net worth	..	..	..	..	..	..	..	..
Financial assets	..	..	..	..	..	..	..	..

Table 2. Financial assets and liabilities of investment funds *(cont.)*

Million HUF

	2009	2010	2011	2012	2013	2014	2015	2016
Currency and deposits	..	..	..	..	..	..	..	..
Debt securities	..	..	..	..	..	..	..	..
Loans	..	..	..	..	..	..	..	..
Equity and investment fund shares	..	..	..	..	..	..	..	..
Equity	..	..	..	..	..	..	..	..
Investment fund shares	..	..	..	..	..	..	..	..
Money market fund shares	..	..	..	..	..	..	..	..
Non-Money market fund shares	..	..	..	..	..	..	..	..
Insurance pension and standardised guarantees	..	..	..	..	..	..	..	..
Financial derivatives and employee stock options	..	..	..	..	..	..	..	..
Other accounts receivable	..	..	..	..	..	..	..	..
Financial liabilities	..	..	..	..	..	..	..	..
Debt securities	..	..	..	..	..	..	..	..
Short-term debt securities	..	..	..	..	..	..	..	..
Long-term debt securities	..	..	..	..	..	..	..	..
Loans	..	..	..	..	..	..	..	..
Short-term loans	..	..	..	..	..	..	..	..
Long-term loans	..	..	..	..	..	..	..	..
Equity and investment fund shares	..	..	..	..	..	..	..	..
Insurance pension and standardised guarantees	..	..	..	..	..	..	..	..
Financial derivatives and employee stock options	..	..	..	..	..	..	..	..
Other accounts payable	..	..	..	..	..	..	..	..
Non-financial assets	..	..	..	..	..	..	..	..
Open-end investment funds								
Financial net worth	..	..	..	..	..	..	..	..
Financial assets	..	..	..	..	..	..	..	..
Currency and deposits	..	..	..	..	..	..	..	..
Debt securities	..	..	..	..	..	..	..	..
Loans	..	..	..	..	..	..	..	..
Equity and investment fund shares	..	..	..	..	..	..	..	..
Equity	..	..	..	..	..	..	..	..
Investment fund shares	..	..	..	..	..	..	..	..
Money market fund shares	..	..	..	..	..	..	..	..
Non-Money market fund shares	..	..	..	..	..	..	..	..
Insurance pension and standardised guarantees	..	..	..	..	..	..	..	..
Financial derivatives and employee stock options	..	..	..	..	..	..	..	..
Other accounts receivable	..	..	..	..	..	..	..	..
Financial liabilities	..	..	..	..	..	..	..	..
Debt securities	..	..	..	..	..	..	..	..
Short-term debt securities	..	..	..	..	..	..	..	..
Long-term debt securities	..	..	..	..	..	..	..	..
Loans	..	..	..	..	..	..	..	..
Short-term loans	..	..	..	..	..	..	..	..
Long-term loans	..	..	..	..	..	..	..	..
Equity and investment fund shares	..	..	..	..	..	..	..	..
Insurance pension and standardised guarantees	..	..	..	..	..	..	..	..
Financial derivatives and employee stock options	..	..	..	..	..	..	..	..
Other accounts payable	..	..	..	..	..	..	..	..
Non-financial assets	..	..	..	..	..	..	..	..

Note: Detailed metadata at: http://metalinks.oecd.org/instinv/20170920/75e8

Table 3. Financial assets and liabilities of insurance corporations and pension funds

Million HUF

	2009	2010	2011	2012	2013	2014	2015	2016
Insurance corporations and pension funds								
Financial net worth	-75 209	-76 736	-174 696	-69 533	-78 630	-43 643	-15 286	5 379
Financial assets	5 878 927	6 485 845	3 410 329	3 543 272	3 665 201	3 977 513	4 129 293	4 337 496
Currency and deposits	279 529	242 713	212 447	172 142	212 288	252 487	265 046	199 574
Debt securities	3 475 654	3 654 838	2 030 279	2 174 370	2 238 054	2 386 935	2 385 013	2 495 597
Loans	23 977	18 228	16 658	10 449	7 755	7 992	8 073	8 063
Equity and investment fund shares	1 938 728	2 392 998	1 003 348	1 027 638	1 054 997	1 177 150	1 309 289	1 471 001
Equity	484 040	448 869	133 573	120 920	112 582	125 361	145 827	187 031
Investment fund shares	1 454 688	1 944 129	869 775	906 718	942 415	1 051 789	1 163 462	1 283 970
Money market fund shares	64 163	78 548	77 130	72 978	77 076	54 223	68 926	52 862
Non-Money market fund shares	1 390 525	1 865 581	792 645	833 740	865 339	997 566	1 094 536	1 231 108
Insurance pension and standardised guarantees	79 689	88 503	89 953	93 929	88 982	92 294	100 164	104 736
Financial derivatives and employee stock options	0	78	75	2	218	4 226	3 743	1 272
Other accounts receivable	81 350	88 487	57 569	64 742	62 907	56 429	57 965	57 253
Financial liabilities	5 954 136	6 562 581	3 585 025	3 612 805	3 743 831	4 021 156	4 144 579	4 332 117
Debt securities	0	0	0	0	26	25	0	0
Short-term debt securities	0	0	0	0	0	0	0	0
Long-term debt securities	0	0	0	0	26	25	0	0
Loans	4 465	4 187	7 853	6 577	5 832	8 111	20 002	5 381
Short-term loans	1 501	1 149	1 533	3 341	1 239	1 818	14 836	130
Long-term loans	2 964	3 038	6 320	3 236	4 593	6 293	5 166	5 251
Equity and investment fund shares	366 674	358 794	332 603	300 311	307 168	307 765	304 553	303 872
Insurance pension and standardised guarantees	5 511 962	6 132 265	3 163 128	3 217 327	3 339 065	3 608 519	3 725 694	3 945 758
Financial derivatives and employee stock options	0	85	1 228	336	56	4 955	3 684	2 282
Other accounts payable	71 035	67 250	80 213	88 254	91 684	91 781	90 646	74 824
Non-financial assets	..	..	..	..	..	..	..	..
Insurance corporations								
Financial net worth	-90 362	-114 867	-149 156	-33 036	-38 362	-14 623	14 397	34 104
Financial assets	2 331 654	2 411 337	2 297 550	2 386 170	2 437 065	2 618 814	2 697 667	2 779 506
Currency and deposits	171 305	158 747	149 104	109 486	123 434	160 378	181 477	125 537
Debt securities	1 366 811	1 281 553	1 314 391	1 426 933	1 442 501	1 498 223	1 443 686	1 505 111
Loans	22 715	16 571	15 019	8 873	6 150	6 337	6 384	6 446
Equity and investment fund shares	639 429	777 476	671 512	682 243	712 903	800 962	904 283	979 717
Equity	116 334	83 432	64 131	57 800	55 435	58 561	56 065	70 438
Investment fund shares	523 095	694 044	607 381	624 443	657 468	742 401	848 218	909 279
Money market fund shares	59 826	73 257	73 575	70 532	74 389	51 016	67 718	50 009
Non-Money market fund shares	463 269	620 787	533 806	553 911	583 079	691 385	780 500	859 270
Insurance pension and standardised guarantees	79 689	88 503	89 953	93 929	88 982	92 294	100 164	104 736
Financial derivatives and employee stock options	0	78	75	2	218	4 226	3 743	884
Other accounts receivable	51 705	88 409	57 496	64 704	62 877	56 394	57 930	57 075
Financial liabilities	2 422 016	2 526 204	2 446 706	2 419 206	2 475 427	2 633 437	2 683 270	2 745 402
Debt securities	0	0	0	0	26	25	0	0
Short-term debt securities	0	0	0	0	0	0	0	0
Long-term debt securities	0	0	0	0	26	25	0	0
Loans	4 465	4 187	7 853	6 577	5 832	8 111	20 002	5 377
Short-term loans	1 501	1 149	1 533	3 341	1 239	1 818	14 836	126
Long-term loans	2 964	3 038	6 320	3 236	4 593	6 293	5 166	5 251
Equity and investment fund shares	351 334	342 938	316 437	283 978	290 538	290 102	284 937	282 304
Insurance pension and standardised guarantees	2 015 735	2 113 867	2 045 389	2 042 932	2 088 549	2 238 849	2 284 451	2 382 520
Financial derivatives and employee stock options	0	85	1 228	336	56	4 955	3 684	1 032
Other accounts payable	50 482	65 127	75 799	85 383	90 426	91 395	90 196	74 169
Non-financial assets	..	..	..	..	..	..	..	..
Pension funds								
Financial net worth	15 153	38 131	-25 540	-36 497	-40 268	-29 020	-29 683	-28 725
Financial assets	3 547 273	4 074 508	1 112 779	1 157 102	1 228 136	1 358 699	1 431 626	1 557 990
Currency and deposits	108 224	83 966	63 343	62 656	88 854	92 109	83 569	74 037
Debt securities	2 108 843	2 373 285	715 888	747 437	795 553	888 712	941 327	990 486
Loans	1 262	1 657	1 639	1 576	1 605	1 655	1 689	1 617
Equity and investment fund shares	1 299 299	1 615 522	331 836	345 395	342 094	375 188	405 006	491 284
Equity	367 706	365 437	69 442	63 120	57 147	65 800	89 762	116 593
Investment fund shares	931 593	1 250 085	262 394	282 275	284 947	309 388	315 244	374 691
Money market fund shares	4 337	5 291	3 555	2 446	2 687	3 207	1 208	2 853
Non-Money market fund shares	927 256	1 244 794	258 839	279 829	282 260	306 181	314 036	371 838
Insurance pension and standardised guarantees	0	0	0	0	0	0	0	0
Financial derivatives and employee stock options	0	0	0	0	0	0	0	388
Other accounts receivable	29 645	78	73	38	30	35	35	178
Financial liabilities	3 532 120	4 036 377	1 138 319	1 193 599	1 268 404	1 387 719	1 461 309	1 586 715
Debt securities	0	0	0	0	0	0	0	0
Short-term debt securities	0	0	0	0	0	0	0	0
Long-term debt securities	0	0	0	0	0	0	0	0
Loans	0	0	0	0	0	0	0	4
Short-term loans	0	0	0	0	0	0	0	4
Long-term loans	0	0	0	0	0	0	0	0
Equity and investment fund shares	15 340	15 856	16 166	16 333	16 630	17 663	19 616	21 568
Insurance pension and standardised guarantees	3 496 227	4 018 398	1 117 739	1 174 395	1 250 516	1 369 670	1 441 243	1 563 238
Financial derivatives and employee stock options	0	0	0	0	0	0	0	1 250
Other accounts payable	20 553	2 123	4 414	2 871	1 258	386	450	655
Non-financial assets	..	..	..	..	..	..	..	..

Note: Detailed metadata at: http://metalinks.oecd.org/instinv/20170920/75e8

Table 4. Portfolio composition by type of investor

As percentage of financial assets and of financial liabilities

Per cent

	2009	2010	2011	2012	2013	2014	2015	2016
Investment funds								
Financial assets	100.0	100.0	100.0	100.0	100.0	100.0	100.0	100.0
Currency and deposits	44.9	37.9	51.3	53.2	45.5	44.1	41.0	38.1
Debt securities	25.5	28.4	24.0	25.1	32.6	32.9	34.7	35.3
Loans	0.0	0.0	0.0	0.0	0.0	0.0	0.0	0.0
Equity and investment fund shares	28.1	31.6	21.9	18.6	17.5	20.7	22.4	24.2
Insurance pension and standardised guarantee schemes	0.0	0.0	0.0	0.0	0.0	0.0	0.0	0.0
Financial derivatives and employee stock options	1.5	1.3	0.9	1.3	1.2	0.8	0.6	0.6
Other accounts receivable	0.0	0.7	2.0	1.9	3.2	1.5	1.4	1.8
Financial liabilities	100.0	100.0	100.0	100.0	100.0	100.0	100.0	100.0
Currency and deposits	0.0	0.0	0.0	0.0	0.0	0.0	0.0	0.0
Debt securities	0.0	0.0	0.0	0.0	0.0	0.0	0.0	0.0
Loans	2.3	1.7	2.3	2.0	1.4	1.4	0.9	1.4
Equity and investment fund shares	97.6	98.1	97.3	96.2	98.4	97.9	98.9	98.3
Insurance pension and standardised guarantee schemes	0.0	0.0	0.0	0.0	0.0	0.0	0.0	0.0
Financial derivatives and employee stock options	0.1	0.2	0.3	0.2	0.1	0.6	0.2	0.2
Other accounts receivable	0.0	0.0	0.1	1.6	0.1	0.1	0.1	0.0
Insurance corporations								
Financial assets	100.0	100.0	100.0	100.0	100.0	100.0	100.0	100.0
Currency and deposits	7.3	6.6	6.5	4.6	5.1	6.1	6.7	4.5
Debt securities	58.6	53.1	57.2	59.8	59.2	57.2	53.5	54.2
Loans	1.0	0.7	0.7	0.4	0.3	0.2	0.2	0.2
Equity and investment fund shares	27.4	32.2	29.2	28.6	29.3	30.6	33.5	35.2
Insurance pension and standardised guarantee schemes	3.4	3.7	3.9	3.9	3.7	3.5	3.7	3.8
Financial derivatives and employee stock options	0.0	0.0	0.0	0.0	0.0	0.2	0.1	0.0
Other accounts receivable	2.2	3.7	2.5	2.7	2.6	2.2	2.1	2.1
Financial liabilities	100.0	100.0	100.0	100.0	100.0	100.0	100.0	100.0
Currency and deposits	0.0	0.0	0.0	0.0	0.0	0.0	0.0	0.0
Debt securities	0.0	0.0	0.0	0.0	0.0	0.0	0.0	0.0
Loans	0.2	0.2	0.3	0.3	0.2	0.3	0.7	0.2
Equity and investment fund shares	14.5	13.6	12.9	11.7	11.7	11.0	10.6	10.3
Insurance pension and standardised guarantee schemes	83.2	83.7	83.6	84.4	84.4	85.0	85.1	86.8
Financial derivatives and employee stock options	0.0	0.0	0.1	0.0	0.0	0.2	0.1	0.0
Other accounts receivable	2.1	2.6	3.1	3.5	3.7	3.5	3.4	2.7
Pension funds								
Financial assets	100.0	100.0	100.0	100.0	100.0	100.0	100.0	100.0
Currency and deposits	3.1	2.1	5.7	5.4	7.2	6.8	5.8	4.8
Debt securities	59.4	58.2	64.3	64.6	64.8	65.4	65.8	63.6
Loans	0.0	0.0	0.1	0.1	0.1	0.1	0.1	0.1
Equity and investment fund shares	36.6	39.6	29.8	29.9	27.9	27.7	28.3	31.5
Insurance pension and standardised guarantee schemes	0.0	0.0	0.0	0.0	0.0	0.0	0.0	0.0
Financial derivatives and employee stock options	0.0	0.0	0.0	0.0	0.0	0.0	0.0	0.0
Other accounts receivable	0.8	0.0	0.0	0.0	0.0	0.0	0.0	0.0
Financial liabilities	100.0	100.0	100.0	100.0	100.0	100.0	100.0	100.0
Currency and deposits	0.0	0.0	0.0	0.0	0.0	0.0	0.0	0.0
Debt securities	0.0	0.0	0.0	0.0	0.0	0.0	0.0	0.0
Loans	0.0	0.0	0.0	0.0	0.0	0.0	0.0	0.0
Equity and investment fund shares	0.4	0.4	1.4	1.4	1.3	1.3	1.3	1.4
Insurance pension and standardised guarantee schemes	99.0	99.6	98.2	98.4	98.6	98.7	98.6	98.5
Financial derivatives and employee stock options	0.0	0.0	0.0	0.0	0.0	0.0	0.0	0.1
Other accounts receivable	0.6	0.1	0.4	0.2	0.1	0.0	0.0	0.0

Note: Detailed metadata at: http://metalinks.oecd.org/instinv/20170920/a49a

Table 1. Financial assets and liabilities of institutional investors, 2016

Million ISK

	Total	Investment funds			
		Non-money market funds			Money market funds
		Total	Open-end non-money market funds	Closed-end non-money market funds	Total
Financial assets	668 211	490 962	340 782	150 180	177 249
Currency and deposits	170 825	29 318	14 620	14 698	141 507
Debt securities	277 617	242 544	185 619	56 925	35 074
Debt securities, short term	12 512	7 082	4 507	2 574	5 430
Debt securities, long term	265 105	235 462	181 112	54 350	29 643
Debt securities issued by residents	277 429	242 355	185 619	56 737	35 074
Debt securities issued by non-residents	188	188	0	188	0
Loans	8 415	8 415	0	8 415	0
Loans, short-term	..	..	..	..	..
Loans, long-term	..	..	..	..	..
Loans granted to residents	..	..	..	..	..
Loans granted to non-residents	..	..	..	..	..
Equity and investment fund shares/units	201 393	201 393	139 925	61 468	0
Equity and investment fund shares issued/units by residents	187 030	187 030	134 460	52 570	0
Equity and investment fund shares/units issued by non residents	14 363	14 363	5 465	8 898	0
Other accounts receivable	6 707	6 038	538	5 501	668

	Total	Investment funds			
		Non-money market funds			Money market funds
		Total	Open-end non-money market funds	Closed-end non-money market funds	Total
Financial liabilities	670 451	493 202	340 783	152 419	177 249
Currency and deposits	..	..	..	..	..
Debt securities	61 249	61 249	0	61 249	0
Debt securities, short term	0	0	0	0	0
Debt securities, long term	61 249	61 249	0	61 249	0
Loans	6 000	6 000	0	6 000	0
Loans, short-term	5 230	5 230	0	5 230	0
Loans, long-term	771	771	0	771	0
Equity and investment fund shares/units	595 370	423 370	339 854	83 517	..
Insurance pension and standardised guaratees	..	..	..	..	..
Financial derivatives and employee stock options	751	751	2	750	0
Other accounts payable	7 079	1 830	927	903	5 249

	Total	Insurance corporations and pension funds			
		Insurance corporations			Pension funds
		Total	Life insurance corporations	Non-life insurance corporations	Total
Financial assets	3 697 616	175 547	16 369	159 177	3 522 069
Currency and deposits	143 423	6 713	1 232	5 431	136 710
Debt securities	1 779 307	71 335	5 770	65 565	1 707 972
Debt securities, short-term	6 779	1 305	229	1 076	5 475
Debt securities, long term	1 772 527	70 030	5 541	64 489	1 702 497
Debt securities issued by residents	1 774 562	67 595	5 735	61 830	1 706 967
Debt securities issued by non-residents	4 744	3 740	5	3 734	1 005
Loans	244 182	1 742	0	1 742	242 441
Loans, short-term	91	..	..	..	91
Loans, long-term	244 092	1 742	0	1 742	242 350
Loans granted to residents	243 983	1 742	0	1 742	242 242
Loans granted to non-residents	199	0	0	0	199
Equity and investment fund shares/units	1 479 814	66 609	2 231	64 378	1 413 204
Equity and investment fund shares/units issued by residents	728 882	60 664	2 166	58 499	668 217
Equity and investment fund shares/units issued by non residents	750 932	5 945	65	5 879	744 987
Other accounts receivable	8 441	3 606	40	3 566	4 835

	Total	Insurance corporations and pension funds			
		Insurance corporations			Pension funds
		Total	Life insurance corporations	Non-life insurance corporations	Total
Financial liabilities	3 701 870	177 456	16 578	160 878	3 524 414
Currency and deposits	..	..	..	..	..
Debt securities	2 070	2 070	0	2 070	..
Debt securities, short term	0	0	0	0	..
Debt securities, long term	2 070	2 070	0	2 070	..
Loans	2 574	2 574	0	2 574	0
Loans, short-term	..	0	0	0	0
Loans, long-term	2 574	2 574	0	2 574	0
Equity and investment fund shares/units	88 619	88 619	6 228	82 391	..
Insurance pension and standardised guarantees	3 592 991	78 715	9 798	68 917	3 514 276
Financial derivatives and employee stock options	13	0	..	..	13
Other accounts payable	15 604	5 478	552	4 926	10 125

Note: Detailed metadata at: http://metalinks.oecd.org/instinv/20170920/75e8

Table 2. Financial assets and liabilities of investment funds

Million ISK

	2009	2010	2011	2012	2013	2014	2015	2016
Investment funds								
Financial net worth	0	0	-3 577	-1 510	-714	-124	-172	-2 240
Financial assets	195 242	284 249	386 382	427 809	468 126	502 500	598 476	668 211
Currency and deposits	18 306	18 087	41 917	35 503	51 558	78 987	117 278	170 825
Debt securities	159 973	236 679	279 886	305 040	285 132	262 187	257 126	277 617
Loans	..	0	0	0	0	0	1 425	8 415
Equity and investment fund shares	16 318	28 234	58 147	85 288	129 033	158 331	213 701	201 393
Equity	6 560	8 832	19 953	39 615	77 810	102 435	152 482	140 906
Investment fund shares	9 758	19 402	38 194	45 673	51 223	55 897	61 220	60 487
Money market fund shares	..	..	..	..	..	..	6 706	4 371
Non-Money market fund shares	..	..	..	..	..	..	54 514	56 116
Insurance pension and standardised guarantees	..	..	..	..	..	..	..	..
Financial derivatives and employee stock options	..	0	1 492	1 455	2 016	2 138	4 529	3 253
Other accounts receivable	646	1 249	4 941	523	387	856	4 418	6 707
Financial liabilities	195 242	284 249	389 960	429 319	468 840	502 624	598 648	670 451
Debt securities	..	0	4 789	26 608	32 451	56 263	57 924	61 249
Short-term debt securities	..	..	..	..	..	..	0	0
Long-term debt securities	..	..	..	..	..	..	57 924	61 249
Loans	..	0	10 071	3 115	3 654	4 416	6 082	6 000
Short-term loans	..	..	..	..	..	..	5 230	5 230
Long-term loans	..	..	..	..	..	..	852	771
Equity and investment fund shares	190 788	280 414	347 714	378 034	414 466	422 661	530 398	595 370
Insurance pension and standardised guarantees	..	..	..	..	..	..	..	..
Financial derivatives and employee stock options	..	0	1 555	96	190	224	753	751
Other accounts payable	4 454	3 835	25 832	21 466	18 077	19 061	3 491	7 079
Non-financial assets	..	0	3 577	1 510	714	124	172	2 240
Money market funds								
Financial net worth	0	0	0	0	0	0	0	0
Financial assets	..	13 391	18 294	19 624	26 449	50 837	92 534	177 249
Currency and deposits	..	6 138	11 479	14 872	22 584	47 838	86 303	141 507
Debt securities	..	7 251	6 801	4 715	3 798	2 890	6 060	35 074
Loans	..	0	0	0	0	0	0	0
Equity and investment fund shares	0	0	0	0	0	0	0	0
Equity	0	0	0	0	0	0	0	0
Investment fund shares	0	0	0	0	0	0	0	0
Money market fund shares	..	..	..	..	..	..	0	0
Non-Money market fund shares	..	..	..	..	..	..	0	0
Insurance pension and standardised guarantees	..	..	..	..	..	..	..	..
Financial derivatives and employee stock options	..	0	0	0	0	0	0	0
Other accounts receivable	..	2	13	37	67	110	170	668
Financial liabilities	..	13 391	18 294	19 624	26 449	50 837	92 534	177 249
Debt securities	..	0	0	0	0	0	0	0
Short-term debt securities	..	..	..	..	..	..	0	0
Long-term debt securities	..	..	..	..	..	..	0	0
Loans	..	0	0	93	0	0	0	0
Short-term loans	..	..	..	..	..	..	0	0
Long-term loans	..	..	..	..	..	..	0	0
Equity and investment fund shares	..	13 377	18 270	19 497	26 422	..	..	..
Insurance pension and standardised guarantees	..	..	..	..	..	..	..	..
Financial derivatives and employee stock options	..	0	0	0	0	0	0	0
Other accounts payable	11	15	24	34	26	53	323	5 249
Non-financial assets	..	0	0	0	0	0	0	0
Non-money market funds								
Financial net worth	0	0	-3 577	-1 510	-714	-124	-172	-2 240
Financial assets	190 512	270 858	368 089	408 185	441 677	451 663	505 943	490 962
Currency and deposits	15 537	11 949	30 437	20 631	28 975	31 149	30 975	29 318
Debt securities	158 013	229 428	273 085	300 325	281 333	259 297	251 066	242 544
Loans	..	0	0	0	0	0	1 425	8 415
Equity and investment fund shares	16 318	28 234	58 147	85 288	129 033	158 331	213 701	201 393
Equity	6 560	8 832	19 953	39 615	77 810	102 435	152 482	140 906
Investment fund shares	9 758	19 402	38 194	45 673	51 223	55 897	61 220	60 487
Money market fund shares	..	..	..	..	..	..	6 706	4 371
Non-Money market fund shares	..	..	..	..	..	..	54 514	56 116
Insurance pension and standardised guarantees	..	..	..	..	..	..	..	..
Financial derivatives and employee stock options	..	0	1 492	1 455	2 016	2 138	4 529	3 253
Other accounts receivable	645	1 247	4 928	485	320	747	4 247	6 038
Financial liabilities	190 512	270 858	371 666	409 695	442 391	451 787	506 115	493 202
Debt securities	..	0	4 789	26 608	32 451	56 263	57 924	61 249
Short-term debt securities	..	..	..	..	..	..	0	0
Long-term debt securities	..	..	..	..	..	..	57 924	61 249
Loans	..	0	10 071	3 022	3 654	4 416	6 082	6 000
Short-term loans	..	..	..	..	..	..	5 230	5 230
Long-term loans	..	..	..	..	..	..	852	771
Equity and investment fund shares	186 068	267 037	329 444	358 537	388 044	371 876	438 187	423 370
Insurance pension and standardised guarantees	..	..	..	..	..	..	..	..
Financial derivatives and employee stock options	..	0	1 555	96	190	224	753	751
Other accounts payable	4 444	3 820	25 808	21 431	18 051	19 008	3 168	1 830
Non-financial assets	..	0	3 577	1 510	714	124	172	2 240
Open-end non-money market funds								
Financial net worth	0	0	-1 070	-447	-110	-20	-77	-1
Financial assets	190 512	270 858	296 547	319 872	340 054	323 700	368 304	340 782

Table 2. Financial assets and liabilities of investment funds *(cont.)*

Million ISK

	2009	2010	2011	2012	2013	2014	2015	2016
Currency and deposits	15 537	11 949	14 510	14 152	22 560	15 162	16 667	14 620
Debt securities	158 013	229 428	246 295	252 614	225 847	199 817	197 031	185 619
Loans	..	0	0	0	0	0	0	0
Equity and investment fund shares	16 318	28 234	33 465	52 696	91 383	108 011	153 403	139 925
Equity	6 560	8 832	11 177	27 168	59 541	73 907	112 890	100 679
Investment fund shares	9 758	19 402	22 287	25 528	31 842	34 104	40 513	39 247
Money market fund shares	..	..	..	..	..	..	1 838	1 012
Non-Money market fund shares	..	..	..	..	..	..	38 675	38 235
Insurance pension and standardised guarantees	..	..	..	..	..	..	..	..
Financial derivatives and employee stock options	..	0	703	0	12	13	50	81
Other accounts receivable	645	1 247	1 573	409	252	698	1 153	538
Financial liabilities	190 512	270 858	297 617	320 318	340 164	323 721	368 381	340 783
Debt securities	..	0	0	0	0	0	0	0
Short-term debt securities	..	..	..	..	..	..	0	0
Long-term debt securities	..	..	..	..	..	..	0	0
Loans	..	0	1 883	669	1	161	0	0
Short-term loans	..	..	..	..	..	..	0	0
Long-term loans	..	..	..	..	..	..	0	0
Equity and investment fund shares	186 068	267 037	279 654	307 669	330 434	315 716	366 534	339 854
Insurance pension and standardised guarantees	..	..	..	..	..	..	..	..
Financial derivatives and employee stock options	..	0	1 554	0	0	9	13	2
Other accounts payable	4 444	3 820	14 525	11 980	9 729	7 836	1 834	927
Non-financial assets	..	0	1 070	447	110	20	77	1
Open-end investment funds								
Financial net worth	0	0	-1 070	-447	-110	-20	-77	-1
Financial assets	195 242	284 249	314 840	339 496	366 503	374 538	460 837	518 031
Currency and deposits	18 306	18 087	25 990	29 024	45 143	63 000	102 970	156 127
Debt securities	159 973	236 679	253 096	257 330	229 645	202 706	203 091	220 692
Loans	..	0	0	0	0	0	0	0
Equity and investment fund shares	16 318	28 234	33 465	52 696	91 383	108 011	153 403	139 925
Equity	6 560	8 832	11 177	27 168	59 541	73 907	112 890	100 679
Investment fund shares	9 758	19 402	22 287	25 528	31 842	34 104	40 513	39 247
Money market fund shares	..	..	..	..	..	..	1 838	1 012
Non-Money market fund shares	..	..	..	..	..	..	38 675	38 235
Insurance pension and standardised guarantees	..	..	..	..	..	..	..	..
Financial derivatives and employee stock options	..	0	703	0	12	13	50	81
Other accounts receivable	646	1 249	1 586	446	319	808	1 323	1 206
Financial liabilities	195 242	284 249	315 911	339 943	366 613	374 558	460 914	518 032
Debt securities	..	0	0	0	0	0	0	0
Short-term debt securities	..	..	..	..	..	..	0	0
Long-term debt securities	..	..	..	..	..	..	0	0
Loans	..	0	1 883	762	1	161	0	0
Short-term loans	..	..	..	..	..	..	0	0
Long-term loans	..	..	..	..	..	..	0	0
Equity and investment fund shares	190 788	280 414	297 924	327 166	356 856	366 500	458 745	511 853
Insurance pension and standardised guarantees	..	..	..	..	..	..	..	..
Financial derivatives and employee stock options	..	0	1 554	0	0	9	13	2
Other accounts payable	4 454	3 835	14 549	12 015	9 756	7 888	2 156	6 176
Non-financial assets	..	0	1 070	447	110	20	77	1

Note: Detailed metadata at: http://metalinks.oecd.org/instinv/20170920/75e8

Table 3. Financial assets and liabilities of insurance corporations and pension funds

Million ISK

	2009	2010	2011	2012	2013	2014	2015	2016
Insurance corporations and pension funds								
Financial net worth	-2 860	-2 733	-5 042	-11 693	-10 335	-10 336	-5 042	-4 254
Financial assets	1 977 202	2 124 243	2 315 595	2 587 644	2 855 350	3 098 164	3 454 444	3 697 616
Currency and deposits	175 635	171 342	170 368	183 380	179 613	144 010	170 737	143 423
Debt securities	923 791	1 094 265	1 208 952	1 305 933	1 401 813	1 486 747	1 581 297	1 779 307
Loans	181 726	177 135	186 050	184 357	184 620	178 808	180 881	244 182
Equity and investment fund shares	647 969	633 917	710 263	877 334	1 048 642	1 247 478	1 476 685	1 479 814
Equity	124 997	142 187	205 831	264 612	378 316	506 991	685 575	658 652
Investment fund shares	522 973	491 730	504 433	612 722	670 326	740 486	791 110	821 162
Money market fund shares	..	..	..	..	..	..	..	..
Non-Money market fund shares	..	..	..	..	..	..	..	..
Insurance pension and standardised guarantees	40 862	40 392	36 159	31 627	34 942	36 004	38 967	42 450
Financial derivatives and employee stock options	172	0	0	0	0	0	0	0
Other accounts receivable	7 048	7 190	3 802	5 013	5 720	5 117	5 878	8 441
Financial liabilities	1 980 063	2 126 976	2 320 637	2 599 338	2 865 685	3 108 500	3 459 486	3 701 870
Debt securities	3 976	4 078	0	0	0	0	2 026	2 070
Short-term debt securities	0	0	0	0	0	0	0	0
Long-term debt securities	3 976	4 078	0	0	0	0	2 026	2 070
Loans	585	455	844	516	151	118	0	2 574
Short-term loans	..	..	..	..	..	..	..	..
Long-term loans	308	238	271	82	70	95	0	2 574
Equity and investment fund shares	53 177	57 988	64 995	72 184	79 851	84 610	86 984	88 619
Insurance pension and standardised guarantees	1 843 957	1 981 275	2 173 761	2 469 525	2 740 835	3 003 095	3 351 115	3 592 991
Financial derivatives and employee stock options	69 865	72 165	60 162	31 941	21 575	2 171	13	13
Other accounts payable	8 503	11 016	20 874	25 171	23 273	18 506	19 348	15 604
Non-financial assets	2 860	2 733	5 042	11 693	10 335	10 336	5 042	4 254
Insurance corporations								
Financial net worth	-1 722	-1 598	-1 647	-6 691	-6 083	-6 615	-2 018	-1 909
Financial assets	129 004	136 528	143 748	147 901	158 612	161 950	169 075	175 547
Currency and deposits	13 106	12 698	13 060	15 493	14 849	8 463	10 406	6 713
Debt securities	45 459	54 920	60 754	65 643	72 049	75 073	70 091	71 335
Loans	7 290	5 246	4 698	3 418	3 078	2 881	1 485	1 742
Equity and investment fund shares	32 540	34 723	39 904	41 358	44 514	50 677	59 878	66 609
Equity	14 866	16 372	20 241	22 153	25 514	35 394	46 244	51 800
Investment fund shares	17 673	18 351	19 663	19 205	18 999	15 283	13 634	14 810
Money market fund shares	..	..	..	..	..	..	..	..
Non-Money market fund shares	..	..	..	..	..	..	..	..
Insurance pension and standardised guarantees	27 030	27 990	24 272	19 675	21 728	22 714	24 650	25 542
Financial derivatives and employee stock options	..	..	..	..	..	..	..	..
Other accounts receivable	3 579	951	1 060	2 315	2 394	2 143	2 564	3 606
Financial liabilities	130 726	138 126	145 395	154 592	164 694	168 565	171 093	177 456
Debt securities	3 976	4 078	0	0	0	0	2 026	2 070
Short-term debt securities	0	0	0	0	0	0	0	0
Long-term debt securities	3 976	4 078	0	0	0	0	2 026	2 070
Loans	308	238	271	82	70	95	0	2 574
Short-term loans	0	0	0	0	0	0	0	0
Long-term loans	308	238	271	82	70	95	0	2 574
Equity and investment fund shares	53 177	57 988	64 995	72 184	79 851	84 610	86 984	88 619
Insurance pension and standardised guarantees	69 233	71 758	75 913	77 383	80 216	78 703	75 215	78 715
Financial derivatives and employee stock options	0	0	0	0	0	0	0	0
Other accounts payable	4 032	4 065	4 216	4 943	4 557	5 156	6 869	5 478
Non-financial assets	1 722	1 598	1 647	6 691	6 083	6 615	2 018	1 909
Pension funds								
Financial net worth	-1 138	-1 135	-3 395	-5 002	-4 253	-3 721	-3 024	-2 345
Financial assets	1 848 199	1 987 715	2 171 846	2 439 744	2 696 738	2 936 214	3 285 369	3 522 069
Currency and deposits	162 529	158 644	157 308	167 887	164 764	135 548	160 331	136 710
Debt securities	878 331	1 039 345	1 148 198	1 240 290	1 329 764	1 411 674	1 511 206	1 707 972
Loans	174 436	171 889	181 352	180 939	181 543	175 927	179 396	242 441
Equity and investment fund shares	615 430	599 195	670 360	835 977	1 004 128	1 196 801	1 416 807	1 413 204
Equity	110 130	125 816	185 590	242 459	352 802	471 597	639 331	606 853
Investment fund shares	505 299	473 379	484 770	593 517	651 326	725 204	777 476	806 352
Money market fund shares	..	..	..	..	..	..	..	..
Non-Money market fund shares	..	..	..	..	..	..	..	..
Insurance pension and standardised guarantees	13 832	12 402	11 887	11 953	13 214	13 291	14 316	16 907
Financial derivatives and employee stock options	172	0	0	0	0	0	0	0
Other accounts receivable	3 469	6 239	2 742	2 698	3 326	2 974	3 314	4 835
Financial liabilities	1 849 337	1 988 850	2 175 242	2 444 746	2 700 991	2 939 935	3 288 393	3 524 414
Debt securities	..	..	..	..	..	..	..	..
Short-term debt securities	..	..	..	..	..	..	..	..
Long-term debt securities	..	..	..	..	..	..	..	..
Loans	277	217	574	435	81	22	0	0
Short-term loans	277	217	574	435	81	22	0	0
Long-term loans	0	0	0	0	0	0	0	0
Equity and investment fund shares	..	..	..	..	..	..	..	..
Insurance pension and standardised guarantees	1 774 723	1 909 517	2 097 849	2 392 142	2 660 618	2 924 392	3 275 901	3 514 276
Financial derivatives and employee stock options	69 865	72 165	60 162	31 941	21 575	2 171	13	13
Other accounts payable	4 471	6 951	16 658	20 228	18 716	13 350	12 480	10 125
Non-financial assets	1 138	1 135	3 395	5 002	4 253	3 721	3 024	2 345

Note: Detailed metadata at: http://metalinks.oecd.org/instinv/20170920/75e8

Table 4. Portfolio composition by type of investor

As percentage of financial assets and of financial liabilities

Per cent

	2009	2010	2011	2012	2013	2014	2015	2016
Investment funds								
Financial assets	100.0	100.0	100.0	100.0	100.0	100.0	100.0	100.0
Currency and deposits	9.4	6.4	10.8	8.3	11.0	15.7	19.6	25.6
Debt securities	81.9	83.3	72.4	71.3	60.9	52.2	43.0	41.5
Loans	0.0	0.0	0.0	0.0	0.0	0.0	0.2	1.3
Equity and investment fund shares	8.4	9.9	15.0	19.9	27.6	31.5	35.7	30.1
Insurance pension and standardised guarantee schemes	0.0	0.0	0.0	0.0	0.0	0.0	0.0	0.0
Financial derivatives and employee stock options	0.0	0.0	0.4	0.3	0.4	0.4	0.8	0.5
Other accounts receivable	0.3	0.4	1.3	0.1	0.1	0.2	0.7	1.0
Financial liabilities	100.0	100.0	100.0	100.0	100.0	100.0	100.0	100.0
Currency and deposits	0.0	0.0	0.0	0.0	0.0	0.0	0.0	0.0
Debt securities	0.0	0.0	1.2	6.2	6.9	11.2	9.7	9.1
Loans	0.0	0.0	2.6	0.7	0.8	0.9	1.0	0.9
Equity and investment fund shares	97.7	98.7	89.2	88.1	88.4	84.1	88.6	88.8
Insurance pension and standardised guarantee schemes	0.0	0.0	0.0	0.0	0.0	0.0	0.0	0.0
Financial derivatives and employee stock options	0.0	0.0	0.4	0.0	0.0	0.0	0.1	0.1
Other accounts receivable	2.3	1.3	6.6	5.0	3.9	3.8	0.6	1.1
Insurance corporations								
Financial assets	100.0	100.0	100.0	100.0	100.0	100.0	100.0	100.0
Currency and deposits	10.2	9.3	9.1	10.5	9.4	5.2	6.2	3.8
Debt securities	35.2	40.2	42.3	44.4	45.4	46.4	41.5	40.6
Loans	5.7	3.8	3.3	2.3	1.9	1.8	0.9	1.0
Equity and investment fund shares	25.2	25.4	27.8	28.0	28.1	31.3	35.4	37.9
Insurance pension and standardised guarantee schemes	21.0	20.5	16.9	13.3	13.7	14.0	14.6	14.6
Financial derivatives and employee stock options	0.0	0.0	0.0	0.0	0.0	0.0	0.0	0.0
Other accounts receivable	2.8	0.7	0.7	1.6	1.5	1.3	1.5	2.1
Financial liabilities	100.0	100.0	100.0	100.0	100.0	100.0	100.0	100.0
Currency and deposits	0.0	0.0	0.0	0.0	0.0	0.0	0.0	0.0
Debt securities	3.0	3.0	0.0	0.0	0.0	0.0	1.2	1.2
Loans	0.2	0.2	0.2	0.1	0.0	0.1	0.0	1.5
Equity and investment fund shares	40.7	42.0	44.7	46.7	48.5	50.2	50.8	49.9
Insurance pension and standardised guarantee schemes	53.0	52.0	52.2	50.1	48.7	46.7	44.0	44.4
Financial derivatives and employee stock options	0.0	0.0	0.0	0.0	0.0	0.0	0.0	0.0
Other accounts receivable	3.1	2.9	2.9	3.2	2.8	3.1	4.0	3.1
Pension funds								
Financial assets	100.0	100.0	100.0	100.0	100.0	100.0	100.0	100.0
Currency and deposits	8.8	8.0	7.2	6.9	6.1	4.6	4.9	3.9
Debt securities	47.5	52.3	52.9	50.8	49.3	48.1	46.0	48.5
Loans	9.4	8.6	8.4	7.4	6.7	6.0	5.5	6.9
Equity and investment fund shares	33.3	30.1	30.9	34.3	37.2	40.8	43.1	40.1
Insurance pension and standardised guarantee schemes	0.7	0.6	0.5	0.5	0.5	0.5	0.4	0.5
Financial derivatives and employee stock options	0.0	0.0	0.0	0.0	0.0	0.0	0.0	0.0
Other accounts receivable	0.2	0.3	0.1	0.1	0.1	0.1	0.1	0.1
Financial liabilities	100.0	100.0	100.0	100.0	100.0	100.0	100.0	100.0
Currency and deposits	0.0	0.0	0.0	0.0	0.0	0.0	0.0	0.0
Debt securities	0.0	0.0	0.0	0.0	0.0	0.0	0.0	0.0
Loans	0.0	0.0	0.0	0.0	0.0	0.0	0.0	0.0
Equity and investment fund shares	0.0	0.0	0.0	0.0	0.0	0.0	0.0	0.0
Insurance pension and standardised guarantee schemes	96.0	96.0	96.4	97.8	98.5	99.5	99.6	99.7
Financial derivatives and employee stock options	3.8	3.6	2.8	1.3	0.8	0.1	0.0	0.0
Other accounts receivable	0.2	0.3	0.8	0.8	0.7	0.5	0.4	0.3

Note: Detailed metadata at: http://metalinks.oecd.org/instinv/20170920/a49a

IRELAND

Table 1. Financial assets and liabilities of institutional investors, 2016

Million EUR (1999 IEP euro)

	Total	Investment funds			
		Non-money market funds			Money market funds
		Total	Open-end non-money market funds	Closed-end non-money market funds	Total
Financial assets	..	1 919 975 e	..	..	..
Currency and deposits	..	67 519 e	..	..	..
Debt securities	..	745 267 e	..	..	..
Debt securities, short term	..	53 949 e	..	..	..
Debt securities, long term	..	691 318 e	..	..	..
Debt securities issued by residents	..	..	..	..	..
Debt securities issued by non-residents	..	..	..	..	..
Loans	..	33 795 e	..	..	..
Loans, short-term	..	..	..	..	..
Loans, long-term	..	33 795 e	..	..	..
Loans granted to residents	..	..	..	..	..
Loans granted to non-residents	..	..	..	..	..
Equity and investment fund shares/units	..	848 788 e	..	..	..
Equity and investment fund shares issued/units by residents	..	..	..	..	..
Equity and investment fund shares/units issued by non residents	..	..	..	..	..
Other accounts receivable	..	63 580 e	..	..	..

	Total	Investment funds			
		Non-money market funds			Money market funds
		Total	Open-end non-money market funds	Closed-end non-money market funds	Total
Financial liabilities	..	1 919 199 e	..	..	..
Currency and deposits	..	0 e	..	..	..
Debt securities	..	0 e	..	..	..
Debt securities, short term	..	0 e	..	..	..
Debt securities, long term	..	0 e	..	..	..
Loans	..	119 940 e	..	..	..
Loans, short-term	..	109 346 e	..	..	..
Loans, long-term	..	10 594 e	..	..	..
Equity and investment fund shares/units	..	1 590 086 e	..	..	..
Insurance pension and standardised guaratees	..	0 e	..	..	..
Financial derivatives and employee stock options	..	153 592 e	..	..	..
Other accounts payable	..	55 581 e	..	..	..

	Total	Insurance corporations and pension funds			
		Insurance corporations			Pension funds
		Total	Life insurance corporations	Non-life insurance corporations	Total
Financial assets	391 213 e	274 452 e	..	..	116 761 e
Currency and deposits	28 641 e	23 580 e	..	..	5 061 e
Debt securities	93 839 e	42 505 e	..	..	51 334 e
Debt securities, short-term	10 499 e	6 832 e	..	..	3 667 e
Debt securities, long term	83 340 e	35 673 e	..	..	47 667 e
Debt securities issued by residents	..	..	..	..	..
Debt securities issued by non-residents	..	..	..	..	..
Loans	1 669 e	1 669 e	..	..	0 e
Loans, short-term	1 138 e	1 138 e	..	..	0 e
Loans, long-term	532 e	532 e	..	..	0 e
Loans granted to residents	..	..	..	..	..
Loans granted to non-residents	..	..	..	..	..
Equity and investment fund shares/units	205 353 e	147 117 e	..	..	58 236 e
Equity and investment fund shares/units issued by residents	..	..	..	..	..
Equity and investment fund shares/units issued by non residents	..	..	..	..	..
Other accounts receivable	23 777 e	21 766 e	..	..	2 011 e

	Total	Insurance corporations and pension funds			
		Insurance corporations			Pension funds
		Total	Life insurance corporations	Non-life insurance corporations	Total
Financial liabilities	400 820 e	284 146 e	..	..	116 674 e
Currency and deposits	0 e	0 e	..	..	0 e
Debt securities	1 933 e	1 933 e	..	..	0 e
Debt securities, short term	0 e	0 e	..	..	0 e
Debt securities, long term	1 933 e	1 933 e	..	..	0 e
Loans	3 573 e	3 539 e	..	..	34 e
Loans, short-term	190 e	181 e	..	..	9 e
Loans, long-term	3 383 e	3 358 e	..	..	25 e
Equity and investment fund shares/units	31 451 e	31 451 e	..	..	0 e
Insurance pension and standardised guarantees	344 514 e	227 874 e	..	..	116 640 e
Financial derivatives and employee stock options	0 e	0 e	..	..	0 e
Other accounts payable	19 349 e	19 349 e	..	..	0 e

Note: Detailed metadata at: http://metalinks.oecd.org/instinv/20170920/75e8

IRELAND

Table 2. Financial assets and liabilities of investment funds

Million EUR

	2009	2010	2011	2012	2013	2014	2015	2016
Investment funds								
Financial net worth	..	..	..	..	..	..	..	..
Financial assets	..	..	..	..	..	..	..	..
Currency and deposits	..	..	..	..	..	..	..	..
Debt securities	..	..	..	..	..	..	..	..
Loans	..	..	..	..	..	..	..	..
Equity and investment fund shares	..	..	..	..	..	..	..	..
Equity	..	..	..	..	..	..	..	..
Investment fund shares	..	..	..	..	..	..	..	..
Money market fund shares	..	..	..	..	..	..	..	..
Non-Money market fund shares	..	..	..	..	..	..	..	..
Insurance pension and standardised guarantees	..	..	..	..	..	..	..	..
Financial derivatives and employee stock options	..	..	..	..	..	..	..	..
Other accounts receivable	..	..	..	..	..	..	..	..
Financial liabilities	..	..	..	..	..	..	..	..
Debt securities	..	..	..	..	..	..	..	..
Short-term debt securities	..	..	..	..	..	..	..	..
Long-term debt securities	..	..	..	..	..	..	..	..
Loans	..	..	..	..	..	..	..	..
Short-term loans	..	..	..	..	..	..	..	..
Long-term loans	..	..	..	..	..	..	..	..
Equity and investment fund shares	..	..	..	..	..	..	..	..
Insurance pension and standardised guarantees	..	..	..	..	..	..	..	..
Financial derivatives and employee stock options	..	..	..	..	..	..	..	..
Other accounts payable	..	..	..	..	..	..	..	..
Non-financial assets	..	..	..	..	..	..	..	..
Money market funds								
Financial net worth	..	..	..	..	..	..	..	..
Financial assets	..	..	..	..	..	..	..	..
Currency and deposits	..	..	..	..	..	..	..	..
Debt securities	..	..	..	..	..	..	..	..
Loans	..	..	..	..	..	..	..	..
Equity and investment fund shares	..	..	..	..	..	..	..	..
Equity	..	..	..	..	..	..	..	..
Investment fund shares	..	..	..	..	..	..	..	..
Money market fund shares	..	..	..	..	..	..	..	..
Non-Money market fund shares	..	..	..	..	..	..	..	..
Insurance pension and standardised guarantees	..	..	..	..	..	..	..	..
Financial derivatives and employee stock options	..	..	..	..	..	..	..	..
Other accounts receivable	..	..	..	..	..	..	..	..
Financial liabilities	..	..	..	..	..	..	..	..
Debt securities	..	..	..	..	..	..	..	..
Short-term debt securities	..	..	..	..	..	..	..	..
Long-term debt securities	..	..	..	..	..	..	..	..
Loans	..	..	..	..	..	..	..	..
Short-term loans	..	..	..	..	..	..	..	..
Long-term loans	..	..	..	..	..	..	..	..
Equity and investment fund shares	..	..	..	..	..	..	..	..
Insurance pension and standardised guarantees	..	..	..	..	..	..	..	..
Financial derivatives and employee stock options	..	..	..	..	..	..	..	..
Other accounts payable	..	..	..	..	..	..	..	..
Non-financial assets	..	..	..	..	..	..	..	..
Non-money market funds								
Financial net worth	..	..	..	..	..	..	..	..
Financial assets	..	613 224 e	789 320 e	1 027 455 e	1 204 707 e	1 525 918 e	1 803 592 e	1 919 975 e
Currency and deposits	..	14 567 e	42 886 e	49 293 e	52 075 e	55 251 e	70 416 e	67 519 e
Debt securities	..	231 013 e	355 204 e	459 271 e	517 807 e	554 030 e	616 171 e	745 267 e
Loans	..	6 668 e	1[illegible] 831 e	31 131 e	23 290 e	15 179 e	31 364 e	33 795 e
Equity and investment fund shares	..	337 394 e	340 748 e	417 717 e	524 418 e	688 070 e	810 230 e	848 788 e
Equity	..	278 592 e	26[illegible] 563 e	330 951 e	413 914 e	502 401 e	591 845 e	619 972 e
Investment fund shares	..	58 802 e	73 185 e	86 766 e	110 504 e	185 668 e	218 386 e	228 816 e
Money market fund shares	..	1 140 e	[illegible] 425 e	1 356 e	1 670 e	17 786 e	27 097 e	30 000 e
Non-Money market fund shares	..	57 662 e	7[illegible] 760 e	85 410 e	108 834 e	167 883 e	191 289 e	198 816 e
Insurance pension and standardised guarantees	..	0 e	0 e	0 e	..	..	..	..
Financial derivatives and employee stock options	..	12 815 e	18 907 e	32 231 e	39 759 e	139 229 e	168 378 e	161 026 e
Other accounts receivable	..	10 768 e	1[illegible] 744 e	37 813 e	47 357 e	74 159 e	107 033 e	63 580 e
Financial liabilities	..	641 318 e	825 228 e	1 015 896 e	1 191 829 e	1 552 474 e	1 778 529 e	1 919 199 e
Debt securities	..	0 e	0 e	0 e	0 e	0 e	0 e	0 e
Short-term debt securities	..	0 e	0 e	0 e	0 e	0 e	0 e	0 e
Long-term debt securities	..	0 e	0 e	0 e	0 e	0 e	0 e	0 e
Loans	..	3 727 e	5 877 e	22 179 e	36 093 e	57 624 e	95 654 e	119 940 e
Short-term loans	..	3 414 e	5 387 e	21 744 e	33 183 e	52 446 e	86 342 e	109 346 e
Long-term loans	..	313 e	490 e	435 e	2 911 e	5 178 e	9 312 e	10 594 e
Equity and investment fund shares	..	601 764 e	775 906 e	921 025 e	1 062 907 e	1 285 078 e	1 419 740 e	1 590 086 e
Insurance pension and standardised guarantees	..	0 e	0 e	0 e	0 e	0 e	0 e	0 e
Financial derivatives and employee stock options	..	9 024 e	10 943 e	34 873 e	40 270 e	131 161 e	161 926 e	153 592 e
Other accounts payable	..	26 802 e	32 503 e	37 819 e	52 559 e	78 612 e	101 209 e	55 581 e
Non-financial assets	..	..	..	..	..	..	..	..
Open-end non-money market funds								
Financial net worth	..	..	..	..	..	..	..	..
Financial assets	..	..	..	..	..	..	..	..

IRELAND

Table 2. Financial assets and liabilities of investment funds *(cont.)*

Million EUR

	2009	2010	2011	2012	2013	2014	2015	2016
Currency and deposits	..	..	..	..	..	..	..	..
Debt securities	..	..	..	..	..	..	..	..
Loans	..	..	..	..	..	..	..	..
Equity and investment fund shares	..	..	..	..	..	..	..	..
Equity	..	..	..	..	..	..	..	..
Investment fund shares	..	..	..	..	..	..	..	..
Money market fund shares	..	..	..	..	..	..	..	..
Non-Money market fund shares	..	..	..	..	..	..	..	..
Insurance pension and standardised guarantees	..	..	..	..	..	..	..	..
Financial derivatives and employee stock options	..	..	..	..	..	..	..	..
Other accounts receivable	..	..	..	..	..	..	..	..
Financial liabilities	..	..	..	..	..	..	..	..
Debt securities	..	..	..	..	..	..	..	..
Short-term debt securities	..	..	..	..	..	..	..	..
Long-term debt securities	..	..	..	..	..	..	..	..
Loans	..	..	..	..	..	..	..	..
Short-term loans	..	..	..	..	..	..	..	..
Long-term loans	..	..	..	..	..	..	..	..
Equity and investment fund shares	..	..	..	..	..	..	..	..
Insurance pension and standardised guarantees	..	..	..	..	..	..	..	..
Financial derivatives and employee stock options	..	..	..	..	..	..	..	..
Other accounts payable	..	..	..	..	..	..	..	..
Non-financial assets	..	..	..	..	..	..	..	..
Open-end investment funds								
Financial net worth	..	..	..	..	..	..	..	..
Financial assets	..	..	..	..	..	..	..	..
Currency and deposits	..	..	..	..	..	..	..	..
Debt securities	..	..	..	..	..	..	..	..
Loans	..	..	..	..	..	..	..	..
Equity and investment fund shares	..	..	..	..	..	..	..	..
Equity	..	..	..	..	..	..	..	..
Investment fund shares	..	..	..	..	..	..	..	..
Money market fund shares	..	..	..	..	..	..	..	..
Non-Money market fund shares	..	..	..	..	..	..	..	..
Insurance pension and standardised guarantees	..	..	..	..	..	..	..	..
Financial derivatives and employee stock options	..	..	..	..	..	..	..	..
Other accounts receivable	..	..	..	..	..	..	..	..
Financial liabilities	..	..	..	..	..	..	..	..
Debt securities	..	..	..	..	..	..	..	..
Short-term debt securities	..	..	..	..	..	..	..	..
Long-term debt securities	..	..	..	..	..	..	..	..
Loans	..	..	..	..	..	..	..	..
Short-term loans	..	..	..	..	..	..	..	..
Long-term loans	..	..	..	..	..	..	..	..
Equity and investment fund shares	..	..	..	..	..	..	..	..
Insurance pension and standardised guarantees	..	..	..	..	..	..	..	..
Financial derivatives and employee stock options	..	..	..	..	..	..	..	..
Other accounts payable	..	..	..	..	..	..	..	..
Non-financial assets	..	..	..	..	..	..	..	..

Note: Detailed metadata at: http://metalinks.oecd.org/instinv/20170920/75e8

IRELAND

Table 3. Financial assets and liabilities of insurance corporations and pension funds

Million EUR

	2009	2010	2011	2012	2013	2014	2015	2016
Insurance corporations and pension funds								
Financial net worth	..	..	..	..	..	..	..	..
Financial assets	..	298 878 e	284 970 e	296 717 e	307 803 e	343 199 e	370 007 e	391 213 e
Currency and deposits	..	24 214 e	24 688 e	25 444 e	24 061 e	24 091 e	27 160 e	28 641 e
Debt securities	..	73 745 e	80 232 e	83 276 e	79 530 e	88 796 e	92 423 e	93 839 e
Loans	..	3 504 e	3 678 e	2 785 e	1 290 e	1 515 e	1 349 e	1 669 e
Equity and investment fund shares	..	135 693 e	127 488 e	138 204 e	152 008 e	176 131 e	191 024 e	205 353 e
Equity	..	65 407 e	62 439 e	67 598 e	70 048 e	76 673 e	76 362 e	78 264 e
Investment fund shares	..	70 286 e	65 049 e	70 606 e	81 960 e	99 458 e	114 661 e	127 089 e
Money market fund shares	..	756 e	706 e	4 305 e	3 211 e	1 550 e	1 467 e	1 460 e
Non-Money market fund shares	..	69 531 e	64 343 e	66 301 e	78 748 e	97 908 e	113 195 e	125 629 e
Insurance pension and standardised guarantees	..	44 055 e	29 978 e	28 352 e	26 698 e	31 991 e	33 734 e	35 968 e
Financial derivatives and employee stock options	..	1 651 e	2 433 e	2 461 e	1 769 e	2 443 e	1 786 e	1 967 e
Other accounts receivable	..	16 017 e	16 472 e	16 196 e	22 448 e	18 232 e	22 532 e	23 777 e
Financial liabilities	..	303 377 e	289 874 e	303 791 e	309 358 e	352 952 e	380 082 e	400 820 e
Debt securities	..	1 294 e	1 169 e	1 152 e	634 e	1 126 e	1 710 e	1 933 e
Short-term debt securities	..	0 e	0 e	0 e	0 e	0 e	0 e	0 e
Long-term debt securities	..	1 294 e	1 169 e	1 152 e	634 e	1 126 e	1 710 e	1 933 e
Loans	..	3 723 e	4 103 e	4 236 e	3 163 e	3 204 e	3 395 e	3 573 e
Short-term loans	..	668 e	743 e	887 e	207 e	143 e	197 e	190 e
Long-term loans	..	3 055 e	3 359 e	3 348 e	2 956 e	3 061 e	3 198 e	3 383 e
Equity and investment fund shares	..	26 626 e	25 919 e	27 241 e	25 156 e	26 949 e	29 191 e	31 451 e
Insurance pension and standardised guarantees	..	261 635 e	244 837 e	257 654 e	265 223 e	305 924 e	327 749 e	344 514 e
Financial derivatives and employee stock options	..	0 e	0 e	0 e	0 e	0 e	0 e	0 e
Other accounts payable	..	10 100 e	13 847 e	13 508 e	15 184 e	15 748 e	18 037 e	19 349 e
Non-financial assets	..	..	..	..	..	..	..	..
Insurance corporations								
Financial net worth	..	..	..	..	..	..	..	..
Financial assets	..	225 113 e	214 971 e	219 876 e	217 800 e	242 516 e	259 277 e	274 452 e
Currency and deposits	..	20 665 e	22 325 e	22 139 e	20 735 e	19 872 e	22 433 e	23 580 e
Debt securities	..	50 678 e	55 341 e	55 247 e	47 534 e	48 649 e	46 079 e	42 505 e
Loans	..	3 504 e	3 678 e	2 785 e	1 290 e	1 515 e	1 349 e	1 669 e
Equity and investment fund shares	..	89 658 e	85 481 e	93 656 e	100 662 e	121 172 e	133 682 e	147 117 e
Equity	..	28 846 e	28 909 e	30 185 e	24 962 e	27 598 e	24 097 e	25 384 e
Investment fund shares	..	60 812 e	56 572 e	63 471 e	75 700 e	93 574 e	109 584 e	121 733 e
Money market fund shares	..	420 e	397 e	4 198 e	3 131 e	1 216 e	1 174 e	1 218 e
Non-Money market fund shares	..	60 392 e	56 175 e	59 273 e	72 568 e	92 358 e	108 411 e	120 515 e
Insurance pension and standardised guarantees	..	44 055 e	29 978 e	28 352 e	26 698 e	31 991 e	33 734 e	35 968 e
Financial derivatives and employee stock options	..	830 e	2 225 e	2 235 e	1 619 e	2 316 e	1 649 e	1 848 e
Other accounts receivable	..	15 723 e	15 942 e	15 462 e	19 262 e	17 001 e	20 353 e	21 766 e
Financial liabilities	..	229 046 e	219 375 e	226 701 e	221 685 e	252 371 e	269 463 e	284 146 e
Debt securities	..	1 294 e	1 169 e	1 152 e	634 e	1 126 e	1 710 e	1 933 e
Short-term debt securities	..	0 e	0 e	0 e	0 e	0 e	0 e	0 e
Long-term debt securities	..	1 294 e	1 169 e	1 152 e	634 e	1 126 e	1 710 e	1 933 e
Loans	..	3 723 e	4 103 e	3 987 e	3 017 e	3 184 e	3 364 e	3 539 e
Short-term loans	..	668 e	743 e	887 e	207 e	123 e	184 e	181 e
Long-term loans	..	3 055 e	3 359 e	3 099 e	2 810 e	3 061 e	3 180 e	3 358 e
Equity and investment fund shares	..	26 626 e	25 919 e	27 241 e	25 137 e	26 930 e	29 191 e	31 451 e
Insurance pension and standardised guarantees	..	187 304 e	174 338 e	180 813 e	177 714 e	205 382 e	217 161 e	227 874 e
Financial derivatives and employee stock options	..	0 e	0 e	0 e	0 e	0 e	0 e	0 e
Other accounts payable	..	10 100 e	13 847 e	13 508 e	15 184 e	15 748 e	18 037 e	19 349 e
Non-financial assets	..	..	..	..	..	..	..	..
Pension funds								
Financial net worth	..	..	..	..	..	..	..	..
Financial assets	..	73 765 e	69 999 e	76 841 e	90 003 e	100 683 e	110 730 e	116 761 e
Currency and deposits	..	3 549 e	2 363 e	3 305 e	3 326 e	4 219 e	4 727 e	5 061 e
Debt securities	..	23 067 e	24 891 e	28 029 e	31 996 e	40 147 e	46 344 e	51 334 e
Loans	..	0 e	0 e	0 e	0 e	0 e	0 e	0 e
Equity and investment fund shares	..	46 035 e	42 007 e	44 548 e	51 346 e	54 959 e	57 342 e	58 236 e
Equity	..	36 561 e	33 530 e	37 413 e	45 086 e	49 075 e	52 265 e	52 880 e
Investment fund shares	..	9 474 e	8 477 e	7 135 e	6 260 e	5 884 e	5 077 e	5 356 e
Money market fund shares	..	336 e	309 e	107 e	80 e	334 e	293 e	242 e
Non-Money market fund shares	..	9 139 e	8 168 e	7 028 e	6 180 e	5 550 e	4 784 e	5 114 e
Insurance pension and standardised guarantees	..	0 e	0 e	0 e	0 e	0 e	0 e	0 e
Financial derivatives and employee stock options	..	821 e	208 e	226 e	150 e	127 e	137 e	119 e
Other accounts receivable	..	294 e	530 e	734 e	3 186 e	1 231 e	2 179 e	2 011 e
Financial liabilities	..	74 331 e	70 499 e	77 090 e	87 673 e	100 581 e	110 619 e	116 674 e
Debt securities	..	0 e	0 e	0 e	0 e	0 e	0 e	0 e
Short-term debt securities	..	0 e	0 e	0 e	0 e	0 e	0 e	0 e
Long-term debt securities	..	0 e	0 e	0 e	0 e	0 e	0 e	0 e
Loans	..	0 e	0 e	249 e	146 e	20 e	31 e	34 e
Short-term loans	..	0 e	0 e	0 e	0 e	20 e	13 e	9 e
Long-term loans	..	0 e	0 e	249 e	146 e	0 e	18 e	25 e
Equity and investment fund shares	..	0 e	0 e	0 e	19 e	19 e	0 e	0 e
Insurance pension and standardised guarantees	..	74 331 e	70 499 e	76 841 e	87 509 e	100 542 e	110 588 e	116 640 e
Financial derivatives and employee stock options	..	0 e	0 e	0 e	0 e	0 e	0 e	0 e
Other accounts payable	..	0 e	0 e	0 e	0 e	0 e	0 e	0 e
Non-financial assets	..	..	..	..	..	..	..	..

Note: Detailed metadata at: http://metalinks.oecd.org/instinv/20170920/75e8

Table 4. Portfolio composition by type of investor

As percentage of financial assets and of financial liabilities

Per cent

	2009	2010	2011	2012	2013	2014	2015	2016
Investment funds								
Financial assets	..	..	..	..	..	..	..	..
Currency and deposits	..	..	..	..	..	..	..	..
Debt securities	..	..	..	..	..	..	..	..
Loans	..	..	..	..	..	..	..	..
Equity and investment fund shares	..	..	..	..	..	..	..	..
Insurance pension and standardised guarantee schemes	..	..	..	..	..	..	..	..
Financial derivatives and employee stock options	..	..	..	..	..	..	..	..
Other accounts receivable	..	..	..	..	..	..	..	..
Financial liabilities	..	..	..	..	..	..	..	..
Currency and deposits	..	..	..	..	..	..	..	..
Debt securities	..	..	..	..	..	..	..	..
Loans	..	..	..	..	..	..	..	..
Equity and investment fund shares	..	..	..	..	..	..	..	..
Insurance pension and standardised guarantee schemes	..	..	..	..	..	..	..	..
Financial derivatives and employee stock options	..	..	..	..	..	..	..	..
Other accounts receivable	..	..	..	..	..	..	..	..
Insurance corporations								
Financial assets	..	100.0	100.0	100.0	100.0	100.0	100.0	100.0
Currency and deposits	..	9.2	10.4	10.1	9.5	8.2	8.7	8.6
Debt securities	..	22.5	25.7	25.1	21.8	20.1	17.8	15.5
Loans	..	1.6	1.7	1.3	0.6	0.6	0.5	0.6
Equity and investment fund shares	..	39.8	39.8	42.6	46.2	50.0	51.6	53.6
Insurance pension and standardised guarantee schemes	..	19.6	13.9	12.9	12.3	13.2	13.0	13.1
Financial derivatives and employee stock options	..	0.4	1.0	1.0	0.7	1.0	0.6	0.7
Other accounts receivable	..	7.0	7.4	7.0	8.8	7.0	7.8	7.9
Financial liabilities	..	100.0	100.0	100.0	100.0	100.0	100.0	100.0
Currency and deposits	..	0.0	0.0	0.0	0.0	0.0	0.0	0.0
Debt securities	..	0.6	0.5	0.5	0.3	0.4	0.6	0.7
Loans	..	1.6	1.9	1.8	1.4	1.3	1.2	1.2
Equity and investment fund shares	..	11.6	11.8	12.0	11.3	10.7	10.8	11.1
Insurance pension and standardised guarantee schemes	..	81.8	79.5	79.8	80.2	81.4	80.6	80.2
Financial derivatives and employee stock options	..	0.0	0.0	0.0	0.0	0.0	0.0	0.0
Other accounts receivable	..	4.4	6.3	6.0	6.8	6.2	6.7	6.8
Pension funds								
Financial assets	..	100.0	100.0	100.0	100.0	100.0	100.0	100.0
Currency and deposits	..	4.8	3.4	4.3	3.7	4.2	4.3	4.3
Debt securities	..	31.3	35.6	36.5	35.5	39.9	41.9	44.0
Loans	..	0.0	0.0	0.0	0.0	0.0	0.0	0.0
Equity and investment fund shares	..	62.4	60.0	58.0	57.0	54.6	51.8	49.9
Insurance pension and standardised guarantee schemes	..	0.0	0.0	0.0	0.0	0.0	0.0	0.0
Financial derivatives and employee stock options	..	1.1	0.3	0.3	0.2	0.1	0.1	0.1
Other accounts receivable	..	0.4	0.8	1.0	3.5	1.2	2.0	1.7
Financial liabilities	..	100.0	100.0	100.0	100.0	100.0	100.0	100.0
Currency and deposits	..	0.0	0.0	0.0	0.0	0.0	0.0	0.0
Debt securities	..	0.0	0.0	0.0	0.0	0.0	0.0	0.0
Loans	..	0.0	0.0	0.3	0.2	0.0	0.0	0.0
Equity and investment fund shares	..	0.0	0.0	0.0	0.0	0.0	0.0	0.0
Insurance pension and standardised guarantee schemes	..	100.0	100.0	99.7	99.8	100.0	100.0	100.0
Financial derivatives and employee stock options	..	0.0	0.0	0.0	0.0	0.0	0.0	0.0
Other accounts receivable	..	0.0	0.0	0.0	0.0	0.0	0.0	0.0

Note: Detailed metadata at: http://metalinks.oecd.org/instinv/20170920/a49a

Table 1. Financial assets and liabilities of institutional investors, 2016

Million ILS

	Investment funds				
	Total	Non-money market funds			Money market funds
		Total	Open-end non-money market funds	Closed-end non-money market funds	Total
Financial assets	214 080	195 196	195 196	..	18 884
Currency and deposits	20 568	13 762	13 762	..	6 805
Debt securities	165 512	153 433	153 433	..	12 079
Debt securities, short term	18 386	10 840	10 840	..	7 546
Debt securities, long term	147 125	142 593	142 593	..	4 533
Debt securities issued by residents	152 230	140 981	140 981	..	11 250
Debt securities issued by non-residents	13 282	12 452	12 452	..	829
Loans	0	0	0	..	0
Loans, short-term	0	0	0	..	0
Loans, long-term	0	0	0	..	0
Loans granted to residents	0	0	0	..	0
Loans granted to non-residents	0	0	0	..	0
Equity and investment fund shares/units	28 059	28 059	28 059	..	0
Equity and investment fund shares issued/units by residents	21 270	21 270	21 270	..	0
Equity and investment fund shares/units issued by non residents	6 790	6 790	6 790	..	0
Other accounts receivable	..	..	..	..	..

	Investment funds				
	Total	Non-money market funds			Money market funds
		Total	Open-end non-money market funds	Closed-end non-money market funds	Total
Financial liabilities	..	..	..	..	..
Currency and deposits	..	..	..	..	..
Debt securities	..	..	..	..	..
Debt securities, short term	..	..	..	..	..
Debt securities, long term	..	..	..	..	..
Loans	..	..	..	..	..
Loans, short-term	..	..	..	..	..
Loans, long-term	..	..	..	..	..
Equity and investment fund shares/units	..	..	..	..	..
Insurance pension and standardised guarantees	..	..	..	..	..
Financial derivatives and employee stock options	..	..	..	..	..
Other accounts payable	..	..	..	..	..

	Insurance corporations and pension funds				
	Total	Insurance corporations			Pension funds
		Total	Life insurance corporations	Non-life insurance corporations	Total
Financial assets	1 386 621	444 817	..	..	941 804
Currency and deposits	107 142	37 845	..	..	69 297
Debt securities	749 440	207 021	..	..	542 420
Debt securities, short-term	29 882	4 164	..	..	25 718
Debt securities, long term	719 559	202 856	..	..	516 702
Debt securities issued by residents	689 377	187 239	..	..	502 138
Debt securities issued by non-residents	60 063	19 782	..	..	40 282
Loans	92 274	39 316	..	..	52 958
Loans, short-term	..	..	..	..	..
Loans, long-term	..	..	..	..	..
Loans granted to residents	85 630	36 134	..	..	49 496
Loans granted to non-residents	6 644	3 181	..	..	3 463
Equity and investment fund shares/units	385 783	119 747	..	..	266 036
Equity and investment fund shares/units issued by residents	181 343	56 269	..	..	125 074
Equity and investment fund shares/units issued by non residents	204 440	63 477	..	..	140 962
Other accounts receivable	30 877	22 701	..	..	8 177

	Insurance corporations and pension funds				
	Total	Insurance corporations			Pension funds
		Total	Life insurance corporations	Non-life insurance corporations	Total
Financial liabilities	..	..	..	..	..
Currency and deposits	..	..	..	..	..
Debt securities	..	..	..	..	..
Debt securities, short term	..	..	..	..	..
Debt securities, long term	..	..	..	..	..
Loans	..	..	..	..	..
Loans, short-term	..	..	..	..	..
Loans, long-term	..	..	..	..	..
Equity and investment fund shares/units	..	..	..	..	..
Insurance pension and standardised guarantees	..	..	..	..	..
Financial derivatives and employee stock options	..	..	..	..	..
Other accounts payable	..	..	..	..	..

Note: Detailed metadata at: http://metalinks.oecd.org/instinv/20170920/2d93
Information on data for Israel: http://oe.cd/israel-disclaimer

Table 2. Financial assets and liabilities of investment funds

Million ILS

	2009	2010	2011	2012	2013	2014	2015	2016
Investment funds								
Financial net worth	..	..	..	..	..	..	..	..
Financial assets	133 200	156 582	142 353	170 099	230 785	261 522	229 155	214 080
Currency and deposits	13 932	14 926	17 173	23 524	42 730	42 192	28 026	20 568
Debt securities	104 230	120 707	112 183	133 809	167 843	194 131	174 598	165 512
Loans	0	0	0	0	0	0	0	0
Equity and investment fund shares	15 020	21 079	13 198	12 863	20 295	25 218	26 690	28 059
Equity	14 726	19 958	12 469	12 028	19 845	24 395	26 130	26 978
Investment fund shares	294	1 121	729	835	450	822	560	1 081
Money market fund shares	..	..	..	..	..	..	..	..
Non-Money market fund shares	..	..	..	..	..	..	..	..
Insurance pension and standardised guarantees	..	..	..	..	..	..	..	..
Financial derivatives and employee stock options	18	-129	-201	-97	-83	-17	-160	-58
Other accounts receivable	..	..	..	..	..	..	..	..
Financial liabilities	..	..	..	..	..	..	..	..
Debt securities	..	..	..	..	..	..	..	..
Short-term debt securities	..	..	..	..	..	..	..	..
Long-term debt securities	..	..	..	..	..	..	..	..
Loans	..	..	..	..	..	..	..	..
Short-term loans	..	..	..	..	..	..	..	..
Long-term loans	..	..	..	..	..	..	..	..
Equity and investment fund shares	..	..	..	..	..	..	..	..
Insurance pension and standardised guarantees	..	..	..	..	..	..	..	..
Financial derivatives and employee stock options	..	..	..	..	..	..	..	..
Other accounts payable	..	..	..	..	..	..	..	..
Non-financial assets	0	0	0	0	0	0	0	0
Money market funds								
Financial net worth	..	..	..	..	..	..	..	..
Financial assets	16 959	17 941	34 076	35 688	61 079	54 035	27 383	18 884
Currency and deposits	7 104	7 736	12 934	16 635	31 060	28 956	14 830	6 805
Debt securities	9 855	10 204	21 141	19 053	30 019	25 078	12 553	12 079
Loans	0	0	0	0	0	0	0	0
Equity and investment fund shares	0	0	0	0	0	0	0	0
Equity	0	0	0	0	0	0	0	0
Investment fund shares	0	0	0	0	0	0	0	0
Money market fund shares	..	..	..	..	..	..	..	..
Non-Money market fund shares	..	..	..	..	..	..	..	..
Insurance pension and standardised guarantees	..	..	..	..	..	..	..	..
Financial derivatives and employee stock options	0	0	0	0	0	0	0	0
Other accounts receivable	..	..	..	..	..	..	..	..
Financial liabilities	..	..	..	..	..	..	..	..
Debt securities	..	..	..	..	..	..	..	..
Short-term debt securities	..	..	..	..	..	..	..	..
Long-term debt securities	..	..	..	..	..	..	..	..
Loans	..	..	..	..	..	..	..	..
Short-term loans	..	..	..	..	..	..	..	..
Long-term loans	..	..	..	..	..	..	..	..
Equity and investment fund shares	..	..	..	..	..	..	..	..
Insurance pension and standardised guarantees	..	..	..	..	..	..	..	..
Financial derivatives and employee stock options	..	..	..	..	..	..	..	..
Other accounts payable	..	..	..	..	..	..	..	..
Non-financial assets	0	0	0	0	0	0	0	0
Non-money market funds								
Financial net worth	..	..	..	..	..	..	..	..
Financial assets	116 240	138 641	108 277	134 411	169 705	207 488	201 771	195 196
Currency and deposits	6 828	7 189	4 239	6 889	11 670	13 235	13 197	13 762
Debt securities	94 375	110 503	91 042	114 756	137 824	169 053	162 045	153 433
Loans	0	0	0	0	0	0	0	0
Equity and investment fund shares	15 020	21 079	13 198	12 863	20 295	25 218	26 690	28 059
Equity	14 726	19 958	12 469	12 028	19 845	24 395	26 130	26 978
Investment fund shares	294	1 121	729	835	450	822	560	1 081
Money market fund shares	..	..	..	..	..	..	..	..
Non-Money market fund shares	..	..	..	..	..	..	..	..
Insurance pension and standardised guarantees	..	..	..	..	..	..	..	..
Financial derivatives and employee stock options	18	-129	-201	-97	-83	-17	-160	-58
Other accounts receivable	..	..	..	..	..	..	..	..
Financial liabilities	..	..	..	..	..	..	..	..
Debt securities	..	..	..	..	..	..	..	..
Short-term debt securities	..	..	..	..	..	..	..	..
Long-term debt securities	..	..	..	..	..	..	..	..
Loans	..	..	..	..	..	..	..	..
Short-term loans	..	..	..	..	..	..	..	..
Long-term loans	..	..	..	..	..	..	..	..
Equity and investment fund shares	..	..	..	..	..	..	..	..
Insurance pension and standardised guarantees	..	..	..	..	..	..	..	..
Financial derivatives and employee stock options	..	..	..	..	..	..	..	..
Other accounts payable	..	..	..	..	..	..	..	..
Non-financial assets	0	0	0	0	0	0	0	0
Open-end non-money market funds								
Financial net worth	..	..	..	..	..	..	..	..
Financial assets	116 240	138 641	108 277	134 411	169 705	207 488	201 771	195 196

Table 2. Financial assets and liabilities of investment funds *(cont.)*

Million ILS

	2009	2010	2011	2012	2013	2014	2015	2016
Currency and deposits	6 828	7 189	4 239	6 889	11 670	13 235	13 197	13 762
Debt securities	94 375	110 503	91 042	114 756	137 824	169 053	162 045	153 433
Loans	0	0	0	0	0	0	0	0
Equity and investment fund shares	15 020	21 079	13 198	12 863	20 295	25 218	26 690	28 059
Equity	14 726	19 958	12 469	12 028	19 845	24 395	26 130	26 978
Investment fund shares	294	1 121	729	835	450	822	560	1 081
Money market fund shares	..	..	..	..	..	..	..	..
Non-Money market fund shares	..	..	..	..	..	..	..	..
Insurance pension and standardised guarantees	..	..	..	..	..	..	..	..
Financial derivatives and employee stock options	18	-129	-201	-97	-83	-17	-160	-58
Other accounts receivable	..	..	..	..	..	..	..	..
Financial liabilities	..	..	..	..	..	..	..	..
Debt securities	..	..	..	..	..	..	..	..
Short-term debt securities	..	..	..	..	..	..	..	..
Long-term debt securities	..	..	..	..	..	..	..	..
Loans	..	..	..	..	..	..	..	..
Short-term loans	..	..	..	..	..	..	..	..
Long-term loans	..	..	..	..	..	..	..	..
Equity and investment fund shares	..	..	..	..	..	..	..	..
Insurance pension and standardised guarantees	..	..	..	..	..	..	..	..
Financial derivatives and employee stock options	..	..	..	..	..	..	..	..
Other accounts payable	..	..	..	..	..	..	..	..
Non-financial assets	0	0	0	0	0	0	0	0
Open-end investment funds								
Financial net worth	..	..	..	..	..	..	..	..
Financial assets	133 200	156 582	142 353	170 099	230 785	261 522	229 155	214 080
Currency and deposits	13 932	14 926	17 173	23 524	42 730	42 192	28 026	20 568
Debt securities	104 230	120 707	112 183	133 809	167 843	194 131	174 598	165 512
Loans	0	0	0	0	0	0	0	0
Equity and investment fund shares	15 020	21 079	13 198	12 863	20 295	25 218	26 690	28 059
Equity	14 726	19 958	12 469	12 028	19 845	24 395	26 130	26 978
Investment fund shares	294	1 121	729	835	450	822	560	1 081
Money market fund shares	..	..	..	..	..	..	..	..
Non-Money market fund shares	..	..	..	..	..	..	..	..
Insurance pension and standardised guarantees	..	..	..	..	..	..	..	..
Financial derivatives and employee stock options	18	-129	-201	-97	-83	-17	-160	-58
Other accounts receivable	..	..	..	..	..	..	..	..
Financial liabilities	..	..	..	..	..	..	..	..
Debt securities	..	..	..	..	..	..	..	..
Short-term debt securities	..	..	..	..	..	..	..	..
Long-term debt securities	..	..	..	..	..	..	..	..
Loans	..	..	..	..	..	..	..	..
Short-term loans	..	..	..	..	..	..	..	..
Long-term loans	..	..	..	..	..	..	..	..
Equity and investment fund shares	..	..	..	..	..	..	..	..
Insurance pension and standardised guarantees	..	..	..	..	..	..	..	..
Financial derivatives and employee stock options	..	..	..	..	..	..	..	..
Other accounts payable	..	..	..	..	..	..	..	..
Non-financial assets	0	0	0	0	0	0	0	0

Note: Detailed metadata at: http://metalinks.oecd.org/instinv/20170920/2d93
Information on data for Israel: http://oe.cd/israel-disclaimer

Table 3. Financial assets and liabilities of insurance corporations and pension funds

Million ILS

	2009	2010	2011	2012	2013	2014	2015	2016
Insurance corporations and pension funds								
Financial net worth	..	..	..	..	..	..	..	..
Financial assets	810 580	897 183	906 865	1 011 560	1 117 101	1 221 043	1 302 591	1 386 621
Currency and deposits	74 364	75 010	68 910	73 576	78 134	82 003	100 245	107 142
Debt securities	511 832	543 987	561 429	607 790	642 423	690 205	722 299	749 440
Loans	19 789	23 405	31 599	41 079	51 951	60 459	73 731	92 274
Equity and investment fund shares	168 253	217 104	208 026	247 784	300 937	343 806	360 762	385 783
Equity	133 935	166 584	149 408	181 334	221 469	250 003	259 311	277 446
Investment fund shares	34 319	50 521	58 618	66 450	79 468	93 803	101 451	108 337
Money market fund shares	..	..	..	..	..	..	..	..
Non-Money market fund shares	..	..	..	..	..	..	..	..
Insurance pension and standardised guarantees	12 521	13 704	14 386	14 639	14 997	14 819	14 015	16 375
Financial derivatives and employee stock options	597	2 745	-504	2 358	4 691	2 154	1 857	4 730
Other accounts receivable	23 225	21 228	23 018	24 334	23 968	27 597	29 682	30 877
Financial liabilities	..	..	..	..	..	..	..	..
Debt securities	..	..	..	..	..	..	..	..
Short-term debt securities	..	..	..	..	..	..	..	..
Long-term debt securities	..	..	..	..	..	..	..	..
Loans	..	..	..	..	..	..	..	..
Short-term loans	..	..	..	..	..	..	..	..
Long-term loans	..	..	..	..	..	..	..	..
Equity and investment fund shares	..	..	..	..	..	..	..	..
Insurance pension and standardised guarantees	..	..	..	..	..	..	..	..
Financial derivatives and employee stock options	..	..	..	..	..	..	..	..
Other accounts payable	..	..	..	..	..	..	..	..
Non-financial assets	10 814	12 396	15 151	17 111	19 996	22 771	24 408	25 535
Insurance corporations								
Financial net worth	..	..	..	..	..	..	..	..
Financial assets	251 815	282 779	292 257	328 405	363 866	395 785	419 748	444 817
Currency and deposits	22 041	22 201	24 361	25 111	26 780	25 346	34 952	37 845
Debt securities	131 346	144 142	149 944	167 129	180 900	194 668	200 576	207 021
Loans	12 598	13 503	16 885	19 832	23 579	25 704	30 733	39 316
Equity and investment fund shares	57 384	72 661	69 613	82 930	97 803	113 666	116 783	119 747
Equity	43 062	52 716	50 347	61 276	71 969	83 613	83 647	83 323
Investment fund shares	14 322	19 945	19 266	21 654	25 835	30 052	33 136	36 423
Money market fund shares	..	..	..	..	..	..	..	..
Non-Money market fund shares	..	..	..	..	..	..	..	..
Insurance pension and standardised guarantees	12 521	13 704	14 386	14 639	14 997	14 819	14 015	16 375
Financial derivatives and employee stock options	391	1 035	373	1 407	1 664	1 486	1 060	1 814
Other accounts receivable	15 535	15 533	16 696	17 358	18 142	20 097	21 628	22 701
Financial liabilities	..	..	..	..	..	..	..	..
Debt securities	..	..	..	..	..	..	..	..
Short-term debt securities	..	..	..	..	..	..	..	..
Long-term debt securities	..	..	..	..	..	..	..	..
Loans	..	..	..	..	..	..	..	..
Short-term loans	..	..	..	..	..	..	..	..
Long-term loans	..	..	..	..	..	..	..	..
Equity and investment fund shares	..	..	..	..	..	..	..	..
Insurance pension and standardised guarantees	..	..	..	..	..	..	..	..
Financial derivatives and employee stock options	..	..	..	..	..	..	..	..
Other accounts payable	..	..	..	..	..	..	..	..
Non-financial assets	8 599	9 937	12 093	13 654	15 955	18 156	19 581	20 729
Pension funds								
Financial net worth	..	..	..	..	..	..	..	..
Financial assets	558 765	614 404	614 608	683 155	753 235	825 258	882 843	941 804
Currency and deposits	52 322	52 809	44 550	48 465	51 354	56 657	65 293	69 297
Debt securities	380 486	399 845	411 485	440 661	461 523	495 537	521 723	542 420
Loans	7 191	9 901	14 715	21 247	28 372	34 755	42 998	52 958
Equity and investment fund shares	110 870	144 443	138 413	164 854	203 134	230 140	243 979	266 036
Equity	90 873	113 867	99 061	120 058	149 501	166 389	175 664	194 123
Investment fund shares	19 997	30 576	39 352	44 796	53 633	63 751	68 315	71 914
Money market fund shares	..	..	..	..	..	..	..	..
Non-Money market fund shares	..	..	..	..	..	..	..	..
Insurance pension and standardised guarantees	0	0	0	0	0	0	0	0
Financial derivatives and employee stock options	206	1 710	-877	951	3 027	668	797	2 916
Other accounts receivable	7 691	5 695	6 322	6 977	5 826	7 500	8 053	8 177
Financial liabilities	..	..	..	..	..	..	..	..
Debt securities	..	..	..	..	..	..	..	..
Short-term debt securities	..	..	..	..	..	..	..	..
Long-term debt securities	..	..	..	..	..	..	..	..
Loans	..	..	..	..	..	..	..	..
Short-term loans	..	..	..	..	..	..	..	..
Long-term loans	..	..	..	..	..	..	..	..
Equity and investment fund shares	..	..	..	..	..	..	..	..
Insurance pension and standardised guarantees	..	..	..	..	..	..	..	..
Financial derivatives and employee stock options	..	..	..	..	..	..	..	..
Other accounts payable	..	..	..	..	..	..	..	..
Non-financial assets	2 214	2 459	3 059	3 457	4 041	4 616	4 828	4 806

Note: Detailed metadata at: http://metalinks.oecd.org/instinv/20170920/2d93
Information on data for Israel: http://oe.cd/israel-disclaimer

Table 4. Portfolio composition by type of investor

As percentage of financial assets and of financial liabilities

Per cent

	2009	2010	2011	2012	2013	2014	2015	2016
Investment funds								
Financial assets	100.0	100.0	100.0	100.0	100.0	100.0	100.0	100.0
Currency and deposits	10.5	9.5	12.1	13.8	18.5	16.1	12.2	9.6
Debt securities	78.3	77.1	78.8	78.7	72.7	74.2	76.2	77.3
Loans	0.0	0.0	0.0	0.0	0.0	0.0	0.0	0.0
Equity and investment fund shares	11.3	13.5	9.3	7.6	8.8	9.6	11.6	13.1
Insurance pension and standardised guarantee schemes	0.0	0.0	0.0	0.0	0.0	0.0	0.0	0.0
Financial derivatives and employee stock options	0.0	-0.1	-0.1	-0.1	0.0	0.0	-0.1	0.0
Other accounts receivable	0.0	0.0	0.0	0.0	0.0	0.0	0.0	0.0
Financial liabilities	..	..	..	..	..	..	..	..
Currency and deposits	..	..	..	..	..	..	..	..
Debt securities	..	..	..	..	..	..	..	..
Loans	..	..	..	..	..	..	..	..
Equity and investment fund shares	..	..	..	..	..	..	..	..
Insurance pension and standardised guarantee schemes	..	..	..	..	..	..	..	..
Financial derivatives and employee stock options	..	..	..	..	..	..	..	..
Other accounts receivable	..	..	..	..	..	..	..	..
Insurance corporations								
Financial assets	100.0	100.0	100.0	100.0	100.0	100.0	100.0	100.0
Currency and deposits	8.8	7.9	8.3	7.6	7.4	6.4	8.3	8.5
Debt securities	52.2	51.0	51.3	50.9	49.7	49.2	47.8	46.5
Loans	5.0	4.8	5.8	6.0	6.5	6.5	7.3	8.8
Equity and investment fund shares	22.8	25.7	23.8	25.3	26.9	28.7	27.8	26.9
Insurance pension and standardised guarantee schemes	5.0	4.8	4.9	4.5	4.1	3.7	3.3	3.7
Financial derivatives and employee stock options	0.2	0.4	0.1	0.4	0.5	0.4	0.3	0.4
Other accounts receivable	6.2	5.5	5.7	5.3	5.0	5.1	5.2	5.1
Financial liabilities	..	..	..	..	..	..	..	..
Currency and deposits	..	..	..	..	..	..	..	..
Debt securities	..	..	..	..	..	..	..	..
Loans	..	..	..	..	..	..	..	..
Equity and investment fund shares	..	..	..	..	..	..	..	..
Insurance pension and standardised guarantee schemes	..	..	..	..	..	..	..	..
Financial derivatives and employee stock options	..	..	..	..	..	..	..	..
Other accounts receivable	..	..	..	..	..	..	..	..
Pension funds								
Financial assets	100.0	100.0	100.0	100.0	100.0	100.0	100.0	100.0
Currency and deposits	9.4	8.6	7.2	7.1	6.8	6.9	7.4	7.4
Debt securities	68.1	65.1	67.0	64.5	61.3	60.0	59.1	57.6
Loans	1.3	1.6	2.4	3.1	3.8	4.2	4.9	5.6
Equity and investment fund shares	19.8	23.5	22.5	24.1	27.0	27.9	27.6	28.2
Insurance pension and standardised guarantee schemes	0.0	0.0	0.0	0.0	0.0	0.0	0.0	0.0
Financial derivatives and employee stock options	0.0	0.3	-0.1	0.1	0.4	0.1	0.1	0.3
Other accounts receivable	1.4	0.9	1.0	1.0	0.8	0.9	0.9	0.9
Financial liabilities	..	..	..	..	..	..	..	..
Currency and deposits	..	..	..	..	..	..	..	..
Debt securities	..	..	..	..	..	..	..	..
Loans	..	..	..	..	..	..	..	..
Equity and investment fund shares	..	..	..	..	..	..	..	..
Insurance pension and standardised guarantee schemes	..	..	..	..	..	..	..	..
Financial derivatives and employee stock options	..	..	..	..	..	..	..	..
Other accounts receivable	..	..	..	..	..	..	..	..

Note: Detailed metadata at: http://metalinks.oecd.org/instinv/20170920/a49a
Information on data for Israel: http://oe.cd/israel-disclaimer

ITALY

Table 1. Financial assets and liabilities of institutional investors, 2016

Million EUR (1999 ITL euro)

	Investment funds				
	Total	Non-money market funds			Money market funds
		Total	Open-end non-money market funds	Closed-end non-money market funds	Total
Financial assets	303 198	298 251	278 855	19 396	4 947
Currency and deposits	..	21 839	16 550	5 289	..
Debt securities	138 619	134 147	134 039	108	4 472
Debt securities, short term	5 779	5 779	5 725	54	0
Debt securities, long term	132 840	128 368	128 314	53	4 472
Debt securities issued by residents	71 140	71 073	70 110	963	67
Debt securities issued by non-residents	67 478	63 074	63 929	-855	4 405
Loans	442	0	0	0	442
Loans, short-term	442	0	0	0	442
Loans, long-term	0	0	0	0	0
Loans granted to residents	442	0	0	0	442
Loans granted to non-residents	0	0	0	0	0
Equity and investment fund shares/units	140 692	140 659	126 660	14 000	33
Equity and investment fund shares issued/units by residents	35 621	35 621	23 972	11 649	0
Equity and investment fund shares/units issued by non residents	105 071	105 038	102 688	2 350	33
Other accounts receivable	0	0	0	0	0

	Investment funds				
	Total	Non-money market funds			Money market funds
		Total	Open-end non-money market funds	Closed-end non-money market funds	Total
Financial liabilities	300 798	296 042	260 549	35 493	4 756
Currency and deposits	0	0	0	0	0
Debt securities	0	0	0	0	0
Debt securities, short term	0	0	0	0	0
Debt securities, long term	0	0	0	0	0
Loans	0	0	0	0	0
Loans, short-term	0	0	0	0	0
Loans, long-term	0	0	0	0	0
Equity and investment fund shares/units	300 798	296 042	260 549	35 493	4 756
Insurance pension and standardised guaratees	0	0	0	0	0
Financial derivatives and employee stock options	0	0	0	0	0
Other accounts payable	0	0	0	0	0

	Insurance corporations and pension funds				
	Total	Insurance corporations			Pension funds
		Total	Life insurance corporations	Non-life insurance corporations	Total
Financial assets	898 604	811 190	732 124	79 066	87 414
Currency and deposits	24 930	19 304	17 422	1 882	5 626
Debt securities	574 678	523 328	472 319	51 008	51 350
Debt securities, short-term	2 462	2 322	2 095	226	140
Debt securities, long term	572 215	521 006	470 224	50 782	51 210
Debt securities issued by residents	388 294	376 581	339 876	36 705	11 713
Debt securities issued by non-residents	186 384	146 747	132 443	14 303	39 637
Loans	9 084	9 084	8 199	885	0
Loans, short-term	1 181	1 181	1 066	115	0
Loans, long-term	7 903	7 903	7 133	770	0
Loans granted to residents	647	631	569	61	16
Loans granted to non-residents	8 437	8 453	7 629	824	-16
Equity and investment fund shares/units	284 840	254 402	229 606	24 796	30 438
Equity and investment fund shares/units issued by residents	56 587	39 904	36 015	3 889	16 683
Equity and investment fund shares/units issued by non residents	..	..	..	..	..
Other accounts receivable	2 214	2 214	1 998	216	0

	Insurance corporations and pension funds				
	Total	Insurance corporations			Pension funds
		Total	Life insurance corporations	Non-life insurance corporations	Total
Financial liabilities	906 910	812 114	732 957	79 156	94 796
Currency and deposits	0	0	0	0	0
Debt securities	16 068	16 068	14 502	1 566	0
Debt securities, short term	0	0	0	0	0
Debt securities, long term	16 068	16 068	14 502	1 566	0
Loans	11 762	11 745	10 600	1 145	17
Loans, short-term	1 474	1 458	1 316	142	16
Loans, long-term	10 288	10 287	9 284	1 003	1
Equity and investment fund shares/units	80 920	80 920	73 032	7 887	0
Insurance pension and standardised guarantees	795 317	700 538	632 257	68 281	94 779
Financial derivatives and employee stock options	249	249	225	24	0
Other accounts payable	2 594	2 594	2 341	253	0

Note: Detailed metadata at: http://metalinks.oecd.org/instinv/20170920/75e8

Table 2. Financial assets and liabilities of investment funds

Million EUR

	2009	2010	2011	2012	2013	2014	2015	2016
Investment funds								
Financial net worth	-21 411	-13 526	-16 742	-18 688	-11 163	-9 845	-523	2 400
Financial assets	221 063	210 872	170 013	164 439	190 901	243 800	285 696	303 198
Currency and deposits	..	..	..	..	..	..	..	..
Debt securities	142 552	126 711	98 563	94 549	102 404	130 241	136 672	138 619
Loans	9 648	2 666	2 925	1 347	749	232	168	442
Equity and investment fund shares	56 773	69 174	55 161	52 278	68 666	94 144	125 165	140 692
Equity	54 523	57 128	44 935	43 478	51 060	68 232	93 951	106 556
Investment fund shares	2 250	12 046	10 226	8 800	17 606	25 912	31 213	34 136
Money market fund shares	..	..	..	..	..	..	..	..
Non-Money market fund shares	..	..	..	..	..	..	..	..
Insurance pension and standardised guarantees	0	0	0	0	0	0	0	0
Financial derivatives and employee stock options	464	361	335	449	884	1 266	1 385	1 606
Other accounts receivable	0	0	0	0	0	0	0	0
Financial liabilities	242 474	224 398	186 755	183 127	202 064	253 645	286 218	300 798
Debt securities	0	0	0	0	0	0	0	0
Short-term debt securities	0	0	0	0	0	0	0	0
Long-term debt securities	0	0	0	0	0	0	0	0
Loans	0	0	0	0	0	0	0	0
Short-term loans	0	0	0	0	0	0	0	0
Long-term loans	0	0	0	0	0	0	0	0
Equity and investment fund shares	242 474	224 398	186 755	183 127	202 064	253 645	286 218	300 798
Insurance pension and standardised guarantees	0	0	0	0	0	0	0	0
Financial derivatives and employee stock options	0	0	0	0	0	0	0	0
Other accounts payable	0	0	0	0	0	0	0	0
Non-financial assets	..	..	..	..	..	..	..	..
Money market funds								
Financial net worth	369	319	604	31	114	22	99	191
Financial assets	55 221	38 664	27 537	9 154	9 636	7 325	6 033	4 947
Currency and deposits	..	..	..	..	..	..	..	..
Debt securities	45 393	35 878	24 485	7 770	8 775	7 093	5 826	4 472
Loans	9 648	2 666	2 925	1 347	749	232	168	442
Equity and investment fund shares	180	120	127	36	112	0	38	33
Equity	154	86	116	36	37	0	38	33
Investment fund shares	26	34	11	0	76	0	0	0
Money market fund shares	..	..	..	..	..	..	..	..
Non-Money market fund shares	..	..	..	..	..	..	..	..
Insurance pension and standardised guarantees	0	0	0	0	0	0	0	0
Financial derivatives and employee stock options	0	0	0	0	0	0	0	0
Other accounts receivable	0	0	0	0	0	0	0	0
Financial liabilities	54 852	38 345	26 933	9 123	9 522	7 303	5 933	4 756
Debt securities	0	0	0	0	0	0	0	0
Short-term debt securities	0	0	0	0	0	0	0	0
Long-term debt securities	0	0	0	0	0	0	0	0
Loans	0	0	0	0	0	0	0	0
Short-term loans	0	0	0	0	0	0	0	0
Long-term loans	0	0	0	0	0	0	0	0
Equity and investment fund shares	54 852	38 345	26 933	9 123	9 522	7 303	5 933	4 756
Insurance pension and standardised guarantees	0	0	0	0	0	0	0	0
Financial derivatives and employee stock options	0	0	0	0	0	0	0	0
Other accounts payable	0	0	0	0	0	0	0	0
Non-financial assets	..	..	..	..	..	..	..	..
Non-money market funds								
Financial net worth	-21 780	-13 845	-17 346	-18 718	-11 277	-9 867	-622	2 209
Financial assets	165 842	172 208	142 475	155 285	181 265	236 475	279 663	298 251
Currency and deposits	11 626	11 960	13 029	15 815	18 198	17 917	22 305	21 839
Debt securities	97 159	90 833	74 078	86 779	93 630	123 148	130 845	134 147
Loans	0	0	0	0	0	0	0	0
Equity and investment fund shares	56 593	69 054	55 034	52 242	68 554	94 144	125 127	140 659
Equity	54 369	57 042	44 819	43 442	51 024	68 232	93 914	106 523
Investment fund shares	2 224	12 013	10 215	8 800	17 530	25 912	31 213	34 136
Money market fund shares	..	..	..	..	..	..	..	..
Non-Money market fund shares	..	..	..	..	..	..	..	..
Insurance pension and standardised guarantees	0	0	0	0	0	0	0	0
Financial derivatives and employee stock options	464	361	335	449	884	1 266	1 385	1 606
Other accounts receivable	0	0	0	0	0	0	0	0
Financial liabilities	187 622	186 054	159 322	174 004	192 543	246 342	280 285	296 042
Debt securities	0	0	0	0	0	0	0	0
Short-term debt securities	0	0	0	0	0	0	0	0
Long-term debt securities	0	0	0	0	0	0	0	0
Loans	0	0	0	0	0	0	0	0
Short-term loans	0	0	0	0	0	0	0	0
Long-term loans	0	0	0	0	0	0	0	0
Equity and investment fund shares	187 622	186 054	159 322	174 004	192 543	246 342	280 285	296 042
Insurance pension and standardised guarantees	0	0	0	0	0	0	0	0
Financial derivatives and employee stock options	0	0	0	0	0	0	0	0
Other accounts payable	0	0	0	0	0	0	0	0
Non-financial assets	..	..	..	..	..	..	..	..
Open-end non-money market funds								
Financial net worth	-4 640	5 384	1 534	-1 792	4 174	6 844	15 609	18 305
Financial assets	163 884	170 512	141 166	153 370	179 492	222 448	264 161	278 855

Table 2. Financial assets and liabilities of investment funds *(cont.)*

Million EUR

	2009	2010	2011	2012	2013	2014	2015	2016
Currency and deposits	11 626	11 960	13 029	15 815	18 198	14 232	18 131	16 550
Debt securities	96 930	90 406	73 886	86 477	93 397	122 787	130 645	134 039
Loans	0	0	0	0	0	0	0	0
Equity and investment fund shares	54 865	67 785	53 916	50 629	67 013	84 163	114 000	126 660
Equity	54 369	57 042	44 819	43 442	51 024	61 554	86 569	97 072
Investment fund shares	497	10 744	9 097	7 187	15 989	22 609	27 431	29 587
Money market fund shares	..	..	..	..	..	..	..	..
Non-Money market fund shares	..	..	..	..	..	..	..	..
Insurance pension and standardised guarantees	0	0	0	0	0	0	0	0
Financial derivatives and employee stock options	464	361	335	449	884	1 266	1 385	1 606
Other accounts receivable	0	0	0	0	0	0	0	0
Financial liabilities	168 525	165 128	139 632	155 162	175 318	215 604	248 552	260 549
Debt securities	0	0	0	0	0	0	0	0
Short-term debt securities	0	0	0	0	0	0	0	0
Long-term debt securities	0	0	0	0	0	0	0	0
Loans	0	0	0	0	0	0	0	0
Short-term loans	0	0	0	0	0	0	0	0
Long-term loans	0	0	0	0	0	0	0	0
Equity and investment fund shares	168 525	165 128	139 632	155 162	175 318	215 604	248 552	260 549
Insurance pension and standardised guarantees	0	0	0	0	0	0	0	0
Financial derivatives and employee stock options	0	0	0	0	0	0	0	0
Other accounts payable	0	0	0	0	0	0	0	0
Non-financial assets	..	..	..	..	..	..	..	..
Open-end investment funds								
Financial net worth	-4 271	5 703	2 138	-1 761	4 288	6 866	15 709	18 496
Financial assets	219 105	209 176	168 703	162 524	189 128	229 773	270 194	283 802
Currency and deposits	11 626	11 960	13 029	15 815	18 198	14 232	18 131	16 550
Debt securities	142 323	126 283	98 371	94 247	102 172	129 881	136 471	138 511
Loans	9 648	2 666	2 925	1 347	749	232	168	442
Equity and investment fund shares	55 045	67 905	54 043	50 665	67 125	84 163	114 038	126 692
Equity	54 523	57 128	44 935	43 478	51 060	61 554	86 607	97 105
Investment fund shares	523	10 778	9 108	7 187	16 065	22 609	27 431	29 587
Money market fund shares	..	..	..	..	..	..	..	..
Non-Money market fund shares	..	..	..	..	..	..	..	..
Insurance pension and standardised guarantees	0	0	0	0	0	0	0	0
Financial derivatives and employee stock options	464	361	335	449	884	1 266	1 385	1 606
Other accounts receivable	0	0	0	0	0	0	0	0
Financial liabilities	223 377	203 473	166 565	164 285	184 840	222 907	254 485	265 306
Debt securities	0	0	0	0	0	0	0	0
Short-term debt securities	0	0	0	0	0	0	0	0
Long-term debt securities	0	0	0	0	0	0	0	0
Loans	0	0	0	0	0	0	0	0
Short-term loans	0	0	0	0	0	0	0	0
Long-term loans	0	0	0	0	0	0	0	0
Equity and investment fund shares	223 377	203 473	166 565	164 285	184 840	222 907	254 485	265 306
Insurance pension and standardised guarantees	0	0	0	0	0	0	0	0
Financial derivatives and employee stock options	0	0	0	0	0	0	0	0
Other accounts payable	0	0	0	0	0	0	0	0
Non-financial assets	..	..	..	..	..	..	..	..

Note: Detailed metadata at: http://metalinks.oecd.org/instinv/20170920/75e8

Table 3. Financial assets and liabilities of insurance corporations and pension funds

Million EUR

	2009	2010	2011	2012	2013	2014	2015	2016
Insurance corporations and pension funds								
Financial net worth	-38 700	-78 983	-82 626	-51 253	-50 707	-28 556	-1 637	-8 305
Financial assets	559 538	543 486	534 948	588 660	643 475	740 319	837 910	898 604
Currency and deposits	18 485	17 584	21 242	27 781	25 655	22 987	29 038	24 930
Debt securities	365 238	356 160	351 523	392 597	430 890	500 873	553 876	574 678
Loans	13 650	13 567	11 412	10 701	9 115	9 002	8 304	9 084
Equity and investment fund shares	158 102	152 728	146 904	153 467	173 493	203 291	241 722	284 840
Equity	85 872	72 631	66 320	65 095	75 028	77 653	81 956	101 505
Investment fund shares	72 230	80 097	80 584	88 372	98 465	125 638	159 766	183 335
Money market fund shares	559	403	292	127	180	160	331	175
Non-Money market fund shares	71 671	79 694	80 292	88 245	98 285	125 477	159 435	183 160
Insurance pension and standardised guarantees	2 148	2 153	2 146	2 122	1 973	1 533	2 555	2 383
Financial derivatives and employee stock options	1 689	1 085	1 567	1 391	1 321	653	477	476
Other accounts receivable	226	208	154	601	1 028	1 980	1 938	2 214
Financial liabilities	598 239	622 469	617 574	639 913	694 182	768 874	839 547	906 910
Debt securities	7 904	6 914	6 334	9 380	9 203	14 118	15 045	16 068
Short-term debt securities	0	0	0	0	0	0	0	0
Long-term debt securities	7 904	6 914	6 334	9 380	9 203	14 118	15 045	16 068
Loans	17 402	15 852	14 080	13 502	12 680	11 149	11 781	11 762
Short-term loans	444	403	622	154	5 644	629	512	1 474
Long-term loans	16 958	15 449	13 458	13 349	7 036	10 520	11 270	10 288
Equity and investment fund shares	59 415	46 770	39 538	41 082	60 330	60 520	69 827	80 920
Insurance pension and standardised guarantees	510 644	550 216	554 283	572 492	608 065	678 910	739 739	795 317
Financial derivatives and employee stock options	1 192	1 039	1 645	1 803	1 350	1 514	645	249
Other accounts payable	1 681	1 678	1 695	1 653	2 554	2 663	2 509	2 594
Non-financial assets	..	..	..	..	..	..	..	..
Insurance corporations								
Financial net worth	-14 764	-53 221	-53 688	-43 593	-39 999	-22 390	477	-923
Financial assets	533 622	512 825	503 318	526 642	577 360	660 504	751 774	811 190
Currency and deposits	15 369	13 037	17 710	24 126	22 254	19 099	24 750	19 304
Debt securities	355 269	345 598	339 906	353 113	388 045	450 553	499 663	523 328
Loans	13 650	13 567	11 412	10 701	9 115	9 002	8 304	9 084
Equity and investment fund shares	145 271	137 176	130 423	134 588	153 624	177 684	214 086	254 402
Equity	79 586	65 353	59 279	55 217	64 907	63 077	66 235	84 822
Investment fund shares	65 685	71 823	71 144	79 371	88 717	114 607	147 851	169 580
Money market fund shares	512	368	265	116	164	147	306	162
Non-Money market fund shares	65 173	71 455	70 879	79 255	88 553	114 460	147 545	169 418
Insurance pension and standardised guarantees	2 148	2 153	2 146	2 122	1 973	1 533	2 555	2 383
Financial derivatives and employee stock options	1 689	1 085	1 567	1 391	1 321	653	477	476
Other accounts receivable	226	208	154	601	1 028	1 980	1 938	2 214
Financial liabilities	548 387	566 046	557 006	570 235	617 359	682 894	751 297	812 114
Debt securities	7 904	6 914	6 334	9 380	9 203	14 118	15 045	16 068
Short-term debt securities	0	0	0	0	0	0	0	0
Long-term debt securities	7 904	6 914	6 334	9 380	9 203	14 118	15 045	16 068
Loans	17 399	15 847	14 072	13 477	12 677	11 145	11 779	11 745
Short-term loans	443	399	614	129	5 642	626	510	1 458
Long-term loans	16 956	15 448	13 458	13 348	7 035	10 519	11 269	10 287
Equity and investment fund shares	59 415	46 770	39 538	41 082	60 330	60 520	69 827	80 920
Insurance pension and standardised guarantees	460 795	493 798	493 723	502 839	531 244	592 933	651 491	700 538
Financial derivatives and employee stock options	1 192	1 039	1 645	1 803	1 350	1 514	645	249
Other accounts payable	1 681	1 678	1 695	1 653	2 554	2 663	2 509	2 594
Non-financial assets	..	..	..	..	..	..	..	..
Pension funds								
Financial net worth	-23 936	-25 762	-28 938	-7 660	-10 708	-6 165	-2 114	-7 382
Financial assets	25 916	30 661	31 630	62 018	66 116	79 815	86 137	87 414
Currency and deposits	3 116	4 547	3 532	3 655	3 401	3 888	4 287	5 626
Debt securities	9 969	10 562	11 616	39 483	42 845	50 320	54 213	51 350
Loans	0	0	0	0	0	0	0	0
Equity and investment fund shares	12 831	15 552	16 481	18 879	19 869	25 607	27 636	30 438
Equity	6 286	7 278	7 041	9 878	10 121	14 576	15 721	16 683
Investment fund shares	6 545	8 274	9 440	9 001	9 748	11 031	11 915	13 755
Money market fund shares	47	35	27	11	16	13	25	13
Non-Money market fund shares	6 498	8 239	9 413	8 990	9 732	11 017	11 890	13 742
Insurance pension and standardised guarantees	0	0	0	0	0	0	0	0
Financial derivatives and employee stock options	0	0	0	0	0	0	0	0
Other accounts receivable	0	0	0	0	0	0	0	0
Financial liabilities	49 852	56 423	60 568	69 678	76 823	85 981	88 250	94 796
Debt securities	0	0	0	0	0	0	0	0
Short-term debt securities	0	0	0	0	0	0	0	0
Long-term debt securities	0	0	0	0	0	0	0	0
Loans	3	5	8	25	2	4	2	17
Short-term loans	1	4	8	24	2	3	2	16
Long-term loans	2	1	1	0	1	0	1	1
Equity and investment fund shares	0	0	0	0	0	0	0	0
Insurance pension and standardised guarantees	49 849	56 418	60 560	69 653	76 821	85 977	88 248	94 779
Financial derivatives and employee stock options	0	0	0	0	0	0	0	0
Other accounts payable	0	0	0	0	0	0	0	0
Non-financial assets	..	..	..	..	..	..	..	..

Note: Detailed metadata at: http://metalinks.oecd.org/instinv/20170920/75e8

Table 4. Portfolio composition by type of investor

As percentage of financial assets and of financial liabilities

Per cent

	2009	2010	2011	2012	2013	2014	2015	2016
Investment funds								
Financial assets	100.0	100.0	100.0	100.0	100.0	100.0	100.0	100.0
Currency and deposits	..	..	..	..	..	..	..	..
Debt securities	64.5	60.1	58.0	57.5	53.6	53.4	47.8	45.7
Loans	4.4	1.3	1.7	0.8	0.4	0.1	0.1	0.1
Equity and investment fund shares	25.7	32.8	32.4	31.8	36.0	38.6	43.8	46.4
Insurance pension and standardised guarantee schemes	0.0	0.0	0.0	0.0	0.0	0.0	0.0	0.0
Financial derivatives and employee stock options	0.2	0.2	0.2	0.3	0.5	0.5	0.5	0.5
Other accounts receivable	0.0	0.0	0.0	0.0	0.0	0.0	0.0	0.0
Financial liabilities	100.0	100.0	100.0	100.0	100.0	100.0	100.0	100.0
Currency and deposits	0.0	0.0	0.0	0.0	0.0	0.0	0.0	0.0
Debt securities	0.0	0.0	0.0	0.0	0.0	0.0	0.0	0.0
Loans	0.0	0.0	0.0	0.0	0.0	0.0	0.0	0.0
Equity and investment fund shares	100.0	100.0	100.0	100.0	100.0	100.0	100.0	100.0
Insurance pension and standardised guarantee schemes	0.0	0.0	0.0	0.0	0.0	0.0	0.0	0.0
Financial derivatives and employee stock options	0.0	0.0	0.0	0.0	0.0	0.0	0.0	0.0
Other accounts receivable	0.0	0.0	0.0	0.0	0.0	0.0	0.0	0.0
Insurance corporations								
Financial assets	100.0	100.0	100.0	100.0	100.0	100.0	100.0	100.0
Currency and deposits	2.9	2.5	3.5	4.6	3.9	2.9	3.3	2.4
Debt securities	66.6	67.4	67.5	67.0	67.2	68.2	66.5	64.5
Loans	2.6	2.6	2.3	2.0	1.6	1.4	1.1	1.1
Equity and investment fund shares	27.2	26.7	25.9	25.6	26.6	26.9	28.5	31.4
Insurance pension and standardised guarantee schemes	0.4	0.4	0.4	0.4	0.3	0.2	0.3	0.3
Financial derivatives and employee stock options	0.3	0.2	0.3	0.3	0.2	0.1	0.1	0.1
Other accounts receivable	0.0	0.0	0.0	0.1	0.2	0.3	0.3	0.3
Financial liabilities	100.0	100.0	100.0	100.0	100.0	100.0	100.0	100.0
Currency and deposits	0.0	0.0	0.0	0.0	0.0	0.0	0.0	0.0
Debt securities	1.4	1.2	1.1	1.6	1.5	2.1	2.0	2.0
Loans	3.2	2.8	2.5	2.4	2.1	1.6	1.6	1.4
Equity and investment fund shares	10.8	8.3	7.1	7.2	9.8	8.9	9.3	10.0
Insurance pension and standardised guarantee schemes	84.0	87.2	88.6	88.2	86.1	86.8	86.7	86.3
Financial derivatives and employee stock options	0.2	0.2	0.3	0.3	0.2	0.2	0.1	0.0
Other accounts receivable	0.3	0.3	0.3	0.3	0.4	0.4	0.3	0.3
Pension funds								
Financial assets	100.0	100.0	100.0	100.0	100.0	100.0	100.0	100.0
Currency and deposits	12.0	14.8	11.2	5.9	5.1	4.9	5.0	6.4
Debt securities	38.5	34.4	36.7	63.7	64.8	63.0	62.9	58.7
Loans	0.0	0.0	0.0	0.0	0.0	0.0	0.0	0.0
Equity and investment fund shares	49.5	50.7	52.1	30.4	30.1	32.1	32.1	34.8
Insurance pension and standardised guarantee schemes	0.0	0.0	0.0	0.0	0.0	0.0	0.0	0.0
Financial derivatives and employee stock options	0.0	0.0	0.0	0.0	0.0	0.0	0.0	0.0
Other accounts receivable	0.0	0.0	0.0	0.0	0.0	0.0	0.0	0.0
Financial liabilities	100.0	100.0	100.0	100.0	100.0	100.0	100.0	100.0
Currency and deposits	0.0	0.0	0.0	0.0	0.0	0.0	0.0	0.0
Debt securities	0.0	0.0	0.0	0.0	0.0	0.0	0.0	0.0
Loans	0.0	0.0	0.0	0.0	0.0	0.0	0.0	0.0
Equity and investment fund shares	0.0	0.0	0.0	0.0	0.0	0.0	0.0	0.0
Insurance pension and standardised guarantee schemes	100.0	100.0	100.0	100.0	100.0	100.0	100.0	100.0
Financial derivatives and employee stock options	0.0	0.0	0.0	0.0	0.0	0.0	0.0	0.0
Other accounts receivable	0.0	0.0	0.0	0.0	0.0	0.0	0.0	0.0

Note: Detailed metadata at: http://metalinks.oecd.org/instinv/20170920/a49a

JAPAN

Table 1. Financial assets and liabilities of institutional investors, 2016

Billion JPY

	Investment funds				
		Non-money market funds			Money market funds
	Total	Total	Open-end non-money market funds	Closed-end non-money market funds	Total
Financial assets	182 476	169 569	..	..	12 907
Currency and deposits	8 917	2 196	..	..	6 722
Debt securities	19 349	13 350	..	..	5 999
Debt securities, short term	..	..	..	..	..
Debt securities, long term	..	..	..	..	..
Debt securities issued by residents	19 349	13 350	..	..	5 999
Debt securities issued by non-residents	..	..	..	..	..
Loans	9 507	9 329	..	..	178
Loans, short-term	..	..	..	..	..
Loans, long-term	..	..	..	..	..
Loans granted to residents	..	..	..	..	..
Loans granted to non-residents	..	..	..	..	..
Equity and investment fund shares/units	40 291	40 291	..	..	0
Equity and investment fund shares issued/units by residents	40 291	40 291	..	..	0
Equity and investment fund shares/units issued by non residents	..	..	..	..	..
Other accounts receivable	103 911	103 902	..	..	9

	Investment funds				
		Non-money market funds			Money market funds
	Total	Total	Open-end non-money market funds	Closed-end non-money market funds	Total
Financial liabilities	182 476	169 570	..	..	12 907
Currency and deposits	0	0	..	..	0
Debt securities	0	0	..	..	0
Debt securities, short term	..	..	..	..	..
Debt securities, long term	..	..	..	..	..
Loans	0	0	..	..	0
Loans, short-term	..	..	..	..	..
Loans, long-term	..	..	..	..	..
Equity and investment fund shares/units	170 738	157 975	..	..	12 763
Insurance pension and standardised guaratees	0	0	..	..	0
Financial derivatives and employee stock options	873	873	..	..	0
Other accounts payable	10 866	10 722	..	..	144

	Insurance corporations and pension funds				
		Insurance corporations			Pension funds
	Total	Total	Life insurance corporations	Non-life insurance corporations	Total
Financial assets	641 708	482 085	435 569	46 516	159 623
Currency and deposits	29 250	18 677	7 189	11 488	10 573
Debt securities	309 909	269 274	257 123	12 151	40 635
Debt securities, short-term	..	..	..	..	..
Debt securities, long term	..	..	..	..	..
Debt securities issued by residents	309 909	269 274	257 123	12 151	40 635
Debt securities issued by non-residents	..	..	..	..	..
Loans	47 661	42 705	40 214	2 492	4 956
Loans, short-term	..	..	..	..	..
Loans, long-term	..	..	..	..	..
Loans granted to residents	..	..	..	..	..
Loans granted to non-residents	..	..	..	..	..
Equity and investment fund shares/units	67 401	43 232	35 831	7 402	24 168
Equity and investment fund shares/units issued by residents	67 401	43 232	35 831	7 402	24 168
Equity and investment fund shares/units issued by non residents	..	..	..	..	..
Other accounts receivable	149 296	104 244	92 890	11 354	45 052

	Insurance corporations and pension funds				
		Insurance corporations			Pension funds
	Total	Total	Life insurance corporations	Non-life insurance corporations	Total
Financial liabilities	576 990	419 308	383 003	36 305	157 682
Currency and deposits	0	0	0	0	0
Debt securities	3 770	3 339	2 546	793	431
Debt securities, short term	..	..	..	..	..
Debt securities, long term	..	..	..	..	..
Loans	15 552	15 459	13 973	1 487	93
Loans, short-term	..	..	..	..	..
Loans, long-term	..	..	..	..	..
Equity and investment fund shares/units	20 079	20 063	7 806	12 257	16
Insurance pension and standardised guarantees	524 979	370 355	351 974	18 381	154 624
Financial derivatives and employee stock options	1 973	917	816	101	1 056
Other accounts payable	10 637	9 174	5 888	3 286	1 463

Note: Detailed metadata at: http://metalinks.oecd.org/instinv/20170920/75e8

Table 2. Financial assets and liabilities of investment funds

Billion JPY

	2009	2010	2011	2012	2013	2014	2015	2016
Investment funds								
Financial net worth	0	-65	0	0	0	0	0	0
Financial assets	93 953	98 618	90 631	102 456	131 673	151 055	173 164	182 476
Currency and deposits	577	588	481	630	620	841	828	8 917
Debt securities	13 656	14 443	13 752	14 242	18 219	21 226	21 870	19 349
Loans	4 199	4 155	4 587	5 467	7 625	8 608	13 389	9 507
Equity and investment fund shares	17 798	17 560	14 975	17 796	27 284	28 929	38 358	40 291
Equity	14 695	14 712	12 695	15 103	24 124	24 849	33 409	35 271
Investment fund shares	3 103	2 849	2 281	2 693	3 160	4 080	4 949	5 020
Money market fund shares	..	..	..	..	..	..	..	..
Non-Money market fund shares	..	..	..	..	..	..	..	..
Insurance pension and standardised guarantees	0	0	0	0	0	0	0	0
Financial derivatives and employee stock options	191	170	139	260	350	422	478	502
Other accounts receivable	57 533	61 702	56 697	64 061	77 575	91 029	98 241	103 911
Financial liabilities	93 953	98 683	90 631	102 457	131 674	151 055	173 164	182 476
Debt securities	0	0	0	0	0	0	0	0
Short-term debt securities	..	..	..	..	..	..	..	..
Long-term debt securities	..	..	..	..	..	..	..	..
Loans	0	0	0	0	0	0	0	0
Short-term loans	..	..	..	..	..	..	..	..
Long-term loans	..	..	..	..	..	..	..	..
Equity and investment fund shares	91 099	94 407	85 930	95 944	122 003	140 435	159 772	170 738
Insurance pension and standardised guarantees	0	0	0	0	0	0	0	0
Financial derivatives and employee stock options	797	760	627	631	631	689	711	873
Other accounts payable	2 057	3 516	4 074	5 882	9 040	9 931	12 682	10 866
Non-financial assets	..	..	..	..	..	..	..	..
Money market funds								
Financial net worth	0	0	0	0	0	0	0	0
Financial assets	8 543	8 639	8 075	8 610	14 237	13 888	13 541	12 907
Currency and deposits	25	14	32	15	13	0	0	6 722
Debt securities	6 562	6 933	6 002	6 628	9 498	9 946	8 243	5 999
Loans	1 424	1 262	1 423	1 454	2 587	2 522	3 997	178
Equity and investment fund shares	0	0	0	0	0	0	0	0
Equity	0	0	0	0	0	0	0	0
Investment fund shares	0	0	0	0	0	0	0	0
Money market fund shares	..	..	..	..	..	..	..	..
Non-Money market fund shares	..	..	..	..	..	..	..	..
Insurance pension and standardised guarantees	0	0	0	0	0	0	0	0
Financial derivatives and employee stock options	0	0	0	0	0	0	0	0
Other accounts receivable	533	430	618	514	2 138	1 420	1 301	9
Financial liabilities	8 543	8 639	8 075	8 610	14 237	13 888	13 541	12 907
Debt securities	0	0	0	0	0	0	0	0
Short-term debt securities	..	..	..	..	..	..	..	..
Long-term debt securities	..	..	..	..	..	..	..	..
Loans	0	0	0	0	0	0	0	0
Short-term loans	..	..	..	..	..	..	..	..
Long-term loans	..	..	..	..	..	..	..	..
Equity and investment fund shares	8 207	8 241	7 624	8 254	13 105	13 100	12 838	12 763
Insurance pension and standardised guarantees	0	0	0	0	0	0	0	0
Financial derivatives and employee stock options	0	0	0	0	0	0	0	0
Other accounts payable	336	398	451	357	1 132	788	703	144
Non-financial assets	..	..	..	..	..	..	..	..
Non-money market funds								
Financial net worth	0	-65	0	0	0	0	0	0
Financial assets	85 411	89 979	82 556	93 846	117 437	137 167	159 623	169 569
Currency and deposits	552	574	450	615	608	841	828	2 196
Debt securities	7 094	7 510	7 750	7 614	8 721	11 280	13 626	13 350
Loans	2 775	2 892	3 164	4 014	5 038	6 086	9 393	9 329
Equity and investment fund shares	17 798	17 560	14 975	17 796	27 284	28 929	38 358	40 291
Equity	14 695	14 712	12 695	15 103	24 124	24 849	33 409	35 271
Investment fund shares	3 103	2 849	2 281	2 693	3 160	4 080	4 949	5 020
Money market fund shares	..	..	..	..	..	..	..	..
Non-Money market fund shares	..	..	..	..	..	..	..	..
Insurance pension and standardised guarantees	0	0	0	0	0	0	0	0
Financial derivatives and employee stock options	191	170	139	260	350	422	478	502
Other accounts receivable	57 001	61 273	56 078	63 548	75 437	89 609	96 940	103 902
Financial liabilities	85 411	90 044	82 556	93 846	117 437	137 167	159 623	169 570
Debt securities	0	0	0	0	0	0	0	0
Short-term debt securities	..	..	..	..	..	..	..	..
Long-term debt securities	..	..	..	..	..	..	..	..
Loans	0	0	0	0	0	0	0	0
Short-term loans	..	..	..	..	..	..	..	..
Long-term loans	..	..	..	..	..	..	..	..
Equity and investment fund shares	82 892	86 166	78 307	87 690	108 898	127 335	146 934	157 975
Insurance pension and standardised guarantees	0	0	0	0	0	0	0	0
Financial derivatives and employee stock options	797	760	627	631	631	689	711	873
Other accounts payable	1 721	3 118	3 623	5 525	7 909	9 143	11 979	10 722
Non-financial assets	..	..	..	..	..	..	..	..
Open-end non-money market funds								
Financial net worth	..	..	..	..	..	..	..	..
Financial assets	..	..	..	..	..	..	..	..

Table 2. Financial assets and liabilities of investment funds *(cont.)*

Billion JPY

	2009	2010	2011	2012	2013	2014	2015	2016
Currency and deposits	..	..	..	..	..	..	..	..
Debt securities	..	..	..	..	..	..	..	..
Loans	..	..	..	..	..	..	..	..
Equity and investment fund shares	..	..	..	..	..	..	..	..
Equity	..	..	..	..	..	..	..	..
Investment fund shares	..	..	..	..	..	..	..	..
Money market fund shares	..	..	..	..	..	..	..	..
Non-Money market fund shares	..	..	..	..	..	..	..	..
Insurance pension and standardised guarantees	..	..	..	..	..	..	..	..
Financial derivatives and employee stock options	..	..	..	..	..	..	..	..
Other accounts receivable	..	..	..	..	..	..	..	..
Financial liabilities	..	..	..	..	..	..	..	..
Debt securities	..	..	..	..	..	..	..	..
Short-term debt securities	..	..	..	..	..	..	..	..
Long-term debt securities	..	..	..	..	..	..	..	..
Loans	..	..	..	..	..	..	..	..
Short-term loans	..	..	..	..	..	..	..	..
Long-term loans	..	..	..	..	..	..	..	..
Equity and investment fund shares	..	..	..	..	..	..	..	..
Insurance pension and standardised guarantees	..	..	..	..	..	..	..	..
Financial derivatives and employee stock options	..	..	..	..	..	..	..	..
Other accounts payable	..	..	..	..	..	..	..	..
Non-financial assets	..	..	..	..	..	..	..	..
Open-end investment funds								
Financial net worth	..	..	..	..	..	..	..	..
Financial assets	..	..	..	..	..	..	..	..
Currency and deposits	..	..	..	..	..	..	..	..
Debt securities	..	..	..	..	..	..	..	..
Loans	..	..	..	..	..	..	..	..
Equity and investment fund shares	..	..	..	..	..	..	..	..
Equity	..	..	..	..	..	..	..	..
Investment fund shares	..	..	..	..	..	..	..	..
Money market fund shares	..	..	..	..	..	..	..	..
Non-Money market fund shares	..	..	..	..	..	..	..	..
Insurance pension and standardised guarantees	..	..	..	..	..	..	..	..
Financial derivatives and employee stock options	..	..	..	..	..	..	..	..
Other accounts receivable	..	..	..	..	..	..	..	..
Financial liabilities	..	..	..	..	..	..	..	..
Debt securities	..	..	..	..	..	..	..	..
Short-term debt securities	..	..	..	..	..	..	..	..
Long-term debt securities	..	..	..	..	..	..	..	..
Loans	..	..	..	..	..	..	..	..
Short-term loans	..	..	..	..	..	..	..	..
Long-term loans	..	..	..	..	..	..	..	..
Equity and investment fund shares	..	..	..	..	..	..	..	..
Insurance pension and standardised guarantees	..	..	..	..	..	..	..	..
Financial derivatives and employee stock options	..	..	..	..	..	..	..	..
Other accounts payable	..	..	..	..	..	..	..	..
Non-financial assets	..	..	..	..	..	..	..	..

Note: Detailed metadata at: http://metalinks.oecd.org/instinv/20170920/75e8

Table 3. Financial assets and liabilities of insurance corporations and pension funds

Billion JPY

	2009	2010	2011	2012	2013	2014	2015	2016
Insurance corporations and pension funds								
Financial net worth	19 620	23 525	24 225	27 352	42 730	58 234	58 677	64 718
Financial assets	517 194	526 620	528 208	553 378	589 151	618 579	626 170	641 708
Currency and deposits	16 049	16 384	18 428	18 250	22 499	24 283	25 683	29 250
Debt securities	249 184	261 436	271 416	283 286	295 883	306 350	302 577	309 909
Loans	60 562	56 915	55 105	52 927	52 066	53 054	53 607	47 661
Equity and investment fund shares	59 467	58 353	49 027	53 401	68 017	68 300	69 972	67 401
Equity	37 561	35 880	28 346	30 533	41 314	41 636	43 733	40 302
Investment fund shares	21 906	22 473	20 681	22 867	26 703	26 664	26 240	27 098
Money market fund shares	..	..	..	..	..	..	..	..
Non-Money market fund shares	..	..	..	..	..	..	..	..
Insurance pension and standardised guarantees	43 649	42 260	47 312	43 853	28 152	28 200	31 097	34 663
Financial derivatives and employee stock options	1 235	1 228	1 766	2 065	1 110	1 596	1 946	3 529
Other accounts receivable	87 048	90 045	85 155	99 599	121 425	136 795	141 288	149 296
Financial liabilities	497 575	503 095	503 982	526 026	546 421	560 345	567 493	576 990
Debt securities	395	350	1 184	1 650	1 993	2 163	2 413	3 770
Short-term debt securities	..	..	..	..	..	..	..	..
Long-term debt securities	..	..	..	..	..	..	..	..
Loans	7 463	8 561	7 189	12 677	14 835	14 932	13 583	15 552
Short-term loans	..	..	..	..	..	..	..	..
Long-term loans	..	..	..	..	..	..	..	..
Equity and investment fund shares	11 585	13 571	11 646	13 382	17 352	18 274	20 853	20 079
Insurance pension and standardised guarantees	470 578	471 593	474 982	488 738	500 048	512 283	518 841	524 979
Financial derivatives and employee stock options	640	853	849	1 399	1 741	3 358	2 270	1 973
Other accounts payable	6 912	8 168	8 132	8 181	10 452	9 334	9 534	10 637
Non-financial assets	..	..	..	..	..	..	..	..
Insurance corporations								
Financial net worth	20 544	24 710	25 221	28 026	41 790	56 904	57 074	62 777
Financial assets	373 826	384 752	385 953	407 139	439 171	460 177	465 551	482 085
Currency and deposits	9 344	10 288	11 457	10 954	13 877	14 955	15 314	18 677
Debt securities	212 678	224 103	234 176	245 357	253 667	262 835	260 388	269 274
Loans	57 976	54 409	51 600	49 428	47 902	48 180	48 264	42 705
Equity and investment fund shares	39 034	37 620	31 729	34 156	42 428	42 971	43 878	43 232
Equity	23 726	22 427	17 934	18 865	25 939	27 759	29 700	28 209
Investment fund shares	15 308	15 193	13 795	15 291	16 489	15 211	14 178	15 023
Money market fund shares	..	..	..	..	..	..	..	..
Non-Money market fund shares	..	..	..	..	..	..	..	..
Insurance pension and standardised guarantees	0	1 440	1 811	1 727	1 623	1 371	1 480	1 350
Financial derivatives and employee stock options	1 013	947	1 268	1 462	544	540	1 029	2 603
Other accounts receivable	53 781	55 947	53 915	64 055	79 130	89 325	95 198	104 244
Financial liabilities	353 282	360 042	360 732	379 114	397 381	403 273	408 477	419 308
Debt securities	395	350	514	980	1 386	1 614	1 928	3 339
Short-term debt securities	..	..	..	..	..	..	..	..
Long-term debt securities	..	..	..	..	..	..	..	..
Loans	7 463	8 561	7 087	12 575	14 747	14 843	13 493	15 459
Short-term loans	..	..	..	..	..	..	..	..
Long-term loans	..	..	..	..	..	..	..	..
Equity and investment fund shares	11 570	13 555	11 630	13 366	17 337	18 258	20 838	20 063
Insurance pension and standardised guarantees	328 351	330 453	334 505	344 559	353 754	358 049	362 973	370 355
Financial derivatives and employee stock options	328	483	277	721	1 080	2 131	1 198	917
Other accounts payable	5 174	6 640	6 718	6 914	9 077	8 378	8 047	9 174
Non-financial assets	..	..	..	..	..	..	..	..
Pension funds								
Financial net worth	-924	-1 186	-996	-673	939	1 330	1 603	1 941
Financial assets	143 369	141 868	142 255	146 239	149 980	158 402	160 619	159 623
Currency and deposits	6 705	6 096	6 971	7 295	8 622	9 328	10 369	10 573
Debt securities	36 506	37 333	37 240	37 929	42 216	43 515	42 189	40 635
Loans	2 586	2 506	3 505	3 499	4 164	4 874	5 343	4 956
Equity and investment fund shares	20 433	20 733	17 298	19 245	25 589	25 329	26 094	24 168
Equity	13 834	13 454	10 412	11 668	15 375	13 876	14 033	12 093
Investment fund shares	6 599	7 279	6 886	7 577	10 214	11 453	12 062	12 075
Money market fund shares	..	..	..	..	..	..	..	..
Non-Money market fund shares	..	..	..	..	..	..	..	..
Insurance pension and standardised guarantees	43 649	40 820	45 502	42 125	26 529	26 829	29 617	33 313
Financial derivatives and employee stock options	222	281	499	602	566	1 056	917	926
Other accounts receivable	33 267	34 098	31 240	35 544	42 295	47 471	46 090	45 052
Financial liabilities	144 293	143 053	143 251	146 912	149 040	157 072	159 017	157 682
Debt securities	0	0	670	671	607	549	485	431
Short-term debt securities	..	..	..	..	..	..	..	..
Long-term debt securities	..	..	..	..	..	..	..	..
Loans	0	0	102	102	88	90	90	93
Short-term loans	..	..	..	..	..	..	..	..
Long-term loans	..	..	..	..	..	..	..	..
Equity and investment fund shares	16	16	16	16	16	16	16	16
Insurance pension and standardised guarantees	142 227	141 139	140 477	144 179	146 294	154 234	155 868	154 624
Financial derivatives and employee stock options	312	370	573	678	661	1 227	1 072	1 056
Other accounts payable	1 738	1 528	1 414	1 267	1 376	957	1 487	1 463
Non-financial assets	..	..	..	..	..	..	..	..

Note: Detailed metadata at: http://metalinks.oecd.org/instinv/20170920/75e8

Table 4. Portfolio composition by type of investor

As percentage of financial assets and of financial liabilities

Per cent

	2009	2010	2011	2012	2013	2014	2015	2016
Investment funds								
Financial assets	100.0	100.0	100.0	100.0	100.0	100.0	100.0	100.0
Currency and deposits	0.6	0.6	0.5	0.6	0.5	0.6	0.5	4.9
Debt securities	14.5	14.6	15.2	13.9	13.8	14.1	12.6	10.6
Loans	4.5	4.2	5.1	5.3	5.8	5.7	7.7	5.2
Equity and investment fund shares	18.9	17.8	16.5	17.4	20.7	19.2	22.2	22.1
Insurance pension and standardised guarantee schemes	0.0	0.0	0.0	0.0	0.0	0.0	0.0	0.0
Financial derivatives and employee stock options	0.2	0.2	0.2	0.3	0.3	0.3	0.3	0.3
Other accounts receivable	61.2	62.6	62.6	62.5	58.9	60.3	56.7	56.9
Financial liabilities	100.0	100.0	100.0	100.0	100.0	100.0	100.0	100.0
Currency and deposits	0.0	0.0	0.0	0.0	0.0	0.0	0.0	0.0
Debt securities	0.0	0.0	0.0	0.0	0.0	0.0	0.0	0.0
Loans	0.0	0.0	0.0	0.0	0.0	0.0	0.0	0.0
Equity and investment fund shares	97.0	95.7	94.8	93.6	92.7	93.0	92.3	93.6
Insurance pension and standardised guarantee schemes	0.0	0.0	0.0	0.0	0.0	0.0	0.0	0.0
Financial derivatives and employee stock options	0.8	0.8	0.7	0.6	0.5	0.5	0.4	0.5
Other accounts receivable	2.2	3.6	4.5	5.7	6.9	6.6	7.3	6.0
Insurance corporations								
Financial assets	100.0	100.0	100.0	100.0	100.0	100.0	100.0	100.0
Currency and deposits	2.5	2.7	3.0	2.7	3.2	3.2	3.3	3.9
Debt securities	56.9	58.2	60.7	60.3	57.8	57.1	55.9	55.9
Loans	15.5	14.1	13.4	12.1	10.9	10.5	10.4	8.9
Equity and investment fund shares	10.4	9.8	8.2	8.4	9.7	9.3	9.4	9.0
Insurance pension and standardised guarantee schemes	0.0	0.4	0.5	0.4	0.4	0.3	0.3	0.3
Financial derivatives and employee stock options	0.3	0.2	0.3	0.4	0.1	0.1	0.2	0.5
Other accounts receivable	14.4	14.5	14.0	15.7	18.0	19.4	20.4	21.6
Financial liabilities	100.0	100.0	100.0	100.0	100.0	100.0	100.0	100.0
Currency and deposits	0.0	0.0	0.0	0.0	0.0	0.0	0.0	0.0
Debt securities	0.1	0.1	0.1	0.3	0.3	0.4	0.5	0.8
Loans	2.1	2.4	2.0	3.3	3.7	3.7	3.3	3.7
Equity and investment fund shares	3.3	3.8	3.2	3.5	4.4	4.5	5.1	4.8
Insurance pension and standardised guarantee schemes	92.9	91.8	92.7	90.9	89.0	88.8	88.9	88.3
Financial derivatives and employee stock options	0.1	0.1	0.1	0.2	0.3	0.5	0.3	0.2
Other accounts receivable	1.5	1.8	1.9	1.8	2.3	2.1	2.0	2.2
Pension funds								
Financial assets	100.0	100.0	100.0	100.0	100.0	100.0	100.0	100.0
Currency and deposits	4.7	4.3	4.9	5.0	5.7	5.9	6.5	6.6
Debt securities	25.5	26.3	26.2	25.9	28.1	27.5	26.3	25.5
Loans	1.8	1.8	2.5	2.4	2.8	3.1	3.3	3.1
Equity and investment fund shares	14.3	14.6	12.2	13.2	17.1	16.0	16.2	15.1
Insurance pension and standardised guarantee schemes	30.4	28.8	32.0	28.8	17.7	16.9	18.4	20.9
Financial derivatives and employee stock options	0.2	0.2	0.4	0.4	0.4	0.7	0.6	0.6
Other accounts receivable	23.2	24.0	22.0	24.3	28.2	30.0	28.7	28.2
Financial liabilities	100.0	100.0	100.0	100.0	100.0	100.0	100.0	100.0
Currency and deposits	0.0	0.0	0.0	0.0	0.0	0.0	0.0	0.0
Debt securities	0.0	0.0	0.5	0.5	0.4	0.3	0.3	0.3
Loans	0.0	0.0	0.1	0.1	0.1	0.1	0.1	0.1
Equity and investment fund shares	0.0	0.0	0.0	0.0	0.0	0.0	0.0	0.0
Insurance pension and standardised guarantee schemes	98.6	98.7	98.1	98.1	98.2	98.2	98.0	98.1
Financial derivatives and employee stock options	0.2	0.3	0.4	0.5	0.4	0.8	0.7	0.7
Other accounts receivable	1.2	1.1	1.0	0.9	0.9	0.6	0.9	0.9

Note: Detailed metadata at: http://metalinks.oecd.org/instinv/20170920/a49a

Table 1. Financial assets and liabilities of institutional investors, 2016

Billion KRW

	Total	Investment funds: Non-money market funds: Total	Open-end non-money market funds	Closed-end non-money market funds	Money market funds: Total
Financial assets	486 351	381 575	..	..	104 777
Currency and deposits	40 877	17 064	..	..	23 812
Debt securities	225 724	147 509	..	..	78 215
Debt securities, short term	73 495	13 299	..	..	60 196
Debt securities, long term	152 228	134 210	..	..	18 019
Debt securities issued by residents	210 531	132 316	..	..	78 215
Debt securities issued by non-residents	15 193	15 193	..	..	0
Loans	18 571	17 626	..	..	945
Loans, short-term	4 106	3 161	..	..	945
Loans, long-term	14 465	14 465	..	..	0
Loans granted to residents	..	..	..	..	..
Loans granted to non-residents	..	..	..	..	..
Equity and investment fund shares/units	124 031	122 581	..	..	1 449
Equity and investment fund shares issued/units by residents	80 311	78 861	..	..	1 449
Equity and investment fund shares/units issued by non residents	43 720	43 720	..	..	0
Other accounts receivable	64 836	64 480	..	..	355

	Total	Investment funds: Non-money market funds: Total	Open-end non-money market funds	Closed-end non-money market funds	Money market funds: Total
Financial liabilities	487 906	382 618	..	..	105 288
Currency and deposits	18 088	17 857	..	..	231
Debt securities	242	242	..	..	0
Debt securities, short term	0	0	..	..	0
Debt securities, long term	242	242	..	..	0
Loans	493	493	..	..	0
Loans, short-term	31	31	..	..	0
Loans, long-term	462	462	..	..	0
Equity and investment fund shares/units	460 356	355 361	..	..	104 996
Insurance pension and standardised guaratees	0	0	..	..	0
Financial derivatives and employee stock options	260	260	..	..	0
Other accounts payable	8 467	8 405	..	..	62

	Total	Insurance corporations and pension funds: Insurance corporations: Total	Life insurance corporations	Non-life insurance corporations	Pension funds: Total
Financial assets	1 272 454	1 111 165	806 848	304 317	161 289
Currency and deposits	114 762	46 134	23 786	22 348	68 627
Debt securities	638 091	604 733	494 408	110 325	33 359
Debt securities, short-term	10 654	9 350	5 583	3 767	1 305
Debt securities, long term	627 437	595 383	488 825	106 558	32 054
Debt securities issued by residents	558 334	525 214	431 041	94 173	33 120
Debt securities issued by non-residents	79 758	79 519	63 367	16 152	239
Loans	205 069	192 533	123 720	68 813	12 537
Loans, short-term	20 785	15 542	12 144	3 398	5 243
Loans, long-term	184 285	176 991	111 576	65 414	7 294
Loans granted to residents	..	..	..	..	..
Loans granted to non-residents	..	..	..	..	..
Equity and investment fund shares/units	201 084	187 362	125 497	61 864	13 722
Equity and investment fund shares/units issued by residents	186 315	172 914	113 729	59 185	13 401
Equity and investment fund shares/units issued by non residents	14 769	14 448	11 768	2 680	322
Other accounts receivable	94 544	72 510	38 529	33 981	22 033

	Total	Insurance corporations and pension funds: Insurance corporations: Total	Life insurance corporations	Non-life insurance corporations	Pension funds: Total
Financial liabilities	1 254 118	1 092 155	790 938	301 218	161 963
Currency and deposits	0	0	0	0	0
Debt securities	3 301	3 301	983	2 319	0
Debt securities, short term	700	700	0	700	0
Debt securities, long term	2 601	2 601	983	1 619	0
Loans	206	206	103	103	0
Loans, short-term	0	0	0	0	0
Loans, long-term	206	206	103	103	0
Equity and investment fund shares/units	69 159	69 159	36 652	32 507	0
Insurance pension and standardised guarantees	1 118 216	961 026	712 276	248 750	157 189
Financial derivatives and employee stock options	6 787	6 546	5 301	1 246	241
Other accounts payable	56 450	51 918	35 623	16 294	4 533

Note: Detailed metadata at: http://metalinks.oecd.org/instinv/20170920/75e8

Table 2. Financial assets and liabilities of investment funds

Billion KRW

	2009	2010	2011	2012	2013	2014	2015	2016
Investment funds								
Financial net worth	-5 444	-2 721	-2 144	-1 723	-1 715	-2 711	-2 007	-1 555
Financial assets	325 846	329 561	286 261	316 742	336 290	381 924	426 176	486 351
Currency and deposits	36 214	33 132	27 305	24 937	22 391	30 627	38 934	40 877
Debt securities	107 388	120 925	98 774	113 715	130 179	156 593	182 011	225 724
Loans	18 067	20 733	18 412	23 138	21 280	15 997	17 059	18 571
Equity and investment fund shares	132 223	125 010	109 094	114 341	118 247	116 741	119 276	124 031
Equity	131 097	121 928	107 167	112 499	115 279	114 730	117 865	121 538
Investment fund shares	1 126	3 083	1 927	1 842	2 968	2 012	1 411	2 493
Money market fund shares	98	73	120	204	291	440	350	1 484
Non-Money market fund shares	1 029	3 010	1 807	1 638	2 677	1 572	1 061	1 009
Insurance pension and standardised guarantees	0	0	0	0	0	0	0	0
Financial derivatives and employee stock options	11 114	10 871	10 663	10 774	11 302	11 428	11 426	12 314
Other accounts receivable	20 840	18 891	22 014	29 838	32 892	50 537	57 470	64 836
Financial liabilities	331 290	332 283	288 406	318 465	338 005	384 635	428 184	487 906
Debt securities	0	0	239	282	343	258	257	242
Short-term debt securities	0	0	0	0	0	0	0	0
Long-term debt securities	0	0	239	282	343	258	257	242
Loans	1 810	2 218	2 319	729	549	470	346	493
Short-term loans	27	203	171	214	276	291	216	31
Long-term loans	1 784	2 016	2 148	515	274	179	130	462
Equity and investment fund shares	319 004	318 652	278 824	308 632	329 843	372 366	412 763	460 356
Insurance pension and standardised guarantees	0	0	0	0	0	0	0	0
Financial derivatives and employee stock options	160	1	0	0	0	0	0	260
Other accounts payable	7 031	8 429	4 917	8 163	5 401	7 385	8 876	8 467
Non-financial assets	..	..	..	..	..	..	..	..
Money market funds								
Financial net worth	-3 590	-1 146	-560	-240	-707	-1 091	-334	-512
Financial assets	69 485	67 123	54 077	64 183	66 742	82 422	94 080	104 777
Currency and deposits	23 782	22 768	16 709	17 059	14 159	20 087	24 654	23 812
Debt securities	42 631	40 944	34 371	42 570	48 285	59 874	66 617	78 215
Loans	2 436	2 670	1 636	3 732	2 118	966	2 256	945
Equity and investment fund shares	50	156	169	252	1 430	568	343	1 449
Equity	0	0	0	0	0	0	0	0
Investment fund shares	50	156	169	252	1 430	568	343	1 449
Money market fund shares	50	54	94	185	267	418	343	1 449
Non-Money market fund shares	0	102	75	67	1 163	150	0	0
Insurance pension and standardised guarantees	0	0	0	0	0	0	0	0
Financial derivatives and employee stock options	0	0	0	0	0	0	0	0
Other accounts receivable	586	585	1 192	570	750	929	209	355
Financial liabilities	73 075	68 269	54 637	64 424	67 448	83 514	94 414	105 288
Debt securities	0	0	0	0	0	0	0	0
Short-term debt securities	0	0	0	0	0	0	0	0
Long-term debt securities	0	0	0	0	0	0	0	0
Loans	0	0	0	0	0	0	0	0
Short-term loans	0	0	0	0	0	0	0	0
Long-term loans	0	0	0	0	0	0	0	0
Equity and investment fund shares	72 425	67 669	54 386	63 985	67 089	83 234	94 073	104 996
Insurance pension and standardised guarantees	0	0	0	0	0	0	0	0
Financial derivatives and employee stock options	0	0	0	0	0	0	0	0
Other accounts payable	606	600	251	439	359	280	283	62
Non-financial assets	..	..	..	..	..	..	..	..
Non-money market funds								
Financial net worth	-1 854	-1 575	-1 584	-1 482	-1 008	-1 620	-1 673	-1 043
Financial assets	256 360	262 439	232 185	252 559	269 548	299 501	332 096	381 575
Currency and deposits	12 432	10 364	10 596	7 877	8 231	10 541	14 280	17 064
Debt securities	64 758	79 981	64 403	71 145	81 895	96 720	115 394	147 509
Loans	15 631	18 063	16 776	19 406	19 162	15 031	14 803	17 626
Equity and investment fund shares	132 172	124 855	108 925	114 089	116 816	116 174	118 933	122 581
Equity	131 097	121 928	107 167	112 499	115 279	114 730	117 865	121 538
Investment fund shares	1 076	2 927	1 759	1 591	1 537	1 444	1 068	1 043
Money market fund shares	47	19	27	19	24	22	7	35
Non-Money market fund shares	1 029	2 908	1 732	1 572	1 514	1 422	1 061	1 009
Insurance pension and standardised guarantees	0	0	0	0	0	0	0	0
Financial derivatives and employee stock options	11 114	10 871	10 663	10 774	11 302	11 428	11 426	12 314
Other accounts receivable	20 254	18 306	20 822	29 268	32 143	49 608	57 261	64 480
Financial liabilities	258 215	264 014	233 769	254 041	270 556	301 121	333 769	382 618
Debt securities	0	0	239	282	343	258	257	242
Short-term debt securities	0	0	0	0	0	0	0	0
Long-term debt securities	0	0	239	282	343	258	257	242
Loans	1 810	2 218	2 319	729	549	470	346	493
Short-term loans	27	203	171	214	276	291	216	31
Long-term loans	1 784	2 016	2 148	515	274	179	130	462
Equity and investment fund shares	246 579	250 984	221 437	244 647	262 754	289 132	318 691	355 361
Insurance pension and standardised guarantees	0	0	0	0	0	0	0	0
Financial derivatives and employee stock options	160	1	0	0	0	0	0	260
Other accounts payable	6 426	7 829	4 666	7 724	5 042	7 105	8 594	8 405
Non-financial assets	..	..	..	..	..	..	..	..
Open-end non-money market funds								
Financial net worth	..	..	..	..	..	..	..	..
Financial assets	..	..	..	..	..	..	..	..

Table 2. Financial assets and liabilities of investment funds *(cont.)*

Billion KRW

	2009	2010	2011	2012	2013	2014	2015	2016
Currency and deposits	..	..	..	..	..	..	..	..
Debt securities	..	..	..	..	..	..	..	..
Loans	..	..	..	..	..	..	..	..
Equity and investment fund shares	..	..	..	..	..	..	..	..
Equity	..	..	..	..	..	..	..	..
Investment fund shares	..	..	..	..	..	..	..	..
Money market fund shares	..	..	..	..	..	..	..	..
Non-Money market fund shares	..	..	..	..	..	..	..	..
Insurance pension and standardised guarantees	..	..	..	..	..	..	..	..
Financial derivatives and employee stock options	..	..	..	..	..	..	..	..
Other accounts receivable	..	..	..	..	..	..	..	..
Financial liabilities	..	..	..	..	..	..	..	..
Debt securities	..	..	..	..	..	..	..	..
Short-term debt securities	..	..	..	..	..	..	..	..
Long-term debt securities	..	..	..	..	..	..	..	..
Loans	..	..	..	..	..	..	..	..
Short-term loans	..	..	..	..	..	..	..	..
Long-term loans	..	..	..	..	..	..	..	..
Equity and investment fund shares	..	..	..	..	..	..	..	..
Insurance pension and standardised guarantees	..	..	..	..	..	..	..	..
Financial derivatives and employee stock options	..	..	..	..	..	..	..	..
Other accounts payable	..	..	..	..	..	..	..	..
Non-financial assets	..	..	..	..	..	..	..	..
Open-end investment funds								
Financial net worth	..	..	..	..	..	..	..	..
Financial assets	..	..	..	..	..	..	..	..
Currency and deposits	..	..	..	..	..	..	..	..
Debt securities	..	..	..	..	..	..	..	..
Loans	..	..	..	..	..	..	..	..
Equity and investment fund shares	..	..	..	..	..	..	..	..
Equity	..	..	..	..	..	..	..	..
Investment fund shares	..	..	..	..	..	..	..	..
Money market fund shares	..	..	..	..	..	..	..	..
Non-Money market fund shares	..	..	..	..	..	..	..	..
Insurance pension and standardised guarantees	..	..	..	..	..	..	..	..
Financial derivatives and employee stock options	..	..	..	..	..	..	..	..
Other accounts receivable	..	..	..	..	..	..	..	..
Financial liabilities	..	..	..	..	..	..	..	..
Debt securities	..	..	..	..	..	..	..	..
Short-term debt securities	..	..	..	..	..	..	..	..
Long-term debt securities	..	..	..	..	..	..	..	..
Loans	..	..	..	..	..	..	..	..
Short-term loans	..	..	..	..	..	..	..	..
Long-term loans	..	..	..	..	..	..	..	..
Equity and investment fund shares	..	..	..	..	..	..	..	..
Insurance pension and standardised guarantees	..	..	..	..	..	..	..	..
Financial derivatives and employee stock options	..	..	..	..	..	..	..	..
Other accounts payable	..	..	..	..	..	..	..	..
Non-financial assets	..	..	..	..	..	..	..	..

Note: Detailed metadata at: http://metalinks.oecd.org/instinv/20170920/75e8

Table 3. Financial assets and liabilities of insurance corporations and pension funds

Billion KRW

	2009	2010	2011	2012	2013	2014	2015	2016
Insurance corporations and pension funds								
Financial net worth	1 911	-15 454	-9 119	2 281	-7 160	6 039	200	18 336
Financial assets	549 333	628 681	711 787	834 819	920 938	1 047 690	1 151 196	1 272 454
Currency and deposits	42 806	54 717	67 999	88 807	87 363	106 019	109 622	114 762
Debt securities	251 965	297 930	344 326	397 271	450 172	513 051	578 196	638 091
Loans	103 448	109 298	113 358	129 919	144 703	161 657	181 328	205 069
Equity and investment fund shares	93 663	108 203	110 390	140 967	156 595	172 577	180 170	201 084
Equity	49 065	56 746	56 999	67 072	73 378	79 874	80 409	94 579
Investment fund shares	44 598	51 457	53 391	73 895	83 217	92 703	99 762	106 505
Money market fund shares	6 404	4 893	4 404	8 359	10 217	15 870	15 327	12 337
Non-Money market fund shares	38 194	46 563	48 988	65 535	73 001	76 833	84 434	94 169
Insurance pension and standardised guarantees	116	177	5 234	5 739	7 015	11 261	14 449	18 337
Financial derivatives and employee stock options	840	1 159	609	1 844	2 326	808	666	567
Other accounts receivable	56 496	57 198	63 872	70 272	72 764	82 317	86 765	94 544
Financial liabilities	547 422	644 135	720 906	832 538	928 097	1 041 650	1 150 996	1 254 118
Debt securities	1 078	1 083	1 236	1 660	2 124	2 107	2 730	3 301
Short-term debt securities	669	548	686	611	296	386	370	700
Long-term debt securities	409	535	550	1 049	1 828	1 721	2 360	2 601
Loans	2 089	1 657	1 448	1 345	805	857	792	206
Short-term loans	280	76	247	343	63	9	16	0
Long-term loans	1 809	1 581	1 202	1 003	742	849	776	206
Equity and investment fund shares	31 471	58 791	56 521	62 221	65 835	69 200	71 722	69 159
Insurance pension and standardised guarantees	481 235	548 088	624 517	725 519	820 437	920 289	1 020 415	1 118 216
Financial derivatives and employee stock options	3 688	2 107	2 586	1 348	1 215	2 405	4 042	6 787
Other accounts payable	27 844	32 402	34 599	40 140	37 662	46 792	51 234	56 450
Non-financial assets	..	..	..	..	..	..	..	..
Insurance corporations								
Financial net worth	1 753	-15 562	-9 511	2 618	-6 590	6 459	-21	19 010
Financial assets	511 068	584 595	654 944	764 577	834 616	932 883	1 014 221	1 111 165
Currency and deposits	29 529	35 099	36 934	47 676	40 385	49 670	47 315	46 134
Debt securities	237 521	285 206	332 210	383 966	432 224	490 346	550 551	604 733
Loans	102 103	108 082	113 248	128 313	142 015	156 647	171 971	192 533
Equity and investment fund shares	89 349	104 253	106 331	136 005	150 112	164 439	167 336	187 362
Equity	48 776	56 463	56 721	66 909	73 301	79 755	80 219	94 110
Investment fund shares	40 573	47 790	49 610	69 096	76 811	84 684	87 117	93 252
Money market fund shares	5 319	3 041	4 145	7 919	9 569	15 186	13 487	11 469
Non-Money market fund shares	35 254	44 749	45 465	61 177	67 242	69 498	73 630	81 783
Insurance pension and standardised guarantees	116	177	5 025	5 429	5 831	6 527	6 878	7 342
Financial derivatives and employee stock options	790	1 144	602	1 811	2 288	787	654	551
Other accounts receivable	51 660	50 634	55 595	61 378	61 762	64 467	69 517	72 510
Financial liabilities	509 315	600 157	664 455	761 959	841 206	926 424	1 014 242	1 092 155
Debt securities	1 078	1 083	1 236	1 660	2 124	2 107	2 730	3 301
Short-term debt securities	669	548	686	611	296	386	370	700
Long-term debt securities	409	535	550	1 049	1 828	1 721	2 360	2 601
Loans	2 089	1 657	1 445	1 342	805	857	792	206
Short-term loans	280	76	247	343	63	9	16	0
Long-term loans	1 809	1 581	1 198	999	742	849	776	206
Equity and investment fund shares	31 471	58 791	56 521	62 221	65 835	69 200	71 722	69 159
Insurance pension and standardised guarantees	445 419	506 361	570 438	656 952	735 656	809 993	887 130	961 026
Financial derivatives and employee stock options	3 688	2 104	2 582	1 348	1 210	2 351	3 902	6 546
Other accounts payable	25 553	30 154	32 235	38 131	35 556	41 917	47 907	51 918
Non-financial assets	..	..	..	..	..	..	..	..
Pension funds								
Financial net worth	157	108	392	-337	-570	-419	221	-674
Financial assets	38 265	44 086	56 843	70 242	86 322	114 807	136 974	161 289
Currency and deposits	13 277	19 618	31 064	41 131	46 978	56 349	62 307	68 627
Debt securities	14 444	12 725	12 116	13 305	17 949	22 706	27 645	33 359
Loans	1 345	1 216	1 110	1 606	2 688	5 011	9 357	12 537
Equity and investment fund shares	4 314	3 950	4 060	4 962	6 483	8 138	12 835	13 722
Equity	289	283	279	163	77	119	190	469
Investment fund shares	4 025	3 667	3 781	4 799	6 407	8 019	12 645	13 253
Money market fund shares	1 085	1 853	259	440	648	684	1 840	868
Non-Money market fund shares	2 940	1 814	3 522	4 359	5 759	7 335	10 804	12 386
Insurance pension and standardised guarantees	0	0	209	310	1 184	4 734	7 571	10 995
Financial derivatives and employee stock options	50	15	8	33	38	21	11	16
Other accounts receivable	4 836	6 563	8 277	8 894	11 002	17 849	17 249	22 033
Financial liabilities	38 107	43 978	56 451	70 579	86 892	115 226	136 753	161 963
Debt securities	0	0	0	0	0	0	0	0
Short-term debt securities	0	0	0	0	0	0	0	0
Long-term debt securities	0	0	0	0	0	0	0	0
Loans	0	0	4	4	0	0	0	0
Short-term loans	0	0	0	0	0	0	0	0
Long-term loans	0	0	4	4	0	0	0	0
Equity and investment fund shares	0	0	0	0	0	0	0	0
Insurance pension and standardised guarantees	35 816	41 726	54 080	68 567	84 781	110 296	133 286	157 189
Financial derivatives and employee stock options	0	3	4	0	5	55	140	241
Other accounts payable	2 291	2 249	2 364	2 009	2 106	4 875	3 327	4 533
Non-financial assets	..	..	..	..	..	..	..	..

Note: Detailed metadata at: http://metalinks.oecd.org/instinv/20170920/75e8

Table 4. Portfolio composition by type of investor

As percentage of financial assets and of financial liabilities

Per cent

	2009	2010	2011	2012	2013	2014	2015	2016
Investment funds								
Financial assets	100.0	100.0	100.0	100.0	100.0	100.0	100.0	100.0
Currency and deposits	11.1	10.1	9.5	7.9	6.7	8.0	9.1	8.4
Debt securities	33.0	36.7	34.5	35.9	38.7	41.0	42.7	46.4
Loans	5.5	6.3	6.4	7.3	6.3	4.2	4.0	3.8
Equity and investment fund shares	40.6	37.9	38.1	36.1	35.2	30.6	28.0	25.5
Insurance pension and standardised guarantee schemes	0.0	0.0	0.0	0.0	0.0	0.0	0.0	0.0
Financial derivatives and employee stock options	3.4	3.3	3.7	3.4	3.4	3.0	2.7	2.5
Other accounts receivable	6.4	5.7	7.7	9.4	9.8	13.2	13.5	13.3
Financial liabilities	100.0	100.0	100.0	100.0	100.0	100.0	100.0	100.0
Currency and deposits	1.0	0.9	0.7	0.2	0.6	1.1	1.4	3.7
Debt securities	0.0	0.0	0.1	0.1	0.1	0.1	0.1	0.0
Loans	0.5	0.7	0.8	0.2	0.2	0.1	0.1	0.1
Equity and investment fund shares	96.3	95.9	96.7	96.9	97.6	96.8	96.4	94.4
Insurance pension and standardised guarantee schemes	0.0	0.0	0.0	0.0	0.0	0.0	0.0	0.0
Financial derivatives and employee stock options	0.0	0.0	0.0	0.0	0.0	0.0	0.0	0.1
Other accounts receivable	2.1	2.5	1.7	2.6	1.6	1.9	2.1	1.7
Insurance corporations								
Financial assets	100.0	100.0	100.0	100.0	100.0	100.0	100.0	100.0
Currency and deposits	5.8	6.0	5.6	6.2	4.8	5.3	4.7	4.2
Debt securities	46.5	48.8	50.7	50.2	51.8	52.6	54.3	54.4
Loans	20.0	18.5	18.1	16.8	17.0	16.8	17.0	17.3
Equity and investment fund shares	17.5	17.8	16.2	17.8	18.0	17.6	16.5	16.9
Insurance pension and standardised guarantee schemes	0.0	0.0	0.8	0.7	0.7	0.7	0.7	0.7
Financial derivatives and employee stock options	0.2	0.2	0.1	0.2	0.3	0.1	0.1	0.0
Other accounts receivable	10.1	8.7	8.5	8.0	7.4	6.9	6.9	6.5
Financial liabilities	100.0	100.0	100.0	100.0	100.0	100.0	100.0	100.0
Currency and deposits	0.0	0.0	0.0	0.0	0.0	0.0	0.0	0.0
Debt securities	0.2	0.2	0.2	0.2	0.3	0.2	0.3	0.3
Loans	0.4	0.3	0.2	0.2	0.1	0.1	0.1	0.0
Equity and investment fund shares	6.2	9.8	8.5	8.2	7.8	7.5	7.1	6.3
Insurance pension and standardised guarantee schemes	87.5	84.4	85.9	86.2	87.5	87.4	87.5	88.0
Financial derivatives and employee stock options	0.7	0.4	0.4	0.2	0.1	0.3	0.4	0.6
Other accounts receivable	5.0	5.0	4.9	5.0	4.2	4.5	4.7	4.8
Pension funds								
Financial assets	100.0	100.0	100.0	100.0	100.0	100.0	100.0	100.0
Currency and deposits	34.7	44.5	54.6	58.6	54.4	49.1	45.5	42.5
Debt securities	37.7	28.9	21.3	18.9	20.8	19.8	20.2	20.7
Loans	3.5	2.8	2.0	2.3	3.1	4.4	6.8	7.8
Equity and investment fund shares	11.3	9.0	7.1	7.1	7.5	7.1	9.4	8.5
Insurance pension and standardised guarantee schemes	0.0	0.0	0.4	0.4	1.4	4.1	5.5	6.8
Financial derivatives and employee stock options	0.1	0.0	0.0	0.0	0.0	0.0	0.0	0.0
Other accounts receivable	12.6	14.9	14.6	12.7	12.7	15.5	12.6	13.7
Financial liabilities	100.0	100.0	100.0	100.0	100.0	100.0	100.0	100.0
Currency and deposits	0.0	0.0	0.0	0.0	0.0	0.0	0.0	0.0
Debt securities	0.0	0.0	0.0	0.0	0.0	0.0	0.0	0.0
Loans	0.0	0.0	0.0	0.0	0.0	0.0	0.0	0.0
Equity and investment fund shares	0.0	0.0	0.0	0.0	0.0	0.0	0.0	0.0
Insurance pension and standardised guarantee schemes	94.0	94.9	95.8	97.1	97.6	95.7	97.5	97.1
Financial derivatives and employee stock options	0.0	0.0	0.0	0.0	0.0	0.0	0.1	0.1
Other accounts receivable	6.0	5.1	4.2	2.8	2.4	4.2	2.4	2.8

Note: Detailed metadata at: http://metalinks.oecd.org/instinv/20170920/a49a

Table 1. Financial assets and liabilities of institutional investors, 2016

Million EUR (2014)

	Investment funds				
	Total	Non-money market funds			Money market funds
		Total	Open-end non-money market funds	Closed-end non-money market funds	Total
Financial assets	..	..	..	..	..
Currency and deposits	..	..	..	..	..
Debt securities	..	..	..	..	..
Debt securities, short term	..	..	..	..	..
Debt securities, long term	..	..	..	..	..
Debt securities issued by residents	..	..	..	..	..
Debt securities issued by non-residents	..	..	..	..	..
Loans	..	..	..	..	..
Loans, short-term	..	..	..	..	..
Loans, long-term	..	..	..	..	..
Loans granted to residents	..	..	..	..	..
Loans granted to non-residents	..	..	..	..	..
Equity and investment fund shares/units	..	..	..	..	..
Equity and investment fund shares issued/units by residents	..	..	..	..	..
Equity and investment fund shares/units issued by non residents	..	..	..	..	..
Other accounts receivable	..	..	..	..	..

	Investment funds				
	Total	Non-money market funds			Money market funds
		Total	Open-end non-money market funds	Closed-end non-money market funds	Total
Financial liabilities	..	..	..	..	..
Currency and deposits	..	..	..	..	..
Debt securities	..	..	..	..	..
Debt securities, short term	..	..	..	..	..
Debt securities, long term	..	..	..	..	..
Loans	..	..	..	..	..
Loans, short-term	..	..	..	..	..
Loans, long-term	..	..	..	..	..
Equity and investment fund shares/units	..	..	..	..	..
Insurance pension and standardised guaratees	..	..	..	..	..
Financial derivatives and employee stock options	..	..	..	..	..
Other accounts payable	..	..	..	..	..

	Insurance corporations and pension funds				
	Total	Insurance corporations			Pension funds
		Total	Life insurance corporations	Non-life insurance corporations	Total
Financial assets	..	..	..	..	3 160
Currency and deposits	..	..	..	..	404
Debt securities	..	..	..	..	1 499
Debt securities, short-term	..	..	..	..	0
Debt securities, long term	..	..	..	..	1 499
Debt securities issued by residents	..	..	..	..	627
Debt securities issued by non-residents	..	..	..	..	872
Loans	..	..	..	..	0
Loans, short-term	..	..	..	..	0
Loans, long-term	..	..	..	..	0
Loans granted to residents	..	..	..	..	0
Loans granted to non-residents	..	..	..	..	0
Equity and investment fund shares/units	..	..	..	..	1 254
Equity and investment fund shares/units issued by residents	..	..	..	..	41
Equity and investment fund shares/units issued by non residents	..	..	..	..	1 213
Other accounts receivable	..	..	..	..	1

	Insurance corporations and pension funds				
	Total	Insurance corporations			Pension funds
		Total	Life insurance corporations	Non-life insurance corporations	Total
Financial liabilities	..	..	..	..	3 160
Currency and deposits	..	..	..	..	0
Debt securities	..	..	..	..	0
Debt securities, short term	..	..	..	..	0
Debt securities, long term	..	..	..	..	0
Loans	..	..	..	..	0
Loans, short-term	..	..	..	..	0
Loans, long-term	..	..	..	..	0
Equity and investment fund shares/units	..	..	..	..	3
Insurance pension and standardised guarantees	..	..	..	..	3 133
Financial derivatives and employee stock options	..	..	..	..	0
Other accounts payable	..	..	..	..	24

Note: Detailed metadata at: http://metalinks.oecd.org/instinv/20170920/727a

Table 3. Financial assets and liabilities of insurance corporations and pension funds

Million EUR

	2009	2010	2011	2012	2013	2014	2015	2016
Insurance corporations and pension funds								
Financial net worth	..	..	..	..	..	..	..	..
Financial assets	..	..	..	..	..	..	..	..
Currency and deposits	..	..	..	..	..	..	..	..
Debt securities	..	..	..	..	..	..	..	..
Loans	..	..	..	..	..	..	..	..
Equity and investment fund shares	..	..	..	..	..	..	..	..
Equity	..	..	..	..	..	..	..	..
Investment fund shares	..	..	..	..	..	..	..	..
Money market fund shares	..	..	..	..	..	..	..	..
Non-Money market fund shares	..	..	..	..	..	..	..	..
Insurance pension and standardised guarantees	..	..	..	..	..	..	..	..
Financial derivatives and employee stock options	..	..	..	..	..	..	..	..
Other accounts receivable	..	..	..	..	..	..	..	..
Financial liabilities	..	..	..	..	..	..	..	..
Debt securities	..	..	..	..	..	..	..	..
Short-term debt securities	..	..	..	..	..	..	..	..
Long-term debt securities	..	..	..	..	..	..	..	..
Loans	..	..	..	..	..	..	..	..
Short-term loans	..	..	..	..	..	..	..	..
Long-term loans	..	..	..	..	..	..	..	..
Equity and investment fund shares	..	..	..	..	..	..	..	..
Insurance pension and standardised guarantees	..	..	..	..	..	..	..	..
Financial derivatives and employee stock options	..	..	..	..	..	..	..	..
Other accounts payable	..	..	..	..	..	..	..	..
Non-financial assets	..	..	..	..	..	..	..	..
Insurance corporations								
Financial net worth	..	..	..	..	..	..	..	..
Financial assets	..	..	..	..	..	..	..	..
Currency and deposits	..	..	..	..	..	..	..	..
Debt securities	..	..	..	..	..	..	..	..
Loans	..	..	..	..	..	..	..	..
Equity and investment fund shares	..	..	..	..	..	..	..	..
Equity	..	..	..	..	..	..	..	..
Investment fund shares	..	..	..	..	..	..	..	..
Money market fund shares	..	..	..	..	..	..	..	..
Non-Money market fund shares	..	..	..	..	..	..	..	..
Insurance pension and standardised guarantees	..	..	..	..	..	..	..	..
Financial derivatives and employee stock options	..	..	..	..	..	..	..	..
Other accounts receivable	..	..	..	..	..	..	..	..
Financial liabilities	..	..	..	..	..	..	..	..
Debt securities	..	..	..	..	..	..	..	..
Short-term debt securities	..	..	..	..	..	..	..	..
Long-term debt securities	..	..	..	..	..	..	..	..
Loans	..	..	..	..	..	..	..	..
Short-term loans	..	..	..	..	..	..	..	..
Long-term loans	..	..	..	..	..	..	..	..
Equity and investment fund shares	..	..	..	..	..	..	..	..
Insurance pension and standardised guarantees	..	..	..	..	..	..	..	..
Financial derivatives and employee stock options	..	..	..	..	..	..	..	..
Other accounts payable	..	..	..	..	..	..	..	..
Non-financial assets	..	..	..	..	..	..	..	..
Pension funds								
Financial net worth	0	0	0	0	0	0	-4	0
Financial assets	1 147	1 343	1 425	1 669	1 907	2 320	2 667	3 160
Currency and deposits	445	519	354	332	296	312	519	404
Debt securities	444	410	580	686	839	1 090	1 229	1 499
Loans	0	0	0	0	0	0	0	0
Equity and investment fund shares	257	413	488	649	735	916	919	1 254
Equity	7	15	10	12	18	25	44	77
Investment fund shares	249	397	478	637	718	891	875	1 177
Money market fund shares	37	73	82	2	2	6	0	0
Non-Money market fund shares	213	325	396	635	715	885	875	1 177
Insurance pension and standardised guarantees	0	0	0	0	0	0	0	0
Financial derivatives and employee stock options	0	0	0	0	0	0	0	2
Other accounts receivable	1	1	3	2	37	1	1	1
Financial liabilities	1 147	1 343	1 426	1 670	1 907	2 320	2 672	3 160
Debt securities	0	0	0	0	0	0	0	0
Short-term debt securities	0	0	0	0	0	0	0	0
Long-term debt securities	0	0	0	0	0	0	0	0
Loans	0	0	0	0	0	0	0	0
Short-term loans	0	0	0	0	0	0	0	0
Long-term loans	0	0	0	0	0	0	0	0
Equity and investment fund shares	2	2	2	3	2	3	3	3
Insurance pension and standardised guarantees	1 137	1 338	1 417	1 664	1 899	2 289	2 656	3 133
Financial derivatives and employee stock options	0	0	1	0	0	1	0	0
Other accounts payable	9	3	5	4	6	27	13	24
Non-financial assets	..	..	..	..	..	..	..	..

Note: Detailed metadata at: http://metalinks.oecd.org/instinv/20170920/727a

LATVIA

Table 4. Portfolio composition by type of investor

As percentage of financial assets and of financial liabilities

Per cent

	2009	2010	2011	2012	2013	2014	2015	2016
Investment funds								
Financial assets	100.0	100.0	100.0	100.0	100.0	100.0	..	..
Currency and deposits	53.3	45.9	32.8	25.1	25.6	19.5	..	..
Debt securities	31.1	28.0	22.3	33.3	40.7	51.5	..	..
Loans	0.0	0.0	6.4	7.6	3.0	5.9	..	..
Equity and investment fund shares	8.2	19.5	37.6	33.4	20.2	21.3	..	..
Insurance pension and standardised guarantee schemes	0.0	0.0	0.0	0.0	0.0	0.0	..	..
Financial derivatives and employee stock options	0.0	0.0	0.0	0.1	0.1	0.0	..	..
Other accounts receivable	7.4	6.5	0.9	0.6	10.3	1.7	..	..
Financial liabilities	100.0	100.0	100.0	100.0	100.0	100.0	..	..
Currency and deposits	0.0	0.0	0.0	0.0	0.0	0.0	..	..
Debt securities	0.0	0.0	0.0	0.0	0.0	0.0	..	..
Loans	0.1	0.1	0.0	1.5	0.0	0.0	..	..
Equity and investment fund shares	99.3	99.3	99.1	98.1	90.9	96.0	..	..
Insurance pension and standardised guarantee schemes	0.0	0.0	0.0	0.0	0.0	0.0	..	..
Financial derivatives and employee stock options	0.2	0.1	0.2	0.0	0.0	0.3	..	..
Other accounts receivable	0.4	0.6	0.7	0.4	9.1	3.6	..	..
Insurance corporations								
Financial assets	..	..	..	..	..	..	..	..
Currency and deposits	..	..	..	..	..	..	..	..
Debt securities	..	..	..	..	..	..	..	..
Loans	..	..	..	..	..	..	..	..
Equity and investment fund shares	..	..	..	..	..	..	..	..
Insurance pension and standardised guarantee schemes	..	..	..	..	..	..	..	..
Financial derivatives and employee stock options	..	..	..	..	..	..	..	..
Other accounts receivable	..	..	..	..	..	..	..	..
Financial liabilities	..	..	..	..	..	..	..	..
Currency and deposits	..	..	..	..	..	..	..	..
Debt securities	..	..	..	..	..	..	..	..
Loans	..	..	..	..	..	..	..	..
Equity and investment fund shares	..	..	..	..	..	..	..	..
Insurance pension and standardised guarantee schemes	..	..	..	..	..	..	..	..
Financial derivatives and employee stock options	..	..	..	..	..	..	..	..
Other accounts receivable	..	..	..	..	..	..	..	..
Pension funds								
Financial assets	100.0	100.0	100.0	100.0	100.0	100.0	100.0	100.0
Currency and deposits	38.8	38.6	24.9	19.9	15.5	13.5	19.4	12.8
Debt securities	38.7	30.5	40.7	41.1	44.0	47.0	46.1	47.4
Loans	0.0	0.0	0.0	0.0	0.0	0.0	0.0	0.0
Equity and investment fund shares	22.4	30.8	34.3	38.9	38.6	39.5	34.5	39.7
Insurance pension and standardised guarantee schemes	0.0	0.0	0.0	0.0	0.0	0.0	0.0	0.0
Financial derivatives and employee stock options	0.0	0.0	0.0	0.0	0.0	0.0	0.0	0.1
Other accounts receivable	0.1	0.1	0.2	0.1	1.9	0.1	0.0	0.0
Financial liabilities	100.0	100.0	100.0	100.0	100.0	100.0	100.0	100.0
Currency and deposits	0.0	0.0	0.0	0.0	0.0	0.0	0.0	0.0
Debt securities	0.0	0.0	0.0	0.0	0.0	0.0	0.0	0.0
Loans	0.0	0.0	0.0	0.0	0.0	0.0	0.0	0.0
Equity and investment fund shares	0.2	0.2	0.2	0.1	0.1	0.1	0.1	0.1
Insurance pension and standardised guarantee schemes	99.1	99.6	99.4	99.6	99.6	98.7	99.4	99.1
Financial derivatives and employee stock options	0.0	0.0	0.1	0.0	0.0	0.0	0.0	0.0
Other accounts receivable	0.7	0.2	0.4	0.2	0.3	1.2	0.5	0.8

Note: Detailed metadata at: http://metalinks.oecd.org/instinv/20170920/a49a

Table 1. Financial assets and liabilities of institutional investors, 2016

Million EUR (1999 LUF euro)

	Investment funds				
	Total	Non-money market funds			Money market funds
		Total	Open-end non-money market funds	Closed-end non-money market funds	Total
Financial assets	4 102 310	3 809 847	3 739 237	70 610	292 462
Currency and deposits	299 257	239 089	228 919	10 169	60 169
Debt securities	1 734 753	1 511 785	1 502 963	8 822	222 968
Debt securities, short term	292 080	121 306	121 280	26	170 775
Debt securities, long term	1 442 673	1 390 479	1 381 683	8 796	52 193
Debt securities issued by residents	62 646	58 212	50 906	7 306	4 434
Debt securities issued by non-residents	1 672 107	1 453 573	1 452 057	1 516	218 534
Loans	0	0	0	0	0
Loans, short-term	0	0	0	0	0
Loans, long-term	0	0	0	0	0
Loans granted to residents	0	0	0	0	0
Loans granted to non-residents	0	0	0	0	0
Equity and investment fund shares/units	1 767 448	1 760 974	1 713 988	46 986	6 474
Equity and investment fund shares issued/units by residents	305 812	300 326	282 423	17 904	5 485
Equity and investment fund shares/units issued by non residents	1 461 636	1 460 648	1 431 566	29 082	989
Other accounts receivable	114 251	111 866	107 937	3 929	2 385

	Investment funds				
	Total	Non-money market funds			Money market funds
		Total	Open-end non-money market funds	Closed-end non-money market funds	Total
Financial liabilities	4 111 713	3 819 251	3 748 164	71 087	292 462
Currency and deposits	0	0	0	0	0
Debt securities	3 259	3 259	3 178	82	0
Debt securities, short term	0	0	0	0	0
Debt securities, long term	3 259	3 259	3 178	82	0
Loans	58 563	57 882	54 893	2 990	681
Loans, short-term	47 367	46 686	44 936	1 750	681
Loans, long-term	11 197	11 197	9 957	1 240	0
Equity and investment fund shares/units	3 758 008	3 470 190	3 405 557	64 634	287 818
Insurance pension and standardised guaratees	0	0	0	0	0
Financial derivatives and employee stock options	166 749	166 433	166 315	118	316
Other accounts payable	125 134	121 486	118 222	3 265	3 648

	Insurance corporations and pension funds				
	Total	Insurance corporations			Pension funds
		Total	Life insurance corporations	Non-life insurance corporations	Total
Financial assets	187 214	185 328	158 961	26 367	1 886
Currency and deposits	16 297	16 241	11 741	4 500	56
Debt securities	41 832	41 092	32 717	8 375	740
Debt securities, short-term	750	750	481	269	0
Debt securities, long term	41 082	40 342	32 236	8 106	740
Debt securities issued by residents	3 538	3 483	3 039	444	55
Debt securities issued by non-residents	38 294	37 609	29 678	7 931	685
Loans	10 250	10 249	7 700	2 549	1
Loans, short-term	2 155	2 154	2	2 152	1
Loans, long-term	8 095	8 095	7 698	397	0
Loans granted to residents	1 224	1 223	64	1 159	1
Loans granted to non-residents	9 027	9 027	7 636	1 391	0
Equity and investment fund shares/units	91 949	90 902	84 621	6 281	1 047
Equity and investment fund shares/units issued by residents	41 283	40 378	35 996	4 383	904
Equity and investment fund shares/units issued by non residents	50 666	50 524	48 626	1 898	143
Other accounts receivable	7 947	7 905	5 040	2 865	42

	Insurance corporations and pension funds				
	Total	Insurance corporations			Pension funds
		Total	Life insurance corporations	Non-life insurance corporations	Total
Financial liabilities	187 455	185 569	159 048	26 520	1 886
Currency and deposits	0	0	0	0	0
Debt securities	377	377	377	0	0
Debt securities, short term	0	0	0	0	0
Debt securities, long term	377	377	377	0	0
Loans	8 303	8 303	7 928	375	0
Loans, short-term	8 303	8 303	7 928	375	0
Loans, long-term	0	0	0	0	0
Equity and investment fund shares/units	4 651	4 651	1 895	2 755	0
Insurance pension and standardised guarantees	159 642	157 784	144 348	13 436	1 857
Financial derivatives and employee stock options	109	109	108	0	0
Other accounts payable	14 375	14 346	4 392	9 953	29

Note: Detailed metadata at: http://metalinks.oecd.org/instinv/20170920/07c7

LUXEMBOURG

Table 2. Financial assets and liabilities of investment funds

Million EUR

	2009	2010	2011	2012	2013	2014	2015	2016
Investment funds								
Financial net worth	-6 853	-11 742	-7 799	-7 776	-8 065	-10 508	-9 729	-9 403
Financial assets	2 009 510	2 415 359	2 361 149	2 650 942	2 921 807	3 381 559	3 845 925	4 102 310
Currency and deposits	159 614	181 513	216 250	204 793	230 406	263 272	253 691	299 257
Debt securities	867 292	984 497	1 004 787	1 175 833	1 206 105	1 461 546	1 610 691	1 734 753
Loans	0	0	0	0	0	0	0	0
Equity and investment fund shares	803 280	1 014 274	871 707	993 919	1 196 586	1 457 147	1 700 922	1 767 448
Equity	607 711	763 939	635 878	724 696	876 831	1 057 227	1 232 138	1 272 422
Investment fund shares	195 569	250 335	235 829	269 223	319 755	399 920	468 784	495 026
Money market fund shares	16 653	16 333	23 391	11 651	17 142	22 103	35 937	35 463
Non-Money market fund shares	178 916	234 002	212 438	257 572	302 614	377 817	432 847	459 563
Insurance pension and standardised guarantees	0	0	0	0	0	0	0	0
Financial derivatives and employee stock options	116 085	162 855	192 169	190 826	203 777	100 561	167 362	186 599
Other accounts receivable	63 238	72 221	76 236	85 572	84 933	99 033	113 259	114 251
Financial liabilities	2 016 363	2 427 101	2 368 949	2 658 718	2 929 872	3 392 067	3 855 654	4 111 713
Debt securities	1 277	1 243	1 691	1 582	2 449	3 307	3 442	3 259
Short-term debt securities	0	0	0	0	0	0	0	0
Long-term debt securities	1 277	1 243	1 691	1 582	2 449	3 307	3 442	3 259
Loans	22 077	25 759	27 744	30 116	48 442	60 729	48 520	58 563
Short-term loans	18 074	22 112	24 599	27 255	45 167	57 170	43 614	47 367
Long-term loans	4 004	3 646	3 145	2 861	3 275	3 559	4 906	11 197
Equity and investment fund shares	1 863 141	2 215 520	2 106 445	2 397 513	2 627 253	3 139 599	3 551 172	3 758 008
Insurance pension and standardised guarantees	0	0	0	0	0	0	0	0
Financial derivatives and employee stock options	55 274	110 672	148 761	142 402	161 744	64 250	147 864	166 749
Other accounts payable	74 594	73 907	84 306	87 103	89 984	124 182	104 657	125 134
Non-financial assets	6 853	11 742	7 799	7 776	8 065	10 508	9 729	9 403
Money market funds								
Financial net worth	0	0	0	0	0	0	0	0
Financial assets	322 716	289 002	305 900	224 286	198 793	223 764	256 099	292 462
Currency and deposits	55 024	57 535	75 450	52 086	43 604	34 372	41 267	60 169
Debt securities	265 385	225 370	223 421	167 631	149 345	182 360	206 947	222 968
Loans	0	0	0	0	0	0	0	0
Equity and investment fund shares	486	786	858	647	3 555	4 157	5 155	6 474
Equity	0	44	20	0	5	0	0	0
Investment fund shares	486	742	838	647	3 550	4 157	5 155	6 474
Money market fund shares	391	505	782	549	3 547	4 157	5 155	6 467
Non-Money market fund shares	95	237	56	98	3	0	0	7
Insurance pension and standardised guarantees	0	0	0	0	0	0	0	0
Financial derivatives and employee stock options	171	1 047	821	28	25	53	114	466
Other accounts receivable	1 651	4 264	5 350	3 894	2 264	2 821	2 615	2 385
Financial liabilities	322 716	289 002	305 900	224 286	198 793	223 764	256 099	292 462
Debt securities	0	0	0	0	0	0	0	0
Short-term debt securities	0	0	0	0	0	0	0	0
Long-term debt securities	0	0	0	0	0	0	0	0
Loans	1 011	809	957	67	594	533	523	681
Short-term loans	1 011	809	957	67	594	533	523	681
Long-term loans	0	0	0	0	0	0	0	0
Equity and investment fund shares	317 849	283 252	298 168	220 251	194 787	214 284	251 772	287 818
Insurance pension and standardised guarantees	0	0	0	0	0	0	0	0
Financial derivatives and employee stock options	209	1 147	845	32	5	13	98	316
Other accounts payable	3 647	3 794	5 930	3 937	3 407	8 934	3 707	3 648
Non-financial assets	0	0	0	0	0	0	0	0
Non-money market funds								
Financial net worth	-6 853	-11 742	-7 799	-7 776	-8 065	-10 508	-9 729	-9 403
Financial assets	1 686 793	2 126 357	2 055 249	2 426 656	2 723 014	3 157 795	3 589 826	3 809 847
Currency and deposits	104 591	123 978	140 800	152 707	186 802	228 901	212 424	239 089
Debt securities	601 908	759 126	781 366	1 008 202	1 056 760	1 279 186	1 403 744	1 511 785
Loans	0	0	0	0	0	0	0	0
Equity and investment fund shares	802 794	1 013 488	870 849	993 272	1 193 031	1 452 989	1 695 767	1 760 974
Equity	607 711	763 895	635 858	724 696	876 826	1 057 227	1 232 138	1 272 422
Investment fund shares	195 083	249 593	234 991	268 576	316 205	395 762	463 629	488 552
Money market fund shares	16 262	15 828	22 609	11 101	13 595	17 946	30 781	28 996
Non-Money market fund shares	178 822	233 765	212 382	257 474	302 610	377 817	432 847	459 556
Insurance pension and standardised guarantees	0	0	0	0	0	0	0	0
Financial derivatives and employee stock options	115 914	161 807	191 347	190 798	203 752	100 508	167 248	186 133
Other accounts receivable	61 587	67 957	70 887	81 678	82 669	96 212	110 644	111 866
Financial liabilities	1 693 647	2 138 099	2 063 048	2 434 432	2 731 079	3 168 303	3 599 555	3 819 251
Debt securities	1 277	1 243	1 691	1 582	2 449	3 307	3 442	3 259
Short-term debt securities	0	0	0	0	0	0	0	0
Long-term debt securities	1 277	1 243	1 691	1 582	2 449	3 307	3 442	3 259
Loans	21 066	24 949	26 787	30 050	47 848	60 195	47 997	57 882
Short-term loans	17 063	21 303	23 642	27 188	44 573	56 636	43 091	46 686
Long-term loans	4 004	3 646	3 145	2 861	3 275	3 559	4 906	11 197
Equity and investment fund shares	1 545 291	1 932 269	1 808 277	2 177 262	2 432 465	2 925 315	3 299 400	3 470 190
Insurance pension and standardised guarantees	0	0	0	0	0	0	0	0
Financial derivatives and employee stock options	55 065	109 524	147 917	142 371	161 739	64 237	147 766	166 433
Other accounts payable	70 947	70 113	78 376	83 167	86 577	115 247	100 951	121 486
Non-financial assets	6 853	11 742	7 799	7 776	8 065	10 508	9 729	9 403
Open-end non-money market funds								
Financial net worth	-6 528	-11 348	-7 691	-7 755	-8 037	-9 308	-9 077	-8 926
Financial assets	1 680 418	2 118 365	2 042 949	2 412 370	2 706 977	3 102 068	3 524 130	3 739 237

Table 2. Financial assets and liabilities of investment funds *(cont.)*

Million EUR

	2009	2010	2011	2012	2013	2014	2015	2016
Currency and deposits	103 527	122 783	138 057	149 686	184 463	221 151	205 061	228 919
Debt securities	601 089	756 885	779 035	1 005 479	1 054 245	1 272 500	1 395 182	1 502 963
Loans	0	0	0	0	0	0	0	0
Equity and investment fund shares	799 449	1 009 521	864 252	985 877	1 183 723	1 415 630	1 650 802	1 713 988
Equity	604 824	760 666	630 959	719 214	870 545	1 038 797	1 209 788	1 246 637
Investment fund shares	194 625	248 854	233 293	266 663	313 179	376 833	441 014	467 351
Money market fund shares	16 161	15 549	22 537	11 032	13 594	17 939	30 769	28 948
Non-Money market fund shares	178 464	233 305	210 756	255 631	299 585	358 894	410 245	438 404
Insurance pension and standardised guarantees	0	0	0	0	0	0	0	0
Financial derivatives and employee stock options	115 904	161 793	191 339	190 796	203 752	100 220	166 565	185 430
Other accounts receivable	60 449	67 383	70 267	80 531	80 794	92 568	106 520	107 937
Financial liabilities	1 686 946	2 129 713	2 050 640	2 420 124	2 715 014	3 111 376	3 533 207	3 748 164
Debt securities	1 277	1 243	1 691	1 582	2 449	3 278	3 256	3 178
Short-term debt securities	0	0	0	0	0	0	0	0
Long-term debt securities	1 277	1 243	1 691	1 582	2 449	3 278	3 256	3 178
Loans	20 518	24 436	26 437	29 135	47 282	58 196	45 114	54 893
Short-term loans	16 933	21 265	23 598	27 129	44 535	55 815	41 421	44 936
Long-term loans	3 585	3 171	2 839	2 006	2 747	2 381	3 693	9 957
Equity and investment fund shares	1 539 704	1 924 978	1 796 830	2 164 687	2 417 568	2 872 869	3 239 056	3 405 557
Insurance pension and standardised guarantees	0	0	0	0	0	0	0	0
Financial derivatives and employee stock options	55 027	109 469	147 887	142 352	161 739	64 205	147 746	166 315
Other accounts payable	70 421	69 587	77 795	82 368	85 976	112 829	98 035	118 222
Non-financial assets	6 528	11 348	7 691	7 755	8 037	9 308	9 077	8 926
Open-end investment funds								
Financial net worth	-6 528	-11 348	-7 691	-7 755	-8 037	-9 308	-9 077	-8 926
Financial assets	2 003 134	2 407 367	2 348 850	2 636 655	2 905 770	3 325 832	3 780 229	4 031 700
Currency and deposits	158 551	180 318	213 507	201 772	228 067	255 522	246 328	289 088
Debt securities	866 474	982 256	1 002 456	1 173 110	1 203 590	1 454 860	1 602 129	1 725 931
Loans	0	0	0	0	0	0	0	0
Equity and investment fund shares	799 935	1 010 306	865 111	986 524	1 187 279	1 419 787	1 655 957	1 720 463
Equity	604 824	760 710	630 980	719 214	870 550	1 038 797	1 209 788	1 246 637
Investment fund shares	195 111	249 596	234 131	267 310	316 729	380 991	446 169	473 826
Money market fund shares	16 552	16 055	23 319	11 581	17 140	22 097	35 924	35 415
Non-Money market fund shares	178 559	233 542	210 812	255 729	299 589	358 894	410 245	438 411
Insurance pension and standardised guarantees	0	0	0	0	0	0	0	0
Financial derivatives and employee stock options	116 075	162 840	192 160	190 824	203 776	100 273	166 680	185 896
Other accounts receivable	62 100	71 646	75 616	84 425	83 058	95 389	109 135	110 322
Financial liabilities	2 009 662	2 418 715	2 356 541	2 644 410	2 913 807	3 335 140	3 789 306	4 040 626
Debt securities	1 277	1 243	1 691	1 582	2 449	3 278	3 256	3 178
Short-term debt securities	0	0	0	0	0	0	0	0
Long-term debt securities	1 277	1 243	1 691	1 582	2 449	3 278	3 256	3 178
Loans	21 529	25 245	27 394	29 202	47 876	58 729	45 636	55 574
Short-term loans	17 944	22 074	24 555	27 196	45 129	56 348	41 944	45 617
Long-term loans	3 585	3 171	2 839	2 006	2 747	2 381	3 693	9 957
Equity and investment fund shares	1 857 553	2 208 230	2 094 998	2 384 938	2 612 355	3 087 153	3 490 828	3 693 374
Insurance pension and standardised guarantees	0	0	0	0	0	0	0	0
Financial derivatives and employee stock options	55 236	110 616	148 732	142 383	161 744	64 217	147 844	166 631
Other accounts payable	74 068	73 381	83 726	86 305	89 383	121 763	101 742	121 869
Non-financial assets	6 528	11 348	7 691	7 755	8 037	9 308	9 077	8 926

Note: Detailed metadata at: http://metalinks.oecd.org/instinv/20170920/07c7

Table 3. Financial assets and liabilities of insurance corporations and pension funds

Million EUR

	2009	2010	2011	2012	2013	2014	2015	2016
Insurance corporations and pension funds								
Financial net worth	341	174	626	913	880	2 094	-173	-241
Financial assets	102 048	121 917	123 153	135 052	143 835	164 411	177 765	187 214
Currency and deposits	9 457	9 385	10 830	11 748	12 210	12 993	15 675	16 297
Debt securities	29 815	36 510	37 256	40 096	39 994	44 641	40 751	41 832
Loans	1 504	1 625	1 786	2 076	1 739	1 982	9 667	10 250
Equity and investment fund shares	47 335	56 215	55 832	62 269	67 364	77 162	87 699	91 949
Equity	11 331	12 557	12 653	12 925	14 308	13 820	16 979	18 153
Investment fund shares	36 004	43 658	43 178	49 343	53 056	63 343	70 721	73 796
Money market fund shares	5 123	4 283	5 500	3 968	3 087	3 602	3 907	4 367
Non-Money market fund shares	30 881	39 375	37 679	45 375	49 969	59 740	66 814	69 429
Insurance pension and standardised guarantees	12 928	16 982	16 312	17 514	21 250	26 212	18 306	18 655
Financial derivatives and employee stock options	0	0	0	0	0	0	333	284
Other accounts receivable	1 009	1 200	1 137	1 350	1 279	1 421	5 334	7 947
Financial liabilities	101 706	121 742	122 527	134 139	142 955	162 317	177 938	187 455
Debt securities	8	4	6	6	3	3	313	377
Short-term debt securities	0	0	0	0	0	0	0	0
Long-term debt securities	8	4	6	6	3	3	313	377
Loans	9 090	11 371	8 729	6 204	6 284	7 764	7 449	8 303
Short-term loans	9 028	11 300	8 655	6 152	6 231	7 702	7 449	8 303
Long-term loans	62	71	75	52	53	62	0	0
Equity and investment fund shares	10 047	9 769	10 416	10 635	9 506	10 170	4 887	4 651
Insurance pension and standardised guarantees	82 120	100 096	102 714	116 546	126 414	143 409	148 973	159 642
Financial derivatives and employee stock options	0	0	0	0	0	0	55	109
Other accounts payable	440	503	662	748	747	971	16 260	14 375
Non-financial assets	240	268	291	230	235	335	178	241
Insurance corporations								
Financial net worth	341	174	626	913	880	2 093	-178	-241
Financial assets	101 204	121 020	122 184	133 963	142 654	162 648	175 928	185 328
Currency and deposits	9 200	9 312	10 789	11 707	12 164	12 909	15 605	16 241
Debt securities	29 623	36 057	36 752	39 554	39 419	43 868	39 994	41 092
Loans	1 502	1 623	1 784	2 075	1 737	1 981	9 666	10 249
Equity and investment fund shares	46 947	55 857	55 425	61 776	66 820	76 274	86 732	90 902
Equity	11 329	12 555	12 652	12 924	14 260	13 820	16 979	18 153
Investment fund shares	35 618	43 302	42 772	48 852	52 560	62 454	69 753	72 749
Money market fund shares	5 068	4 249	5 448	3 929	3 058	3 552	3 846	4 350
Non-Money market fund shares	30 550	39 053	37 324	44 923	49 502	58 902	65 907	68 399
Insurance pension and standardised guarantees	12 928	16 982	16 312	17 514	21 250	26 212	18 306	18 655
Financial derivatives and employee stock options	0	0	0	0	0	0	333	284
Other accounts receivable	1 004	1 190	1 122	1 338	1 264	1 405	5 293	7 905
Financial liabilities	100 863	120 846	121 558	133 050	141 775	160 554	176 106	185 569
Debt securities	8	4	6	6	3	3	313	377
Short-term debt securities	0	0	0	0	0	0	0	0
Long-term debt securities	8	4	6	6	3	3	313	377
Loans	9 090	11 371	8 729	6 204	6 284	7 764	7 449	8 303
Short-term loans	9 028	11 300	8 655	6 152	6 231	7 702	7 449	8 303
Long-term loans	62	71	75	52	53	62	0	0
Equity and investment fund shares	10 047	9 769	10 416	10 635	9 506	10 170	4 887	4 651
Insurance pension and standardised guarantees	81 279	99 205	101 753	115 462	125 241	141 689	147 170	157 784
Financial derivatives and employee stock options	0	0	0	0	0	0	55	109
Other accounts payable	437	498	654	743	740	928	16 231	14 346
Non-financial assets	240	268	291	230	235	335	178	241
Pension funds								
Financial net worth	0	0	0	0	0	0	5	0
Financial assets	844	896	969	1 089	1 181	1 763	1 837	1 886
Currency and deposits	256	73	41	41	46	84	70	56
Debt securities	193	453	503	542	575	773	757	740
Loans	2	2	2	1	1	1	1	1
Equity and investment fund shares	388	359	407	493	544	889	968	1 047
Equity	2	2	1	2	48	0	0	0
Investment fund shares	386	356	406	491	496	889	968	1 047
Money market fund shares	55	35	52	40	29	51	61	17
Non-Money market fund shares	331	321	355	452	467	838	907	1 030
Insurance pension and standardised guarantees	0	0	0	0	0	0	0	0
Financial derivatives and employee stock options	0	0	0	0	0	0	0	0
Other accounts receivable	5	11	16	12	15	17	42	42
Financial liabilities	843	896	968	1 089	1 180	1 763	1 832	1 886
Debt securities	0	0	0	0	0	0	0	0
Short-term debt securities	0	0	0	0	0	0	0	0
Long-term debt securities	0	0	0	0	0	0	0	0
Loans	0	0	0	0	0	0	0	0
Short-term loans	0	0	0	0	0	0	0	0
Long-term loans	0	0	0	0	0	0	0	0
Equity and investment fund shares	0	0	0	0	0	0	0	0
Insurance pension and standardised guarantees	841	891	961	1 084	1 173	1 720	1 803	1 857
Financial derivatives and employee stock options	0	0	0	0	0	0	0	0
Other accounts payable	2	5	8	5	7	43	29	29
Non-financial assets	0	0	0	0	0	0	0	0

Note: Detailed metadata at: http://metalinks.oecd.org/instinv/20170920/07c7

Table 4. Portfolio composition by type of investor

As percentage of financial assets and of financial liabilities

Per cent

	2009	2010	2011	2012	2013	2014	2015	2016
Investment funds								
Financial assets	100.0	100.0	100.0	100.0	100.0	100.0	100.0	100.0
Currency and deposits	7.9	7.5	9.2	7.7	7.9	7.8	6.6	7.3
Debt securities	43.2	40.8	42.6	44.4	41.3	43.2	41.9	42.3
Loans	0.0	0.0	0.0	0.0	0.0	0.0	0.0	0.0
Equity and investment fund shares	40.0	42.0	36.9	37.5	41.0	43.1	44.2	43.1
Insurance pension and standardised guarantee schemes	0.0	0.0	0.0	0.0	0.0	0.0	0.0	0.0
Financial derivatives and employee stock options	5.8	6.7	8.1	7.2	7.0	3.0	4.4	4.5
Other accounts receivable	3.1	3.0	3.2	3.2	2.9	2.9	2.9	2.8
Financial liabilities	100.0	100.0	100.0	100.0	100.0	100.0	100.0	100.0
Currency and deposits	0.0	0.0	0.0	0.0	0.0	0.0	0.0	0.0
Debt securities	0.1	0.1	0.1	0.1	0.1	0.1	0.1	0.1
Loans	1.1	1.1	1.2	1.1	1.7	1.8	1.3	1.4
Equity and investment fund shares	92.4	91.3	88.9	90.2	89.7	92.6	92.1	91.4
Insurance pension and standardised guarantee schemes	0.0	0.0	0.0	0.0	0.0	0.0	0.0	0.0
Financial derivatives and employee stock options	2.7	4.6	6.3	5.4	5.5	1.9	3.8	4.1
Other accounts receivable	3.7	3.0	3.6	3.3	3.1	3.7	2.7	3.0
Insurance corporations								
Financial assets	100.0	100.0	100.0	100.0	100.0	100.0	100.0	100.0
Currency and deposits	9.1	7.7	8.8	8.7	8.5	7.9	8.9	8.8
Debt securities	29.3	29.8	30.1	29.5	27.6	27.0	22.7	22.2
Loans	1.5	1.3	1.5	1.5	1.2	1.2	5.5	5.5
Equity and investment fund shares	46.4	46.2	45.4	46.1	46.8	46.9	49.3	49.0
Insurance pension and standardised guarantee schemes	12.8	14.0	13.4	13.1	14.9	16.1	10.4	10.1
Financial derivatives and employee stock options	0.0	0.0	0.0	0.0	0.0	0.0	0.2	0.2
Other accounts receivable	1.0	1.0	0.9	1.0	0.9	0.9	3.0	4.3
Financial liabilities	100.0	100.0	100.0	100.0	100.0	100.0	100.0	100.0
Currency and deposits	0.0	0.0	0.0	0.0	0.0	0.0	0.0	0.0
Debt securities	0.0	0.0	0.0	0.0	0.0	0.0	0.2	0.2
Loans	9.0	9.4	7.2	4.7	4.4	4.8	4.2	4.5
Equity and investment fund shares	10.0	8.1	8.6	8.0	6.7	6.3	2.8	2.5
Insurance pension and standardised guarantee schemes	80.6	82.1	83.7	86.8	88.3	88.2	83.6	85.0
Financial derivatives and employee stock options	0.0	0.0	0.0	0.0	0.0	0.0	0.0	0.1
Other accounts receivable	0.4	0.4	0.5	0.6	0.5	0.6	9.2	7.7
Pension funds								
Financial assets	100.0	100.0	100.0	100.0	100.0	100.0	100.0	100.0
Currency and deposits	30.4	8.1	4.2	3.8	3.9	4.8	3.8	3.0
Debt securities	22.8	50.5	52.0	49.8	48.7	43.8	41.2	39.3
Loans	0.2	0.2	0.2	0.1	0.1	0.1	0.1	0.1
Equity and investment fund shares	46.0	40.0	42.0	45.3	46.1	50.4	52.7	55.5
Insurance pension and standardised guarantee schemes	0.0	0.0	0.0	0.0	0.0	0.0	0.0	0.0
Financial derivatives and employee stock options	0.0	0.0	0.0	0.0	0.0	0.0	0.0	0.0
Other accounts receivable	0.6	1.2	1.6	1.1	1.3	0.9	2.3	2.2
Financial liabilities	100.0	100.0	100.0	100.0	100.0	100.0	100.0	100.0
Currency and deposits	0.0	0.0	0.0	0.0	0.0	0.0	0.0	0.0
Debt securities	0.0	0.0	0.0	0.0	0.0	0.0	0.0	0.0
Loans	0.0	0.0	0.0	0.0	0.0	0.0	0.0	0.0
Equity and investment fund shares	0.0	0.0	0.0	0.0	0.0	0.0	0.0	0.0
Insurance pension and standardised guarantee schemes	99.7	99.5	99.2	99.5	99.4	97.6	98.4	98.5
Financial derivatives and employee stock options	0.0	0.0	0.0	0.0	0.0	0.0	0.0	0.0
Other accounts receivable	0.3	0.5	0.8	0.5	0.6	2.4	1.6	1.5

Note: Detailed metadata at: http://metalinks.oecd.org/instinv/20170920/a49a

NETHERLANDS

Table 1. Financial assets and liabilities of institutional investors, 2016

Million EUR (1999 NLD euro)

	Total	Investment funds			
		Non-money market funds			Money market funds
		Total	Open-end non-money market funds	Closed-end non-money market funds	Total
Financial assets	..	792 894	..	..	..
Currency and deposits	..	10 465	..	..	..
Debt securities	..	250 004	..	..	..
Debt securities, short term	..	4 880	..	..	..
Debt securities, long term	..	245 124	..	..	..
Debt securities issued by residents	..	18 739	..	..	..
Debt securities issued by non-residents	..	231 265	..	..	..
Loans	..	66 529	..	..	..
Loans, short-term	..	28 546	..	..	..
Loans, long-term	..	37 983	..	..	..
Loans granted to residents	..	55 584	..	..	..
Loans granted to non-residents	..	10 945	..	..	..
Equity and investment fund shares/units	..	460 425	..	..	..
Equity and investment fund shares issued/units by residents	..	43 973	..	..	..
Equity and investment fund shares/units issued by non residents	..	416 452	..	..	..
Other accounts receivable	..	6 886	..	..	..

	Total	Investment funds			
		Non-money market funds			Money market funds
		Total	Open-end non-money market funds	Closed-end non-money market funds	Total
Financial liabilities	..	824 009	..	..	..
Currency and deposits	..	..	..	..	..
Debt securities	..	804	..	..	..
Debt securities, short term	..	41	..	..	..
Debt securities, long term	..	763	..	..	..
Loans	..	15 054	..	..	..
Loans, short-term	..	5 834	..	..	..
Loans, long-term	..	9 220	..	..	..
Equity and investment fund shares/units	..	802 193	..	..	..
Insurance pension and standardised guaratees	..	..	..	..	..
Financial derivatives and employee stock options	..	145	..	..	..
Other accounts payable	..	5 813	..	..	..

	Total	Insurance corporations and pension funds			
		Insurance corporations			Pension funds
		Total	Life insurance corporations	Non-life insurance corporations	Total
Financial assets	1 850 531	489 477	..	..	1 361 054
Currency and deposits	26 631	17 236	..	..	9 395
Debt securities	541 631	201 627	..	..	340 004
Debt securities, short-term	8 172	4 613	..	..	3 559
Debt securities, long term	533 459	197 014	..	..	336 445
Debt securities issued by residents	120 111	53 040	..	..	67 071
Debt securities issued by non-residents	421 520	148 587	..	..	272 933
Loans	123 816	95 671	..	..	28 145
Loans, short-term	20 831	8 709	..	..	12 122
Loans, long-term	102 985	86 962	..	..	16 023
Loans granted to residents	117 229	90 580	..	..	26 649
Loans granted to non-residents	6 587	5 091	..	..	1 496
Equity and investment fund shares/units	1 043 588	114 622	..	..	928 966
Equity and investment fund shares/units issued by residents	765 695	90 014	..	..	675 681
Equity and investment fund shares/units issued by non residents	277 893	24 608	..	..	253 285
Other accounts receivable	35 312	30 869	..	..	4 443

	Total	Insurance corporations and pension funds			
		Insurance corporations			Pension funds
		Total	Life insurance corporations	Non-life insurance corporations	Total
Financial liabilities	1 822 027	498 417	..	..	1 323 610
Currency and deposits	..	..	..	..	..
Debt securities	630	630	..	..	0
Debt securities, short term	0	0	..	..	0
Debt securities, long term	630	630	..	..	0
Loans	42 549	15 509	..	..	27 040
Loans, short-term	38 364	12 568	..	..	25 796
Loans, long-term	4 185	2 941	..	..	1 244
Equity and investment fund shares/units	64 677	64 677	..	..	0
Insurance pension and standardised guarantees	1 648 471	380 123	..	..	1 268 348
Financial derivatives and employee stock options	179	107	..	..	72
Other accounts payable	65 521	37 371	..	..	28 150

Note: Detailed metadata at: http://metalinks.oecd.org/instinv/20170920/75e8

Table 2. Financial assets and liabilities of investment funds

Million EUR

	2009	2010	2011	2012	2013	2014	2015	2016
Investment funds								
Financial net worth	..	..	..	..	..	..	..	..
Financial assets	..	..	..	..	..	..	..	..
Currency and deposits	..	..	..	..	..	..	..	..
Debt securities	..	..	..	..	..	..	..	..
Loans	..	..	..	..	..	..	..	..
Equity and investment fund shares	..	..	..	..	..	..	..	..
Equity	..	..	..	..	..	..	..	..
Investment fund shares	..	..	..	..	..	..	..	..
Money market fund shares	..	..	..	..	..	..	..	..
Non-Money market fund shares	..	..	..	..	..	..	..	..
Insurance pension and standardised guarantees	..	..	..	..	..	..	..	..
Financial derivatives and employee stock options	..	..	..	..	..	..	..	..
Other accounts receivable	..	..	..	..	..	..	..	..
Financial liabilities	..	..	..	..	..	..	..	..
Debt securities	..	..	..	..	..	..	..	..
Short-term debt securities	..	..	..	..	..	..	..	..
Long-term debt securities	..	..	..	..	..	..	..	..
Loans	..	..	..	..	..	..	..	..
Short-term loans	..	..	..	..	..	..	..	..
Long-term loans	..	..	..	..	..	..	..	..
Equity and investment fund shares	..	..	..	..	..	..	..	..
Insurance pension and standardised guarantees	..	..	..	..	..	..	..	..
Financial derivatives and employee stock options	..	..	..	..	..	..	..	..
Other accounts payable	..	..	..	..	..	..	..	..
Non-financial assets	..	..	..	..	..	..	..	..
Money market funds								
Financial net worth	..	..	..	..	..	..	..	..
Financial assets	..	..	..	..	..	..	..	..
Currency and deposits	..	..	..	..	..	..	..	..
Debt securities	..	..	..	..	..	..	..	..
Loans	..	..	..	..	..	..	..	..
Equity and investment fund shares	..	..	..	..	..	..	..	..
Equity	..	..	..	..	..	..	..	..
Investment fund shares	..	..	..	..	..	..	..	..
Money market fund shares	..	..	..	..	..	..	..	..
Non-Money market fund shares	..	..	..	..	..	..	..	..
Insurance pension and standardised guarantees	..	..	..	..	..	..	..	..
Financial derivatives and employee stock options	..	..	..	..	..	..	..	..
Other accounts receivable	..	..	..	..	..	..	..	..
Financial liabilities	..	..	..	..	..	..	..	..
Debt securities	..	..	..	..	..	..	..	..
Short-term debt securities	..	..	..	..	..	..	..	..
Long-term debt securities	..	..	..	..	..	..	..	..
Loans	..	..	..	..	..	..	..	..
Short-term loans	..	..	..	..	..	..	..	..
Long-term loans	..	..	..	..	..	..	..	..
Equity and investment fund shares	..	..	..	..	..	..	..	..
Insurance pension and standardised guarantees	..	..	..	..	..	..	..	..
Financial derivatives and employee stock options	..	..	..	..	..	..	..	..
Other accounts payable	..	..	..	..	..	..	..	..
Non-financial assets	..	..	..	..	..	..	..	..
Non-money market funds								
Financial net worth	-25 097	-31 238	-31 993	-31 241	-29 712	-28 306	-29 138	-31 115
Financial assets	435 011	467 130	481 027	558 381	619 582	724 521	729 968	792 894
Currency and deposits	16 323	11 486	8 789	9 820	9 195	12 604	12 548	10 465
Debt securities	154 405	156 176	169 133	198 116	211 039	233 685	245 707	250 004
Loans	39 180	31 718	32 851	43 076	50 691	53 019	56 013	66 529
Equity and investment fund shares	218 215	258 191	264 136	300 312	332 166	413 915	410 117	460 425
Equity	172 712	191 877	197 546	231 923	257 697	314 786	300 601	339 297
Investment fund shares	45 503	66 314	66 590	68 389	74 469	99 129	109 516	121 128
Money market fund shares	203	957	1 111	1 182	1 119	5 108	6 420	5 498
Non-Money market fund shares	45 300	65 357	65 479	67 207	73 350	94 021	103 096	115 630
Insurance pension and standardised guarantees	0	0	0	0	0	0	0	0
Financial derivatives and employee stock options	-883	-473	-356	2 312	584	72	902	-1 415
Other accounts receivable	7 771	10 032	6 474	4 745	15 907	11 226	4 681	6 886
Financial liabilities	460 108	498 368	513 020	589 622	649 294	752 827	759 106	824 009
Debt securities	588	1 685	1 405	1 614	2 215	3 051	770	804
Short-term debt securities	0	0	0	0	128	413	41	41
Long-term debt securities	588	1 685	1 405	1 614	2 087	2 638	729	763
Loans	37 149	19 237	17 995	19 036	14 868	20 095	17 479	15 054
Short-term loans	26 927	7 916	7 113	8 951	4 672	11 471	8 815	5 834
Long-term loans	10 222	11 321	10 882	10 085	10 196	8 624	8 664	9 220
Equity and investment fund shares	411 499	465 288	487 806	562 231	615 812	717 180	733 310	802 193
Insurance pension and standardised guarantees	..	..	..	..	..	..	..	..
Financial derivatives and employee stock options	13	219	173	275	223	339	197	145
Other accounts payable	10 859	11 939	5 641	6 466	16 176	12 162	7 350	5 813
Non-financial assets	24 197	30 307	31 088	30 374	29 106	27 731	29 774	31 266
Open-end non-money market funds								
Financial net worth	..	..	..	..	..	..	..	..
Financial assets	..	..	..	..	..	..	..	..

NETHERLANDS

Table 2. Financial assets and liabilities of investment funds *(cont.)*

Million EUR

	2009	2010	2011	2012	2013	2014	2015	2016
Currency and deposits	..	..	..	..	..	..	..	..
Debt securities	..	..	..	..	..	..	..	..
Loans	..	..	..	..	..	..	..	..
Equity and investment fund shares	..	..	..	..	..	..	..	..
Equity	..	..	..	..	..	..	..	..
Investment fund shares	..	..	..	..	..	..	..	..
Money market fund shares	..	..	..	..	..	..	..	..
Non-Money market fund shares	..	..	..	..	..	..	..	..
Insurance pension and standardised guarantees	..	..	..	..	..	..	..	..
Financial derivatives and employee stock options	..	..	..	..	..	..	..	..
Other accounts receivable	..	..	..	..	..	..	..	..
Financial liabilities	..	..	..	..	..	..	..	..
Debt securities	..	..	..	..	..	..	..	..
Short-term debt securities	..	..	..	..	..	..	..	..
Long-term debt securities	..	..	..	..	..	..	..	..
Loans	..	..	..	..	..	..	..	..
Short-term loans	..	..	..	..	..	..	..	..
Long-term loans	..	..	..	..	..	..	..	..
Equity and investment fund shares	..	..	..	..	..	..	..	..
Insurance pension and standardised guarantees	..	..	..	..	..	..	..	..
Financial derivatives and employee stock options	..	..	..	..	..	..	..	..
Other accounts payable	..	..	..	..	..	..	..	..
Non-financial assets	..	..	..	..	..	..	..	..
Open-end investment funds								
Financial net worth	..	..	..	..	..	..	..	..
Financial assets	..	..	..	..	..	..	..	..
Currency and deposits	..	..	..	..	..	..	..	..
Debt securities	..	..	..	..	..	..	..	..
Loans	..	..	..	..	..	..	..	..
Equity and investment fund shares	..	..	..	..	..	..	..	..
Equity	..	..	..	..	..	..	..	..
Investment fund shares	..	..	..	..	..	..	..	..
Money market fund shares	..	..	..	..	..	..	..	..
Non-Money market fund shares	..	..	..	..	..	..	..	..
Insurance pension and standardised guarantees	..	..	..	..	..	..	..	..
Financial derivatives and employee stock options	..	..	..	..	..	..	..	..
Other accounts receivable	..	..	..	..	..	..	..	..
Financial liabilities	..	..	..	..	..	..	..	..
Debt securities	..	..	..	..	..	..	..	..
Short-term debt securities	..	..	..	..	..	..	..	..
Long-term debt securities	..	..	..	..	..	..	..	..
Loans	..	..	..	..	..	..	..	..
Short-term loans	..	..	..	..	..	..	..	..
Long-term loans	..	..	..	..	..	..	..	..
Equity and investment fund shares	..	..	..	..	..	..	..	..
Insurance pension and standardised guarantees	..	..	..	..	..	..	..	..
Financial derivatives and employee stock options	..	..	..	..	..	..	..	..
Other accounts payable	..	..	..	..	..	..	..	..
Non-financial assets	..	..	..	..	..	..	..	..

Note: Detailed metadata at: http://metalinks.oecd.org/instinv/20170920/75e8

Table 3. Financial assets and liabilities of insurance corporations and pension funds

Million EUR

	2009	2010	2011	2012	2013	2014	2015	2016
Insurance corporations and pension funds								
Financial net worth	20 673	29 856	-31 685	3 851	49 429	79 887	36 295	28 504
Financial assets	1 111 510	1 198 549	1 290 926	1 448 914	1 447 209	1 716 787	1 721 147	1 850 531
Currency and deposits	30 792	27 527	26 869	29 745	17 227	23 324	21 026	26 631
Debt securities	339 694	347 270	378 432	434 893	422 599	507 161	514 805	541 631
Loans	98 477	108 079	106 525	104 731	105 094	116 656	117 507	123 816
Equity and investment fund shares	560 938	626 055	650 151	744 698	806 251	929 361	955 285	1 043 588
Equity	128 802	145 984	133 442	154 394	164 491	184 784	201 692	220 584
Investment fund shares	432 136	480 071	516 709	590 304	641 760	744 577	753 593	823 004
Money market fund shares	9 401	6 357	5 183	8 682	7 666	8 903	7 942	9 766
Non-Money market fund shares	422 735	473 714	511 526	581 622	634 094	735 674	745 651	813 238
Insurance pension and standardised guarantees	29 359	29 720	34 077	34 058	35 123	30 539	30 103	25 427
Financial derivatives and employee stock options	12 695	17 736	58 851	67 408	31 488	79 180	50 847	54 126
Other accounts receivable	39 555	42 162	36 021	33 381	29 427	30 566	31 574	35 312
Financial liabilities	1 090 837	1 168 693	1 322 611	1 445 063	1 397 780	1 636 900	1 684 852	1 822 027
Debt securities	0	0	419	553	705	850	607	630
Short-term debt securities	0	0	0	0	0	0	0	0
Long-term debt securities	0	0	419	553	705	850	607	630
Loans	61 794	43 028	46 044	39 520	29 716	40 984	35 185	42 549
Short-term loans	52 472	34 041	39 084	32 244	24 760	35 552	30 912	38 364
Long-term loans	9 322	8 987	6 960	7 276	4 956	5 432	4 273	4 185
Equity and investment fund shares	43 827	48 038	51 104	54 945	53 322	61 575	62 707	64 677
Insurance pension and standardised guarantees	953 874	1 043 655	1 174 326	1 275 072	1 252 722	1 449 560	1 509 809	1 648 471
Financial derivatives and employee stock options	403	593	556	677	812	806	202	179
Other accounts payable	30 939	33 379	50 162	74 296	60 503	83 125	76 342	65 521
Non-financial assets	26 575	18 264	16 761	16 050	14 040	13 093	12 366	13 096
Insurance corporations								
Financial net worth	-17 744	-2 817	-4 216	-1 931	-2 031	-2 345	-1 949	-8 940
Financial assets	379 796	408 044	432 844	453 693	435 748	487 437	474 869	489 477
Currency and deposits	14 038	14 744	17 290	17 506	7 903	12 800	11 284	17 236
Debt securities	164 012	170 892	177 957	200 514	180 434	204 124	196 523	201 627
Loans	67 243	68 073	74 582	70 712	77 564	83 208	90 911	95 671
Equity and investment fund shares	78 865	98 144	97 535	103 070	117 235	124 328	118 461	114 622
Equity	35 724	39 628	36 447	37 778	34 714	29 128	30 001	30 737
Investment fund shares	43 141	58 516	61 088	65 292	82 521	95 200	88 460	83 885
Money market fund shares	1 038	1 426	732	2 942	2 719	1 751	1 383	1 279
Non-Money market fund shares	42 103	57 090	60 356	62 350	79 802	93 449	87 077	82 606
Insurance pension and standardised guarantees	15 131	15 448	19 881	20 215	21 308	20 363	19 918	17 365
Financial derivatives and employee stock options	4 364	6 216	14 216	13 548	6 909	17 146	10 100	12 087
Other accounts receivable	36 143	34 527	31 383	28 128	24 395	25 468	27 672	30 869
Financial liabilities	397 540	410 861	437 060	455 624	437 779	489 782	476 818	498 417
Debt securities	0	0	419	553	705	850	607	630
Short-term debt securities	0	0	0	0	0	0	0	0
Long-term debt securities	0	0	419	553	705	850	607	630
Loans	29 385	26 525	22 591	18 739	14 287	16 496	14 766	15 509
Short-term loans	21 385	18 821	17 244	13 174	11 107	13 057	11 768	12 568
Long-term loans	8 000	7 704	5 347	5 565	3 180	3 439	2 998	2 941
Equity and investment fund shares	43 827	48 038	51 104	54 945	53 322	61 575	62 707	64 677
Insurance pension and standardised guarantees	301 504	307 590	325 740	340 114	331 001	367 364	357 953	380 123
Financial derivatives and employee stock options	133	155	350	422	373	447	55	107
Other accounts payable	22 691	28 553	36 856	40 851	38 091	43 050	40 730	37 371
Non-financial assets	10 906	8 972	7 691	7 372	5 609	5 435	4 922	5 121
Pension funds								
Financial net worth	38 417	32 673	-27 469	5 782	51 460	82 232	38 244	37 444
Financial assets	731 714	790 505	858 082	995 221	1 011 461	1 229 350	1 246 278	1 361 054
Currency and deposits	16 754	12 783	9 579	12 239	9 324	10 524	9 742	9 395
Debt securities	175 682	176 378	200 475	234 379	242 165	303 037	318 282	340 004
Loans	31 234	40 006	31 943	34 019	27 530	33 448	26 596	28 145
Equity and investment fund shares	482 073	527 911	552 616	641 628	689 016	805 033	836 824	928 966
Equity	93 078	106 356	96 995	116 616	129 777	155 656	171 691	189 847
Investment fund shares	388 995	421 555	455 621	525 012	559 239	649 377	665 133	739 119
Money market fund shares	8 363	4 931	4 451	5 740	4 947	7 152	6 559	8 487
Non-Money market fund shares	380 632	416 624	451 170	519 272	554 292	642 225	658 574	730 632
Insurance pension and standardised guarantees	14 228	14 272	14 196	13 843	13 815	10 176	10 185	8 062
Financial derivatives and employee stock options	8 331	11 520	44 635	53 860	24 579	62 034	40 747	42 039
Other accounts receivable	3 412	7 635	4 638	5 253	5 032	5 098	3 902	4 443
Financial liabilities	693 297	757 832	885 551	989 439	960 001	1 147 118	1 208 034	1 323 610
Debt securities	0	0	0	0	0	0	0	0
Short-term debt securities	0	0	0	0	0	0	0	0
Long-term debt securities	0	0	0	0	0	0	0	0
Loans	32 409	16 503	23 453	20 781	15 429	24 488	20 419	27 040
Short-term loans	31 087	15 220	21 840	19 070	13 653	22 495	19 144	25 796
Long-term loans	1 322	1 283	1 613	1 711	1 776	1 993	1 275	1 244
Equity and investment fund shares	0	0	0	0	0	0	0	0
Insurance pension and standardised guarantees	652 370	736 065	848 586	934 958	921 721	1 082 196	1 151 856	1 268 348
Financial derivatives and employee stock options	270	438	206	255	439	359	147	72
Other accounts payable	8 248	4 826	13 306	33 445	22 412	40 075	35 612	28 150
Non-financial assets	15 669	9 292	9 070	8 678	8 431	7 658	7 444	7 975

Note: Detailed metadata at: http://metalinks.oecd.org/instinv/20170920/75e8

Table 4. Portfolio composition by type of investor

As percentage of financial assets and of financial liabilities

Per cent

	2009	2010	2011	2012	2013	2014	2015	2016
Investment funds								
Financial assets	..	..	..	..	..	..	..	..
Currency and deposits	..	..	..	..	..	..	..	..
Debt securities	..	..	..	..	..	..	..	..
Loans	..	..	..	..	..	..	..	..
Equity and investment fund shares	..	..	..	..	..	..	..	..
Insurance pension and standardised guarantee schemes	..	..	..	..	..	..	..	..
Financial derivatives and employee stock options	..	..	..	..	..	..	..	..
Other accounts receivable	..	..	..	..	..	..	..	..
Financial liabilities	..	..	..	..	..	..	..	..
Currency and deposits	..	..	..	..	..	..	..	..
Debt securities	..	..	..	..	..	..	..	..
Loans	..	..	..	..	..	..	..	..
Equity and investment fund shares	..	..	..	..	..	..	..	..
Insurance pension and standardised guarantee schemes	..	..	..	..	..	..	..	..
Financial derivatives and employee stock options	..	..	..	..	..	..	..	..
Other accounts receivable	..	..	..	..	..	..	..	..
Insurance corporations								
Financial assets	100.0	100.0	100.0	100.0	100.0	100.0	100.0	100.0
Currency and deposits	3.7	3.6	4.0	3.9	1.8	2.6	2.4	3.5
Debt securities	43.2	41.9	41.1	44.2	41.4	41.9	41.4	41.2
Loans	17.7	16.7	17.2	15.6	17.8	17.1	19.1	19.5
Equity and investment fund shares	20.8	24.1	22.5	22.7	26.9	25.5	24.9	23.4
Insurance pension and standardised guarantee schemes	4.0	3.8	4.6	4.5	4.9	4.2	4.2	3.5
Financial derivatives and employee stock options	1.1	1.5	3.3	3.0	1.6	3.5	2.1	2.5
Other accounts receivable	9.5	8.5	7.3	6.2	5.6	5.2	5.8	6.3
Financial liabilities	100.0	100.0	100.0	100.0	100.0	100.0	100.0	100.0
Currency and deposits	0.0	0.0	0.0	0.0	0.0	0.0	0.0	0.0
Debt securities	0.0	0.0	0.1	0.1	0.2	0.2	0.1	0.1
Loans	7.4	6.5	5.2	4.1	3.3	3.4	3.1	3.1
Equity and investment fund shares	11.0	11.7	11.7	12.1	12.2	12.6	13.2	13.0
Insurance pension and standardised guarantee schemes	75.8	74.9	74.5	74.6	75.6	75.0	75.1	76.3
Financial derivatives and employee stock options	0.0	0.0	0.1	0.1	0.1	0.1	0.0	0.0
Other accounts receivable	5.7	6.9	8.4	9.0	8.7	8.8	8.5	7.5
Pension funds								
Financial assets	100.0	100.0	100.0	100.0	100.0	100.0	100.0	100.0
Currency and deposits	2.3	1.6	1.1	1.2	0.9	0.9	0.8	0.7
Debt securities	24.0	22.3	23.4	23.6	23.9	24.7	25.5	25.0
Loans	4.3	5.1	3.7	3.4	2.7	2.7	2.1	2.1
Equity and investment fund shares	65.9	66.8	64.4	64.5	68.1	65.5	67.1	68.3
Insurance pension and standardised guarantee schemes	1.9	1.8	1.7	1.4	1.4	0.8	0.8	0.6
Financial derivatives and employee stock options	1.1	1.5	5.2	5.4	2.4	5.0	3.3	3.1
Other accounts receivable	0.5	1.0	0.5	0.5	0.5	0.4	0.3	0.3
Financial liabilities	100.0	100.0	100.0	100.0	100.0	100.0	100.0	100.0
Currency and deposits	0.0	0.0	0.0	0.0	0.0	0.0	0.0	0.0
Debt securities	0.0	0.0	0.0	0.0	0.0	0.0	0.0	0.0
Loans	4.7	2.2	2.6	2.1	1.6	2.1	1.7	2.0
Equity and investment fund shares	0.0	0.0	0.0	0.0	0.0	0.0	0.0	0.0
Insurance pension and standardised guarantee schemes	94.1	97.1	95.8	94.5	96.0	94.3	95.3	95.8
Financial derivatives and employee stock options	0.0	0.1	0.0	0.0	0.0	0.0	0.0	0.0
Other accounts receivable	1.2	0.6	1.5	3.4	2.3	3.5	2.9	2.1

Note: Detailed metadata at: http://metalinks.oecd.org/instinv/20170920/a49a

NEW ZEALAND

Table 1. Financial assets and liabilities of institutional investors, 2016

Million NZD

	Investment funds				
	Total	Non-money market funds			Money market funds
		Total	Open-end non-money market funds	Closed-end non-money market funds	Total
Financial assets	116 152	103 091	..	..	13 061
Currency and deposits	24 391	16 178	..	..	8 213
Debt securities	36 562	31 713	..	..	4 849
Debt securities, short term	8 085	4 022	..	..	4 063
Debt securities, long term	28 477	27 692	..	..	785
Debt securities issued by residents	22 405	17 556	..	..	4 849
Debt securities issued by non-residents	14 157	14 157	..	..	0
Loans	4	4	..	..	0
Loans, short-term	..	..	..	..	..
Loans, long-term	..	..	..	..	..
Loans granted to residents	4	4	..	..	0
Loans granted to non-residents	0	0	..	..	0
Equity and investment fund shares/units	54 194	54 194	..	..	0
Equity and investment fund shares issued/units by residents	18 500	18 500	..	..	0
Equity and investment fund shares/units issued by non residents	35 695	35 695	..	..	0
Other accounts receivable	623	623	..	..	0

	Investment funds				
	Total	Non-money market funds			Money market funds
		Total	Open-end non-money market funds	Closed-end non-money market funds	Total
Financial liabilities	..	..	..	..	..
Currency and deposits	..	..	..	..	..
Debt securities	..	..	..	..	..
Debt securities, short term	..	..	..	..	..
Debt securities, long term	..	..	..	..	..
Loans	..	..	..	..	..
Loans, short-term	..	..	..	..	..
Loans, long-term	..	..	..	..	..
Equity and investment fund shares/units	..	..	..	..	..
Insurance pension and standardised guaratees	..	..	..	..	..
Financial derivatives and employee stock options	..	..	..	..	..
Other accounts payable	..	..	..	..	..

	Insurance corporations and pension funds				
	Total	Insurance corporations			Pension funds
		Total	Life insurance corporations	Non-life insurance corporations	Total
Financial assets	..	..	..	..	64 621
Currency and deposits	..	..	..	..	4 555
Debt securities	..	..	..	..	14 508
Debt securities, short-term	..	..	..	..	1 502
Debt securities, long term	..	..	..	..	13 006
Debt securities issued by residents	..	..	..	..	6 773
Debt securities issued by non-residents	..	..	..	..	7 735
Loans	..	..	..	..	7
Loans, short-term	..	..	..	..	..
Loans, long-term	..	..	..	..	..
Loans granted to residents	..	..	..	..	7
Loans granted to non-residents	..	..	..	..	0
Equity and investment fund shares/units	..	..	..	..	44 791
Equity and investment fund shares/units issued by residents	..	..	..	..	21 672
Equity and investment fund shares/units issued by non residents	..	..	..	..	23 118
Other accounts receivable	..	..	..	..	427

	Insurance corporations and pension funds				
	Total	Insurance corporations			Pension funds
		Total	Life insurance corporations	Non-life insurance corporations	Total
Financial liabilities	..	..	..	..	..
Currency and deposits	..	..	..	..	..
Debt securities	..	..	..	..	..
Debt securities, short term	..	..	..	..	..
Debt securities, long term	..	..	..	..	..
Loans	..	..	..	..	..
Loans, short-term	..	..	..	..	..
Loans, long-term	..	..	..	..	..
Equity and investment fund shares/units	..	..	..	..	..
Insurance pension and standardised guarantees	..	..	..	..	..
Financial derivatives and employee stock options	..	..	..	..	..
Other accounts payable	..	..	..	..	..

Note: Detailed metadata at: http://metalinks.oecd.org/instinv/20170920/75e8

Table 2. Financial assets and liabilities of investment funds

Million NZD

	2009	2010	2011	2012	2013	2014	2015	2016
Investment funds								
Financial net worth	..	..	..	..	..	..	..	..
Financial assets	..	..	..	..	..	87 605	102 435	116 152
Currency and deposits	..	..	..	..	..	20 519	22 092	24 391
Debt securities	..	..	..	..	..	25 060	30 848	36 562
Loans	..	..	..	..	..	75	47	4
Equity and investment fund shares	..	..	..	..	..	41 110	48 401	54 194
Equity	..	..	..	..	..	22 496	26 504	32 898
Investment fund shares	..	..	..	..	..	18 614	21 897	21 297
Money market fund shares	..	..	..	..	..	..	..	..
Non-Money market fund shares	..	..	..	..	..	..	..	..
Insurance pension and standardised guarantees	..	..	..	..	..	..	..	..
Financial derivatives and employee stock options	..	..	..	..	..	296	448	378
Other accounts receivable	..	..	..	..	..	545	601	623
Financial liabilities	..	..	..	..	..	..	..	..
Debt securities	..	..	..	..	..	..	..	..
Short-term debt securities	..	..	..	..	..	..	..	..
Long-term debt securities	..	..	..	..	..	..	..	..
Loans	..	..	..	..	..	..	..	..
Short-term loans	..	..	..	..	..	..	..	..
Long-term loans	..	..	..	..	..	..	..	..
Equity and investment fund shares	..	..	..	..	..	..	..	..
Insurance pension and standardised guarantees	..	..	..	..	..	..	..	..
Financial derivatives and employee stock options	..	..	..	..	..	..	..	..
Other accounts payable	..	..	..	..	..	..	..	..
Non-financial assets	..	..	..	..	..	1	1	1
Money market funds								
Financial net worth	..	..	..	..	..	..	..	..
Financial assets	..	..	..	..	..	10 216	12 017	13 061
Currency and deposits	..	..	..	..	..	7 994	8 370	8 213
Debt securities	..	..	..	..	..	2 222	3 647	4 849
Loans	..	..	..	..	..	0	0	0
Equity and investment fund shares	..	..	..	..	..	0	0	0
Equity	..	..	..	..	..	0	0	0
Investment fund shares	..	..	..	..	..	0	0	0
Money market fund shares	..	..	..	..	..	..	..	..
Non-Money market fund shares	..	..	..	..	..	..	..	..
Insurance pension and standardised guarantees	..	..	..	..	..	..	..	..
Financial derivatives and employee stock options	..	..	..	..	..	0	0	0
Other accounts receivable	..	..	..	..	..	0	0	0
Financial liabilities	..	..	..	..	..	..	..	..
Debt securities	..	..	..	..	..	..	..	..
Short-term debt securities	..	..	..	..	..	..	..	..
Long-term debt securities	..	..	..	..	..	..	..	..
Loans	..	..	..	..	..	..	..	..
Short-term loans	..	..	..	..	..	..	..	..
Long-term loans	..	..	..	..	..	..	..	..
Equity and investment fund shares	..	..	..	..	..	..	..	..
Insurance pension and standardised guarantees	..	..	..	..	..	..	..	..
Financial derivatives and employee stock options	..	..	..	..	..	..	..	..
Other accounts payable	..	..	..	..	..	..	..	..
Non-financial assets	..	..	..	..	..	0	0	0
Non-money market funds								
Financial net worth	..	..	..	..	..	..	..	..
Financial assets	..	..	..	..	..	77 389	90 418	103 091
Currency and deposits	..	..	..	..	..	12 525	13 721	16 178
Debt securities	..	..	..	..	..	22 838	27 201	31 713
Loans	..	..	..	..	..	75	47	4
Equity and investment fund shares	..	..	..	..	..	41 110	48 401	54 194
Equity	..	..	..	..	..	22 496	26 504	32 898
Investment fund shares	..	..	..	..	..	18 614	21 897	21 297
Money market fund shares	..	..	..	..	..	..	..	..
Non-Money market fund shares	..	..	..	..	..	..	..	..
Insurance pension and standardised guarantees	..	..	..	..	..	..	..	..
Financial derivatives and employee stock options	..	..	..	..	..	296	448	378
Other accounts receivable	..	..	..	..	..	545	601	623
Financial liabilities	..	..	..	..	..	..	..	..
Debt securities	..	..	..	..	..	..	..	..
Short-term debt securities	..	..	..	..	..	..	..	..
Long-term debt securities	..	..	..	..	..	..	..	..
Loans	..	..	..	..	..	..	..	..
Short-term loans	..	..	..	..	..	..	..	..
Long-term loans	..	..	..	..	..	..	..	..
Equity and investment fund shares	..	..	..	..	..	..	..	..
Insurance pension and standardised guarantees	..	..	..	..	..	..	..	..
Financial derivatives and employee stock options	..	..	..	..	..	..	..	..
Other accounts payable	..	..	..	..	..	..	..	..
Non-financial assets	..	..	..	..	..	1	1	1
Open-end non-money market funds								
Financial net worth	..	..	..	..	..	..	..	..
Financial assets	..	..	..	..	..	..	..	..

Table 2. Financial assets and liabilities of investment funds *(cont.)*

Million NZD

	2009	2010	2011	2012	2013	2014	2015	2016
Currency and deposits	..	..	..	..	..	..	..	..
Debt securities	..	..	..	..	..	..	..	..
Loans	..	..	..	..	..	..	..	..
Equity and investment fund shares	..	..	..	..	..	..	..	..
Equity	..	..	..	..	..	..	..	..
Investment fund shares	..	..	..	..	..	..	..	..
Money market fund shares	..	..	..	..	..	..	..	..
Non-Money market fund shares	..	..	..	..	..	..	..	..
Insurance pension and standardised guarantees	..	..	..	..	..	..	..	..
Financial derivatives and employee stock options	..	..	..	..	..	..	..	..
Other accounts receivable	..	..	..	..	..	..	..	..
Financial liabilities	..	..	..	..	..	..	..	..
Debt securities	..	..	..	..	..	..	..	..
Short-term debt securities	..	..	..	..	..	..	..	..
Long-term debt securities	..	..	..	..	..	..	..	..
Loans	..	..	..	..	..	..	..	..
Short-term loans	..	..	..	..	..	..	..	..
Long-term loans	..	..	..	..	..	..	..	..
Equity and investment fund shares	..	..	..	..	..	..	..	..
Insurance pension and standardised guarantees	..	..	..	..	..	..	..	..
Financial derivatives and employee stock options	..	..	..	..	..	..	..	..
Other accounts payable	..	..	..	..	..	..	..	..
Non-financial assets	..	..	..	..	..	..	..	..
Open-end investment funds								
Financial net worth	..	..	..	..	..	..	..	..
Financial assets	..	..	..	..	..	..	..	..
Currency and deposits	..	..	..	..	..	..	..	..
Debt securities	..	..	..	..	..	..	..	..
Loans	..	..	..	..	..	..	..	..
Equity and investment fund shares	..	..	..	..	..	..	..	..
Equity	..	..	..	..	..	..	..	..
Investment fund shares	..	..	..	..	..	..	..	..
Money market fund shares	..	..	..	..	..	..	..	..
Non-Money market fund shares	..	..	..	..	..	..	..	..
Insurance pension and standardised guarantees	..	..	..	..	..	..	..	..
Financial derivatives and employee stock options	..	..	..	..	..	..	..	..
Other accounts receivable	..	..	..	..	..	..	..	..
Financial liabilities	..	..	..	..	..	..	..	..
Debt securities	..	..	..	..	..	..	..	..
Short-term debt securities	..	..	..	..	..	..	..	..
Long-term debt securities	..	..	..	..	..	..	..	..
Loans	..	..	..	..	..	..	..	..
Short-term loans	..	..	..	..	..	..	..	..
Long-term loans	..	..	..	..	..	..	..	..
Equity and investment fund shares	..	..	..	..	..	..	..	..
Insurance pension and standardised guarantees	..	..	..	..	..	..	..	..
Financial derivatives and employee stock options	..	..	..	..	..	..	..	..
Other accounts payable	..	..	..	..	..	..	..	..
Non-financial assets	..	..	..	..	..	..	..	..

Note: Detailed metadata at: http://metalinks.oecd.org/instinv/20170920/75e8

NEW ZEALAND

Table 3. Financial assets and liabilities of insurance corporations and pension funds

Million NZD

	2009	2010	2011	2012	2013	2014	2015	2016
Insurance corporations and pension funds								
Financial net worth	..	..	..	..	..	..	..	..
Financial assets	..	..	..	..	..	..	..	..
Currency and deposits	..	..	..	..	..	..	..	..
Debt securities	..	..	..	..	..	..	..	..
Loans	..	..	..	..	..	..	..	..
Equity and investment fund shares	..	..	..	..	..	..	..	..
Equity	..	..	..	..	..	..	..	..
Investment fund shares	..	..	..	..	..	..	..	..
Money market fund shares	..	..	..	..	..	..	..	..
Non-Money market fund shares	..	..	..	..	..	..	..	..
Insurance pension and standardised guarantees	..	..	..	..	..	..	..	..
Financial derivatives and employee stock options	..	..	..	..	..	..	..	..
Other accounts receivable	..	..	..	..	..	..	..	..
Financial liabilities	..	..	..	..	..	..	..	..
Debt securities	..	..	..	..	..	..	..	..
Short-term debt securities	..	..	..	..	..	..	..	..
Long-term debt securities	..	..	..	..	..	..	..	..
Loans	..	..	..	..	..	..	..	..
Short-term loans	..	..	..	..	..	..	..	..
Long-term loans	..	..	..	..	..	..	..	..
Equity and investment fund shares	..	..	..	..	..	..	..	..
Insurance pension and standardised guarantees	..	..	..	..	..	..	..	..
Financial derivatives and employee stock options	..	..	..	..	..	..	..	..
Other accounts payable	..	..	..	..	..	..	..	..
Non-financial assets	..	..	..	..	..	..	..	..
Insurance corporations								
Financial net worth	..	..	..	..	..	..	..	..
Financial assets	..	..	..	..	..	..	..	..
Currency and deposits	..	..	..	..	..	..	..	..
Debt securities	..	..	..	..	..	..	..	..
Loans	..	..	..	..	..	..	..	..
Equity and investment fund shares	..	..	..	..	..	..	..	..
Equity	..	..	..	..	..	..	..	..
Investment fund shares	..	..	..	..	..	..	..	..
Money market fund shares	..	..	..	..	..	..	..	..
Non-Money market fund shares	..	..	..	..	..	..	..	..
Insurance pension and standardised guarantees	..	..	..	..	..	..	..	..
Financial derivatives and employee stock options	..	..	..	..	..	..	..	..
Other accounts receivable	..	..	..	..	..	..	..	..
Financial liabilities	..	..	..	..	..	..	..	..
Debt securities	..	..	..	..	..	..	..	..
Short-term debt securities	..	..	..	..	..	..	..	..
Long-term debt securities	..	..	..	..	..	..	..	..
Loans	..	..	..	..	..	..	..	..
Short-term loans	..	..	..	..	..	..	..	..
Long-term loans	..	..	..	..	..	..	..	..
Equity and investment fund shares	..	..	..	..	..	..	..	..
Insurance pension and standardised guarantees	..	..	..	..	..	..	..	..
Financial derivatives and employee stock options	..	..	..	..	..	..	..	..
Other accounts payable	..	..	..	..	..	..	..	..
Non-financial assets	..	..	..	..	..	..	..	..
Pension funds								
Financial net worth	..	..	..	..	..	..	..	..
Financial assets	..	..	..	..	..	51 365	57 612	64 621
Currency and deposits	..	..	..	..	..	3 775	3 957	4 555
Debt securities	..	..	..	..	..	11 469	12 781	14 508
Loans	..	..	..	..	..	22	10	7
Equity and investment fund shares	..	..	..	..	..	35 550	40 012	44 791
Equity	..	..	..	..	..	14 110	15 486	19 035
Investment fund shares	..	..	..	..	..	21 440	24 525	25 756
Money market fund shares	..	..	..	..	..	..	..	..
Non-Money market fund shares	..	..	..	..	..	..	..	..
Insurance pension and standardised guarantees	..	..	..	..	..	..	..	..
Financial derivatives and employee stock options	..	..	..	..	..	305	585	333
Other accounts receivable	..	..	..	..	..	244	268	427
Financial liabilities	..	..	..	..	..	..	..	..
Debt securities	..	..	..	..	..	..	..	..
Short-term debt securities	..	..	..	..	..	..	..	..
Long-term debt securities	..	..	..	..	..	..	..	..
Loans	..	..	..	..	..	..	..	..
Short-term loans	..	..	..	..	..	..	..	..
Long-term loans	..	..	..	..	..	..	..	..
Equity and investment fund shares	..	..	..	..	..	..	..	..
Insurance pension and standardised guarantees	..	..	..	..	..	..	..	..
Financial derivatives and employee stock options	..	..	..	..	..	..	..	..
Other accounts payable	..	..	..	..	..	..	..	..
Non-financial assets	..	..	..	..	..	114	111	117

Note: Detailed metadata at: http://metalinks.oecd.org/instinv/20170920/75e8

Table 4. Portfolio composition by type of investor

As percentage of financial assets and of financial liabilities

Per cent

	2009	2010	2011	2012	2013	2014	2015	2016
Investment funds								
Financial assets	..	..	..	..	..	100.0	100.0	100.0
Currency and deposits	..	..	..	..	..	23.4	21.6	21.0
Debt securities	..	..	..	..	..	28.6	30.1	31.5
Loans	..	..	..	..	..	0.1	0.0	0.0
Equity and investment fund shares	..	..	..	..	..	46.9	47.2	46.7
Insurance pension and standardised guarantee schemes	..	..	..	..	..	0.0	0.0	0.0
Financial derivatives and employee stock options	..	..	..	..	..	0.3	0.4	0.3
Other accounts receivable	..	..	..	..	..	0.6	0.6	0.5
Financial liabilities	..	..	..	..	..	..	..	..
Currency and deposits	..	..	..	..	..	..	..	..
Debt securities	..	..	..	..	..	..	..	..
Loans	..	..	..	..	..	..	..	..
Equity and investment fund shares	..	..	..	..	..	..	..	..
Insurance pension and standardised guarantee schemes	..	..	..	..	..	..	..	..
Financial derivatives and employee stock options	..	..	..	..	..	..	..	..
Other accounts receivable	..	..	..	..	..	..	..	..
Insurance corporations								
Financial assets	..	..	..	..	..	..	..	..
Currency and deposits	..	..	..	..	..	..	..	..
Debt securities	..	..	..	..	..	..	..	..
Loans	..	..	..	..	..	..	..	..
Equity and investment fund shares	..	..	..	..	..	..	..	..
Insurance pension and standardised guarantee schemes	..	..	..	..	..	..	..	..
Financial derivatives and employee stock options	..	..	..	..	..	..	..	..
Other accounts receivable	..	..	..	..	..	..	..	..
Financial liabilities	..	..	..	..	..	..	..	..
Currency and deposits	..	..	..	..	..	..	..	..
Debt securities	..	..	..	..	..	..	..	..
Loans	..	..	..	..	..	..	..	..
Equity and investment fund shares	..	..	..	..	..	..	..	..
Insurance pension and standardised guarantee schemes	..	..	..	..	..	..	..	..
Financial derivatives and employee stock options	..	..	..	..	..	..	..	..
Other accounts receivable	..	..	..	..	..	..	..	..
Pension funds								
Financial assets	..	..	..	..	..	100.0	100.0	100.0
Currency and deposits	..	..	..	..	..	7.3	6.9	7.0
Debt securities	..	..	..	..	..	22.3	22.2	22.5
Loans	..	..	..	..	..	0.0	0.0	0.0
Equity and investment fund shares	..	..	..	..	..	69.2	69.5	69.3
Insurance pension and standardised guarantee schemes	..	..	..	..	..	0.0	0.0	0.0
Financial derivatives and employee stock options	..	..	..	..	..	0.6	1.0	0.5
Other accounts receivable	..	..	..	..	..	0.5	0.5	0.7
Financial liabilities	..	..	..	..	..	..	..	..
Currency and deposits	..	..	..	..	..	..	..	..
Debt securities	..	..	..	..	..	..	..	..
Loans	..	..	..	..	..	..	..	..
Equity and investment fund shares	..	..	..	..	..	..	..	..
Insurance pension and standardised guarantee schemes	..	..	..	..	..	..	..	..
Financial derivatives and employee stock options	..	..	..	..	..	..	..	..
Other accounts receivable	..	..	..	..	..	..	..	..

Note: Detailed metadata at: http://metalinks.oecd.org/instinv/20170920/a49a

NORWAY

Table 1. Financial assets and liabilities of institutional investors, 2016

Million NOK

	Investment funds				
	Total	Non-money market funds			Money market funds
		Total	Open-end non-money market funds	Closed-end non-money market funds	Total
Financial assets	..	..	959 198	..	95 884
Currency and deposits	..	..	25 035	..	10 267
Debt securities	..	..	328 862	..	77 986
Debt securities, short term	..	..	12 299	..	14 196
Debt securities, long term	..	..	316 563	..	63 790
Debt securities issued by residents	..	..	193 458	..	74 623
Debt securities issued by non-residents	..	..	135 404	..	3 363
Loans	..	..	0	..	..
Loans, short-term	..	..	..	..	..
Loans, long-term	..	..	0	..	..
Loans granted to residents	..	..	0	..	..
Loans granted to non-residents	..	..	..	..	..
Equity and investment fund shares/units	..	..	596 377	..	7 295
Equity and investment fund shares issued/units by residents	..	..	243 948	..	7 282
Equity and investment fund shares/units issued by non residents	..	..	352 429	..	..
Other accounts receivable	..	..	14 447	..	336

	Investment funds				
	Total	Non-money market funds			Money market funds
		Total	Open-end non-money market funds	Closed-end non-money market funds	Total
Financial liabilities	..	..	955 321	..	95 778
Currency and deposits	..	..	..	..	..
Debt securities	..	..	..	..	..
Debt securities, short term	..	..	..	..	..
Debt securities, long term	..	..	..	..	..
Loans	..	..	435	..	..
Loans, short-term	..	..	435	..	..
Loans, long-term	..	..	..	..	..
Equity and investment fund shares/units	..	..	950 878	..	95 450
Insurance pension and standardised guaratees	..	..	..	..	..
Financial derivatives and employee stock options	..	..	..	..	..
Other accounts payable	..	..	4 008	..	328

	Insurance corporations and pension funds				
	Total	Insurance corporations			Pension funds
		Total	Life insurance corporations	Non-life insurance corporations	Total
Financial assets	1 935 438	1 609 668	1 378 482	231 186	325 770
Currency and deposits	41 759	34 468	25 515	8 953	7 291
Debt securities	753 338	620 627	523 016	97 611	132 711
Debt securities, short-term	39 458	33 304	20 199	13 105	6 154
Debt securities, long term	713 880	587 323	502 817	84 506	126 557
Debt securities issued by residents	423 336	309 002	242 299	66 703	114 334
Debt securities issued by non-residents	330 002	311 625	280 717	30 908	18 377
Loans	118 123	116 090	114 230	1 860	2 033
Loans, short-term	0	0	0	0	..
Loans, long-term	118 123	116 090	114 230	1 860	2 033
Loans granted to residents	108 226	106 196	104 336	1 860	2 030
Loans granted to non-residents	9 897	9 894	9 894	0	3
Equity and investment fund shares/units	936 167	754 383	705 713	48 670	181 784
Equity and investment fund shares/units issued by residents	665 317	556 666	534 040	22 626	108 651
Equity and investment fund shares/units issued by non residents	270 850	197 717	171 673	26 044	73 133
Other accounts receivable	61 724	60 002	5 792	54 210	1 722

	Insurance corporations and pension funds				
	Total	Insurance corporations			Pension funds
		Total	Life insurance corporations	Non-life insurance corporations	Total
Financial liabilities	1 987 155	1 653 032	1 380 428	272 604	334 123
Currency and deposits	..	..	-	..	..
Debt securities	20 596	20 596	17 577	3 019	0
Debt securities, short term	..	..	-	..	..
Debt securities, long term	20 596	20 596	17 577	3 019	0
Loans	12 381	11 957	11 579	378	424
Loans, short-term	1 099	1 099	1 096	3	..
Loans, long-term	11 282	10 858	10 483	375	424
Equity and investment fund shares/units	260 738	229 521	93 281	136 240	31 217
Insurance pension and standardised guarantees	1 660 970	1 360 447	1 240 852	119 595	300 523
Financial derivatives and employee stock options	8 190	7 067	6 185	882	1 123
Other accounts payable	24 280	23 444	10 954	12 490	836

Note: Detailed metadata at: http://metalinks.oecd.org/instinv/20170920/75e8

Table 2. Financial assets and liabilities of investment funds

Million NOK

	2009	2010	2011	2012	2013	2014	2015	2016
Investment funds								
Financial net worth	..	..	..	..	..	..	..	..
Financial assets	..	..	..	..	..	..	..	..
Currency and deposits	..	..	..	..	..	..	..	..
Debt securities	..	..	..	..	..	..	..	..
Loans	..	..	..	..	..	..	..	..
Equity and investment fund shares	..	..	..	..	..	..	..	..
Equity	..	..	..	..	..	..	..	..
Investment fund shares	..	..	..	..	..	..	..	..
Money market fund shares	..	..	..	..	..	..	..	..
Non-Money market fund shares	..	..	..	..	..	..	..	..
Insurance pension and standardised guarantees	..	..	..	..	..	..	..	..
Financial derivatives and employee stock options	..	..	..	..	..	..	..	..
Other accounts receivable	..	..	..	..	..	..	..	..
Financial liabilities	..	..	..	..	..	..	..	..
Debt securities	..	..	..	..	..	..	..	..
Short-term debt securities	..	..	..	..	..	..	..	..
Long-term debt securities	..	..	..	..	..	..	..	..
Loans	..	..	..	..	..	..	..	..
Short-term loans	..	..	..	..	..	..	..	..
Long-term loans	..	..	..	..	..	..	..	..
Equity and investment fund shares	..	..	..	..	..	..	..	..
Insurance pension and standardised guarantees	..	..	..	..	..	..	..	..
Financial derivatives and employee stock options	..	..	..	..	..	..	..	..
Other accounts payable	..	..	..	..	..	..	..	..
Non-financial assets	..	..	..	..	..	..	..	..
Money market funds								
Financial net worth	85	-1 318	265	-42	38	48	58	106
Financial assets	111 816	109 163	120 275	95 718	90 646	86 717	82 313	95 884
Currency and deposits	6 525	6 845	5 494	10 993	12 715	13 422	10 216	10 267
Debt securities	89 737	85 875	98 069	76 512	68 000	66 345	65 384	77 986
Loans	..	..	..	..	..	..	..	..
Equity and investment fund shares	14 694	15 488	16 006	7 605	8 614	6 505	6 377	7 295
Equity	..	..	..	..	..	..	..	..
Investment fund shares	14 694	15 488	16 006	7 605	8 614	6 505	6 377	7 295
Money market fund shares	14 694	15 488	16 006	7 592	8 560	6 468	6 364	7 282
Non-Money market fund shares	..	..	..	..	..	..	..	..
Insurance pension and standardised guarantees	..	..	..	..	..	..	..	..
Financial derivatives and employee stock options	..	..	..	..	..	..	..	..
Other accounts receivable	860	955	706	608	1 317	445	336	336
Financial liabilities	111 731	110 481	120 010	95 760	90 608	86 669	82 255	95 778
Debt securities	..	..	..	..	..	..	..	..
Short-term debt securities	..	..	..	..	..	..	..	..
Long-term debt securities	..	..	..	..	..	..	..	..
Loans	..	..	..	..	..	..	..	..
Short-term loans	..	..	..	..	..	..	..	..
Long-term loans	..	..	..	..	..	..	..	..
Equity and investment fund shares	111 078	110 146	119 472	95 520	89 545	86 236	81 929	95 450
Insurance pension and standardised guarantees	..	..	..	..	..	..	..	..
Financial derivatives and employee stock options	..	..	..	..	..	..	..	..
Other accounts payable	653	335	538	240	1 063	433	326	328
Non-financial assets	..	..	..	..	..	..	..	..
Non-money market funds								
Financial net worth	..	..	..	..	..	..	..	..
Financial assets	..	..	..	..	..	..	..	..
Currency and deposits	..	..	..	..	..	..	..	..
Debt securities	..	..	..	..	..	..	..	..
Loans	..	..	..	..	..	..	..	..
Equity and investment fund shares	..	..	..	..	..	..	..	..
Equity	..	..	..	..	..	..	..	..
Investment fund shares	..	..	..	..	..	..	..	..
Money market fund shares	..	..	..	..	..	..	..	..
Non-Money market fund shares	..	..	..	..	..	..	..	..
Insurance pension and standardised guarantees	..	..	..	..	..	..	..	..
Financial derivatives and employee stock options	..	..	..	..	..	..	..	..
Other accounts receivable	..	..	..	..	..	..	..	..
Financial liabilities	..	..	..	..	..	..	..	..
Debt securities	..	..	..	..	..	..	..	..
Short-term debt securities	..	..	..	..	..	..	..	..
Long-term debt securities	..	..	..	..	..	..	..	..
Loans	..	..	..	..	..	..	..	..
Short-term loans	..	..	..	..	..	..	..	..
Long-term loans	..	..	..	..	..	..	..	..
Equity and investment fund shares	..	..	..	..	..	..	..	..
Insurance pension and standardised guarantees	..	..	..	..	..	..	..	..
Financial derivatives and employee stock options	..	..	..	..	..	..	..	..
Other accounts payable	..	..	..	..	..	..	..	..
Non-financial assets	..	..	..	..	..	..	..	..
Open-end non-money market funds								
Financial net worth	3 129	4 194	2 719	539	526	13	783	3 877
Financial assets	340 850	435 788	409 383	518 095	641 172	824 695	884 689	959 198

Table 2. Financial assets and liabilities of investment funds *(cont.)*

Million NOK

	2009	2010	2011	2012	2013	2014	2015	2016
Currency and deposits	16 142	13 080	16 470	16 293	18 721	26 214	26 810	25 035
Debt securities	62 562	89 792	107 306	158 407	178 526	293 483	314 650	328 862
Loans	0	0	0	0	0	0	0	0
Equity and investment fund shares	258 601	327 629	282 251	330 722	438 402	498 837	536 726	596 377
Equity	212 733	273 308	232 679	260 330	342 826	379 600	399 051	437 232
Investment fund shares	45 868	54 321	49 572	70 392	95 576	119 237	137 675	159 145
Money market fund shares	0	0	0	6 274	4 895	5 977	6 372	6 816
Non-Money market fund shares	45 868	54 321	49 572	64 118	90 681	113 260	131 303	152 329
Insurance pension and standardised guarantees	..	..	..	..	..	..	..	..
Financial derivatives and employee stock options	0	0	0	705	-190	-5 349	-5 523	-5 523
Other accounts receivable	3 545	5 287	3 356	11 968	5 713	11 510	12 026	14 447
Financial liabilities	337 721	431 594	406 664	517 556	640 646	824 682	883 906	955 321
Debt securities	..	..	..	..	..	..	..	..
Short-term debt securities	..	..	..	..	..	..	..	..
Long-term debt securities	..	..	..	..	..	..	..	..
Loans	0	0	0	1 113	650	1 978	3 743	435
Short-term loans	0	0	0	1 113	650	1 978	3 743	435
Long-term loans	..	..	..	..	..	..	..	..
Equity and investment fund shares	337 661	431 521	406 598	513 910	636 305	818 518	876 168	950 878
Insurance pension and standardised guarantees	..	..	..	..	..	..	..	..
Financial derivatives and employee stock options	..	..	..	..	..	..	..	..
Other accounts payable	60	73	66	2 533	3 691	4 186	3 995	4 008
Non-financial assets	..	..	..	..	..	..	..	..
Open-end investment funds								
Financial net worth	3 214	2 876	2 984	497	564	61	841	3 983
Financial assets	452 666	544 951	529 658	613 813	731 818	911 412	967 002	1 055 082
Currency and deposits	22 667	19 925	21 964	27 286	31 436	39 636	37 026	35 302
Debt securities	152 299	175 667	205 375	234 919	246 526	359 828	380 034	406 848
Loans	0	0	0	0	0	0	0	0
Equity and investment fund shares	273 295	343 117	298 257	338 327	447 016	505 342	543 103	603 672
Equity	212 733	273 308	232 679	260 330	342 826	379 600	399 051	437 232
Investment fund shares	60 562	69 809	65 578	77 997	104 190	125 742	144 052	166 440
Money market fund shares	14 694	15 488	16 006	13 866	13 455	12 445	12 736	14 098
Non-Money market fund shares	45 868	54 321	49 572	64 131	90 735	113 297	131 316	152 342
Insurance pension and standardised guarantees	..	..	..	..	..	..	..	..
Financial derivatives and employee stock options	0	0	0	705	-190	-5 349	-5 523	-5 523
Other accounts receivable	4 405	6 242	4 062	12 576	7 030	11 955	12 362	14 783
Financial liabilities	449 452	542 075	526 674	613 316	731 254	911 351	966 161	1 051 099
Debt securities	..	..	..	..	..	..	..	..
Short-term debt securities	..	..	..	..	..	..	..	..
Long-term debt securities	..	..	..	..	..	..	..	..
Loans	0	0	0	1 113	650	1 978	3 743	435
Short-term loans	0	0	0	1 113	650	1 978	3 743	435
Long-term loans	..	..	..	..	..	..	..	..
Equity and investment fund shares	448 739	541 667	526 070	609 430	725 850	904 754	958 097	1 046 328
Insurance pension and standardised guarantees	..	..	..	..	..	..	..	..
Financial derivatives and employee stock options	..	..	..	..	..	..	..	..
Other accounts payable	713	408	604	2 773	4 754	4 619	4 321	4 336
Non-financial assets	..	..	..	..	..	..	..	..

Note: Detailed metadata at: http://metalinks.oecd.org/instinv/20170920/75e8

Table 3. Financial assets and liabilities of insurance corporations and pension funds

Million NOK

	2009	2010	2011	2012	2013	2014	2015	2016
Insurance corporations and pension funds								
Financial net worth	28 110	26 183	19 050	-21 296	-35 308	-32 621	-47 574	-51 717
Financial assets	1 107 812	1 209 650	1 273 579	1 410 105	1 554 349	1 717 289	1 825 987	1 935 438
Currency and deposits	40 412	39 519	38 768	44 030	54 388	45 782	46 960	41 759
Debt securities	543 148	550 608	615 902	670 544	731 358	702 241	732 544	753 338
Loans	73 691	57 450	54 059	53 658	64 870	84 510	94 911	118 123
Equity and investment fund shares	379 281	485 463	492 237	567 562	626 038	802 131	868 178	936 167
Equity	203 521	260 160	218 490	242 316	246 444	270 419	287 519	299 242
Investment fund shares	175 760	225 303	273 747	325 246	379 594	531 712	580 659	636 925
Money market fund shares	31 291	32 236	41 235	36 833	32 472	30 393	26 770	27 492
Non-Money market fund shares	144 469	193 067	232 512	288 413	347 122	501 319	553 889	609 433
Insurance pension and standardised guarantees	14 888	13 369	13 065	14 209	16 270	16 147	18 599	18 949
Financial derivatives and employee stock options	1 844	3 856	1 509	5 572	3 829	4 928	3 917	5 378
Other accounts receivable	54 548	59 385	58 039	54 530	57 596	61 550	60 878	61 724
Financial liabilities	1 079 702	1 183 467	1 254 529	1 431 401	1 589 657	1 749 910	1 873 561	1 987 155
Debt securities	8 199	11 147	10 994	11 016	11 377	13 162	20 197	20 596
Short-term debt securities	..	..	..	..	..	..	..	..
Long-term debt securities	8 199	11 147	10 994	11 016	11 377	13 162	20 197	20 596
Loans	9 619	4 320	4 393	4 775	3 859	4 565	11 237	12 381
Short-term loans	1	5	0	37	25	31	375	1 099
Long-term loans	9 618	4 315	4 393	4 738	3 834	4 534	10 862	11 282
Equity and investment fund shares	40 988	71 243	90 483	175 478	208 510	227 550	261 072	260 738
Insurance pension and standardised guarantees	991 606	1 076 188	1 120 210	1 214 058	1 336 457	1 460 755	1 544 172	1 660 970
Financial derivatives and employee stock options	2 169	1 699	2 083	2 241	4 141	18 398	12 398	8 190
Other accounts payable	27 121	18 870	26 366	23 833	25 313	25 480	24 485	24 280
Non-financial assets	..	..	..	..	..	..	..	..
Insurance corporations								
Financial net worth	53 893	54 485	47 435	-14 551	-31 223	-32 623	-50 005	-43 364
Financial assets	941 613	1 027 696	1 088 313	1 186 317	1 297 941	1 426 697	1 509 629	1 609 668
Currency and deposits	32 610	33 745	32 732	38 011	48 304	38 262	39 701	34 468
Debt securities	447 094	451 003	502 667	555 786	607 928	570 467	594 558	620 627
Loans	71 562	55 191	51 949	51 131	61 935	81 978	92 878	116 090
Equity and investment fund shares	325 019	417 530	434 270	469 566	503 374	655 369	701 057	754 383
Equity	178 703	228 707	193 022	208 176	206 167	226 911	240 235	251 821
Investment fund shares	146 316	188 823	241 248	261 390	297 207	428 458	460 822	502 562
Money market fund shares	31 291	32 236	41 235	32 278	26 499	23 474	18 930	19 482
Non-Money market fund shares	115 025	156 587	200 013	229 112	270 708	404 984	441 892	483 080
Insurance pension and standardised guarantees	14 888	13 369	13 065	14 209	16 270	16 147	18 599	18 949
Financial derivatives and employee stock options	1 844	3 856	1 509	4 996	3 611	4 612	3 660	5 149
Other accounts receivable	48 596	53 002	52 121	52 618	56 519	59 862	59 176	60 002
Financial liabilities	887 720	973 211	1 040 878	1 200 868	1 329 164	1 459 320	1 559 634	1 653 032
Debt securities	8 199	11 147	10 994	10 779	11 030	13 161	20 197	20 596
Short-term debt securities	..	..	..	..	..	..	..	..
Long-term debt securities	8 199	11 147	10 994	10 779	11 030	13 161	20 197	20 596
Loans	9 619	4 320	4 393	4 280	3 347	4 118	10 813	11 957
Short-term loans	1	5	0	37	25	31	375	1 099
Long-term loans	9 618	4 315	4 393	4 243	3 322	4 087	10 438	10 858
Equity and investment fund shares	25 992	53 848	72 861	153 807	184 076	200 584	229 855	229 521
Insurance pension and standardised guarantees	816 249	884 472	925 684	1 007 028	1 102 384	1 201 068	1 264 069	1 360 447
Financial derivatives and employee stock options	2 169	1 699	2 083	2 169	3 810	15 939	11 051	7 067
Other accounts payable	25 492	17 725	24 863	22 805	24 517	24 450	23 649	23 444
Non-financial assets	..	..	..	..	..	..	..	..
Pension funds								
Financial net worth	-25 783	-28 302	-28 385	-6 745	-4 085	2	2 431	-8 353
Financial assets	166 199	181 954	185 266	223 788	256 408	290 592	316 358	325 770
Currency and deposits	7 802	5 774	6 036	6 019	6 084	7 520	7 259	7 291
Debt securities	96 054	99 605	113 235	114 758	123 430	131 774	137 986	132 711
Loans	2 129	2 259	2 110	2 527	2 935	2 532	2 033	2 033
Equity and investment fund shares	54 262	67 933	57 967	97 996	122 664	146 762	167 121	181 784
Equity	24 818	31 453	25 468	34 140	40 277	43 508	47 284	47 421
Investment fund shares	29 444	36 480	32 499	63 856	82 387	103 254	119 837	134 363
Money market fund shares	0	0	0	4 555	5 973	6 919	7 840	8 010
Non-Money market fund shares	29 444	36 480	32 499	59 301	76 414	96 335	111 997	126 353
Insurance pension and standardised guarantees	..	..	..	..	..	..	..	..
Financial derivatives and employee stock options	0	0	0	576	218	316	257	229
Other accounts receivable	5 952	6 383	5 918	1 912	1 077	1 688	1 702	1 722
Financial liabilities	191 982	210 256	213 651	230 533	260 493	290 590	313 927	334 123
Debt securities	0	0	0	237	347	1	0	0
Short-term debt securities	..	..	..	..	..	..	..	..
Long-term debt securities	0	0	0	237	347	1	0	0
Loans	0	0	0	495	512	447	424	424
Short-term loans	..	..	..	..	..	..	..	..
Long-term loans	0	0	0	495	512	447	424	424
Equity and investment fund shares	14 996	17 395	17 622	21 671	24 434	26 966	31 217	31 217
Insurance pension and standardised guarantees	175 357	191 716	194 526	207 030	234 073	259 687	280 103	300 523
Financial derivatives and employee stock options	0	0	0	72	331	2 459	1 347	1 123
Other accounts payable	1 629	1 145	1 503	1 028	796	1 030	836	836
Non-financial assets	..	..	..	..	..	..	..	..

Note: Detailed metadata at: http://metalinks.oecd.org/instinv/20170920/75e8

Table 4. Portfolio composition by type of investor

As percentage of financial assets and of financial liabilities

Per cent

	2009	2010	2011	2012	2013	2014	2015	2016
Investment funds								
Financial assets	..	..	..	..	..	..	..	..
Currency and deposits	..	..	..	..	..	..	..	..
Debt securities	..	..	..	..	..	..	..	..
Loans	..	..	..	..	..	..	..	..
Equity and investment fund shares	..	..	..	..	..	..	..	..
Insurance pension and standardised guarantee schemes	..	..	..	..	..	..	..	..
Financial derivatives and employee stock options	..	..	..	..	..	..	..	..
Other accounts receivable	..	..	..	..	..	..	..	..
Financial liabilities	..	..	..	..	..	..	..	..
Currency and deposits	..	..	..	..	..	..	..	..
Debt securities	..	..	..	..	..	..	..	..
Loans	..	..	..	..	..	..	..	..
Equity and investment fund shares	..	..	..	..	..	..	..	..
Insurance pension and standardised guarantee schemes	..	..	..	..	..	..	..	..
Financial derivatives and employee stock options	..	..	..	..	..	..	..	..
Other accounts receivable	..	..	..	..	..	..	..	..
Insurance corporations								
Financial assets	100.0	100.0	100.0	100.0	100.0	100.0	100.0	100.0
Currency and deposits	3.5	3.3	3.0	3.2	3.7	2.7	2.6	2.1
Debt securities	47.5	43.9	46.2	46.8	46.8	40.0	39.4	38.6
Loans	7.6	5.4	4.8	4.3	4.8	5.7	6.2	7.2
Equity and investment fund shares	34.5	40.6	39.9	39.6	38.8	45.9	46.4	46.9
Insurance pension and standardised guarantee schemes	1.6	1.3	1.2	1.2	1.3	1.1	1.2	1.2
Financial derivatives and employee stock options	0.2	0.4	0.1	0.4	0.3	0.3	0.2	0.3
Other accounts receivable	5.2	5.2	4.8	4.4	4.4	4.2	3.9	3.7
Financial liabilities	100.0	100.0	100.0	100.0	100.0	100.0	100.0	100.0
Currency and deposits	0.0	0.0	0.0	0.0	0.0	0.0	0.0	0.0
Debt securities	0.9	1.1	1.1	0.9	0.8	0.9	1.3	1.2
Loans	1.1	0.4	0.4	0.4	0.3	0.3	0.7	0.7
Equity and investment fund shares	2.9	5.5	7.0	12.8	13.8	13.7	14.7	13.9
Insurance pension and standardised guarantee schemes	91.9	90.9	88.9	83.9	82.9	82.3	81.0	82.3
Financial derivatives and employee stock options	0.2	0.2	0.2	0.2	0.3	1.1	0.7	0.4
Other accounts receivable	2.9	1.8	2.4	1.9	1.8	1.7	1.5	1.4
Pension funds								
Financial assets	100.0	100.0	100.0	100.0	100.0	100.0	100.0	100.0
Currency and deposits	4.7	3.2	3.3	2.7	2.4	2.6	2.3	2.2
Debt securities	57.8	54.7	61.1	51.3	48.1	45.3	43.6	40.7
Loans	1.3	1.2	1.1	1.1	1.1	0.9	0.6	0.6
Equity and investment fund shares	32.6	37.3	31.3	43.8	47.8	50.5	52.8	55.8
Insurance pension and standardised guarantee schemes	0.0	0.0	0.0	0.0	0.0	0.0	0.0	0.0
Financial derivatives and employee stock options	0.0	0.0	0.0	0.3	0.1	0.1	0.1	0.1
Other accounts receivable	3.6	3.5	3.2	0.9	0.4	0.6	0.5	0.5
Financial liabilities	100.0	100.0	100.0	100.0	100.0	100.0	100.0	100.0
Currency and deposits	0.0	0.0	0.0	0.0	0.0	0.0	0.0	0.0
Debt securities	0.0	0.0	0.0	0.1	0.1	0.0	0.0	0.0
Loans	0.0	0.0	0.0	0.2	0.2	0.2	0.1	0.1
Equity and investment fund shares	7.8	8.3	8.2	9.4	9.4	9.3	9.9	9.3
Insurance pension and standardised guarantee schemes	91.3	91.2	91.0	89.8	89.9	89.4	89.2	89.9
Financial derivatives and employee stock options	0.0	0.0	0.0	0.0	0.1	0.8	0.4	0.3
Other accounts receivable	0.8	0.5	0.7	0.4	0.3	0.4	0.3	0.3

Note: Detailed metadata at: http://metalinks.oecd.org/instinv/20170920/a49a

POLAND

Table 1. Financial assets and liabilities of institutional investors, 2016

Million PLN

	Total	Investment funds			
		Non-money market funds			Money market funds
		Total	Open-end non-money market funds	Closed-end non-money market funds	Total
Financial assets	..	285 975	137 573	148 402	..
Currency and deposits	..	20 358	9 713	10 645	..
Debt securities	..	119 317	81 034	38 283	..
Debt securities, short term	..	2 095	758	1 337	..
Debt securities, long term	..	117 222	80 276	36 946	..
Debt securities issued by residents	..	104 905	70 527	34 378	..
Debt securities issued by non-residents	..	14 412	10 507	3 905	..
Loans	..	14 581	..	14 579	..
Loans, short-term	..	..	..	312	..
Loans, long-term	..	14 267	0	14 267	..
Loans granted to residents	..	..	..	4 449	..
Loans granted to non-residents	..	..	0	..	..
Equity and investment fund shares/units	..	..	45 312	58 456	..
Equity and investment fund shares issued/units by residents	..	54 654	28 196	26 458	..
Equity and investment fund shares/units issued by non residents	..	49 114	17 116	31 998	..
Other accounts receivable	..	27 602	1 398	26 204	..

	Total	Investment funds			
		Non-money market funds			Money market funds
		Total	Open-end non-money market funds	Closed-end non-money market funds	Total
Financial liabilities	..	..	137 573	152 523	..
Currency and deposits	..	..	..	..	..
Debt securities	..	..	..	..	..
Debt securities, short term	..	..	..	..	..
Debt securities, long term	..	..	..	..	..
Loans	..	7 369	6 679	690	..
Loans, short-term	..	7 099	6 679	420	..
Loans, long-term	..	270	0	270	..
Equity and investment fund shares/units	..	271 720	126 206	145 514	..
Insurance pension and standardised guaratees	..	..	..	..	..
Financial derivatives and employee stock options	..	179	116	63	..
Other accounts payable	..	10 827	4 572	6 255	..

	Total	Insurance corporations and pension funds			
		Insurance corporations			Pension funds
		Total	Life insurance corporations	Non-life insurance corporations	Total
Financial assets	339 497	183 715	102 777	80 938	155 782
Currency and deposits	22 265	9 844	6 340	3 505	12 421
Debt securities	87 830	72 813	35 308	37 505	15 017
Debt securities, short-term	0	0	0	0	0 e
Debt securities, long term	87 830	72 813	35 308	37 505	15 017 e
Debt securities issued by residents	83 378	68 632	33 373	35 260	14 746 e
Debt securities issued by non-residents	4 452	4 181	1 935	2 245	271 e
Loans	2 850	2 850	603	2 247	0
Loans, short-term	..	1 471	165	1 306	0
Loans, long-term	..	1 379	438	941	0
Loans granted to residents	2 721	2 721	603	2 118	0
Loans granted to non-residents	129	129	0	129	0
Equity and investment fund shares/units	192 936	65 202	45 505	19 697	127 734
Equity and investment fund shares/units issued by residents	175 137	58 302	39 589	18 712	116 835 e
Equity and investment fund shares/units issued by non residents	17 800	6 901	5 916	985	10 899 e
Other accounts receivable	26 558	25 947	14 148 e	11 799	611

	Total	Insurance corporations and pension funds			
		Insurance corporations			Pension funds
		Total	Life insurance corporations	Non-life insurance corporations	Total
Financial liabilities	341 148	185 366	103 193	82 173	155 782
Currency and deposits	1 618	1 618 e	148 e	1 470 e	0
Debt securities	..	..	..	..	0
Debt securities, short term	..	..	..	..	0
Debt securities, long term	..	..	..	..	0
Loans	..	..	..	..	0
Loans, short-term	..	..	..	..	0
Loans, long-term	..	..	..	..	0
Equity and investment fund shares/units	..	..	..	..	0
Insurance pension and standardised guarantees	297 935	142 729	87 359	55 370	155 206
Financial derivatives and employee stock options	..	..	..	..	0
Other accounts payable	..	..	..	..	576

Note: Detailed metadata at: http://metalinks.oecd.org/instinv/20170920/06e1

Table 2. Financial assets and liabilities of investment funds

Million PLN

	2009	2010	2011	2012	2013	2014	2015	2016
Investment funds								
Financial net worth	..	..	..	..	..	..	..	..
Financial assets	..	..	..	..	..	..	..	..
Currency and deposits	..	..	..	..	..	..	..	..
Debt securities	..	..	..	..	..	..	..	..
Loans	..	..	..	..	..	..	..	..
Equity and investment fund shares	..	..	..	..	..	..	..	..
Equity	..	..	..	..	..	..	..	..
Investment fund shares	..	..	..	..	..	..	..	..
Money market fund shares	..	..	..	..	..	..	..	..
Non-Money market fund shares	..	..	..	..	..	..	..	..
Insurance pension and standardised guarantees	..	..	..	..	..	..	..	..
Financial derivatives and employee stock options	..	..	..	..	..	..	..	..
Other accounts receivable	..	..	..	..	..	..	..	..
Financial liabilities	..	..	..	..	..	..	..	..
Debt securities	..	..	..	..	..	..	..	..
Short-term debt securities	..	..	..	..	..	..	..	..
Long-term debt securities	..	..	..	..	..	..	..	..
Loans	..	..	..	..	..	..	..	..
Short-term loans	..	..	..	..	..	..	..	..
Long-term loans	..	..	..	..	..	..	..	..
Equity and investment fund shares	..	..	..	..	..	..	..	..
Insurance pension and standardised guarantees	..	..	..	..	..	..	..	..
Financial derivatives and employee stock options	..	..	..	..	..	..	..	..
Other accounts payable	..	..	..	..	..	..	..	..
Non-financial assets	..	..	..	..	..	..	..	..
Money market funds								
Financial net worth	..	..	..	..	..	..	..	..
Financial assets	..	..	..	..	..	..	..	..
Currency and deposits	..	..	..	..	..	..	..	..
Debt securities	..	..	..	..	..	..	..	..
Loans	..	..	..	..	..	..	..	..
Equity and investment fund shares	..	..	..	..	..	..	..	..
Equity	..	..	..	..	..	..	..	..
Investment fund shares	..	..	..	..	..	..	..	..
Money market fund shares	..	..	..	..	..	..	..	..
Non-Money market fund shares	..	..	..	..	..	..	..	..
Insurance pension and standardised guarantees	..	..	..	..	..	..	..	..
Financial derivatives and employee stock options	..	..	..	..	..	..	..	..
Other accounts receivable	..	..	..	..	..	..	..	..
Financial liabilities	..	..	..	..	..	..	..	..
Debt securities	..	..	..	..	..	..	..	..
Short-term debt securities	..	..	..	..	..	..	..	..
Long-term debt securities	..	..	..	..	..	..	..	..
Loans	..	..	..	..	..	..	..	..
Short-term loans	..	..	..	..	..	..	..	..
Long-term loans	..	..	..	..	..	..	..	..
Equity and investment fund shares	..	..	..	..	..	..	..	..
Insurance pension and standardised guarantees	..	..	..	..	..	..	..	..
Financial derivatives and employee stock options	..	..	..	..	..	..	..	..
Other accounts payable	..	..	..	..	..	..	..	..
Non-financial assets	..	..	..	..	..	..	..	..
Non-money market funds								
Financial net worth	..	-2	-4	-3	-749	-2 498	-2 533	-4 121
Financial assets	..	133 201	123 794	158 821	209 923	237 992	290 227	285 975
Currency and deposits	..	7 644	8 510	12 150	18 749	17 330	21 771	20 358
Debt securities	..	54 247	52 946	66 395	86 207	107 560	109 602	119 317
Loans	..	317	294	402	895	3 796	14 139	14 581
Equity and investment fund shares	..	67 654	55 869	67 500	88 632	90 023	119 453	..
Equity	..	59 437	48 172	59 602	79 090	74 532	102 432	86 089
Investment fund shares	..	8 217	7 697	7 898	9 542	15 491	17 021	17 679
Money market fund shares	..	192	151	0	0	2	6	..
Non-Money market fund shares	..	8 025	7 546	7 898	9 542	15 489	17 015	17 679
Insurance pension and standardised guarantees	..	..	..	..	..	..	..	..
Financial derivatives and employee stock options	..	172	144	119	279	297	360	349
Other accounts receivable	..	3 167	6 031	12 255	15 161	18 986	24 902	27 602
Financial liabilities	..	133 203	123 798	158 824	210 672	240 490	292 760	..
Debt securities	..	..	..	..	..	..	..	..
Short-term debt securities	..	..	..	..	..	..	..	..
Long-term debt securities	..	..	..	..	..	..	..	..
Loans	..	9 179	4 023	3 627	6 240	11 106	9 777	7 369
Short-term loans	..	9 179	3 850	3 627	6 166	11 012	9 660	7 099
Long-term loans	..	0	173	0	74	94	117	270
Equity and investment fund shares	..	121 013	116 991	150 428	192 273	216 134	269 914	271 720
Insurance pension and standardised guarantees	..	..	..	..	..	..	..	..
Financial derivatives and employee stock options	..	86	113	144	120	534	141	179
Other accounts payable	..	2 924	2 670	4 627	12 038	12 715	12 928	10 827
Non-financial assets	..	1	1	0	748	2 496	2 535	4 121
Open-end non-money market funds								
Financial net worth	..	-1	-2	-1	-1	-2	1	0
Financial assets	..	107 252	87 657	106 075	128 591	142 814	144 289	137 573

Table 2. Financial assets and liabilities of investment funds *(cont.)*

Million PLN

	2009	2010	2011	2012	2013	2014	2015	2016
Currency and deposits	..	6 062	5 781	8 777	13 373	12 328	11 685	9 713
Debt securities	..	51 147	48 649	60 927	69 103	84 334	84 718	81 034
Loans	..	0	0	2	3	2	2	..
Equity and investment fund shares	..	48 734	31 334	34 143	44 069	43 700	45 919	45 312
Equity	..	42 528	25 657	28 172	35 747	32 304	30 991	30 825
Investment fund shares	..	6 206	5 677	5 971	8 322	11 396	14 928	14 487
Money market fund shares	..	191	150	0	0	2	6	..
Non-Money market fund shares	..	6 015	5 527	5 971	8 322	11 394	14 922	14 487
Insurance pension and standardised guarantees	..	..	..	..	..	..	..	..
Financial derivatives and employee stock options	..	117	102	70	185	69	182	114
Other accounts receivable	..	1 192	1 791	2 156	1 858	2 381	1 783	1 398
Financial liabilities	..	107 253	87 659	106 076	128 592	142 816	144 288	137 573
Debt securities	..	..	..	..	..	..	..	..
Short-term debt securities	..	..	..	..	..	..	..	..
Long-term debt securities	..	..	..	..	..	..	..	..
Loans	..	9 136	3 772	3 539	5 442	8 137	8 392	6 679
Short-term loans	..	9 136	3 676	3 539	5 416	8 137	8 392	6 679
Long-term loans	..	0	96	0	26	0	0	0
Equity and investment fund shares	..	96 079	82 463	99 293	115 358	127 583	129 829	126 206
Insurance pension and standardised guarantees	..	..	..	..	..	..	..	..
Financial derivatives and employee stock options	..	12	42	67	55	420	113	116
Other accounts payable	..	2 025	1 381	3 178	7 737	6 675	5 953	4 572
Non-financial assets	..	0	0	0	0	0	0	0
Open-end investment funds								
Financial net worth	..	..	..	..	..	..	..	..
Financial assets	..	..	..	..	..	..	..	..
Currency and deposits	..	..	..	..	..	..	..	..
Debt securities	..	..	..	..	..	..	..	..
Loans	..	..	..	..	..	..	..	..
Equity and investment fund shares	..	..	..	..	..	..	..	..
Equity	..	..	..	..	..	..	..	..
Investment fund shares	..	..	..	..	..	..	..	..
Money market fund shares	..	..	..	..	..	..	..	..
Non-Money market fund shares	..	..	..	..	..	..	..	..
Insurance pension and standardised guarantees	..	..	..	..	..	..	..	..
Financial derivatives and employee stock options	..	..	..	..	..	..	..	..
Other accounts receivable	..	..	..	..	..	..	..	..
Financial liabilities	..	..	..	..	..	..	..	..
Debt securities	..	..	..	..	..	..	..	..
Short-term debt securities	..	..	..	..	..	..	..	..
Long-term debt securities	..	..	..	..	..	..	..	..
Loans	..	..	..	..	..	..	..	..
Short-term loans	..	..	..	..	..	..	..	..
Long-term loans	..	..	..	..	..	..	..	..
Equity and investment fund shares	..	..	..	..	..	..	..	..
Insurance pension and standardised guarantees	..	..	..	..	..	..	..	..
Financial derivatives and employee stock options	..	..	..	..	..	..	..	..
Other accounts payable	..	..	..	..	..	..	..	..
Non-financial assets	..	..	..	..	..	..	..	..

Note: Detailed metadata at: http://metalinks.oecd.org/instinv/20170920/06e1

Table 3. Financial assets and liabilities of insurance corporations and pension funds

Million PLN

	2009	2010	2011	2012	2013	2014	2015	2016
Insurance corporations and pension funds								
Financial net worth	-2 166	-2 208	-2 253	-2 340	-2 496	-2 831	-3 045	-1 651
Financial assets	323 133	373 247	373 542	441 731	474 234	334 184	329 381	339 497
Currency and deposits	21 152	24 072	23 402	36 249	29 340	24 153	21 380	22 265
Debt securities	189 378	198 804	211 036	223 591	222 296	80 118	79 760	87 830
Loans	913	2 124	2 107	3 410	5 116	5 347	3 976	2 850
Equity and investment fund shares	95 223	127 572	115 163	155 137	192 442	197 425	194 438	192 936
Equity	69 628	96 182	84 156	110 518	137 230	138 276	133 099	142 091
Investment fund shares	25 595	31 390	31 007	44 620	55 212	59 150	61 339	50 845
Money market fund shares	..	..	..	..	..	..	..	..
Non-Money market fund shares	..	..	..	..	..	..	..	..
Insurance pension and standardised guarantees	4 642	5 500	5 639	7 024	6 271	7 194	9 715	6 447
Financial derivatives and employee stock options	165	313	443	641	653	915	853	611
Other accounts receivable	11 660	14 861	15 749	15 678	18 118	19 030	19 259	26 558
Financial liabilities	325 300	375 455	380 795	444 071	476 730	337 015	332 425	341 148
Debt securities	..	..	..	..	..	..	..	..
Short-term debt securities	..	..	..	..	..	..	..	..
Long-term debt securities	..	..	..	..	..	..	..	..
Loans	..	..	..	..	..	..	..	..
Short-term loans	..	..	..	..	..	..	..	..
Long-term loans	..	..	..	..	..	..	..	..
Equity and investment fund shares	..	..	..	..	..	..	..	..
Insurance pension and standardised guarantees	280 047	332 570	335 563	392 259	428 089	283 800	279 398	297 935
Financial derivatives and employee stock options	..	..	..	..	..	..	..	..
Other accounts payable	..	..	..	..	..	..	..	..
Non-financial assets	2 166	2 208	2 253	2 340	2 496	2 839	3 045	1 651
Insurance corporations								
Financial net worth	-2 166	-2 208	-2 253	-2 340	-2 496	-2 831	-3 045	-1 651 e
Financial assets	141 260	148 414	149 520	167 538	171 365	182 993	186 680	183 715
Currency and deposits	16 943	15 086	16 103	16 575	12 995	13 281	11 590	9 844
Debt securities	68 178	65 929	66 507	66 380	62 893	64 883	65 008	72 813
Loans	913	2 124	2 107	3 410	5 116	5 347	3 976	2 850
Equity and investment fund shares	39 279	45 206	43 821	58 074	66 157	72 842	76 711	65 202
Equity	14 836	15 104	13 988	14 520	11 575	13 992	15 587	14 458
Investment fund shares	24 443	30 101	29 833	43 555	54 582	58 851	61 124	50 744
Money market fund shares	..	..	..	..	..	..	..	..
Non-Money market fund shares	..	..	..	..	..	..	..	..
Insurance pension and standardised guarantees	4 642	5 500	5 639	7 024	6 271	7 194	9 715	6 447
Financial derivatives and employee stock options	163	313	370	639	651	911	852	611
Other accounts receivable	11 142	14 255	14 971	15 434	17 284	18 534	18 827	25 947
Financial liabilities	143 427	150 622	151 773	169 878	173 861	185 824	189 724	185 366
Debt securities	..	..	..	..	..	..	..	..
Short-term debt securities	..	..	..	..	..	..	..	..
Long-term debt securities	..	..	..	..	..	..	..	..
Loans	..	..	..	..	..	..	..	..
Short-term loans	..	..	..	..	..	..	..	..
Long-term loans	..	..	..	..	..	..	..	..
Equity and investment fund shares	..	..	..	..	..	..	..	..
Insurance pension and standardised guarantees	100 084	109 763	109 285	120 780	126 778	132 971	137 107	142 729
Financial derivatives and employee stock options	..	..	..	..	..	..	..	..
Other accounts payable	..	..	..	..	..	..	..	..
Non-financial assets	2 166	2 208	2 253	2 340	2 496	2 839	3 045	1 651
Pension funds								
Financial net worth	0	0	0	0	0	0	0	0
Financial assets	181 873	224 833	229 022	274 193	302 869	151 191	142 701	155 782
Currency and deposits	4 209	8 986	12 299	19 674	16 345	10 872	9 790	12 421
Debt securities	121 200	132 875	144 529	157 211	159 403	15 235	14 752	15 017
Loans	0	0	0	0	0	0	0	0
Equity and investment fund shares	55 944	82 366	71 342	97 063	126 285	124 583	117 727	127 734
Equity	54 792	81 078	70 168	95 998	125 655	124 284	117 512	127 633
Investment fund shares	1 152	1 289	1 174	1 065	630	299	215	101
Money market fund shares	..	..	..	..	..	..	..	..
Non-Money market fund shares	..	..	..	..	..	..	..	..
Insurance pension and standardised guarantees	0	0	0	0	0	0	0	0
Financial derivatives and employee stock options	2	0	73	2	2	4	1	0
Other accounts receivable	518	606	778	244	834	496	432	611
Financial liabilities	181 873	224 833	229 022	274 193	302 869	151 191	142 701	155 782
Debt securities	0	0	0	0	0	0	0	0
Short-term debt securities	0	0	0	0	0	0	0	0
Long-term debt securities	0	0	0	0	0	0	0	0
Loans	584	958	1 190	2 116	759	0	0	0
Short-term loans	..	..	..	..	..	0	0	0
Long-term loans	..	..	..	..	..	0	0	0
Equity and investment fund shares	0	0	0	0	0	0	0	0
Insurance pension and standardised guarantees	179 963	222 807	226 278	271 479	301 311	150 829	142 291	155 206
Financial derivatives and employee stock options	0	0	0	0	0	0	0	0
Other accounts payable	1 326	1 069	1 554	598	798	362	410	576
Non-financial assets	0	0	0	0	0	0	0	0

Note: Detailed metadata at: http://metalinks.oecd.org/instinv/20170920/06e1

Table 4. Portfolio composition by type of investor

As percentage of financial assets and of financial liabilities

Per cent

	2009	2010	2011	2012	2013	2014	2015	2016
Investment funds								
Financial assets	..	..	..	..	..	..	..	..
Currency and deposits	..	..	..	..	..	..	..	..
Debt securities	..	..	..	..	..	..	..	..
Loans	..	..	..	..	..	..	..	..
Equity and investment fund shares	..	..	..	..	..	..	..	..
Insurance pension and standardised guarantee schemes	..	..	..	..	..	..	..	..
Financial derivatives and employee stock options	..	..	..	..	..	..	..	..
Other accounts receivable	..	..	..	..	..	..	..	..
Financial liabilities	..	..	..	..	..	..	..	..
Currency and deposits	..	..	..	..	..	..	..	..
Debt securities	..	..	..	..	..	..	..	..
Loans	..	..	..	..	..	..	..	..
Equity and investment fund shares	..	..	..	..	..	..	..	..
Insurance pension and standardised guarantee schemes	..	..	..	..	..	..	..	..
Financial derivatives and employee stock options	..	..	..	..	..	..	..	..
Other accounts receivable	..	..	..	..	..	..	..	..
Insurance corporations								
Financial assets	100.0	100.0	100.0	100.0	100.0	100.0	100.0	100.0
Currency and deposits	12.0	10.2	10.8	9.9	7.6	7.3	6.2	5.4
Debt securities	48.3	44.4	44.5	39.6	36.7	35.5	34.8	39.6
Loans	0.6	1.4	1.4	2.0	3.0	2.9	2.1	1.6
Equity and investment fund shares	27.8	30.5	29.3	34.7	38.6	39.8	41.1	35.5
Insurance pension and standardised guarantee schemes	3.3	3.7	3.8	4.2	3.7	3.9	5.2	3.5
Financial derivatives and employee stock options	0.1	0.2	0.2	0.4	0.4	0.5	0.5	0.3
Other accounts receivable	7.9	9.6	10.0	9.2	10.1	10.1	10.1	14.1
Financial liabilities	100.0	100.0	100.0	100.0	100.0	100.0	100.0	100.0
Currency and deposits	1.2	1.4	1.3	1.5	1.1	0.8	0.7	0.9
Debt securities	..	..	..	..	..	..	..	..
Loans	..	..	..	..	..	..	..	..
Equity and investment fund shares	..	..	..	..	..	..	..	..
Insurance pension and standardised guarantee schemes	69.8	72.9	72.0	71.1	72.9	71.6	72.3	77.0
Financial derivatives and employee stock options	..	..	..	..	..	..	..	..
Other accounts receivable	..	..	..	..	..	..	..	..
Pension funds								
Financial assets	100.0	100.0	100.0	100.0	100.0	100.0	100.0	100.0
Currency and deposits	2.3	4.0	5.4	7.2	5.4	7.2	6.9	8.0
Debt securities	66.6	59.1	63.1	57.3	52.6	10.1	10.3	9.6
Loans	0.0	0.0	0.0	0.0	0.0	0.0	0.0	0.0
Equity and investment fund shares	30.8	36.6	31.2	35.4	41.7	82.4	82.5	82.0
Insurance pension and standardised guarantee schemes	0.0	0.0	0.0	0.0	0.0	0.0	0.0	0.0
Financial derivatives and employee stock options	0.0	0.0	0.0	0.0	0.0	0.0	0.0	0.0
Other accounts receivable	0.3	0.3	0.3	0.1	0.3	0.3	0.3	0.4
Financial liabilities	100.0	100.0	100.0	100.0	100.0	100.0	100.0	100.0
Currency and deposits	0.0	0.0	0.0	0.0	0.0	0.0	0.0	0.0
Debt securities	0.0	0.0	0.0	0.0	0.0	0.0	0.0	0.0
Loans	0.3	0.4	0.5	0.8	0.3	0.0	0.0	0.0
Equity and investment fund shares	0.0	0.0	0.0	0.0	0.0	0.0	0.0	0.0
Insurance pension and standardised guarantee schemes	98.9	99.1	98.8	99.0	99.5	99.8	99.7	99.6
Financial derivatives and employee stock options	0.0	0.0	0.0	0.0	0.0	0.0	0.0	0.0
Other accounts receivable	0.7	0.5	0.7	0.2	0.3	0.2	0.3	0.4

Note: Detailed metadata at: http://metalinks.oecd.org/instinv/20170920/a49a

PORTUGAL

Table 1. Financial assets and liabilities of institutional investors, 2016

Million EUR (1999 PTE euro)

	Total	Investment funds			
		Non-money market funds			Money market funds
		Total	Open-end non-money market funds	Closed-end non-money market funds	Total
Financial assets	..	..	..	..	..
Currency and deposits	..	..	..	..	..
Debt securities	..	3 570	..	..	..
Debt securities, short term	..	..	..	..	..
Debt securities, long term	..	..	..	..	..
Debt securities issued by residents	..	721	..	..	..
Debt securities issued by non-residents	..	2 849	..	..	..
Loans	..	..	..	..	..
Loans, short-term	..	..	..	..	..
Loans, long-term	..	..	..	..	..
Loans granted to residents	..	..	..	..	..
Loans granted to non-residents	..	..	..	..	..
Equity and investment fund shares/units	..	..	..	..	..
Equity and investment fund shares issued/units by residents	..	1 720	..	..	..
Equity and investment fund shares/units issued by non residents	..	3 593	..	..	..
Other accounts receivable	..	..	..	..	..

	Total	Investment funds			
		Non-money market funds			Money market funds
		Total	Open-end non-money market funds	Closed-end non-money market funds	Total
Financial liabilities	..	..	..	..	..
Currency and deposits	..	..	..	..	..
Debt securities	..	..	..	..	..
Debt securities, short term	..	..	..	..	..
Debt securities, long term	..	..	..	..	..
Loans	..	1 667	..	..	..
Loans, short-term	..	..	..	..	..
Loans, long-term	..	..	..	..	..
Equity and investment fund shares/units	25 417	23 082	..	..	2 336
Insurance pension and standardised guaratees	..	..	..	..	..
Financial derivatives and employee stock options	..	..	..	..	..
Other accounts payable	..	..	..	..	..

	Total	Insurance corporations and pension funds			
		Insurance corporations			Pension funds
		Total	Life insurance corporations	Non-life insurance corporations	Total
Financial assets	..	..	..	..	..
Currency and deposits	6 026	..	..	..	..
Debt securities	49 630	..	..	..	..
Debt securities, short-term	1 859	..	..	..	..
Debt securities, long term	47 772	..	..	..	..
Debt securities issued by residents	..	..	..	..	..
Debt securities issued by non-residents	..	..	..	..	..
Loans	..	..	..	..	..
Loans, short-term	..	..	..	..	..
Loans, long-term	127	..	..	..	..
Loans granted to residents	..	..	..	..	..
Loans granted to non-residents	..	..	..	..	..
Equity and investment fund shares/units	16 993	..	..	..	..
Equity and investment fund shares/units issued by residents	..	..	..	..	..
Equity and investment fund shares/units issued by non residents	..	..	..	..	..
Other accounts receivable	3 140	..	..	..	..

	Total	Insurance corporations and pension funds			
		Insurance corporations			Pension funds
		Total	Life insurance corporations	Non-life insurance corporations	Total
Financial liabilities	..	..	..	..	..
Currency and deposits	..	..	..	..	..
Debt securities	201	..	..	..	..
Debt securities, short term	0	..	..	..	..
Debt securities, long term	201	..	..	..	..
Loans	545	..	..	..	..
Loans, short-term	166	..	..	..	..
Loans, long-term	379	..	..	..	..
Equity and investment fund shares/units	5 188	..	..	..	..
Insurance pension and standardised guarantees	69 194	..	..	..	..
Financial derivatives and employee stock options	..	..	..	..	..
Other accounts payable	1 342	..	..	..	..

Note: Detailed metadata at: http://metalinks.oecd.org/instinv/20170920/75e8

Table 2. Financial assets and liabilities of investment funds

Million EUR

	2009	2010	2011	2012	2013	2014	2015	2016
Investment funds								
Financial net worth	..	..	..	..	..	..	..	..
Financial assets	..	..	..	..	..	..	..	..
Currency and deposits	..	..	..	..	..	..	..	..
Debt securities	..	..	..	..	..	..	..	..
Loans	..	..	..	..	..	..	..	..
Equity and investment fund shares	..	..	..	..	..	..	..	..
Equity	..	..	..	..	..	..	..	..
Investment fund shares	..	..	..	..	..	..	..	..
Money market fund shares	..	..	..	..	..	..	..	..
Non-Money market fund shares	..	..	..	..	..	..	..	..
Insurance pension and standardised guarantees	..	..	..	..	..	..	..	..
Financial derivatives and employee stock options	..	..	..	..	..	..	..	..
Other accounts receivable	..	..	..	..	..	..	..	..
Financial liabilities	..	..	..	..	..	..	..	..
Debt securities	..	..	..	..	..	..	..	..
Short-term debt securities	..	..	..	..	..	..	..	..
Long-term debt securities	..	..	..	..	..	..	..	..
Loans	..	..	..	..	..	..	..	..
Short-term loans	..	..	..	..	..	..	..	..
Long-term loans	..	..	..	..	..	..	..	..
Equity and investment fund shares	30 290	28 078	24 731	26 914	28 398	27 117	27 003	25 417
Insurance pension and standardised guarantees	..	..	..	..	..	..	..	..
Financial derivatives and employee stock options	..	..	..	..	..	..	..	..
Other accounts payable	..	..	..	..	..	..	..	..
Non-financial assets	..	..	..	..	..	..	..	..
Money market funds								
Financial net worth	..	..	..	..	..	..	..	..
Financial assets	..	..	..	..	..	..	..	..
Currency and deposits	..	..	..	..	..	..	..	..
Debt securities	..	..	..	..	..	..	..	..
Loans	..	..	..	..	..	..	..	..
Equity and investment fund shares	..	..	..	..	..	..	..	..
Equity	..	..	..	..	..	..	..	..
Investment fund shares	..	..	..	..	..	..	..	..
Money market fund shares	..	..	..	..	..	..	..	..
Non-Money market fund shares	..	..	..	..	..	..	..	..
Insurance pension and standardised guarantees	..	..	..	..	..	..	..	..
Financial derivatives and employee stock options	..	..	..	..	..	..	..	..
Other accounts receivable	..	..	..	..	..	..	..	..
Financial liabilities	..	..	..	..	..	..	..	..
Debt securities	..	..	..	..	..	..	..	..
Short-term debt securities	..	..	..	..	..	..	..	..
Long-term debt securities	..	..	..	..	..	..	..	..
Loans	..	..	..	..	..	..	..	..
Short-term loans	..	..	..	..	..	..	..	..
Long-term loans	..	..	..	..	..	..	..	..
Equity and investment fund shares	12	46	65	1 308	2 383	2 497	3 053	2 336
Insurance pension and standardised guarantees	..	..	..	..	..	..	..	..
Financial derivatives and employee stock options	..	..	..	..	..	..	..	..
Other accounts payable	..	..	..	..	..	..	..	..
Non-financial assets	..	..	..	..	..	..	..	..
Non-money market funds								
Financial net worth	..	..	..	..	..	..	..	..
Financial assets	..	..	..	..	..	..	..	..
Currency and deposits	..	..	..	..	..	..	..	..
Debt securities	10 581	8 325	6 357	6 773	5 634	4 442	3 757	3 570
Loans	..	..	..	..	..	..	..	..
Equity and investment fund shares	..	..	..	..	..	..	..	..
Equity	3 662	3 877	2 663	2 576	2 484	2 597	2 584	2 600
Investment fund shares	1 736	1 741	1 773	1 688	1 963	2 308	2 927	2 712
Money market fund shares	..	..	..	..	..	..	..	..
Non-Money market fund shares	..	..	..	..	..	..	..	..
Insurance pension and standardised guarantees	..	..	..	..	..	..	..	..
Financial derivatives and employee stock options	..	..	..	..	..	..	..	..
Other accounts receivable	..	..	..	..	..	..	..	..
Financial liabilities	..	..	..	..	..	..	..	..
Debt securities	..	..	..	..	..	..	..	..
Short-term debt securities	..	..	..	..	..	..	..	..
Long-term debt securities	..	..	..	..	..	..	..	..
Loans	2 825	3 064	3 326	3 193	2 737	2 383	1 930	1 667
Short-term loans	..	..	..	..	..	..	..	..
Long-term loans	..	..	..	..	..	..	..	..
Equity and investment fund shares	30 278	28 032	24 666	25 606	26 015	24 620	23 950	23 082
Insurance pension and standardised guarantees	..	..	..	..	..	..	..	..
Financial derivatives and employee stock options	..	..	..	..	..	..	..	..
Other accounts payable	..	..	..	..	..	..	..	..
Non-financial assets	13 666	14 471	14 743	14 651	14 572	13 476	12 082	11 329
Open-end non-money market funds								
Financial net worth	..	..	..	..	..	..	..	..
Financial assets	..	..	..	..	..	..	..	..

Table 2. Financial assets and liabilities of investment funds *(cont.)*

Million EUR

	2009	2010	2011	2012	2013	2014	2015	2016
Currency and deposits	..	..	..	..	..	..	..	..
Debt securities	..	..	..	..	..	..	..	..
Loans	..	..	..	..	..	..	..	..
Equity and investment fund shares	..	..	..	..	..	..	..	..
Equity	..	..	..	..	..	..	..	..
Investment fund shares	..	..	..	..	..	..	..	..
Money market fund shares	..	..	..	..	..	..	..	..
Non-Money market fund shares	..	..	..	..	..	..	..	..
Insurance pension and standardised guarantees	..	..	..	..	..	..	..	..
Financial derivatives and employee stock options	..	..	..	..	..	..	..	..
Other accounts receivable	..	..	..	..	..	..	..	..
Financial liabilities	..	..	..	..	..	..	..	..
Debt securities	..	..	..	..	..	..	..	..
Short-term debt securities	..	..	..	..	..	..	..	..
Long-term debt securities	..	..	..	..	..	..	..	..
Loans	..	..	..	..	..	..	..	..
Short-term loans	..	..	..	..	..	..	..	..
Long-term loans	..	..	..	..	..	..	..	..
Equity and investment fund shares	..	..	..	..	..	..	..	..
Insurance pension and standardised guarantees	..	..	..	..	..	..	..	..
Financial derivatives and employee stock options	..	..	..	..	..	..	..	..
Other accounts payable	..	..	..	..	..	..	..	..
Non-financial assets	..	..	..	..	..	..	..	..
Open-end investment funds								
Financial net worth	..	..	..	..	..	..	..	..
Financial assets	..	..	..	..	..	..	..	..
Currency and deposits	..	..	..	..	..	..	..	..
Debt securities	..	..	..	..	..	..	..	..
Loans	..	..	..	..	..	..	..	..
Equity and investment fund shares	..	..	..	..	..	..	..	..
Equity	..	..	..	..	..	..	..	..
Investment fund shares	..	..	..	..	..	..	..	..
Money market fund shares	..	..	..	..	..	..	..	..
Non-Money market fund shares	..	..	..	..	..	..	..	..
Insurance pension and standardised guarantees	..	..	..	..	..	..	..	..
Financial derivatives and employee stock options	..	..	..	..	..	..	..	..
Other accounts receivable	..	..	..	..	..	..	..	..
Financial liabilities	..	..	..	..	..	..	..	..
Debt securities	..	..	..	..	..	..	..	..
Short-term debt securities	..	..	..	..	..	..	..	..
Long-term debt securities	..	..	..	..	..	..	..	..
Loans	..	..	..	..	..	..	..	..
Short-term loans	..	..	..	..	..	..	..	..
Long-term loans	..	..	..	..	..	..	..	..
Equity and investment fund shares	..	..	..	..	..	..	..	..
Insurance pension and standardised guarantees	..	..	..	..	..	..	..	..
Financial derivatives and employee stock options	..	..	..	..	..	..	..	..
Other accounts payable	..	..	..	..	..	..	..	..
Non-financial assets	..	..	..	..	..	..	..	..

Note: Detailed metadata at: http://metalinks.oecd.org/instinv/20170920/75e8

Table 3. Financial assets and liabilities of insurance corporations and pension funds

Million EUR

	2009	2010	2011	2012	2013	2014	2015	2016
Insurance corporations and pension funds								
Financial net worth	..	..	..	..	..	..	..	..
Financial assets	..	..	..	..	..	..	..	..
Currency and deposits	7 171	8 499	8 603	9 753	8 908	9 491	8 330	6 026
Debt securities	57 585	57 261	47 293	48 804	48 328	51 657	49 936	49 630
Loans	346	354	436	396	..	..	..	..
Equity and investment fund shares	14 691	14 559	12 892	12 375	13 969	15 456	16 716	16 993
Equity	5 788	5 425	4 344	4 364	4 874	5 789	7 216	6 831
Investment fund shares	8 903	9 134	8 548	8 012	9 095	9 667	9 500	10 162
Money market fund shares	10	16	10	14	30	30	54	88
Non-Money market fund shares	8 892	9 118	8 538	7 997	9 064	9 637	9 446	10 074
Insurance pension and standardised guarantees	1 666	964	920	856	804	771	795	793
Financial derivatives and employee stock options	..	..	..	..	..	..	..	..
Other accounts receivable	3 461	3 818	3 069	1 983	3 470	2 943	2 937	3 140
Financial liabilities	..	..	..	..	..	..	..	..
Debt securities	210	204	211	196	186	193	223	201
Short-term debt securities	0	0	0	0	0	0	0	0
Long-term debt securities	210	204	211	196	186	193	223	201
Loans	800	1 185	1 884	1 670	387	557	466	545
Short-term loans	674	1 066	1 698	1 458	83	138	90	166
Long-term loans	126	119	186	213	304	419	376	379
Equity and investment fund shares	4 631	4 487	4 145	5 747	5 751	5 822	5 891	5 188
Insurance pension and standardised guarantees	77 101	79 382	65 902	64 604	66 708	71 121	70 375	69 194
Financial derivatives and employee stock options	..	..	..	..	..	..	..	..
Other accounts payable	1 558	1 308	3 918	1 612	1 775	1 504	1 269	1 342
Non-financial assets	..	..	..	..	..	..	..	..
Insurance corporations								
Financial net worth	..	..	..	..	..	..	..	..
Financial assets	..	..	..	..	..	..	..	..
Currency and deposits	..	..	..	..	..	..	..	..
Debt securities	..	..	..	..	..	..	..	..
Loans	..	..	..	..	..	..	..	..
Equity and investment fund shares	..	..	..	..	..	..	..	..
Equity	..	..	..	..	..	..	..	..
Investment fund shares	..	..	..	..	..	..	..	..
Money market fund shares	..	..	..	..	..	..	..	..
Non-Money market fund shares	..	..	..	..	..	..	..	..
Insurance pension and standardised guarantees	..	..	..	..	..	..	..	..
Financial derivatives and employee stock options	..	..	..	..	..	..	..	..
Other accounts receivable	..	..	..	..	..	..	..	..
Financial liabilities	..	..	..	..	..	..	..	..
Debt securities	..	..	..	..	..	..	..	..
Short-term debt securities	..	..	..	..	..	..	..	..
Long-term debt securities	..	..	..	..	..	..	..	..
Loans	..	..	..	..	..	..	..	..
Short-term loans	..	..	..	..	..	..	..	..
Long-term loans	..	..	..	..	..	..	..	..
Equity and investment fund shares	..	..	..	..	..	..	..	..
Insurance pension and standardised guarantees	..	..	..	..	..	..	..	..
Financial derivatives and employee stock options	..	..	..	..	..	..	..	..
Other accounts payable	..	..	..	..	..	..	..	..
Non-financial assets	..	..	..	..	..	..	..	..
Pension funds								
Financial net worth	..	..	..	..	..	..	..	..
Financial assets	..	..	..	..	..	..	..	..
Currency and deposits	..	..	..	..	..	..	..	..
Debt securities	..	..	..	..	..	..	..	..
Loans	..	..	..	..	..	..	..	..
Equity and investment fund shares	..	..	..	..	..	..	..	..
Equity	..	..	..	..	..	..	..	..
Investment fund shares	..	..	..	..	..	..	..	..
Money market fund shares	..	..	..	..	..	..	..	..
Non-Money market fund shares	..	..	..	..	..	..	..	..
Insurance pension and standardised guarantees	..	..	..	..	..	..	..	..
Financial derivatives and employee stock options	..	..	..	..	..	..	..	..
Other accounts receivable	..	..	..	..	..	..	..	..
Financial liabilities	..	..	..	..	..	..	..	..
Debt securities	..	..	..	..	..	..	..	..
Short-term debt securities	..	..	..	..	..	..	..	..
Long-term debt securities	..	..	..	..	..	..	..	..
Loans	..	..	..	..	..	..	..	..
Short-term loans	..	..	..	..	..	..	..	..
Long-term loans	..	..	..	..	..	..	..	..
Equity and investment fund shares	..	..	..	..	..	..	..	..
Insurance pension and standardised guarantees	..	..	..	..	..	..	..	..
Financial derivatives and employee stock options	..	..	..	..	..	..	..	..
Other accounts payable	..	..	..	..	..	..	..	..
Non-financial assets	..	..	..	..	..	..	..	..

Note: Detailed metadata at: http://metalinks.oecd.org/instinv/20170920/75e8

SLOVAK REPUBLIC

Table 1. Financial assets and liabilities of institutional investors, 2016

Million EUR (2009 SKK euro)

	Total	Investment funds: Non-money market funds: Total	Open-end non-money market funds	Closed-end non-money market funds	Money market funds: Total
Financial assets	..	6 015	6 015	..	..
Currency and deposits	..	1 575	1 575	..	..
Debt securities	..	1 191	1 191	..	..
Debt securities, short term	..	9	9	..	..
Debt securities, long term	..	1 182	1 182	..	..
Debt securities issued by residents	..	..	..	..	..
Debt securities issued by non-residents	..	..	..	..	..
Loans	..	138	138	..	..
Loans, short-term	..	0	0	..	..
Loans, long-term	..	138	138	..	..
Loans granted to residents	..	..	..	..	..
Loans granted to non-residents	..	..	..	..	..
Equity and investment fund shares/units	..	3 020	3 020	..	..
Equity and investment fund shares issued/units by residents	..	..	..	..	..
Equity and investment fund shares/units issued by non residents	..	..	..	..	..
Other accounts receivable	..	90	90	..	..

	Total	Investment funds: Non-money market funds: Total	Open-end non-money market funds	Closed-end non-money market funds	Money market funds: Total
Financial liabilities	..	6 174	6 174	..	..
Currency and deposits	..	..	..	..	..
Debt securities	..	0	0	..	..
Debt securities, short term	..	0	0	..	..
Debt securities, long term	..	0	0	..	..
Loans	..	3	3	..	..
Loans, short-term	..	3	3	..	..
Loans, long-term	..	0	0	..	..
Equity and investment fund shares/units	..	6 091	6 091	..	..
Insurance pension and standardised guaratees	..	0	0	..	..
Financial derivatives and employee stock options	..	2	2	..	..
Other accounts payable	..	77	77	..	..

	Total	Insurance corporations and pension funds: Insurance corporations: Total	Life insurance corporations	Non-life insurance corporations	Pension funds: Total
Financial assets	15 772	7 494	..	..	8 278
Currency and deposits	1 165	257	..	..	908
Debt securities	10 461	4 887	..	..	5 573
Debt securities, short-term	0	0	..	..	0
Debt securities, long term	10 461	4 887	..	..	5 573
Debt securities issued by residents	..	..	..	..	..
Debt securities issued by non-residents	..	..	..	..	..
Loans	24	24	..	..	0
Loans, short-term	0	0	..	..	0
Loans, long-term	23	23	..	..	0
Loans granted to residents	..	..	..	..	..
Loans granted to non-residents	..	..	..	..	..
Equity and investment fund shares/units	3 374	1 585	..	..	1 788
Equity and investment fund shares/units issued by residents	..	..	..	..	..
Equity and investment fund shares/units issued by non residents	..	..	..	..	..
Other accounts receivable	343	338	..	..	4

	Total	Insurance corporations and pension funds: Insurance corporations: Total	Life insurance corporations	Non-life insurance corporations	Pension funds: Total
Financial liabilities	15 927	7 251	..	..	8 676
Currency and deposits	..	..	..	..	..
Debt securities	1	1	..	..	0
Debt securities, short term	0	0	..	..	0
Debt securities, long term	1	1	..	..	0
Loans	0	0	..	..	0
Loans, short-term	0	0	..	..	0
Loans, long-term	0	0	..	..	0
Equity and investment fund shares/units	1 492	1 492	..	..	0
Insurance pension and standardised guaratees	13 983	5 332	..	..	8 651
Financial derivatives and employee stock options	9	4	..	..	5
Other accounts payable	441	421	..	..	20

Note: Detailed metadata at: http://metalinks.oecd.org/instinv/20170920/0082

Table 2. Financial assets and liabilities of investment funds

Million EUR

	2009	2010	2011	2012	2013	2014	2015	2016
Investment funds								
Financial net worth	..	..	..	..	..	..	..	..
Financial assets	..	..	..	..	..	..	..	..
Currency and deposits	..	..	..	..	..	..	..	..
Debt securities	..	..	..	..	..	..	..	..
Loans	..	..	..	..	..	..	..	..
Equity and investment fund shares	..	..	..	..	..	..	..	..
Equity	..	..	..	..	..	..	..	..
Investment fund shares	..	..	..	..	..	..	..	..
Money market fund shares	..	..	..	..	..	..	..	..
Non-Money market fund shares	..	..	..	..	..	..	..	..
Insurance pension and standardised guarantees	..	..	..	..	..	..	..	..
Financial derivatives and employee stock options	..	..	..	..	..	..	..	..
Other accounts receivable	..	..	..	..	..	..	..	..
Financial liabilities	..	..	..	..	..	..	..	..
Debt securities	..	..	..	..	..	..	..	..
Short-term debt securities	..	..	..	..	..	..	..	..
Long-term debt securities	..	..	..	..	..	..	..	..
Loans	..	..	..	..	..	..	..	..
Short-term loans	..	..	..	..	..	..	..	..
Long-term loans	..	..	..	..	..	..	..	..
Equity and investment fund shares	..	..	..	..	..	..	..	..
Insurance pension and standardised guarantees	..	..	..	..	..	..	..	..
Financial derivatives and employee stock options	..	..	..	..	..	..	..	..
Other accounts payable	..	..	..	..	..	..	..	..
Non-financial assets	..	..	..	..	..	..	..	..
Money market funds								
Financial net worth	..	..	..	..	..	..	..	..
Financial assets	..	..	..	..	..	..	..	..
Currency and deposits	..	..	..	..	..	..	..	..
Debt securities	..	..	..	..	..	..	..	..
Loans	..	..	..	..	..	..	..	..
Equity and investment fund shares	..	..	..	..	..	..	..	..
Equity	..	..	..	..	..	..	..	..
Investment fund shares	..	..	..	..	..	..	..	..
Money market fund shares	..	..	..	..	..	..	..	..
Non-Money market fund shares	..	..	..	..	..	..	..	..
Insurance pension and standardised guarantees	..	..	..	..	..	..	..	..
Financial derivatives and employee stock options	..	..	..	..	..	..	..	..
Other accounts receivable	..	..	..	..	..	..	..	..
Financial liabilities	..	..	..	..	..	..	..	..
Debt securities	..	..	..	..	..	..	..	..
Short-term debt securities	..	..	..	..	..	..	..	..
Long-term debt securities	..	..	..	..	..	..	..	..
Loans	..	..	..	..	..	..	..	..
Short-term loans	..	..	..	..	..	..	..	..
Long-term loans	..	..	..	..	..	..	..	..
Equity and investment fund shares	..	..	..	..	..	..	..	..
Insurance pension and standardised guarantees	..	..	..	..	..	..	..	..
Financial derivatives and employee stock options	..	..	..	..	..	..	..	..
Other accounts payable	..	..	..	..	..	..	..	..
Non-financial assets	..	..	..	..	..	..	..	..
Non-money market funds								
Financial net worth	..	..	..	-1 937	-2 320	-2 604	-381	-159
Financial assets	..	..	..	1 425	2 067	2 809	5 592	6 015
Currency and deposits	..	..	..	0	0	0	1 717	1 575
Debt securities	..	..	..	843	956	1 401	1 234	1 191
Loans	..	..	..	126	223	184	131	138
Equity and investment fund shares	..	..	..	404	831	1 176	2 440	3 020
Equity	..	..	..	146	387	377	779	971
Investment fund shares	..	..	..	258	444	799	1 661	2 049
Money market fund shares	..	..	..	258	0	0	26	12
Non-Money market fund shares	..	..	..	0	444	799	1 636	2 037
Insurance pension and standardised guarantees	..	..	..	2	2	0	0	0
Financial derivatives and employee stock options	..	..	..	0	0	0	0	0
Other accounts receivable	..	..	..	50	54	48	70	90
Financial liabilities	..	..	..	3 363	4 387	5 413	5 973	6 174
Debt securities	..	..	..	0	0	0	0	0
Short-term debt securities	..	..	..	0	0	0	0	0
Long-term debt securities	..	..	..	0	0	0	0	0
Loans	..	..	..	0	0	0	0	3
Short-term loans	..	..	..	0	0	0	0	3
Long-term loans	..	..	..	0	0	0	0	0
Equity and investment fund shares	..	..	..	3 337	4 356	5 399	5 888	6 091
Insurance pension and standardised guarantees	..	..	..	0	0	0	0	0
Financial derivatives and employee stock options	..	..	..	1	0	0	2	2
Other accounts payable	..	..	..	24	31	13	82	77
Non-financial assets	..	..	..	..	..	..	..	..
Open-end non-money market funds								
Financial net worth	..	..	..	-1 937	-2 320	-2 604	-381	-159
Financial assets	..	..	..	1 425	2 067	2 809	5 592	6 015

Table 2. Financial assets and liabilities of investment funds *(cont.)*

Million EUR

	2009	2010	2011	2012	2013	2014	2015	2016
Currency and deposits	..	..	..	0	0	0	1 717	1 575
Debt securities	..	..	..	843	956	1 401	1 234	1 191
Loans	..	..	..	126	223	184	131	138
Equity and investment fund shares	..	..	..	404	831	1 176	2 440	3 020
Equity	..	..	..	146	387	377	779	971
Investment fund shares	..	..	..	258	444	799	1 661	2 049
Money market fund shares	..	..	..	258	0	0	26	12
Non-Money market fund shares	..	..	..	0	444	799	1 636	2 037
Insurance pension and standardised guarantees	..	..	..	2	2	0	0	0
Financial derivatives and employee stock options	..	..	..	0	0	0	0	0
Other accounts receivable	..	..	..	50	54	48	70	90
Financial liabilities	..	..	..	3 363	4 387	5 413	5 973	6 174
Debt securities	..	..	..	0	0	0	0	0
Short-term debt securities	..	..	..	0	0	0	0	0
Long-term debt securities	..	..	..	0	0	0	0	0
Loans	..	..	..	0	0	0	0	3
Short-term loans	..	..	..	0	0	0	0	3
Long-term loans	..	..	..	0	0	0	0	0
Equity and investment fund shares	..	..	..	3 337	4 356	5 399	5 888	6 091
Insurance pension and standardised guarantees	..	..	..	0	0	0	0	0
Financial derivatives and employee stock options	..	..	..	1	0	0	2	2
Other accounts payable	..	..	..	24	31	13	82	77
Non-financial assets	..	..	..	..	..	..	..	..
Open-end investment funds								
Financial net worth	..	..	..	..	..	..	..	..
Financial assets	..	..	..	..	..	..	..	..
Currency and deposits	..	..	..	..	..	..	..	..
Debt securities	..	..	..	..	..	..	..	..
Loans	..	..	..	..	..	..	..	..
Equity and investment fund shares	..	..	..	..	..	..	..	..
Equity	..	..	..	..	..	..	..	..
Investment fund shares	..	..	..	..	..	..	..	..
Money market fund shares	..	..	..	..	..	..	..	..
Non-Money market fund shares	..	..	..	..	..	..	..	..
Insurance pension and standardised guarantees	..	..	..	..	..	..	..	..
Financial derivatives and employee stock options	..	..	..	..	..	..	..	..
Other accounts receivable	..	..	..	..	..	..	..	..
Financial liabilities	..	..	..	..	..	..	..	..
Debt securities	..	..	..	..	..	..	..	..
Short-term debt securities	..	..	..	..	..	..	..	..
Long-term debt securities	..	..	..	..	..	..	..	..
Loans	..	..	..	..	..	..	..	..
Short-term loans	..	..	..	..	..	..	..	..
Long-term loans	..	..	..	..	..	..	..	..
Equity and investment fund shares	..	..	..	..	..	..	..	..
Insurance pension and standardised guarantees	..	..	..	..	..	..	..	..
Financial derivatives and employee stock options	..	..	..	..	..	..	..	..
Other accounts payable	..	..	..	..	..	..	..	..
Non-financial assets	..	..	..	..	..	..	..	..

Note: Detailed metadata at: http://metalinks.oecd.org/instinv/20170920/0082

Table 3. Financial assets and liabilities of insurance corporations and pension funds

Million EUR

	2009	2010	2011	2012	2013	2014	2015	2016
Insurance corporations and pension funds								
Financial net worth	..	..	..	..	..	..	..	..
Financial assets	..	..	..	11 735	13 760	14 504	14 567	15 772
Currency and deposits	..	..	..	873	1 838	1 639	1 428	1 165
Debt securities	..	..	..	9 065	9 400	9 871	9 656	10 461
Loans	..	..	..	88	28	46	37	24
Equity and investment fund shares	..	..	..	1 263	2 054	2 424	2 792	3 374
Equity	..	..	..	232	361	332	331	417
Investment fund shares	..	..	..	1 030	1 693	2 092	2 462	2 956
Money market fund shares	..	..	..	3	5	10	3	0
Non-Money market fund shares	..	..	..	1 027	1 688	2 081	2 459	2 956
Insurance pension and standardised guarantees	..	..	..	91	99	193	343	399
Financial derivatives and employee stock options	..	..	..	4	6	5	6	8
Other accounts receivable	..	..	..	350	335	326	304	343
Financial liabilities	..	..	..	12 632	12 850	14 116	14 618	15 927
Debt securities	..	..	..	0	0	0	1	1
Short-term debt securities	..	..	..	0	0	0	0	0
Long-term debt securities	..	..	..	0	0	0	1	1
Loans	..	..	..	51	58	59	89	0
Short-term loans	..	..	..	0	0	0	0	0
Long-term loans	..	..	..	51	57	58	89	0
Equity and investment fund shares	..	..	..	442	405	462	1 480	1 492
Insurance pension and standardised guarantees	..	..	..	11 746	11 982	13 195	12 611	13 983
Financial derivatives and employee stock options	..	..	..	6	8	9	4	9
Other accounts payable	..	..	..	387	396	391	433	441
Non-financial assets	..	..	..	..	..	..	..	..
Insurance corporations								
Financial net worth	..	..	..	2 298	247	546	-23	243
Financial assets	..	..	..	8 147	5 982	6 780	6 717	7 494
Currency and deposits	..	..	..	448	360	296	267	257
Debt securities	..	..	..	6 395	4 040	4 664	4 486	4 887
Loans	..	..	..	88	28	46	37	24
Equity and investment fund shares	..	..	..	774	1 127	1 256	1 287	1 585
Equity	..	..	..	191	179	168	170	217
Investment fund shares	..	..	..	583	948	1 088	1 116	1 368
Money market fund shares	..	..	..	3	5	10	3	0
Non-Money market fund shares	..	..	..	580	943	1 078	1 114	1 368
Insurance pension and standardised guarantees	..	..	..	91	99	193	343	399
Financial derivatives and employee stock options	..	..	..	4	5	5	6	3
Other accounts receivable	..	..	..	347	324	320	292	338
Financial liabilities	..	..	..	5 849	5 735	6 234	6 740	7 251
Debt securities	..	..	..	0	0	0	1	1
Short-term debt securities	..	..	..	0	0	0	0	0
Long-term debt securities	..	..	..	0	0	0	1	1
Loans	..	..	..	51	58	59	89	0
Short-term loans	..	..	..	0	0	0	0	0
Long-term loans	..	..	..	51	57	58	89	0
Equity and investment fund shares	..	..	..	442	405	462	1 480	1 492
Insurance pension and standardised guarantees	..	..	..	4 968	4 893	5 325	4 765	5 332
Financial derivatives and employee stock options	..	..	..	6	4	8	2	4
Other accounts payable	..	..	..	382	375	381	404	421
Non-financial assets	..	..	..	..	..	..	..	..
Pension funds								
Financial net worth	..	..	..	-3 195	663	-158	-28	-398
Financial assets	..	..	..	3 588	7 777	7 723	7 850	8 278
Currency and deposits	..	..	..	425	1 479	1 343	1 161	908
Debt securities	..	..	..	2 671	5 360	5 206	5 170	5 573
Loans	..	..	..	0	0	0	0	0
Equity and investment fund shares	..	..	..	488	926	1 168	1 505	1 788
Equity	..	..	..	41	181	164	160	200
Investment fund shares	..	..	..	447	745	1 003	1 345	1 588
Money market fund shares	..	..	..	0	0	0	0	0
Non-Money market fund shares	..	..	..	447	745	1 003	1 345	1 588
Insurance pension and standardised guarantees	..	..	..	0	0	0	0	0
Financial derivatives and employee stock options	..	..	..	0	1	0	1	5
Other accounts receivable	..	..	..	4	11	5	13	4
Financial liabilities	..	..	..	6 784	7 115	7 882	7 878	8 676
Debt securities	..	..	..	0	0	0	0	0
Short-term debt securities	..	..	..	0	0	0	0	0
Long-term debt securities	..	..	..	0	0	0	0	0
Loans	..	..	..	0	0	0	0	0
Short-term loans	..	..	..	0	0	0	0	0
Long-term loans	..	..	..	0	0	0	0	0
Equity and investment fund shares	..	..	..	0	0	0	0	0
Insurance pension and standardised guarantees	..	..	..	6 779	7 089	7 870	7 847	8 651
Financial derivatives and employee stock options	..	..	..	0	4	1	3	5
Other accounts payable	..	..	..	5	21	10	29	20
Non-financial assets	..	..	..	..	..	..	..	..

Note: Detailed metadata at: http://metalinks.oecd.org/instinv/20170920/0082

Table 4. Portfolio composition by type of investor

As percentage of financial assets and of financial liabilities

Per cent

	2009	2010	2011	2012	2013	2014	2015	2016
Investment funds								
Financial assets	..	..	..	..	..	..	..	..
Currency and deposits	..	..	..	..	..	..	..	..
Debt securities	..	..	..	..	..	..	..	..
Loans	..	..	..	..	..	..	..	..
Equity and investment fund shares	..	..	..	..	..	..	..	..
Insurance pension and standardised guarantee schemes	..	..	..	..	..	..	..	..
Financial derivatives and employee stock options	..	..	..	..	..	..	..	..
Other accounts receivable	..	..	..	..	..	..	..	..
Financial liabilities	..	..	..	..	..	..	..	..
Currency and deposits	..	..	..	..	..	..	..	..
Debt securities	..	..	..	..	..	..	..	..
Loans	..	..	..	..	..	..	..	..
Equity and investment fund shares	..	..	..	..	..	..	..	..
Insurance pension and standardised guarantee schemes	..	..	..	..	..	..	..	..
Financial derivatives and employee stock options	..	..	..	..	..	..	..	..
Other accounts receivable	..	..	..	..	..	..	..	..
Insurance corporations								
Financial assets	..	..	..	100.0	100.0	100.0	100.0	100.0
Currency and deposits	..	..	..	5.5	6.0	4.4	4.0	3.4
Debt securities	..	..	..	78.5	67.5	68.8	66.8	65.2
Loans	..	..	..	1.1	0.5	0.7	0.6	0.3
Equity and investment fund shares	..	..	..	9.5	18.8	18.5	19.2	21.2
Insurance pension and standardised guarantee schemes	..	..	..	1.1	1.7	2.8	5.1	5.3
Financial derivatives and employee stock options	..	..	..	0.0	0.1	0.1	0.1	0.0
Other accounts receivable	..	..	..	4.3	5.4	4.7	4.3	4.5
Financial liabilities	..	..	..	100.0	100.0	100.0	100.0	100.0
Currency and deposits	..	..	..	0.0	0.0	0.0	0.0	0.0
Debt securities	..	..	..	0.0	0.0	0.0	0.0	0.0
Loans	..	..	..	0.9	1.0	0.9	1.3	0.0
Equity and investment fund shares	..	..	..	7.6	7.1	7.4	22.0	20.6
Insurance pension and standardised guarantee schemes	..	..	..	84.9	85.3	85.4	70.7	73.5
Financial derivatives and employee stock options	..	..	..	0.1	0.1	0.1	0.0	0.1
Other accounts receivable	..	..	..	6.5	6.5	6.1	6.0	5.8
Pension funds								
Financial assets	..	..	..	100.0	100.0	100.0	100.0	100.0
Currency and deposits	..	..	..	11.9	19.0	17.4	14.8	11.0
Debt securities	..	..	..	74.4	68.9	67.4	65.9	67.3
Loans	..	..	..	0.0	0.0	0.0	0.0	0.0
Equity and investment fund shares	..	..	..	13.6	11.9	15.1	19.2	21.6
Insurance pension and standardised guarantee schemes	..	..	..	0.0	0.0	0.0	0.0	0.0
Financial derivatives and employee stock options	..	..	..	0.0	0.0	0.0	0.0	0.1
Other accounts receivable	..	..	..	0.1	0.1	0.1	0.2	0.0
Financial liabilities	..	..	..	100.0	100.0	100.0	100.0	100.0
Currency and deposits	..	..	..	0.0	0.0	0.0	0.0	0.0
Debt securities	..	..	..	0.0	0.0	0.0	0.0	0.0
Loans	..	..	..	0.0	0.0	0.0	0.0	0.0
Equity and investment fund shares	..	..	..	0.0	0.0	0.0	0.0	0.0
Insurance pension and standardised guarantee schemes	..	..	..	99.9	99.6	99.9	99.6	99.7
Financial derivatives and employee stock options	..	..	..	0.0	0.1	0.0	0.0	0.1
Other accounts receivable	..	..	..	0.1	0.3	0.1	0.4	0.2

Note: Detailed metadata at: http://metalinks.oecd.org/instinv/20170920/a49a

SLOVENIA

Table 1. Financial assets and liabilities of institutional investors, 2016

Million EUR (2007 SIT euro)

	Total	Investment funds			Money market funds
		Non-money market funds			
		Total	Open-end non-money market funds	Closed-end non-money market funds	Total
Financial assets	2 474	2 374	2 374	..	100
Currency and deposits	192	124	124	..	68
Debt securities	425	393	393	..	32
Debt securities, short term	48	16	16	..	32
Debt securities, long term	377	377	377	..	0
Debt securities issued by residents	63	57	57	..	6
Debt securities issued by non-residents	362	335	335	..	27
Loans	..	..	..	..	..
Loans, short-term	..	..	..	..	..
Loans, long-term	..	..	..	..	..
Loans granted to residents	..	..	..	..	..
Loans granted to non-residents	..	..	..	..	..
Equity and investment fund shares/units	1 845	1 845	1 845	..	..
Equity and investment fund shares issued/units by residents	113	113	113	..	..
Equity and investment fund shares/units issued by non residents	1 732	1 732	1 732	..	..
Other accounts receivable	11	11	11	..	0

	Total	Investment funds			Money market funds
		Non-money market funds			
		Total	Open-end non-money market funds	Closed-end non-money market funds	Total
Financial liabilities	2 474	2 374	2 374	..	100
Currency and deposits	..	..	..	..	..
Debt securities	..	..	..	..	..
Debt securities, short term	..	..	..	..	..
Debt securities, long term	..	..	..	..	..
Loans	0	0	0	..	..
Loans, short-term	0	0	0	..	..
Loans, long-term	..	..	..	..	..
Equity and investment fund shares/units	2 464	2 364	2 364	..	99
Insurance pension and standardised guaratees	..	..	..	..	..
Financial derivatives and employee stock options	0	0	0	..	..
Other accounts payable	11	9	9	..	1

	Total	Insurance corporations and pension funds			Pension funds
		Insurance corporations			
		Total	Life insurance corporations	Non-life insurance corporations	Total
Financial assets	9 980	7 416	..	..	2 564
Currency and deposits	660	286	..	..	374
Debt securities	6 026	4 486	..	..	1 540
Debt securities, short-term	154	34	..	..	120
Debt securities, long term	5 872	4 452	..	..	1 420
Debt securities issued by residents	2 004	1 216	..	..	788
Debt securities issued by non-residents	4 023	3 270	..	..	753
Loans	124	99	..	..	25
Loans, short-term	34	14	..	..	20
Loans, long-term	89	85	..	..	4
Loans granted to residents	101	77	..	..	24
Loans granted to non-residents	23	22	..	..	1
Equity and investment fund shares/units	2 677	2 060	..	..	616
Equity and investment fund shares/units issued by residents	1 465	1 367	..	..	98
Equity and investment fund shares/units issued by non residents	1 211	693	..	..	518
Other accounts receivable	311	303	..	..	8

	Total	Insurance corporations and pension funds			Pension funds
		Insurance corporations			
		Total	Life insurance corporations	Non-life insurance corporations	Total
Financial liabilities	9 848	7 276	..	..	2 572
Currency and deposits	0	0	..	..	0
Debt securities	84	84	..	..	0
Debt securities, short term	0	0	..	..	0
Debt securities, long term	84	84	..	..	0
Loans	26	26	..	..	0
Loans, short-term	1	1	..	..	0
Loans, long-term	25	25	..	..	0
Equity and investment fund shares/units	1 696	1 651	..	..	45
Insurance pension and standardised guarantees	7 810	5 301	..	..	2 509
Financial derivatives and employee stock options	0	0	..	..	0
Other accounts payable	233	214	..	..	18

Note: Detailed metadata at: http://metalinks.oecd.org/instinv/20170920/475d

SLOVENIA

Table 2. Financial assets and liabilities of investment funds

Million EUR

	2009	2010	2011	2012	2013	2014	2015	2016
Investment funds								
Financial net worth	..	..	..	..	..	..	..	..
Financial assets	2 234	2 289	1 811	1 831	1 855	2 151	2 319	2 474
Currency and deposits	190	163	147	136	110	136	166	192
Debt securities	223	234	248	250	220	263	351	425
Loans	..	..	..	..	..	..	..	..
Equity and investment fund shares	1 814	1 881	1 407	1 433	1 516	1 746	1 795	1 845
Equity	1 632	1 700	1 250	1 280	1 348	1 598	1 641	1 690
Investment fund shares	182	181	157	153	168	149	154	156
Money market fund shares	0	0	0	0	0	0	0	2
Non-Money market fund shares	182	181	157	153	168	149	154	154
Insurance pension and standardised guarantees	..	..	..	..	..	..	..	..
Financial derivatives and employee stock options	0	0	0	0	0	0	1	1
Other accounts receivable	7	11	9	12	9	6	5	11
Financial liabilities	2 234	2 289	1 811	1 831	1 855	2 151	2 319	2 474
Debt securities	..	..	..	..	..	..	..	..
Short-term debt securities	..	..	..	..	..	..	..	..
Long-term debt securities	..	..	..	..	..	..	..	..
Loans	16	13	8	0	0	0	0	0
Short-term loans	16	13	8	0	0	0	0	0
Long-term loans	..	..	..	..	..	..	..	..
Equity and investment fund shares	2 195	2 252	1 790	1 817	1 840	2 143	2 309	2 464
Insurance pension and standardised guarantees	..	..	..	..	..	..	..	..
Financial derivatives and employee stock options	0	0	0	0	0	0	0	0
Other accounts payable	22	24	13	13	16	8	10	11
Non-financial assets	..	..	..	..	..	..	..	..
Money market funds								
Financial net worth	..	..	..	..	..	..	..	..
Financial assets	14	12	26	26	37	37	58	100
Currency and deposits	14	12	20	15	23	24	32	68
Debt securities	0	0	6	10	14	13	25	32
Loans	..	..	..	..	..	..	..	..
Equity and investment fund shares	..	..	..	..	..	..	..	..
Equity	..	..	..	..	..	..	..	..
Investment fund shares	..	..	..	..	..	..	..	..
Money market fund shares	..	..	..	..	..	..	..	..
Non-Money market fund shares	..	..	..	..	..	..	..	..
Insurance pension and standardised guarantees	..	..	..	..	..	..	..	..
Financial derivatives and employee stock options	..	..	..	..	..	..	..	..
Other accounts receivable	0	0	0	0	0	0	0	0
Financial liabilities	14	12	26	26	37	37	58	100
Debt securities	..	..	..	..	..	..	..	..
Short-term debt securities	..	..	..	..	..	..	..	..
Long-term debt securities	..	..	..	..	..	..	..	..
Loans	..	..	..	..	..	..	..	..
Short-term loans	..	..	..	..	..	..	..	..
Long-term loans	..	..	..	..	..	..	..	..
Equity and investment fund shares	14	12	26	24	36	37	56	99
Insurance pension and standardised guarantees	..	..	..	..	..	..	..	..
Financial derivatives and employee stock options	..	..	..	..	..	..	..	..
Other accounts payable	0	0	0	2	0	1	1	1
Non-financial assets	..	..	..	..	..	..	..	..
Non-money market funds								
Financial net worth	..	..	..	..	..	..	..	..
Financial assets	2 220	2 276	1 785	1 805	1 819	2 113	2 261	2 374
Currency and deposits	176	151	127	121	87	111	134	124
Debt securities	223	234	242	239	206	250	326	393
Loans	..	..	..	..	..	..	..	..
Equity and investment fund shares	1 814	1 881	1 407	1 433	1 516	1 746	1 795	1 845
Equity	1 632	1 700	1 250	1 280	1 348	1 598	1 641	1 690
Investment fund shares	182	181	157	153	168	149	154	156
Money market fund shares	0	0	0	0	0	0	0	2
Non-Money market fund shares	182	181	157	153	168	149	154	154
Insurance pension and standardised guarantees	..	..	..	..	..	..	..	..
Financial derivatives and employee stock options	0	0	0	0	0	0	1	1
Other accounts receivable	7	11	9	12	9	6	5	11
Financial liabilities	2 220	2 276	1 785	1 805	1 819	2 113	2 261	2 374
Debt securities	..	..	..	..	..	..	..	..
Short-term debt securities	..	..	..	..	..	..	..	..
Long-term debt securities	..	..	..	..	..	..	..	..
Loans	16	13	8	0	0	0	0	0
Short-term loans	16	13	8	0	0	0	0	0
Long-term loans	..	..	..	..	..	..	..	..
Equity and investment fund shares	2 182	2 239	1 764	1 794	1 803	2 106	2 253	2 364
Insurance pension and standardised guarantees	..	..	..	..	..	..	..	..
Financial derivatives and employee stock options	0	0	0	0	0	0	0	0
Other accounts payable	22	24	13	11	16	7	8	9
Non-financial assets	..	..	..	..	..	..	..	..
Open-end non-money market funds								
Financial net worth	..	..	..	..	..	..	..	..
Financial assets	1 842	2 036	1 785	1 805	1 819	2 113	2 261	2 374

Table 2. Financial assets and liabilities of investment funds *(cont.)*

Million EUR

	2009	2010	2011	2012	2013	2014	2015	2016
Currency and deposits	155	127	127	121	87	111	134	124
Debt securities	197	222	242	239	206	250	326	393
Loans	..	..	..	..	..	..	..	..
Equity and investment fund shares	1 484	1 675	1 407	1 433	1 516	1 746	1 795	1 845
Equity	1 319	1 500	1 250	1 280	1 348	1 598	1 641	1 690
Investment fund shares	165	176	157	153	168	149	154	156
Money market fund shares	0	0	0	0	0	0	0	2
Non-Money market fund shares	165	175	157	153	168	149	154	154
Insurance pension and standardised guarantees	..	..	..	..	..	..	..	..
Financial derivatives and employee stock options	0	0	0	0	0	0	1	1
Other accounts receivable	6	11	9	12	9	6	5	11
Financial liabilities	1 842	2 036	1 785	1 805	1 819	2 113	2 261	2 374
Debt securities	..	..	..	..	..	..	..	..
Short-term debt securities	..	..	..	..	..	..	..	..
Long-term debt securities	..	..	..	..	..	..	..	..
Loans	0	0	8	0	0	0	0	0
Short-term loans	0	0	8	0	0	0	0	0
Long-term loans	..	..	..	..	..	..	..	..
Equity and investment fund shares	1 828	2 017	1 764	1 794	1 803	2 106	2 253	2 364
Insurance pension and standardised guarantees	..	..	..	..	..	..	..	..
Financial derivatives and employee stock options	0	0	0	0	0	0	0	0
Other accounts payable	14	19	13	11	16	7	8	9
Non-financial assets	..	..	..	..	..	..	..	..
Open-end investment funds								
Financial net worth	..	..	..	..	..	..	..	..
Financial assets	1 856	2 048	1 811	1 831	1 855	2 151	2 319	2 474
Currency and deposits	169	140	147	136	110	136	166	192
Debt securities	197	222	248	250	220	263	351	425
Loans	..	..	..	..	..	..	..	..
Equity and investment fund shares	1 484	1 675	1 407	1 433	1 516	1 746	1 795	1 845
Equity	1 319	1 500	1 250	1 280	1 348	1 598	1 641	1 690
Investment fund shares	165	176	157	153	168	149	154	156
Money market fund shares	0	0	0	0	0	0	0	2
Non-Money market fund shares	165	175	157	153	168	149	154	154
Insurance pension and standardised guarantees	..	..	..	..	..	..	..	..
Financial derivatives and employee stock options	0	0	0	0	0	0	1	1
Other accounts receivable	6	11	9	12	9	6	5	11
Financial liabilities	1 856	2 048	1 811	1 831	1 855	2 151	2 319	2 474
Debt securities	..	..	..	..	..	..	..	..
Short-term debt securities	..	..	..	..	..	..	..	..
Long-term debt securities	..	..	..	..	..	..	..	..
Loans	0	0	8	0	0	0	0	0
Short-term loans	0	0	8	0	0	0	0	0
Long-term loans	..	..	..	..	..	..	..	..
Equity and investment fund shares	1 842	2 030	1 790	1 817	1 840	2 143	2 309	2 464
Insurance pension and standardised guarantees	..	..	..	..	..	..	..	..
Financial derivatives and employee stock options	0	0	0	0	0	0	0	0
Other accounts payable	14	19	13	13	16	8	10	11
Non-financial assets	..	..	..	..	..	..	..	..

Note: Detailed metadata at: http://metalinks.oecd.org/instinv/20170920/475d

SLOVENIA

Table 3. Financial assets and liabilities of insurance corporations and pension funds

Million EUR

	2009	2010	2011	2012	2013	2014	2015	2016
Insurance corporations and pension funds								
Financial net worth	-269	-78	-41	164	213	181	42	132
Financial assets	6 705	7 344	7 533	8 275	8 614	9 370	9 486	9 980
Currency and deposits	739	967	1 151	950	686	781	669	660
Debt securities	3 700	3 938	3 889	4 440	4 882	5 344	5 693	6 026
Loans	145	151	196	174	166	150	113	124
Equity and investment fund shares	1 634	1 830	1 841	2 153	2 307	2 597	2 580	2 677
Equity	826	761	779	827	858	929	840	775
Investment fund shares	808	1 069	1 062	1 326	1 449	1 667	1 741	1 901
Money market fund shares	..	..	..	..	..	..	..	..
Non-Money market fund shares	..	..	..	..	..	..	..	..
Insurance pension and standardised guarantees	218	184	183	225	201	216	177	182
Financial derivatives and employee stock options	4	4	4	4	2	0	0	0
Other accounts receivable	266	269	270	330	370	282	253	311
Financial liabilities	6 974	7 422	7 574	8 111	8 401	9 189	9 444	9 848
Debt securities	56	49	49	45	37	38	35	84
Short-term debt securities	0	0	0	0	0	0	0	0
Long-term debt securities	56	49	49	45	37	38	35	84
Loans	60	61	57	37	31	26	26	26
Short-term loans	14	11	20	3	5	0	0	1
Long-term loans	46	51	38	34	26	26	26	25
Equity and investment fund shares	1 148	973	972	1 215	1 348	1 690	1 659	1 696
Insurance pension and standardised guarantees	5 544	6 155	6 297	6 553	6 684	7 209	7 498	7 810
Financial derivatives and employee stock options	0	0	0	0	0	0	0	0
Other accounts payable	166	184	200	262	301	226	227	233
Non-financial assets	..	..	..	..	..	..	..	..
Insurance corporations								
Financial net worth	-300	-69	-32	174	207	180	34	140
Financial assets	5 020	5 396	5 491	6 197	6 475	7 031	6 999	7 416
Currency and deposits	374	488	594	488	365	327	314	286
Debt securities	2 640	2 819	2 750	3 256	3 590	4 083	4 157	4 486
Loans	96	105	129	121	112	112	86	99
Equity and investment fund shares	1 424	1 529	1 563	1 779	1 852	2 019	2 016	2 060
Equity	706	647	703	754	794	830	775	711
Investment fund shares	718	883	860	1 025	1 058	1 189	1 241	1 350
Money market fund shares	..	..	..	..	..	..	..	..
Non-Money market fund shares	..	..	..	..	..	..	..	..
Insurance pension and standardised guarantees	218	184	183	225	201	216	177	182
Financial derivatives and employee stock options	4	4	4	4	2	0	0	0
Other accounts receivable	263	266	267	324	354	273	249	303
Financial liabilities	5 320	5 465	5 523	6 023	6 268	6 851	6 965	7 276
Debt securities	56	49	49	45	37	38	35	84
Short-term debt securities	0	0	0	0	0	0	0	0
Long-term debt securities	56	49	49	45	37	38	35	84
Loans	60	60	57	37	31	26	26	26
Short-term loans	14	11	20	3	5	0	0	1
Long-term loans	46	49	38	34	26	26	26	25
Equity and investment fund shares	1 118	939	936	1 176	1 308	1 648	1 615	1 651
Insurance pension and standardised guarantees	3 926	4 240	4 308	4 512	4 599	4 927	5 070	5 301
Financial derivatives and employee stock options	0	0	0	0	0	0	0	0
Other accounts payable	160	177	173	252	293	213	220	214
Non-financial assets	..	..	..	..	..	..	..	..
Pension funds								
Financial net worth	31	-9	-9	-11	6	2	8	-8
Financial assets	1 685	1 948	2 042	2 078	2 139	2 339	2 487	2 564
Currency and deposits	365	479	556	462	322	454	356	374
Debt securities	1 059	1 119	1 139	1 184	1 292	1 261	1 537	1 540
Loans	48	46	67	53	54	37	27	25
Equity and investment fund shares	210	301	277	374	455	578	565	616
Equity	120	114	76	73	64	99	64	64
Investment fund shares	90	186	201	301	391	479	500	552
Money market fund shares	..	..	..	..	..	..	..	..
Non-Money market fund shares	..	..	..	..	..	..	..	..
Insurance pension and standardised guarantees	0	0	0	0	0	0	0	0
Financial derivatives and employee stock options	0	0	0	0	0	0	0	0
Other accounts receivable	3	3	3	6	15	9	4	8
Financial liabilities	1 654	1 957	2 052	2 089	2 133	2 337	2 479	2 572
Debt securities	0	0	0	0	0	0	0	0
Short-term debt securities	0	0	0	0	0	0	0	0
Long-term debt securities	0	0	0	0	0	0	0	0
Loans	0	2	0	0	0	0	0	0
Short-term loans	0	0	0	0	0	0	0	0
Long-term loans	0	2	0	0	0	0	0	0
Equity and investment fund shares	30	34	36	39	40	43	44	45
Insurance pension and standardised guarantees	1 618	1 914	1 989	2 041	2 085	2 281	2 428	2 509
Financial derivatives and employee stock options	0	0	0	0	0	0	0	0
Other accounts payable	6	7	26	10	8	13	7	18
Non-financial assets	..	..	..	..	..	..	..	..

Note: Detailed metadata at: http://metalinks.oecd.org/instinv/20170920/475d

Table 4. Portfolio composition by type of investor

As percentage of financial assets and of financial liabilities

Per cent

	2009	2010	2011	2012	2013	2014	2015	2016
Investment funds								
Financial assets	100.0	100.0	100.0	100.0	100.0	100.0	100.0	100.0
Currency and deposits	8.5	7.1	8.1	7.4	5.9	6.3	7.1	7.8
Debt securities	10.0	10.2	13.7	13.6	11.9	12.2	15.2	17.2
Loans	0.0	0.0	0.0	0.0	0.0	0.0	0.0	0.0
Equity and investment fund shares	81.2	82.2	77.7	78.3	81.7	81.2	77.4	74.6
Insurance pension and standardised guarantee schemes	0.0	0.0	0.0	0.0	0.0	0.0	0.0	0.0
Financial derivatives and employee stock options	0.0	0.0	0.0	0.0	0.0	0.0	0.0	0.0
Other accounts receivable	0.3	0.5	0.5	0.7	0.5	0.3	0.2	0.4
Financial liabilities	100.0	100.0	100.0	100.0	100.0	100.0	100.0	100.0
Currency and deposits	0.0	0.0	0.0	0.0	0.0	0.0	0.0	0.0
Debt securities	0.0	0.0	0.0	0.0	0.0	0.0	0.0	0.0
Loans	0.7	0.6	0.4	0.0	0.0	0.0	0.0	0.0
Equity and investment fund shares	98.3	98.4	98.8	99.3	99.1	99.6	99.6	99.6
Insurance pension and standardised guarantee schemes	0.0	0.0	0.0	0.0	0.0	0.0	0.0	0.0
Financial derivatives and employee stock options	0.0	0.0	0.0	0.0	0.0	0.0	0.0	0.0
Other accounts receivable	1.0	1.1	0.7	0.7	0.9	0.4	0.4	0.4
Insurance corporations								
Financial assets	100.0	100.0	100.0	100.0	100.0	100.0	100.0	100.0
Currency and deposits	7.4	9.0	10.8	7.9	5.6	4.7	4.5	3.9
Debt securities	52.6	52.2	50.1	52.5	55.4	58.1	59.4	60.5
Loans	1.9	1.9	2.4	2.0	1.7	1.6	1.2	1.3
Equity and investment fund shares	28.4	28.3	28.5	28.7	28.6	28.7	28.8	27.8
Insurance pension and standardised guarantee schemes	4.3	3.4	3.3	3.6	3.1	3.1	2.5	2.5
Financial derivatives and employee stock options	0.1	0.1	0.1	0.1	0.0	0.0	0.0	0.0
Other accounts receivable	5.2	4.9	4.9	5.2	5.5	3.9	3.6	4.1
Financial liabilities	100.0	100.0	100.0	100.0	100.0	100.0	100.0	100.0
Currency and deposits	0.0	0.0	0.0	0.0	0.0	0.0	0.0	0.0
Debt securities	1.1	0.9	0.9	0.8	0.6	0.6	0.5	1.2
Loans	1.1	1.1	1.0	0.6	0.5	0.4	0.4	0.4
Equity and investment fund shares	21.0	17.2	16.9	19.5	20.9	24.0	23.2	22.7
Insurance pension and standardised guarantee schemes	73.8	77.6	78.0	74.9	73.4	71.9	72.8	72.8
Financial derivatives and employee stock options	0.0	0.0	0.0	0.0	0.0	0.0	0.0	0.0
Other accounts receivable	3.0	3.2	3.1	4.2	4.7	3.1	3.2	2.9
Pension funds								
Financial assets	100.0	100.0	100.0	100.0	100.0	100.0	100.0	100.0
Currency and deposits	21.7	24.6	27.2	22.2	15.0	19.4	14.3	14.6
Debt securities	62.9	57.4	55.8	57.0	60.4	53.9	61.8	60.1
Loans	2.9	2.4	3.3	2.5	2.5	1.6	1.1	1.0
Equity and investment fund shares	12.5	15.4	13.6	18.0	21.3	24.7	22.7	24.0
Insurance pension and standardised guarantee schemes	0.0	0.0	0.0	0.0	0.0	0.0	0.0	0.0
Financial derivatives and employee stock options	0.0	0.0	0.0	0.0	0.0	0.0	0.0	0.0
Other accounts receivable	0.2	0.2	0.1	0.3	0.7	0.4	0.2	0.3
Financial liabilities	100.0	100.0	100.0	100.0	100.0	100.0	100.0	100.0
Currency and deposits	0.0	0.0	0.0	0.0	0.0	0.0	0.0	0.0
Debt securities	0.0	0.0	0.0	0.0	0.0	0.0	0.0	0.0
Loans	0.0	0.1	0.0	0.0	0.0	0.0	0.0	0.0
Equity and investment fund shares	1.8	1.7	1.8	1.8	1.9	1.8	1.8	1.7
Insurance pension and standardised guarantee schemes	97.8	97.8	97.0	97.7	97.7	97.6	97.9	97.5
Financial derivatives and employee stock options	0.0	0.0	0.0	0.0	0.0	0.0	0.0	0.0
Other accounts receivable	0.4	0.4	1.3	0.5	0.4	0.6	0.3	0.7

Note: Detailed metadata at: http://metalinks.oecd.org/instinv/20170920/a49a

SPAIN

Table 1. Financial assets and liabilities of institutional investors, 2016

Million EUR (1999 ESP euro)

		Investment funds			
		Non-money market funds			Money market funds
	Total	Total	Open-end non-money market funds	Closed-end non-money market funds	Total
Financial assets	274 498	264 767	264 376	391	9 731
Currency and deposits	44 124	41 397	41 322	75	2 726
Debt securities	123 592	116 628	116 628	0	6 964
Debt securities, short term	14 298	7 335	7 335	0	6 964
Debt securities, long term	109 294	109 294	109 294	0	0
Debt securities issued by residents	69 592	66 814	66 814	0	2 778
Debt securities issued by non-residents	54 000	49 814	49 814	0	4 186
Loans	0	..	..	0	0
Loans, short-term	0	..	..	0	0
Loans, long-term	0	..	..	0	..
Loans granted to residents	0	..	..	0	0
Loans granted to non-residents	0	..	..	0	0
Equity and investment fund shares/units	102 918	102 885	102 881	4	34
Equity and investment fund shares issued/units by residents	19 251	19 247	19 244	4	3
Equity and investment fund shares/units issued by non residents	83 667	83 637	83 637	0	30
Other accounts receivable	2 525	2 517	2 205	312	8

		Investment funds			
		Non-money market funds			Money market funds
	Total	Total	Open-end non-money market funds	Closed-end non-money market funds	Total
Financial liabilities	275 786	266 055	264 376	1 679	9 731
Currency and deposits	0	..	..	0	..
Debt securities	0	..	..	0	..
Debt securities, short term	0	..	..	0	..
Debt securities, long term	0	..	..	0	..
Loans	522	513	0	513	9
Loans, short-term	522	513	0	513	9
Loans, long-term	0	..	..	0	0
Equity and investment fund shares/units	273 059	263 337	262 252	1 085	9 722
Insurance pension and standardised guarantees	0	..	..	0	..
Financial derivatives and employee stock options	412	412	412	0	..
Other accounts payable	1 793	1 793	1 712	80	0

		Insurance corporations and pension funds			
		Insurance corporations			Pension funds
	Total	Total	Life insurance corporations	Non-life insurance corporations	Total
Financial assets	444 897	311 242	..	..	133 655
Currency and deposits	42 696	28 368	..	..	14 328
Debt securities	287 254	218 405	..	..	68 849
Debt securities, short-term	2 742	1 105	..	..	1 637
Debt securities, long term	284 513	217 301	..	..	67 212
Debt securities issued by residents	197 072	157 361	..	..	39 711
Debt securities issued by non-residents	90 182	61 044	..	..	29 138
Loans	3 538	3 529	..	..	9
Loans, short-term	2 005	2 005	..	..	0
Loans, long-term	1 532	1 523	..	..	9
Loans granted to residents	2 000	..	..	..	9
Loans granted to non-residents	1 538	1 538	..	..	..
Equity and investment fund shares/units	77 231	36 194	..	..	41 037
Equity and investment fund shares/units issued by residents	29 855	22 044	..	..	7 811
Equity and investment fund shares/units issued by non residents	47 377	14 150	..	..	33 226
Other accounts receivable	17 928	17 619	..	..	309

		Insurance corporations and pension funds			
		Insurance corporations			Pension funds
	Total	Total	Life insurance corporations	Non-life insurance corporations	Total
Financial liabilities	444 519	312 634	..	..	131 885
Currency and deposits	..	..	..	..	..
Debt securities	169	169	..	..	0
Debt securities, short term	0	0	..	..	0
Debt securities, long term	169	169	..	..	0
Loans	5 836	5 836	..	..	0
Loans, short-term	4 716	4 716	..	..	0
Loans, long-term	1 121	1 121	..	..	0
Equity and investment fund shares/units	47 327	47 327	..	..	0
Insurance pension and standardised guarantees	385 817	254 522	..	..	131 295
Financial derivatives and employee stock options	0	0	..	..	0
Other accounts payable	5 370	4 780	..	..	590

Note: Detailed metadata at: http://metalinks.oecd.org/instinv/20170920/558c

Table 2. Financial assets and liabilities of investment funds

Million EUR

	2009	2010	2011	2012	2013	2014	2015	2016
Investment funds								
Financial net worth	-7 306	-7 036	-5 375	-5 028	-5 346	-1 478	-1 434	-1 288
Financial assets	199 694	172 952	157 190	150 185	187 089	233 630	259 583	274 498
Currency and deposits	44 687	37 142	28 326	27 388	39 500	43 527	46 474	44 124
Debt securities	112 614	92 223	94 234	87 273	98 663	119 003	110 939	123 592
Loans	18	67	10	23	1	0	0	0
Equity and investment fund shares	38 339	40 417	32 261	32 812	45 430	67 410	98 267	102 918
Equity	18 927	18 997	15 769	16 440	23 661	30 372	37 315	37 418
Investment fund shares	19 412	21 419	16 492	16 371	21 769	37 038	60 952	65 500
Money market fund shares	1 310	999	1 114	875	722	563	1 330	1 464
Non-Money market fund shares	18 102	20 420	15 378	15 497	21 047	36 475	59 621	64 036
Insurance pension and standardised guarantees	0	0	0	0	0	0	0	0
Financial derivatives and employee stock options	2 297	1 596	1 102	1 159	1 440	1 327	1 123	1 340
Other accounts receivable	1 739	1 508	1 255	1 532	2 054	2 363	2 780	2 525
Financial liabilities	207 000	179 988	162 565	155 213	192 435	235 108	261 017	275 786
Debt securities	0	0	0	0	0	0	0	0
Short-term debt securities	0	0	0	0	0	0	0	0
Long-term debt securities	0	0	0	0	0	0	0	0
Loans	631	648	538	534	864	456	529	522
Short-term loans	631	648	538	534	864	456	529	522
Long-term loans	0	0	0	0	0	0	0	0
Equity and investment fund shares	204 182	177 509	160 555	153 296	190 028	232 871	258 847	273 059
Insurance pension and standardised guarantees	0	0	0	0	0	0	0	0
Financial derivatives and employee stock options	958	671	637	521	363	417	377	412
Other accounts payable	1 229	1 160	835	863	1 180	1 363	1 264	1 793
Non-financial assets	7 238	6 975	5 292	4 939	5 258	1 478	1 434	1 287
Money market funds								
Financial net worth	-68	-61	-83	-89	-88	0	0	0
Financial assets	13 458	8 107	7 972	6 903	8 343	7 309	8 328	9 731
Currency and deposits	5 147	3 952	2 855	1 825	2 695	2 559	3 510	2 726
Debt securities	8 293	4 088	5 104	5 055	5 644	4 702	4 784	6 964
Loans	18	67	10	23	1	0	0	0
Equity and investment fund shares	0	0	2	1	3	6	3	34
Equity	..	..	..	..	..	..	..	..
Investment fund shares	0	0	2	1	3	6	3	34
Money market fund shares	0	0	2	1	3	4	3	34
Non-Money market fund shares	0	0	0	0	0	2	0	0
Insurance pension and standardised guarantees	..	..	..	..	..	..	..	..
Financial derivatives and employee stock options	..	..	..	..	..	..	..	..
Other accounts receivable	0	0	0	0	0	42	32	8
Financial liabilities	13 526	8 168	8 055	6 992	8 432	7 309	8 328	9 731
Debt securities	..	..	..	..	..	..	..	..
Short-term debt securities	..	..	..	..	..	..	..	..
Long-term debt securities	..	..	..	..	..	..	..	..
Loans	21	9	19	9	11	9	8	9
Short-term loans	21	9	19	9	11	9	8	9
Long-term loans	0	0	0	0	0	0	0	0
Equity and investment fund shares	13 486	8 154	8 036	6 979	8 420	7 299	8 320	9 722
Insurance pension and standardised guarantees	..	..	..	..	..	..	..	..
Financial derivatives and employee stock options	..	..	..	..	..	..	..	..
Other accounts payable	19	5	0	4	1	1	0	0
Non-financial assets	0	0	0	0	0	0	0	0
Non-money market funds								
Financial net worth	-7 238	-6 975	-5 292	-4 939	-5 258	-1 478	-1 434	-1 288
Financial assets	186 236	164 845	149 218	143 282	178 745	226 321	251 254	264 767
Currency and deposits	39 540	33 190	25 471	25 563	36 805	40 968	42 964	41 397
Debt securities	104 321	88 135	89 130	82 218	93 019	114 301	106 155	116 628
Loans	..	..	..	..	..	..	..	..
Equity and investment fund shares	38 339	40 417	32 259	32 811	45 427	67 404	98 264	102 885
Equity	18 927	18 997	15 769	16 440	23 661	30 372	37 315	37 418
Investment fund shares	19 412	21 419	16 490	16 371	21 766	37 032	60 949	65 466
Money market fund shares	1 310	999	1 112	874	719	559	1 327	1 430
Non-Money market fund shares	18 102	20 420	15 378	15 497	21 047	36 473	59 621	64 036
Insurance pension and standardised guarantees	..	..	..	..	..	..	..	..
Financial derivatives and employee stock options	2 297	1 596	1 102	1 159	1 440	1 327	1 123	1 340
Other accounts receivable	1 739	1 508	1 255	1 532	2 054	2 321	2 748	2 517
Financial liabilities	193 474	171 820	154 510	148 221	184 003	227 799	252 688	266 055
Debt securities	..	..	..	..	..	..	..	..
Short-term debt securities	..	..	..	..	..	..	..	..
Long-term debt securities	..	..	..	..	..	..	..	..
Loans	610	639	520	525	853	447	520	513
Short-term loans	610	639	520	525	853	447	520	513
Long-term loans	..	..	..	..	..	..	..	..
Equity and investment fund shares	190 696	169 355	152 519	146 316	181 608	225 573	250 527	263 337
Insurance pension and standardised guarantees	..	..	..	..	..	..	..	..
Financial derivatives and employee stock options	958	671	637	521	363	417	377	412
Other accounts payable	1 210	1 156	834	859	1 179	1 363	1 264	1 793
Non-financial assets	7 238	6 975	5 292	4 939	5 258	1 478	1 434	1 287
Open-end non-money market funds								
Financial net worth	0	0	0	0	0	0	0	0
Financial assets	185 877	164 509	149 040	143 077	178 394	226 056	250 971	264 376

Table 2. Financial assets and liabilities of investment funds *(cont.)*

Million EUR

	2009	2010	2011	2012	2013	2014	2015	2016
Currency and deposits	39 359	33 015	25 358	25 421	36 555	40 928	42 893	41 322
Debt securities	104 304	88 131	89 127	82 218	93 018	114 297	106 155	116 628
Loans	..	..	..	..	..	..	..	..
Equity and investment fund shares	38 333	40 408	32 259	32 810	45 416	67 392	98 253	102 881
Equity	18 921	18 988	15 769	16 440	23 656	30 371	37 315	37 418
Investment fund shares	19 412	21 419	16 490	16 371	21 760	37 021	60 938	65 463
Money market fund shares	1 310	999	1 112	874	719	559	1 327	1 430
Non-Money market fund shares	18 102	20 420	15 378	15 497	21 041	36 462	59 611	64 032
Insurance pension and standardised guarantees	..	..	..	..	..	..	..	..
Financial derivatives and employee stock options	2 297	1 596	1 102	1 159	1 440	1 327	1 123	1 340
Other accounts receivable	1 585	1 360	1 193	1 469	1 965	2 111	2 547	2 205
Financial liabilities	185 878	164 509	149 040	143 078	178 394	226 056	250 971	264 376
Debt securities	..	..	..	..	..	..	..	..
Short-term debt securities	..	..	..	..	..	..	..	..
Long-term debt securities	..	..	..	..	..	..	..	..
Loans	0	1	10	37	3	5	4	0
Short-term loans	0	1	10	37	3	5	4	0
Long-term loans	..	..	..	..	..	..	..	..
Equity and investment fund shares	183 922	162 917	147 712	141 831	177 072	224 346	249 404	262 252
Insurance pension and standardised guarantees	..	..	..	..	..	..	..	..
Financial derivatives and employee stock options	958	671	637	521	363	417	377	412
Other accounts payable	997	919	681	689	956	1 288	1 186	1 712
Non-financial assets	0	0	0	0	0	0	0	0
Open-end investment funds								
Financial net worth	-68	-61	-83	-89	-89	0	0	0
Financial assets	199 336	172 616	157 011	149 981	186 738	233 364	259 299	274 107
Currency and deposits	44 506	36 967	28 213	27 246	39 250	43 487	46 403	44 048
Debt securities	112 597	92 219	94 231	87 273	98 662	118 999	110 939	123 592
Loans	18	67	10	23	1	0	0	0
Equity and investment fund shares	38 333	40 408	32 261	32 811	45 418	67 398	98 256	102 914
Equity	18 921	18 988	15 769	16 440	23 656	30 371	37 315	37 418
Investment fund shares	19 412	21 419	16 492	16 371	21 763	37 027	60 941	65 496
Money market fund shares	1 310	999	1 114	875	722	563	1 330	1 464
Non-Money market fund shares	18 102	20 420	15 378	15 497	21 041	36 464	59 611	64 032
Insurance pension and standardised guarantees	0	0	0	0	0	0	0	0
Financial derivatives and employee stock options	2 297	1 596	1 102	1 159	1 440	1 327	1 123	1 340
Other accounts receivable	1 585	1 360	1 193	1 469	1 965	2 153	2 579	2 213
Financial liabilities	199 404	172 677	157 095	150 070	186 826	233 365	259 300	274 107
Debt securities	0	0	0	0	0	0	0	0
Short-term debt securities	0	0	0	0	0	0	0	0
Long-term debt securities	0	0	0	0	0	0	0	0
Loans	21	10	28	46	14	14	13	9
Short-term loans	21	10	28	46	14	14	13	9
Long-term loans	0	0	0	0	0	0	0	0
Equity and investment fund shares	197 409	171 071	155 748	148 810	185 492	231 645	257 723	271 974
Insurance pension and standardised guarantees	..	..	..	..	..	..	..	..
Financial derivatives and employee stock options	958	671	637	521	363	417	377	412
Other accounts payable	1 016	924	681	693	957	1 288	1 186	1 712
Non-financial assets	0	0	0	0	0	0	0	0

Note: Detailed metadata at: http://metalinks.oecd.org/instinv/20170920/558c

Table 3. Financial assets and liabilities of insurance corporations and pension funds

Million EUR

	2009	2010	2011	2012	2013	2014	2015	2016
Insurance corporations and pension funds								
Financial net worth	1 782	-2 016	-6 253	-3 533	-14 006	-15 157	2 482	377
Financial assets	349 184	349 659	357 430	371 806	382 456	415 596	434 704	444 897
Currency and deposits	65 178	65 374	63 969	63 176	63 157	59 695	59 089	42 696
Debt securities	200 339	194 794	204 283	217 165	223 990	259 472	273 812	287 254
Loans	5 567	7 493	7 724	7 742	7 356	4 521	2 979	3 538
Equity and investment fund shares	46 792	49 481	48 641	46 093	53 555	58 788	65 982	77 231
Equity	29 592	27 746	27 501	26 866	27 628	30 074	28 667	32 802
Investment fund shares	17 199	21 735	21 141	19 227	25 927	28 714	37 314	44 430
Money market fund shares	590	357	351	305	367	319	364	425
Non-Money market fund shares	16 609	21 378	20 789	18 923	25 559	28 395	36 951	44 005
Insurance pension and standardised guarantees	16 651	17 099	16 949	17 629	15 365	14 966	15 025	15 803
Financial derivatives and employee stock options	0	0	1 247	915	936	826	446	
Other accounts receivable	14 657	15 417	15 863	18 754	18 118	17 219	16 991	17 928
Financial liabilities	347 402	351 675	363 682	375 339	396 462	430 753	432 222	444 519
Debt securities	311	296	296	146	146	0	0	169
Short-term debt securities	0	0	0	0	0	0	0	0
Long-term debt securities	311	296	296	146	146	0	0	169
Loans	10 969	12 366	19 248	17 579	17 320	19 171	17 726	5 836
Short-term loans	9 144	11 264	17 841	16 547	16 139	17 497	16 323	4 716
Long-term loans	1 824	1 102	1 408	1 031	1 181	1 674	1 402	1 121
Equity and investment fund shares	31 412	30 967	31 925	34 835	41 173	44 335	44 601	47 327
Insurance pension and standardised guarantees	299 754	300 553	305 456	315 767	331 140	360 548	363 938	385 817
Financial derivatives and employee stock options	0	0	0	0	0	0	0	0
Other accounts payable	4 957	7 492	6 756	7 013	6 683	6 699	5 959	5 370
Non-financial assets	9 830	10 513	9 977	10 241	10 582	10 705	10 944	10 636
Insurance corporations								
Financial net worth	2 463	-1 436	-5 597	-2 839	-8 617	-10 191	5 425	-1 392
Financial assets	245 667	244 235	253 512	263 514	271 946	295 984	309 024	311 242
Currency and deposits	48 104	47 431	50 504	48 179	49 049	45 406	42 648	28 368
Debt securities	140 805	137 215	141 880	155 979	158 374	188 945	205 893	218 405
Loans	5 298	7 345	7 650	7 704	7 325	4 512	2 968	3 529
Equity and investment fund shares	28 929	29 723	30 927	24 618	30 925	32 569	33 929	36 194
Equity	18 279	15 987	17 493	15 846	17 009	17 786	17 409	16 918
Investment fund shares	10 650	13 736	13 435	8 772	13 916	14 784	16 520	19 276
Money market fund shares	441	267	251	204	246	215	260	321
Non-Money market fund shares	10 209	13 469	13 183	8 569	13 669	14 569	16 260	18 955
Insurance pension and standardised guarantees	8 190	7 487	6 955	7 226	7 429	6 587	6 077	6 681
Financial derivatives and employee stock options	0	0	1 247	915	936	826	446	
Other accounts receivable	14 342	15 033	15 595	18 561	17 930	17 029	16 683	17 619
Financial liabilities	243 204	245 671	259 108	266 353	280 563	306 175	303 599	312 634
Debt securities	311	296	296	146	146	0	0	169
Short-term debt securities	0	0	0	0	0	0	0	0
Long-term debt securities	311	296	296	146	146	0	0	169
Loans	10 969	12 366	19 248	17 579	17 320	19 171	17 726	5 836
Short-term loans	9 144	11 264	17 841	16 547	16 139	17 497	16 323	4 716
Long-term loans	1 824	1 102	1 408	1 031	1 181	1 674	1 402	1 121
Equity and investment fund shares	31 412	30 967	31 925	34 835	41 173	44 335	44 601	47 327
Insurance pension and standardised guarantees	195 787	195 005	201 149	206 997	215 488	236 371	235 707	254 522
Financial derivatives and employee stock options	0	0	0	0	0	0	0	0
Other accounts payable	4 726	7 036	6 490	6 797	6 436	6 298	5 567	4 780
Non-financial assets	9 607	10 273	9 747	10 012	10 382	10 527	10 773	10 460
Pension funds								
Financial net worth	-681	-580	-656	-694	-5 389	-4 966	-2 943	1 769
Financial assets	103 517	105 424	103 918	108 292	110 510	119 612	125 680	133 655
Currency and deposits	17 074	17 943	13 465	14 997	14 108	14 289	16 441	14 328
Debt securities	59 534	57 579	62 403	61 186	65 616	70 527	67 919	68 849
Loans	269	148	74	38	31	8	12	9
Equity and investment fund shares	17 863	19 758	17 714	21 475	22 630	26 219	32 053	41 037
Equity	11 313	11 759	10 008	11 020	10 619	12 290	11 258	15 884
Investment fund shares	6 549	7 999	7 706	10 455	12 011	13 930	20 794	25 154
Money market fund shares	149	90	100	101	121	104	104	104
Non-Money market fund shares	6 400	7 909	7 606	10 354	11 890	13 826	20 691	25 050
Insurance pension and standardised guarantees	8 461	9 612	9 994	10 403	7 936	8 379	8 948	9 122
Financial derivatives and employee stock options	0	0	0	0	0	0	0	0
Other accounts receivable	317	384	268	193	190	190	308	309
Financial liabilities	104 198	106 004	104 574	108 986	115 899	124 578	128 623	131 885
Debt securities	0	0	0	0	0	0	0	0
Short-term debt securities	0	0	0	0	0	0	0	0
Long-term debt securities	0	0	0	0	0	0	0	0
Loans	0	0	0	0	0	0	0	0
Short-term loans	0	0	0	0	0	0	0	0
Long-term loans	0	0	0	0	0	0	0	0
Equity and investment fund shares	0	0	0	0	0	0	0	0
Insurance pension and standardised guarantees	103 967	105 548	104 307	108 770	115 652	124 177	128 231	131 295
Financial derivatives and employee stock options	0	0	0	0	0	0	0	0
Other accounts payable	231	456	266	216	247	401	392	590
Non-financial assets	223	240	230	229	200	178	172	176

Note: Detailed metadata at: http://metalinks.oecd.org/instinv/20170920/558c

Table 4. Portfolio composition by type of investor

As percentage of financial assets and of financial liabilities

Per cent

	2009	2010	2011	2012	2013	2014	2015	2016
Investment funds								
Financial assets	100.0	100.0	100.0	100.0	100.0	100.0	100.0	100.0
Currency and deposits	22.4	21.5	18.0	18.2	21.1	18.6	17.9	16.1
Debt securities	56.4	53.3	59.9	58.1	52.7	50.9	42.7	45.0
Loans	0.0	0.0	0.0	0.0	0.0	0.0	0.0	0.0
Equity and investment fund shares	19.2	23.4	20.5	21.8	24.3	28.9	37.9	37.5
Insurance pension and standardised guarantee schemes	0.0	0.0	0.0	0.0	0.0	0.0	0.0	0.0
Financial derivatives and employee stock options	1.2	0.9	0.7	0.8	0.8	0.6	0.4	0.5
Other accounts receivable	0.9	0.9	0.8	1.0	1.1	1.0	1.1	0.9
Financial liabilities	100.0	100.0	100.0	100.0	100.0	100.0	100.0	100.0
Currency and deposits	0.0	0.0	0.0	0.0	0.0	0.0	0.0	0.0
Debt securities	0.0	0.0	0.0	0.0	0.0	0.0	0.0	0.0
Loans	0.3	0.4	0.3	0.3	0.4	0.2	0.2	0.2
Equity and investment fund shares	98.6	98.6	98.8	98.8	98.7	99.0	99.2	99.0
Insurance pension and standardised guarantee schemes	0.0	0.0	0.0	0.0	0.0	0.0	0.0	0.0
Financial derivatives and employee stock options	0.5	0.4	0.4	0.3	0.2	0.2	0.1	0.1
Other accounts receivable	0.6	0.6	0.5	0.6	0.6	0.6	0.5	0.6
Insurance corporations								
Financial assets	100.0	100.0	100.0	100.0	100.0	100.0	100.0	100.0
Currency and deposits	19.6	19.4	19.9	18.3	18.0	15.3	13.8	9.1
Debt securities	57.3	56.2	56.0	59.2	58.2	63.8	66.6	70.2
Loans	2.2	3.0	3.0	2.9	2.7	1.5	1.0	1.1
Equity and investment fund shares	11.8	12.2	12.2	9.3	11.4	11.0	11.0	11.6
Insurance pension and standardised guarantee schemes	3.3	3.1	2.7	2.7	2.7	2.2	2.0	2.1
Financial derivatives and employee stock options	0.0	0.0	0.0	0.5	0.3	0.3	0.3	0.1
Other accounts receivable	5.8	6.2	6.2	7.0	6.6	5.8	5.4	5.7
Financial liabilities	100.0	100.0	100.0	100.0	100.0	100.0	100.0	100.0
Currency and deposits	0.0	0.0	0.0	0.0	0.0	0.0	0.0	0.0
Debt securities	0.1	0.1	0.1	0.1	0.1	0.0	0.0	0.1
Loans	4.5	5.0	7.4	6.6	6.2	6.3	5.8	1.9
Equity and investment fund shares	12.9	12.6	12.3	13.1	14.7	14.5	14.7	15.1
Insurance pension and standardised guarantee schemes	80.5	79.4	77.6	77.7	76.8	77.2	77.6	81.4
Financial derivatives and employee stock options	0.0	0.0	0.0	0.0	0.0	0.0	0.0	0.0
Other accounts receivable	1.9	2.9	2.5	2.6	2.3	2.1	1.8	1.5
Pension funds								
Financial assets	100.0	100.0	100.0	100.0	100.0	100.0	100.0	100.0
Currency and deposits	16.5	17.0	13.0	13.8	12.8	11.9	13.1	10.7
Debt securities	57.5	54.6	60.1	56.5	59.4	59.0	54.0	51.5
Loans	0.3	0.1	0.1	0.0	0.0	0.0	0.0	0.0
Equity and investment fund shares	17.3	18.7	17.0	19.8	20.5	21.9	25.5	30.7
Insurance pension and standardised guarantee schemes	8.2	9.1	9.6	9.6	7.2	7.0	7.1	6.8
Financial derivatives and employee stock options	0.0	0.0	0.0	0.0	0.0	0.0	0.0	0.0
Other accounts receivable	0.3	0.4	0.3	0.2	0.2	0.2	0.2	0.2
Financial liabilities	100.0	100.0	100.0	100.0	100.0	100.0	100.0	100.0
Currency and deposits	0.0	0.0	0.0	0.0	0.0	0.0	0.0	0.0
Debt securities	0.0	0.0	0.0	0.0	0.0	0.0	0.0	0.0
Loans	0.0	0.0	0.0	0.0	0.0	0.0	0.0	0.0
Equity and investment fund shares	0.0	0.0	0.0	0.0	0.0	0.0	0.0	0.0
Insurance pension and standardised guarantee schemes	99.8	99.6	99.7	99.8	99.8	99.7	99.7	99.6
Financial derivatives and employee stock options	0.0	0.0	0.0	0.0	0.0	0.0	0.0	0.0
Other accounts receivable	0.2	0.4	0.3	0.2	0.2	0.3	0.3	0.4

Note: Detailed metadata at: http://metalinks.oecd.org/instinv/20170920/a49a

Table 1. Financial assets and liabilities of institutional investors, 2016

Million SEK

	Investment funds				
	Total	Non-money market funds			Money market funds
		Total	Open-end non-money market funds	Closed-end non-money market funds	Total
Financial assets	3 602 738	3 583 840	..	..	18 898
Currency and deposits	100 631	99 973	..	..	658
Debt securities	827 527	809 354	..	..	18 173
Debt securities, short term	46 705	46 020	..	..	685
Debt securities, long term	780 822	763 334	..	..	17 488
Debt securities issued by residents	665 056	647 661	..	..	17 395
Debt securities issued by non-residents	162 471	161 693	..	..	778
Loans	..	..	..	..	..
Loans, short-term	..	..	..	..	..
Loans, long-term	..	..	..	..	..
Loans granted to residents	..	..	..	..	..
Loans granted to non-residents	..	..	..	..	..
Equity and investment fund shares/units	2 539 086	2 539 086	..	..	..
Equity and investment fund shares issued/units by residents	1 081 040	1 081 040	..	..	..
Equity and investment fund shares/units issued by non residents	1 458 046	1 458 046	..	..	..
Other accounts receivable	95 053	94 986	..	..	67

	Investment funds				
	Total	Non-money market funds			Money market funds
		Total	Open-end non-money market funds	Closed-end non-money market funds	Total
Financial liabilities	3 602 738	3 583 840	..	..	18 898
Currency and deposits			..	..	
Debt securities	..	..	..	..	..
Debt securities, short term	..	..	..	..	..
Debt securities, long term	..	..	..	..	..
Loans	18 916	18 916	..	..	..
Loans, short-term	18 899	18 899	..	..	..
Loans, long-term	17	17	..	..	..
Equity and investment fund shares/units	3 345 569	3 326 738	..	..	18 831
Insurance pension and standardised guaratees	..	..	..	..	..
Financial derivatives and employee stock options	28 459	28 459	..	..	..
Other accounts payable	209 794	209 727	..	..	67

	Insurance corporations and pension funds				
	Total	Insurance corporations			Pension funds
		Total	Life insurance corporations	Non-life insurance corporations	Total
Financial assets	5 483 346	1 435 855	..	..	4 047 491
Currency and deposits	158 397	61 114	..	..	97 283
Debt securities	1 459 505	388 598	..	..	1 070 907
Debt securities, short-term	14 428	6 866	..	..	7 562
Debt securities, long term	1 445 077	381 732	..	..	1 063 345
Debt securities issued by residents	1 072 696	316 703	..	..	755 993
Debt securities issued by non-residents	386 809	71 895	..	..	314 914
Loans	70 073	28 270	..	..	41 803
Loans, short-term	0	0	..	..	0
Loans, long-term	70 073	28 270	..	..	41 803
Loans granted to residents	53 977	16 727	..	..	37 250
Loans granted to non-residents	16 096	11 543	..	..	4 553
Equity and investment fund shares/units	3 696 335	920 124	..	..	2 776 211
Equity and investment fund shares/units issued by residents	2 472 623	624 430	..	..	1 848 193
Equity and investment fund shares/units issued by non residents	1 223 712	295 694	..	..	928 018
Other accounts receivable	46 598	11 226	..	..	35 372

	Insurance corporations and pension funds				
	Total	Insurance corporations			Pension funds
		Total	Life insurance corporations	Non-life insurance corporations	Total
Financial liabilities	5 006 966	1 119 004	..	..	3 887 962
Currency and deposits	..	..	..	..	..
Debt securities	2 574	2 474	..	..	100
Debt securities, short term	0	0	..	..	..
Debt securities, long term	2 574	2 474	..	..	100
Loans	48 382	22 960	..	..	25 422
Loans, short-term	39 210	18 736	..	..	20 474
Loans, long-term	9 172	4 224	..	..	4 948
Equity and investment fund shares/units	377 082	118 646	..	..	258 436
Insurance pension and standardised guarantees	4 545 682	965 912	..	..	3 579 770
Financial derivatives and employee stock options	20 490	2 108	..	..	18 382
Other accounts payable	12 756	6 904	..	..	5 852

Note: Detailed metadata at: http://metalinks.oecd.org/instinv/20170920/5811

SWEDEN

Table 2. Financial assets and liabilities of investment funds

Million SEK

	2009	2010	2011	2012	2013	2014	2015	2016
Investment funds								
Financial net worth	0	0	0	0	0	0	0	0
Financial assets	1 529 605	1 790 498	1 641 931	1 898 888	2 370 648	3 013 996	3 201 560	3 602 738
Currency and deposits	49 109	47 935	56 495	64 412	68 292	83 751	94 600	100 631
Debt securities	343 160	369 068	395 474	401 403	488 305	756 278	747 892	827 527
Loans	..	..	..	..	..	..	..	..
Equity and investment fund shares	1 065 120	1 285 368	1 119 224	1 327 329	1 698 569	2 062 603	2 256 773	2 539 086
Equity	922 813	1 095 259	919 966	1 053 080	1 315 861	1 588 209	1 729 009	1 982 252
Investment fund shares	142 307	190 109	199 258	274 249	382 708	474 394	527 764	556 834
Money market fund shares	621	658	8 814	5 591	5 478	17 058	13 130	10 987
Non-Money market fund shares	141 686	189 451	190 444	268 658	377 230	457 336	514 634	545 847
Insurance pension and standardised guarantees	..	..	..	..	..	..	..	..
Financial derivatives and employee stock options	8 927	9 773	16 227	14 974	20 993	28 746	31 136	40 441
Other accounts receivable	63 289	78 354	54 511	90 770	94 489	82 618	71 159	95 053
Financial liabilities	1 529 605	1 790 498	1 641 931	1 898 888	2 370 648	3 013 996	3 201 560	3 602 738
Debt securities	..	..	..	..	..	..	..	..
Short-term debt securities	..	..	..	..	..	..	..	..
Long-term debt securities	..	..	..	..	..	..	..	..
Loans	20 066	19 486	10 775	6 623	6 543	15 106	9 649	18 916
Short-term loans	15 774	19 440	10 728	6 600	6 528	15 087	9 639	18 899
Long-term loans	4 292	46	47	23	15	19	10	17
Equity and investment fund shares	1 393 334	1 635 074	1 534 584	1 737 409	2 158 151	2 769 988	3 039 287	3 345 569
Insurance pension and standardised guarantees	..	..	..	..	..	..	..	..
Financial derivatives and employee stock options	7 472	5 717	13 540	13 204	14 892	29 678	27 826	28 459
Other accounts payable	108 733	130 221	83 032	141 652	191 062	199 224	124 798	209 794
Non-financial assets	..	..	..	..	..	..	..	..
Money market funds								
Financial net worth	0	0	0	0	0	0	0	0
Financial assets	70 245	70 983	99 680	22 192	19 439	22 983	23 636	18 898
Currency and deposits	1 397	1 105	2 236	167	237	563	793	658
Debt securities	68 758	69 585	97 335	21 580	18 759	22 346	22 773	18 173
Loans	..	..	..	..	..	..	..	..
Equity and investment fund shares	..	..	..	..	..	..	..	..
Equity	..	..	..	..	..	..	..	..
Investment fund shares	..	..	..	..	..	..	..	..
Money market fund shares	..	..	..	..	..	..	..	..
Non-Money market fund shares	..	..	..	..	..	..	..	..
Insurance pension and standardised guarantees	..	..	..	..	..	..	..	..
Financial derivatives and employee stock options	..	21	..	6	..	1	..	..
Other accounts receivable	90	272	109	439	443	73	70	67
Financial liabilities	70 245	70 983	99 680	22 192	19 439	22 983	23 636	18 898
Debt securities	..	..	..	..	..	..	..	..
Short-term debt securities	..	..	..	..	..	..	..	..
Long-term debt securities	..	..	..	..	..	..	..	..
Loans	164	138	2	..	..	..	..	..
Short-term loans	164	138	2	..	..	..	..	..
Long-term loans	0	0	0	..	..	..	..	..
Equity and investment fund shares	69 632	70 578	99 456	22 103	19 349	22 715	23 572	18 831
Insurance pension and standardised guarantees	..	..	..	..	..	..	..	..
Financial derivatives and employee stock options	..	..	1	5	..	1	..	..
Other accounts payable	449	267	221	84	90	267	64	67
Non-financial assets	..	..	..	..	..	..	..	..
Non-money market funds								
Financial net worth	0	0	0	0	0	0	0	0
Financial assets	1 459 360	1 719 515	1 542 251	1 876 696	2 351 209	2 991 013	3 177 924	3 583 840
Currency and deposits	47 712	46 830	54 259	64 245	68 055	83 188	93 807	99 973
Debt securities	274 402	299 483	298 139	379 823	469 546	733 932	725 119	809 354
Loans	..	..	..	..	..	..	..	..
Equity and investment fund shares	1 065 120	1 285 368	1 119 224	1 327 329	1 698 569	2 062 603	2 256 773	2 539 086
Equity	922 813	1 095 259	919 966	1 053 080	1 315 861	1 588 209	1 729 009	1 982 252
Investment fund shares	142 307	190 109	199 258	274 249	382 708	474 394	527 764	556 834
Money market fund shares	621	658	8 814	5 591	5 478	17 058	13 130	10 987
Non-Money market fund shares	141 686	189 451	190 444	268 658	377 230	457 336	514 634	545 847
Insurance pension and standardised guarantees	..	..	..	..	..	..	..	..
Financial derivatives and employee stock options	8 927	9 752	16 227	14 968	20 993	28 745	31 136	40 441
Other accounts receivable	63 199	78 082	54 402	90 331	94 046	82 545	71 089	94 986
Financial liabilities	1 459 360	1 719 515	1 542 251	1 876 696	2 351 209	2 991 013	3 177 924	3 583 840
Debt securities	..	..	..	..	..	..	..	..
Short-term debt securities	..	..	..	..	..	..	..	..
Long-term debt securities	..	..	..	..	..	..	..	..
Loans	19 902	19 348	10 773	6 623	6 543	15 106	9 649	18 916
Short-term loans	15 610	19 302	10 726	6 600	6 528	15 087	9 639	18 899
Long-term loans	4 292	46	47	23	15	19	10	17
Equity and investment fund shares	1 323 702	1 564 496	1 435 128	1 715 306	2 138 802	2 747 273	3 015 715	3 326 738
Insurance pension and standardised guarantees	..	..	..	..	..	..	..	..
Financial derivatives and employee stock options	7 472	5 717	13 539	13 199	14 892	29 677	27 826	28 459
Other accounts payable	108 284	129 954	82 811	141 568	190 972	198 957	124 734	209 727
Non-financial assets	..	..	..	..	..	..	..	..
Open-end non-money market funds								
Financial net worth	..	..	..	..	..	..	..	..
Financial assets	..	..	..	..	..	..	..	..

Table 2. Financial assets and liabilities of investment funds *(cont.)*

Million SEK

	2009	2010	2011	2012	2013	2014	2015	2016
Currency and deposits	..	..	..	..	..	..	..	..
Debt securities	..	..	..	..	..	..	..	..
Loans	..	..	..	..	..	..	..	..
Equity and investment fund shares	..	..	..	..	..	..	..	..
Equity	..	..	..	..	..	..	..	..
Investment fund shares	..	..	..	..	..	..	..	..
Money market fund shares	..	..	..	..	..	..	..	..
Non-Money market fund shares	..	..	..	..	..	..	..	..
Insurance pension and standardised guarantees	..	..	..	..	..	..	..	..
Financial derivatives and employee stock options	..	..	..	..	..	..	..	..
Other accounts receivable	..	..	..	..	..	..	..	..
Financial liabilities	..	..	..	..	..	..	..	..
Debt securities	..	..	..	..	..	..	..	..
Short-term debt securities	..	..	..	..	..	..	..	..
Long-term debt securities	..	..	..	..	..	..	..	..
Loans	..	..	..	..	..	..	..	..
Short-term loans	..	..	..	..	..	..	..	..
Long-term loans	..	..	..	..	..	..	..	..
Equity and investment fund shares	..	..	..	..	..	..	..	..
Insurance pension and standardised guarantees	..	..	..	..	..	..	..	..
Financial derivatives and employee stock options	..	..	..	..	..	..	..	..
Other accounts payable	..	..	..	..	..	..	..	..
Non-financial assets	..	..	..	..	..	..	..	..
Open-end investment funds								
Financial net worth	..	..	..	..	..	..	..	..
Financial assets	..	..	..	..	..	..	..	..
Currency and deposits	..	..	..	..	..	..	..	..
Debt securities	..	..	..	..	..	..	..	..
Loans	..	..	..	..	..	..	..	..
Equity and investment fund shares	..	..	..	..	..	..	..	..
Equity	..	..	..	..	..	..	..	..
Investment fund shares	..	..	..	..	..	..	..	..
Money market fund shares	..	..	..	..	..	..	..	..
Non-Money market fund shares	..	..	..	..	..	..	..	..
Insurance pension and standardised guarantees	..	..	..	..	..	..	..	..
Financial derivatives and employee stock options	..	..	..	..	..	..	..	..
Other accounts receivable	..	..	..	..	..	..	..	..
Financial liabilities	..	..	..	..	..	..	..	..
Debt securities	..	..	..	..	..	..	..	..
Short-term debt securities	..	..	..	..	..	..	..	..
Long-term debt securities	..	..	..	..	..	..	..	..
Loans	..	..	..	..	..	..	..	..
Short-term loans	..	..	..	..	..	..	..	..
Long-term loans	..	..	..	..	..	..	..	..
Equity and investment fund shares	..	..	..	..	..	..	..	..
Insurance pension and standardised guarantees	..	..	..	..	..	..	..	..
Financial derivatives and employee stock options	..	..	..	..	..	..	..	..
Other accounts payable	..	..	..	..	..	..	..	..
Non-financial assets	..	..	..	..	..	..	..	..

Note: Detailed metadata at: http://metalinks.oecd.org/instinv/20170920/5811

SWEDEN

Table 3. Financial assets and liabilities of insurance corporations and pension funds

Million SEK

	2009	2010	2011	2012	2013	2014	2015	2016
Insurance corporations and pension funds								
Financial net worth	229 256	180 362	-69 089	228 507	417 786	461 000	443 015	476 380
Financial assets	3 228 484	3 560 107	3 508 654	3 823 335	4 203 014	4 876 244	5 111 030	5 483 346
Currency and deposits	98 109	124 813	143 986	133 180	132 335	150 550	153 929	158 397
Debt securities	1 244 521	1 211 861	1 340 473	1 381 949	1 349 994	1 452 043	1 470 003	1 459 505
Loans	54 080	58 899	63 628	71 319	70 540	74 275	63 468	70 073
Equity and investment fund shares	1 743 293	2 069 281	1 847 381	2 120 623	2 556 520	3 077 624	3 324 208	3 696 335
Equity	705 212	864 567	714 543	839 000	980 463	1 125 674	1 190 459	1 308 304
Investment fund shares	1 038 081	1 204 714	1 132 838	1 281 623	1 576 057	1 951 950	2 133 749	2 388 031
Money market fund shares	40 755	42 326	62 013	53 856	65 825	65 887	70 756	69 846
Non-Money market fund shares	997 326	1 162 388	1 070 825	1 227 767	1 510 232	1 886 063	2 062 993	2 318 185
Insurance pension and standardised guarantees	33 600	31 643	33 570	32 157	29 225	31 228	27 618	24 529
Financial derivatives and employee stock options	16 393	24 268	29 166	36 975	16 279	28 363	28 873	27 909
Other accounts receivable	38 488	39 342	50 450	47 132	48 121	62 161	42 931	46 598
Financial liabilities	2 999 228	3 379 745	3 577 743	3 594 828	3 785 228	4 415 244	4 668 015	5 006 966
Debt securities	7 678	6 260	5 431	5 347	5 422	4 659	3 231	2 574
Short-term debt securities	0	0	0	0	0	0	0	0
Long-term debt securities	7 678	6 260	5 431	5 347	5 422	4 659	3 231	2 574
Loans	56 240	81 376	88 679	71 631	21 788	48 832	38 545	48 382
Short-term loans	20 622	42 846	43 148	37 911	20 012	37 571	33 183	39 210
Long-term loans	35 618	38 530	45 531	33 720	1 776	11 261	5 362	9 172
Equity and investment fund shares	368 786	373 410	363 708	368 208	377 082	377 082	377 082	377 082
Insurance pension and standardised guarantees	2 542 586	2 901 250	3 094 655	3 125 615	3 359 611	3 940 024	4 221 348	4 545 682
Financial derivatives and employee stock options	11 279	6 484	14 029	13 345	11 117	33 361	14 741	20 490
Other accounts payable	12 659	10 965	11 241	10 682	10 208	11 286	13 068	12 756
Non-financial assets	..	..	..	..	..	..	..	..
Insurance corporations								
Financial net worth	100 339	71 232	39 336	154 174	225 963	254 063	294 566	316 851
Financial assets	973 533	1 045 699	1 020 870	1 100 174	1 167 293	1 329 202	1 374 825	1 435 855
Currency and deposits	43 234	37 509	41 521	52 663	48 929	66 135	63 359	61 114
Debt securities	396 288	382 809	408 873	393 959	372 587	393 474	393 450	388 598
Loans	17 482	18 151	25 602	34 252	28 351	32 581	25 678	28 270
Equity and investment fund shares	463 041	556 014	490 880	565 854	668 184	782 154	846 878	920 124
Equity	196 456	227 682	187 208	210 507	251 027	282 608	297 369	317 446
Investment fund shares	266 585	328 332	303 672	355 347	417 157	499 546	549 509	602 678
Money market fund shares	16 051	16 179	24 749	21 277	26 011	25 286	26 263	27 158
Non-Money market fund shares	250 534	312 153	278 923	334 070	391 146	474 260	523 246	575 520
Insurance pension and standardised guarantees	33 600	31 643	33 570	32 157	29 225	31 228	27 618	24 529
Financial derivatives and employee stock options	5 577	5 497	6 002	6 213	2 428	5 130	3 220	1 994
Other accounts receivable	14 311	14 076	14 422	15 076	17 589	18 500	14 622	11 226
Financial liabilities	873 194	974 467	981 534	946 000	941 330	1 075 139	1 080 259	1 119 004
Debt securities	5 978	4 560	3 731	3 647	3 722	3 862	2 433	2 474
Short-term debt securities	0	0	0	0	0	0	0	0
Long-term debt securities	5 978	4 560	3 731	3 647	3 722	3 862	2 433	2 474
Loans	50 749	77 897	79 542	64 398	19 240	45 821	19 556	22 960
Short-term loans	19 500	41 740	41 712	34 726	18 216	36 409	18 664	18 736
Long-term loans	31 249	36 157	37 330	29 672	1 024	9 412	892	4 224
Equity and investment fund shares	118 646	118 646	118 646	118 646	118 646	118 646	118 646	118 646
Insurance pension and standardised guarantees	686 563	764 252	769 460	751 452	792 700	897 879	931 746	965 912
Financial derivatives and employee stock options	4 497	2 151	3 521	1 340	969	2 806	1 298	2 108
Other accounts payable	6 761	6 961	6 634	6 517	6 053	6 125	6 580	6 904
Non-financial assets	..	..	..	..	..	..	..	..
Pension funds								
Financial net worth	128 917	109 130	-108 425	74 333	191 823	206 937	148 449	159 529
Financial assets	2 254 951	2 514 408	2 487 784	2 723 161	3 035 721	3 547 042	3 736 205	4 047 491
Currency and deposits	54 875	87 304	102 465	80 517	83 406	84 415	90 570	97 283
Debt securities	848 233	829 052	931 600	987 990	977 407	1 058 569	1 076 553	1 070 907
Loans	36 598	40 748	38 026	37 067	42 189	41 694	37 790	41 803
Equity and investment fund shares	1 280 252	1 513 267	1 356 501	1 554 769	1 888 336	2 295 470	2 477 330	2 776 211
Equity	508 756	636 885	527 335	628 493	729 436	843 066	893 090	990 858
Investment fund shares	771 496	876 382	829 166	926 276	1 158 900	1 452 404	1 584 240	1 785 353
Money market fund shares	24 704	26 147	37 264	32 579	39 814	40 601	44 493	42 688
Non-Money market fund shares	746 792	850 235	791 902	893 697	1 119 086	1 411 803	1 539 747	1 742 665
Insurance pension and standardised guarantees	..	..	..	..	..	..	..	..
Financial derivatives and employee stock options	10 816	18 771	23 164	30 762	13 851	23 233	25 653	25 915
Other accounts receivable	24 177	25 266	36 028	32 056	30 532	43 661	28 309	35 372
Financial liabilities	2 126 034	2 405 278	2 596 209	2 648 828	2 843 898	3 340 105	3 587 756	3 887 962
Debt securities	1 700	1 700	1 700	1 700	1 700	797	798	100
Short-term debt securities	..	..	..	..	..	..	..	..
Long-term debt securities	1 700	1 700	1 700	1 700	1 700	797	798	100
Loans	5 491	3 479	9 137	7 233	2 548	3 011	18 989	25 422
Short-term loans	1 122	1 106	1 436	3 185	1 796	1 162	14 519	20 474
Long-term loans	4 369	2 373	7 701	4 048	752	1 849	4 470	4 948
Equity and investment fund shares	250 140	254 764	245 062	249 562	258 436	258 436	258 436	258 436
Insurance pension and standardised guarantees	1 856 023	2 136 998	2 325 195	2 374 163	2 566 911	3 042 145	3 289 602	3 579 770
Financial derivatives and employee stock options	6 782	4 333	10 508	12 005	10 148	30 555	13 443	18 382
Other accounts payable	5 898	4 004	4 607	4 165	4 155	5 161	6 488	5 852
Non-financial assets	..	..	..	..	..	..	..	..

Note: Detailed metadata at: http://metalinks.oecd.org/instinv/20170920/5811

Table 4. Portfolio composition by type of investor

As percentage of financial assets and of financial liabilities

Per cent

	2009	2010	2011	2012	2013	2014	2015	2016
Investment funds								
Financial assets	100.0	100.0	100.0	100.0	100.0	100.0	100.0	100.0
Currency and deposits	3.2	2.7	3.4	3.4	2.9	2.8	3.0	2.8
Debt securities	22.4	20.6	24.1	21.1	20.6	25.1	23.4	23.0
Loans	0.0	0.0	0.0	0.0	0.0	0.0	0.0	0.0
Equity and investment fund shares	69.6	71.8	68.2	69.9	71.6	68.4	70.5	70.5
Insurance pension and standardised guarantee schemes	0.0	0.0	0.0	0.0	0.0	0.0	0.0	0.0
Financial derivatives and employee stock options	0.6	0.5	1.0	0.8	0.9	1.0	1.0	1.1
Other accounts receivable	4.1	4.4	3.3	4.8	4.0	2.7	2.2	2.6
Financial liabilities	100.0	100.0	100.0	100.0	100.0	100.0	100.0	100.0
Currency and deposits	0.0	0.0	0.0	0.0	0.0	0.0	0.0	0.0
Debt securities	0.0	0.0	0.0	0.0	0.0	0.0	0.0	0.0
Loans	1.3	1.1	0.7	0.3	0.3	0.5	0.3	0.5
Equity and investment fund shares	91.1	91.3	93.5	91.5	91.0	91.9	94.9	92.9
Insurance pension and standardised guarantee schemes	0.0	0.0	0.0	0.0	0.0	0.0	0.0	0.0
Financial derivatives and employee stock options	0.5	0.3	0.8	0.7	0.6	1.0	0.9	0.8
Other accounts receivable	7.1	7.3	5.1	7.5	8.1	6.6	3.9	5.8
Insurance corporations								
Financial assets	100.0	100.0	100.0	100.0	100.0	100.0	100.0	100.0
Currency and deposits	4.4	3.6	4.1	4.8	4.2	5.0	4.6	4.3
Debt securities	40.7	36.6	40.1	35.8	31.9	29.6	28.6	27.1
Loans	1.8	1.7	2.5	3.1	2.4	2.5	1.9	2.0
Equity and investment fund shares	47.6	53.2	48.1	51.4	57.2	58.8	61.6	64.1
Insurance pension and standardised guarantee schemes	3.5	3.0	3.3	2.9	2.5	2.3	2.0	1.7
Financial derivatives and employee stock options	0.6	0.5	0.6	0.6	0.2	0.4	0.2	0.1
Other accounts receivable	1.5	1.3	1.4	1.4	1.5	1.4	1.1	0.8
Financial liabilities	100.0	100.0	100.0	100.0	100.0	100.0	100.0	100.0
Currency and deposits	0.0	0.0	0.0	0.0	0.0	0.0	0.0	0.0
Debt securities	0.7	0.5	0.4	0.4	0.4	0.4	0.2	0.2
Loans	5.8	8.0	8.1	6.8	2.0	4.3	1.8	2.1
Equity and investment fund shares	13.6	12.2	12.1	12.5	12.6	11.0	11.0	10.6
Insurance pension and standardised guarantee schemes	78.6	78.4	78.4	79.4	84.2	83.5	86.3	86.3
Financial derivatives and employee stock options	0.5	0.2	0.4	0.1	0.1	0.3	0.1	0.2
Other accounts receivable	0.8	0.7	0.7	0.7	0.6	0.6	0.6	0.6
Pension funds								
Financial assets	100.0	100.0	100.0	100.0	100.0	100.0	100.0	100.0
Currency and deposits	2.4	3.5	4.1	3.0	2.7	2.4	2.4	2.4
Debt securities	37.6	33.0	37.4	36.3	32.2	29.8	28.8	26.5
Loans	1.6	1.6	1.5	1.4	1.4	1.2	1.0	1.0
Equity and investment fund shares	56.8	60.2	54.5	57.1	62.2	64.7	66.3	68.6
Insurance pension and standardised guarantee schemes	0.0	0.0	0.0	0.0	0.0	0.0	0.0	0.0
Financial derivatives and employee stock options	0.5	0.7	0.9	1.1	0.5	0.7	0.7	0.6
Other accounts receivable	1.1	1.0	1.4	1.2	1.0	1.2	0.8	0.9
Financial liabilities	100.0	100.0	100.0	100.0	100.0	100.0	100.0	100.0
Currency and deposits	0.0	0.0	0.0	0.0	0.0	0.0	0.0	0.0
Debt securities	0.1	0.1	0.1	0.1	0.1	0.0	0.0	0.0
Loans	0.3	0.1	0.4	0.3	0.1	0.1	0.5	0.7
Equity and investment fund shares	11.8	10.6	9.4	9.4	9.1	7.7	7.2	6.6
Insurance pension and standardised guarantee schemes	87.3	88.8	89.6	89.6	90.3	91.1	91.7	92.1
Financial derivatives and employee stock options	0.3	0.2	0.4	0.5	0.4	0.9	0.4	0.5
Other accounts receivable	0.3	0.2	0.2	0.2	0.1	0.2	0.2	0.2

Note: Detailed metadata at: http://metalinks.oecd.org/instinv/20170920/a49a

SWITZERLAND

Table 1. Financial assets and liabilities of institutional investors, 2015

Million CHF

	Investment funds				
	Total	Non-money market funds			Money market funds
		Total	Open-end non-money market funds	Closed-end non-money market funds	Total
Financial assets	..	..	648 819	..	30 548
Currency and deposits	..	..	16 215	..	2 234
Debt securities	..	..	313 460	..	28 245
Debt securities, short term	..	..	1 985	..	14 874
Debt securities, long term	..	..	311 475	..	13 371
Debt securities issued by residents	..	..	100 440	..	4 198
Debt securities issued by non-residents	..	..	213 020	..	24 047
Loans	..	..	..	..	..
Loans, short-term	..	..	..	..	..
Loans, long-term	..	..	..	..	..
Loans granted to residents	..	..	..	..	..
Loans granted to non-residents	..	..	..	..	..
Equity and investment fund shares/units	..	..	319 144	..	69
Equity and investment fund shares issued/units by residents	..	..	159 226	..	60
Equity and investment fund shares/units issued by non residents	..	..	159 918	..	9
Other accounts receivable	..	..	..	..	..

	Investment funds				
	Total	Non-money market funds			Money market funds
		Total	Open-end non-money market funds	Closed-end non-money market funds	Total
Financial liabilities	..	..	717 922	..	32 313
Currency and deposits	..	..	..	..	..
Debt securities	..	..	..	..	..
Debt securities, short term	..	..	..	..	..
Debt securities, long term	..	..	..	..	..
Loans	..	..	10 948	..	259
Loans, short-term	..	..	..	..	..
Loans, long-term	..	..	..	..	..
Equity and investment fund shares/units	..	..	706 974	..	32 054
Insurance pension and standardised guaratees	..	..	..	..	..
Financial derivatives and employee stock options	..	..	..	..	..
Other accounts payable	..	..	..	..	..

	Insurance corporations and pension funds				
	Total	Insurance corporations			Pension funds
		Total	Life insurance corporations	Non-life insurance corporations	Total
Financial assets	1 277 057	561 105	..	..	715 952
Currency and deposits	76 508	33 318	..	..	43 190
Debt securities	298 471	171 906	..	..	126 565
Debt securities, short-term	10 908	9 244	..	..	1 664
Debt securities, long term	287 563	162 662	..	..	124 901
Debt securities issued by residents	130 736	65 292	..	..	65 444
Debt securities issued by non-residents	167 735	106 614	..	..	61 121
Loans	65 638	53 227	..	..	12 411
Loans, short-term	..	..	..	..	..
Loans, long-term	..	..	..	..	..
Loans granted to residents	46 338	33 927	..	..	12 411
Loans granted to non-residents	19 300	19 300	..	..	..
Equity and investment fund shares/units	833 198	302 654	..	..	530 544
Equity and investment fund shares/units issued by residents	575 826	137 227	..	..	438 599
Equity and investment fund shares/units issued by non residents	257 372	165 427	..	..	91 945
Other accounts receivable	..	..	..	..	..

	Insurance corporations and pension funds				
	Total	Insurance corporations			Pension funds
		Total	Life insurance corporations	Non-life insurance corporations	Total
Financial liabilities	..	..	..	..	734 721
Currency and deposits	..	..	..	..	..
Debt securities	13 482	13 482	..	..	..
Debt securities, short term	..	..	..	..	..
Debt securities, long term	13 482	13 482	..	..	..
Loans	12 917	11 416	..	..	1 501
Loans, short-term	..	..	..	..	..
Loans, long-term	..	..	..	..	..
Equity and investment fund shares/units	..	..	..	..	..
Insurance pension and standardised guarantees	1 113 837	380 617	..	..	733 220
Financial derivatives and employee stock options	..	..	..	..	..
Other accounts payable	..	..	..	..	..

SWITZERLAND

Table 2. Financial assets and liabilities of investment funds

Million CHF

	2009	2010	2011	2012	2013	2014	2015	2016
Investment funds								
Financial net worth	..	..	..	..	..	..	..	..
Financial assets	..	..	..	..	..	..	..	..
Currency and deposits	..	..	..	..	..	..	..	..
Debt securities	..	..	..	..	..	..	..	..
Loans	..	..	..	..	..	..	..	..
Equity and investment fund shares	..	..	..	..	..	..	..	..
Equity	..	..	..	..	..	..	..	..
Investment fund shares	..	..	..	..	..	..	..	..
Money market fund shares	..	..	..	..	..	..	..	..
Non-Money market fund shares	..	..	..	..	..	..	..	..
Insurance pension and standardised guarantees	..	..	..	..	..	..	..	..
Financial derivatives and employee stock options	..	..	..	..	..	..	..	..
Other accounts receivable	..	..	..	..	..	..	..	..
Financial liabilities	..	..	..	..	..	..	..	..
Debt securities	..	..	..	..	..	..	..	..
Short-term debt securities	..	..	..	..	..	..	..	..
Long-term debt securities	..	..	..	..	..	..	..	..
Loans	..	..	..	..	..	..	..	..
Short-term loans	..	..	..	..	..	..	..	..
Long-term loans	..	..	..	..	..	..	..	..
Equity and investment fund shares	..	..	..	..	..	..	..	..
Insurance pension and standardised guarantees	..	..	..	..	..	..	..	..
Financial derivatives and employee stock options	..	..	..	..	..	..	..	..
Other accounts payable	..	..	..	..	..	..	..	..
Non-financial assets	..	..	..	..	..	..	..	..
Money market funds								
Financial net worth	-3 020	-1 850	-823	-2 372	-236	-272	-1 765	..
Financial assets	37 474	32 021	35 724	33 845	36 075	36 595	30 548	..
Currency and deposits	1 901	1 436	2 583	2 514	2 562	2 630	2 234	..
Debt securities	34 889	30 106	32 899	31 120	33 284	33 783	28 245	..
Loans	..	..	..	..	..	..	..	..
Equity and investment fund shares	684	479	242	211	229	182	69	..
Equity	528	34	18	22	29	34	34	..
Investment fund shares	156	445	224	189	200	148	35	..
Money market fund shares	..	..	..	..	..	..	..	..
Non-Money market fund shares	..	..	..	..	..	..	..	..
Insurance pension and standardised guarantees	..	..	..	..	..	..	..	..
Financial derivatives and employee stock options	..	..	..	..	..	..	..	..
Other accounts receivable	..	..	..	..	..	..	..	..
Financial liabilities	40 494	33 871	36 547	36 217	36 311	36 867	32 313	..
Debt securities	..	..	..	..	..	..	..	..
Short-term debt securities	..	..	..	..	..	..	..	..
Long-term debt securities	..	..	..	..	..	..	..	..
Loans	20	153	25	89	64	37	259	..
Short-term loans	..	..	..	..	..	..	..	..
Long-term loans	..	..	..	..	..	..	..	..
Equity and investment fund shares	40 474	33 718	36 522	36 128	36 247	36 830	32 054	..
Insurance pension and standardised guarantees	..	..	..	..	..	..	..	..
Financial derivatives and employee stock options	..	..	..	..	..	..	..	..
Other accounts payable	..	..	..	..	..	..	..	..
Non-financial assets	..	..	..	..	..	..	..	..
Non-money market funds								
Financial net worth	..	..	..	..	..	..	..	..
Financial assets	..	..	..	..	..	..	..	..
Currency and deposits	..	..	..	..	..	..	..	..
Debt securities	..	..	..	..	..	..	..	..
Loans	..	..	..	..	..	..	..	..
Equity and investment fund shares	..	..	..	..	..	..	..	..
Equity	..	..	..	..	..	..	..	..
Investment fund shares	..	..	..	..	..	..	..	..
Money market fund shares	..	..	..	..	..	..	..	..
Non-Money market fund shares	..	..	..	..	..	..	..	..
Insurance pension and standardised guarantees	..	..	..	..	..	..	..	..
Financial derivatives and employee stock options	..	..	..	..	..	..	..	..
Other accounts receivable	..	..	..	..	..	..	..	..
Financial liabilities	..	..	..	..	..	..	..	..
Debt securities	..	..	..	..	..	..	..	..
Short-term debt securities	..	..	..	..	..	..	..	..
Long-term debt securities	..	..	..	..	..	..	..	..
Loans	..	..	..	..	..	..	..	..
Short-term loans	..	..	..	..	..	..	..	..
Long-term loans	..	..	..	..	..	..	..	..
Equity and investment fund shares	..	..	..	..	..	..	..	..
Insurance pension and standardised guarantees	..	..	..	..	..	..	..	..
Financial derivatives and employee stock options	..	..	..	..	..	..	..	..
Other accounts payable	..	..	..	..	..	..	..	..
Non-financial assets	..	..	..	..	..	..	..	..
Open-end non-money market funds								
Financial net worth	-45 130	-55 329	-59 111	-72 780	-57 435	-59 601	-69 103	..
Financial assets	351 402	390 382	402 174	455 825	512 309	598 344	648 819	..

SWITZERLAND

Table 2. Financial assets and liabilities of investment funds *(cont.)*

Million CHF

	2009	2010	2011	2012	2013	2014	2015	2016
Currency and deposits	8 959	10 505	13 916	14 426	13 337	14 041	16 215	..
Debt securities	182 935	205 504	220 250	236 940	247 866	290 117	313 460	..
Loans	..	..	..	..	..	..	..	..
Equity and investment fund shares	159 508	174 373	165 008	204 459	251 106	294 186	319 144	..
Equity	120 413	132 979	126 558	149 956	180 666	207 476	219 330	..
Investment fund shares	39 095	41 394	4[illegible] 450	54 503	70 440	86 710	99 814	..
Money market fund shares	..	..	..	..	..	..	..	..
Non-Money market fund shares	..	..	..	..	..	..	..	..
Insurance pension and standardised guarantees	..	..	..	..	..	..	..	..
Financial derivatives and employee stock options	..	..	..	..	..	..	..	..
Other accounts receivable	..	..	..	..	..	..	..	..
Financial liabilities	396 532	445 711	46[illegible] 285	528 605	569 744	657 945	717 922	..
Debt securities	..	..	..	..	..	..	..	..
Short-term debt securities	..	..	..	..	..	..	..	..
Long-term debt securities	..	..	..	..	..	..	..	..
Loans	2 737	4 004	6 374	8 171	7 440	10 672	10 948	..
Short-term loans	..	..	..	..	..	..	..	..
Long-term loans	..	..	..	..	..	..	..	..
Equity and investment fund shares	393 795	441 707	454 911	520 434	562 304	647 273	706 974	..
Insurance pension and standardised guarantees	..	..	..	..	..	..	..	..
Financial derivatives and employee stock options	..	..	..	..	..	..	..	..
Other accounts payable	..	..	..	..	..	..	..	..
Non-financial assets	26 756	29 022	3[illegible] 853	36 202	39 884	45 811	49 340	..
Open-end investment funds								
Financial net worth	-48 150	-57 179	-59 934	-75 152	-57 671	-59 873	-70 868	..
Financial assets	388 876	422 403	437 898	489 670	548 384	634 939	679 367	..
Currency and deposits	10 860	11 941	16 499	16 940	15 899	16 671	18 449	..
Debt securities	217 824	235 610	253 149	268 060	281 150	323 900	341 705	..
Loans	..	..	..	..	..	..	..	..
Equity and investment fund shares	160 192	174 852	168 250	204 670	251 335	294 368	319 213	..
Equity	120 941	133 013	126 576	149 978	180 695	207 510	219 364	..
Investment fund shares	39 251	41 839	4[illegible] 674	54 692	70 640	86 858	99 849	..
Money market fund shares	..	..	..	..	..	..	..	..
Non-Money market fund shares	..	..	..	..	..	..	..	..
Insurance pension and standardised guarantees	..	..	..	..	..	..	..	..
Financial derivatives and employee stock options	..	..	..	..	..	..	..	..
Other accounts receivable	..	..	..	..	..	..	..	..
Financial liabilities	437 026	479 582	497 832	564 822	606 055	694 812	750 235	..
Debt securities	..	..	..	..	..	..	..	..
Short-term debt securities	..	..	..	..	..	..	..	..
Long-term debt securities	..	..	..	..	..	..	..	..
Loans	2 757	4 157	6 399	8 260	7 504	10 709	11 207	..
Short-term loans	..	..	..	..	..	..	..	..
Long-term loans	..	..	..	..	..	..	..	..
Equity and investment fund shares	434 269	475 425	49[illegible] 433	556 562	598 551	684 103	739 028	..
Insurance pension and standardised guarantees	..	..	..	..	..	..	..	..
Financial derivatives and employee stock options	..	..	..	..	..	..	..	..
Other accounts payable	..	..	..	..	..	..	..	..
Non-financial assets	26 756	29 022	3[illegible] 853	36 202	39 884	45 811	49 340	..

Table 3. Financial assets and liabilities of insurance corporations and pension funds

Million CHF

	2009	2010	2011	2012	2013	2014	2015	2016
Insurance corporations and pension funds								
Financial net worth	..	..	..	..	..	..	..	..
Financial assets	1 008 231	1 050 094	1 080 959	1 154 128	1 189 102	1 268 077	1 277 057	..
Currency and deposits	64 400	65 307	74 287	81 377	84 221	84 171	76 508	..
Debt securities	329 455	324 772	327 333	338 092	319 496	322 738	298 471	..
Loans	63 109	62 012	61 588	61 727	63 787	63 290	65 638	..
Equity and investment fund shares	542 475	590 811	608 081	665 506	712 469	794 636	833 198	..
Equity	216 758	220 355	224 408	245 542	240 710	231 908	229 260	..
Investment fund shares	325 717	370 456	383 673	419 964	471 759	562 728	603 938	..
Money market fund shares	..	..	..	..	..	..	..	..
Non-Money market fund shares	..	..	..	..	..	..	..	..
Insurance pension and standardised guarantees	8 792	7 192	9 670	7 426	9 129	3 242	3 242	..
Financial derivatives and employee stock options	..	..	..	..	..	..	..	..
Other accounts receivable	..	..	..	..	..	..	..	..
Financial liabilities	..	..	..	..	..	..	..	..
Debt securities	4 932	6 052	7 455	9 255	9 258	13 447	13 482	..
Short-term debt securities	..	..	..	..	..	..	..	..
Long-term debt securities	4 932	6 052	7 455	9 255	9 258	13 447	13 482	..
Loans	14 087	20 877	13 885	14 306	15 574	13 191	12 917	..
Short-term loans	..	..	..	..	..	..	..	..
Long-term loans	..	..	..	..	..	..	..	..
Equity and investment fund shares	..	..	..	..	..	..	..	..
Insurance pension and standardised guarantees	923 597	941 309	969 376	1 008 677	1 044 038	1 085 336	1 113 837	..
Financial derivatives and employee stock options	..	..	..	..	..	..	..	..
Other accounts payable	..	..	..	..	..	..	..	..
Non-financial assets	95 398	98 566	102 753	107 523	110 279	115 227	..	..
Insurance corporations								
Financial net worth	..	..	..	..	..	..	..	..
Financial assets	474 006	489 213	513 601	545 714	535 032	563 029	561 105	..
Currency and deposits	29 758	29 238	34 109	36 395	31 130	33 072	33 318	..
Debt securities	176 539	182 548	186 009	198 874	188 201	188 597	171 906	..
Loans	49 679	49 591	49 740	51 221	52 922	51 498	53 227	..
Equity and investment fund shares	218 030	227 836	243 743	259 224	262 779	289 862	302 654	..
Equity	133 583	135 689	147 002	155 613	152 351	156 230	159 437	..
Investment fund shares	84 447	92 147	96 741	103 611	110 428	133 632	143 217	..
Money market fund shares	..	..	..	..	..	..	..	..
Non-Money market fund shares	..	..	..	..	..	..	..	..
Insurance pension and standardised guarantees	..	..	..	..	..	..	..	..
Financial derivatives and employee stock options	..	..	..	..	..	..	..	..
Other accounts receivable	..	..	..	..	..	..	..	..
Financial liabilities	..	..	..	..	..	..	..	..
Debt securities	4 932	6 052	7 455	9 255	9 258	13 447	13 482	..
Short-term debt securities	..	..	..	..	..	..	..	..
Long-term debt securities	4 932	6 052	7 455	9 255	9 258	13 447	13 482	..
Loans	12 052	17 786	11 508	12 444	12 661	11 291	11 416	..
Short-term loans	..	..	..	..	..	..	..	..
Long-term loans	..	..	..	..	..	..	..	..
Equity and investment fund shares	..	..	..	..	..	..	..	..
Insurance pension and standardised guarantees	327 636	332 113	340 506	353 635	360 938	371 332	380 617	..
Financial derivatives and employee stock options	..	..	..	..	..	..	..	..
Other accounts payable	..	..	..	..	..	..	..	..
Non-financial assets	36 554	37 988	38 610	40 792	41 703	43 111	44 933	..
Pension funds								
Financial net worth	-63 771	-51 406	-63 889	-48 490	-31 943	-10 856	-18 769	..
Financial assets	534 225	560 881	567 358	608 414	654 070	705 048	715 952	..
Currency and deposits	34 642	36 069	40 178	44 982	53 091	51 099	43 190	..
Debt securities	152 916	142 224	141 324	139 218	131 295	134 141	126 565	..
Loans	13 430	12 421	11 848	10 506	10 865	11 792	12 411	..
Equity and investment fund shares	324 445	362 975	364 338	406 282	449 690	504 774	530 544	..
Equity	83 175	84 666	77 406	89 929	88 359	75 678	69 823	..
Investment fund shares	241 270	278 309	286 932	316 353	361 331	429 096	460 721	..
Money market fund shares	..	..	..	..	..	..	..	..
Non-Money market fund shares	..	..	..	..	..	..	..	..
Insurance pension and standardised guarantees	8 792	7 192	9 670	7 426	9 129	3 242	3 242	..
Financial derivatives and employee stock options	..	..	..	..	..	..	..	..
Other accounts receivable	..	..	..	..	..	..	..	..
Financial liabilities	597 996	612 287	631 247	656 904	686 013	715 904	734 721	..
Debt securities	..	..	..	..	..	..	..	..
Short-term debt securities	..	..	..	..	..	..	..	..
Long-term debt securities	..	..	..	..	..	..	..	..
Loans	2 035	3 091	2 377	1 862	2 913	1 900	1 501	..
Short-term loans	..	..	..	..	..	..	..	..
Long-term loans	..	..	..	..	..	..	..	..
Equity and investment fund shares	..	..	..	..	..	..	..	..
Insurance pension and standardised guarantees	595 961	609 196	628 870	655 042	683 100	714 004	733 220	..
Financial derivatives and employee stock options	..	..	..	..	..	..	..	..
Other accounts payable	..	..	..	..	..	..	..	..
Non-financial assets	58 844	60 578	64 143	66 731	68 576	72 116	..	..

Table 4. Portfolio composition by type of investor

As percentage of financial assets and of financial liabilities

Per cent

	2009	2010	2011	2012	2013	2014	2015	2016
Investment funds								
Financial assets	..	..	..	..	..	..	..	..
Currency and deposits	..	..	..	..	..	..	..	..
Debt securities	..	..	..	..	..	..	..	..
Loans	..	..	..	..	..	..	..	..
Equity and investment fund shares	..	..	..	..	..	..	..	..
Insurance pension and standardised guarantee schemes	..	..	..	..	..	..	..	..
Financial derivatives and employee stock options	..	..	..	..	..	..	..	..
Other accounts receivable	..	..	..	..	..	..	..	..
Financial liabilities	..	..	..	..	..	..	..	..
Currency and deposits	..	..	..	..	..	..	..	..
Debt securities	..	..	..	..	..	..	..	..
Loans	..	..	..	..	..	..	..	..
Equity and investment fund shares	..	..	..	..	..	..	..	..
Insurance pension and standardised guarantee schemes	..	..	..	..	..	..	..	..
Financial derivatives and employee stock options	..	..	..	..	..	..	..	..
Other accounts receivable	..	..	..	..	..	..	..	..
Insurance corporations								
Financial assets	100.0	100.0	100.0	100.0	100.0	100.0	100.0	..
Currency and deposits	6.3	6.0	6.6	6.7	5.8	5.9	5.9	..
Debt securities	37.2	37.3	36.2	36.4	35.2	33.5	30.6	..
Loans	10.5	10.1	9.7	9.4	9.9	9.1	9.5	..
Equity and investment fund shares	46.0	46.6	47.5	47.5	49.1	51.5	53.9	..
Insurance pension and standardised guarantee schemes	0.0	0.0	0.0	0.0	0.0	0.0	0.0	..
Financial derivatives and employee stock options	0.0	0.0	0.0	0.0	0.0	0.0	0.0	..
Other accounts receivable	0.0	0.0	0.0	0.0	0.0	0.0	0.0	..
Financial liabilities	..	..	..	..	..	..	..	..
Currency and deposits	..	..	..	..	..	..	..	..
Debt securities	..	..	..	..	..	..	..	..
Loans	..	..	..	..	..	..	..	..
Equity and investment fund shares	..	..	..	..	..	..	..	..
Insurance pension and standardised guarantee schemes	..	..	..	..	..	..	..	..
Financial derivatives and employee stock options	..	..	..	..	..	..	..	..
Other accounts receivable	..	..	..	..	..	..	..	..
Pension funds								
Financial assets	100.0	100.0	100.0	100.0	100.0	100.0	100.0	..
Currency and deposits	6.5	6.4	7.1	7.4	8.1	7.2	6.0	..
Debt securities	28.6	25.4	24.9	22.9	20.1	19.0	17.7	..
Loans	2.5	2.2	2.1	1.7	1.7	1.7	1.7	..
Equity and investment fund shares	60.7	64.7	64.2	66.8	68.8	71.6	74.1	..
Insurance pension and standardised guarantee schemes	1.6	1.3	1.7	1.2	1.4	0.5	0.5	..
Financial derivatives and employee stock options	0.0	0.0	0.0	0.0	0.0	0.0	0.0	..
Other accounts receivable	0.0	0.0	0.0	0.0	0.0	0.0	0.0	..
Financial liabilities	100.0	100.0	100.0	100.0	100.0	100.0	100.0	..
Currency and deposits	0.0	0.0	0.0	0.0	0.0	0.0	0.0	..
Debt securities	0.0	0.0	0.0	0.0	0.0	0.0	0.0	..
Loans	0.3	0.5	0.4	0.3	0.4	0.3	0.2	..
Equity and investment fund shares	0.0	0.0	0.0	0.0	0.0	0.0	0.0	..
Insurance pension and standardised guarantee schemes	99.7	99.5	99.6	99.7	99.6	99.7	99.8	..
Financial derivatives and employee stock options	0.0	0.0	0.0	0.0	0.0	0.0	0.0	..
Other accounts receivable	0.0	0.0	0.0	0.0	0.0	0.0	0.0	..

TURKEY

Table 1. Financial assets and liabilities of institutional investors, 2016

Million TRY

	Investment funds				
	Total	Non-money market funds			Money market funds
		Total	Open-end non-money market funds	Closed-end non-money market funds	Total
Financial assets	46 865	34 240	32 346	1 894	12 625
Currency and deposits	13 202	5 761	5 259	502	7 441
Debt securities	29 823	24 639	23 810	829	5 184
Debt securities, short term	18 146	13 343	13 040	304	4 803
Debt securities, long term	11 677	11 296	10 771	526	381
Debt securities issued by residents	29 722	24 538	23 708	829	5 184
Debt securities issued by non-residents	102	102	102	0	0
Loans	..	..	..	..	..
Loans, short-term	..	..	..	..	..
Loans, long-term	..	..	..	..	..
Loans granted to residents	..	..	..	..	..
Loans granted to non-residents	..	..	..	..	..
Equity and investment fund shares/units	3 840	3 840	3 277	563	0
Equity and investment fund shares issued/units by residents	3 495	3 495	2 932	563	0
Equity and investment fund shares/units issued by non residents	345	345	345	0	0
Other accounts receivable	..	..	..	..	..

	Investment funds				
	Total	Non-money market funds			Money market funds
		Total	Open-end non-money market funds	Closed-end non-money market funds	Total
Financial liabilities	..	..	..	..	..
Currency and deposits	..	..	..	..	..
Debt securities	..	..	..	..	..
Debt securities, short term	..	..	..	..	..
Debt securities, long term	..	..	..	..	..
Loans	..	..	..	..	..
Loans, short-term	..	..	..	..	..
Loans, long-term	..	..	..	..	..
Equity and investment fund shares/units	..	..	..	..	..
Insurance pension and standardised guaratees	..	..	..	..	..
Financial derivatives and employee stock options	..	..	..	..	..
Other accounts payable	..	..	..	..	..

	Insurance corporations and pension funds				
	Total	Insurance corporations			Pension funds
		Total	Life insurance corporations	Non-life insurance corporations	Total
Financial assets	121 046	60 578	14 500	46 078	60 467
Currency and deposits	42 285	27 458	7 358	20 100	14 827
Debt securities	47 782	15 087	5 312	9 776	32 695
Debt securities, short-term	..	15 083	5 310	9 773	..
Debt securities, long term	..	4	2	2	..
Debt securities issued by residents	..	0	..	..	..
Debt securities issued by non-residents	..	0	..	..	..
Loans	..	195	195	0	..
Loans, short-term	..	61	61	..	..
Loans, long-term	..	134	134	..	..
Loans granted to residents	..	0	..	..	..
Loans granted to non-residents	..	0	..	..	..
Equity and investment fund shares/units	10 653	3 488	377	3 111	7 165
Equity and investment fund shares/units issued by residents	..	0	..	..	..
Equity and investment fund shares/units issued by non residents	..	0	..	..	..
Other accounts receivable	20 130	14 349	1 258	13 091	5 781

	Insurance corporations and pension funds				
	Total	Insurance corporations			Pension funds
		Total	Life insurance corporations	Non-life insurance corporations	Total
Financial liabilities	..	122 012	76 541	..	..
Currency and deposits	..	0	..	..	..
Debt securities	..	0	0	..	..
Debt securities, short term	..	0	..	..	..
Debt securities, long term	..	0	..	..	..
Loans	..	742	172	570	..
Loans, short-term	..	742	172	570	..
Loans, long-term	..	0	0	0	..
Equity and investment fund shares/units	..	15 375	5 710	9 664	..
Insurance pension and standardised guarantees	..	100 376	70 147	30 229	..
Financial derivatives and employee stock options	..	0	..	..	..
Other accounts payable	..	5 519	511	5 008	..

Note: Detailed metadata at: http://metalinks.oecd.org/instinv/20170920/75e8

Table 2. Financial assets and liabilities of investment funds

Million TRY

	2009	2010	2011	2012	2013	2014	2015	2016
Investment funds								
Financial net worth	..	..	..	..	..	..	..	..
Financial assets	..	..	..	..	..	45 383	40 267	46 865
Currency and deposits	..	..	..	..	..	23 058	11 524	13 202
Debt securities	..	..	..	..	..	19 979	25 353	29 823
Loans	..	..	..	..	..	..	..	..
Equity and investment fund shares	..	..	..	..	..	2 346	3 390	3 840
Equity	..	..	..	..	..	2 244	3 250	3 510
Investment fund shares	..	..	..	..	..	102	140	330
Money market fund shares	..	..	..	..	..	56	30	3
Non-Money market fund shares	..	..	..	..	..	46	110	328
Insurance pension and standardised guarantees	..	..	..	..	..	..	..	..
Financial derivatives and employee stock options	..	..	..	..	..	..	..	..
Other accounts receivable	..	..	..	..	..	..	..	..
Financial liabilities	..	..	..	..	..	..	..	..
Debt securities	..	..	..	..	..	..	..	..
Short-term debt securities	..	..	..	..	..	..	..	..
Long-term debt securities	..	..	..	..	..	..	..	..
Loans	..	..	..	..	..	..	..	..
Short-term loans	..	..	..	..	..	..	..	..
Long-term loans	..	..	..	..	..	..	..	..
Equity and investment fund shares	..	..	..	..	..	..	..	..
Insurance pension and standardised guarantees	..	..	..	..	..	..	..	..
Financial derivatives and employee stock options	..	..	..	..	..	..	..	..
Other accounts payable	..	..	..	..	..	..	..	..
Non-financial assets	..	..	..	..	..	32 264	41 236	50 709
Money market funds								
Financial net worth	..	..	..	..	..	..	..	..
Financial assets	..	..	..	..	..	12 622	11 933	12 625
Currency and deposits	..	..	..	..	..	8 901	7 378	7 441
Debt securities	..	..	..	..	..	3 721	4 555	5 184
Loans	..	..	..	..	..	..	..	..
Equity and investment fund shares	..	..	..	..	..	0	0	0
Equity	..	..	..	..	..	0	0	0
Investment fund shares	..	..	..	..	..	0	0	0
Money market fund shares	..	..	..	..	..	0	0	0
Non-Money market fund shares	..	..	..	..	..	0	0	0
Insurance pension and standardised guarantees	..	..	..	..	..	..	..	..
Financial derivatives and employee stock options	..	..	..	..	..	..	..	..
Other accounts receivable	..	..	..	..	..	..	..	..
Financial liabilities	..	..	..	..	..	..	..	..
Debt securities	..	..	..	..	..	..	..	..
Short-term debt securities	..	..	..	..	..	..	..	..
Long-term debt securities	..	..	..	..	..	..	..	..
Loans	..	..	..	..	..	..	..	..
Short-term loans	..	..	..	..	..	..	..	..
Long-term loans	..	..	..	..	..	..	..	..
Equity and investment fund shares	..	..	..	..	..	..	..	..
Insurance pension and standardised guarantees	..	..	..	..	..	..	..	..
Financial derivatives and employee stock options	..	..	..	..	..	..	..	..
Other accounts payable	..	..	..	..	..	..	..	..
Non-financial assets	..	..	..	..	..	0	0	0
Non-money market funds								
Financial net worth	..	..	..	..	..	..	..	..
Financial assets	..	..	..	..	..	32 761	28 334	34 240
Currency and deposits	..	..	..	..	..	14 157	4 145	5 761
Debt securities	..	..	..	..	..	16 258	20 798	24 639
Loans	..	..	..	..	..	..	..	..
Equity and investment fund shares	..	..	..	..	..	2 346	3 390	3 840
Equity	..	..	..	..	..	2 244	3 250	3 510
Investment fund shares	..	..	..	..	..	102	140	330
Money market fund shares	..	..	..	..	..	56	30	3
Non-Money market fund shares	..	..	..	..	..	46	110	328
Insurance pension and standardised guarantees	..	..	..	..	..	..	..	..
Financial derivatives and employee stock options	..	..	..	..	..	..	..	..
Other accounts receivable	..	..	..	..	..	..	..	..
Financial liabilities	..	..	..	..	..	..	..	..
Debt securities	..	..	..	..	..	..	..	..
Short-term debt securities	..	..	..	..	..	..	..	..
Long-term debt securities	..	..	..	..	..	..	..	..
Loans	..	..	..	..	..	..	..	..
Short-term loans	..	..	..	..	..	..	..	..
Long-term loans	..	..	..	..	..	..	..	..
Equity and investment fund shares	..	..	..	..	..	..	..	..
Insurance pension and standardised guarantees	..	..	..	..	..	..	..	..
Financial derivatives and employee stock options	..	..	..	..	..	..	..	..
Other accounts payable	..	..	..	..	..	..	..	..
Non-financial assets	..	..	..	..	..	32 264	41 236	50 709
Open-end non-money market funds								
Financial net worth	..	..	..	..	..	..	..	..
Financial assets	..	..	..	..	..	31 676	26 822	32 346

Table 2. Financial assets and liabilities of investment funds *(cont.)*

Million TRY

	2009	2010	2011	2012	2013	2014	2015	2016
Currency and deposits	..	..	..	..	..	13 983	3 920	5 259
Debt securities	..	..	..	..	..	15 509	20 072	23 810
Loans	..	..	..	..	..	..	..	..
Equity and investment fund shares	..	..	..	..	..	2 184	2 829	3 277
Equity	..	..	..	..	..	2 138	2 719	2 949
Investment fund shares	..	..	..	..	..	46	110	328
Money market fund shares	..	..	..	..	..	0	0	0
Non-Money market fund shares	..	..	..	..	..	46	110	328
Insurance pension and standardised guarantees	..	..	..	..	..	..	..	..
Financial derivatives and employee stock options	..	..	..	..	..	..	..	..
Other accounts receivable	..	..	..	..	..	..	..	..
Financial liabilities	..	..	..	..	..	..	..	..
Debt securities	..	..	..	..	..	..	..	..
Short-term debt securities	..	..	..	..	..	..	..	..
Long-term debt securities	..	..	..	..	..	..	..	..
Loans	..	..	..	..	..	..	..	..
Short-term loans	..	..	..	..	..	..	..	..
Long-term loans	..	..	..	..	..	..	..	..
Equity and investment fund shares	..	..	..	..	..	..	..	..
Insurance pension and standardised guarantees	..	..	..	..	..	..	..	..
Financial derivatives and employee stock options	..	..	..	..	..	..	..	..
Other accounts payable	..	..	..	..	..	..	..	..
Non-financial assets	..	..	..	..	..	0	0	0
Open-end investment funds								
Financial net worth	..	..	..	..	..	..	..	..
Financial assets	..	..	..	..	..	44 298	38 755	44 970
Currency and deposits	..	..	..	..	..	22 884	11 299	12 700
Debt securities	..	..	..	..	..	19 230	24 627	28 994
Loans	..	..	..	..	..	..	..	..
Equity and investment fund shares	..	..	..	..	..	2 184	2 829	3 277
Equity	..	..	..	..	..	2 138	2 719	2 949
Investment fund shares	..	..	..	..	..	46	110	328
Money market fund shares	..	..	..	..	..	0	0	0
Non-Money market fund shares	..	..	..	..	..	46	110	328
Insurance pension and standardised guarantees	..	..	..	..	..	..	..	..
Financial derivatives and employee stock options	..	..	..	..	..	..	..	..
Other accounts receivable	..	..	..	..	..	..	..	..
Financial liabilities	..	..	..	..	..	..	..	..
Debt securities	..	..	..	..	..	..	..	..
Short-term debt securities	..	..	..	..	..	..	..	..
Long-term debt securities	..	..	..	..	..	..	..	..
Loans	..	..	..	..	..	..	..	..
Short-term loans	..	..	..	..	..	..	..	..
Long-term loans	..	..	..	..	..	..	..	..
Equity and investment fund shares	..	..	..	..	..	..	..	..
Insurance pension and standardised guarantees	..	..	..	..	..	..	..	..
Financial derivatives and employee stock options	..	..	..	..	..	..	..	..
Other accounts payable	..	..	..	..	..	..	..	..
Non-financial assets	..	..	..	..	..	0	0	0

Note: Detailed metadata at: http://metalinks.oecd.org/instinv/20170920/75e8

Table 3. Financial assets and liabilities of insurance corporations and pension funds

Million TRY

	2009	2010	2011	2012	2013	2014	2015	2016
Insurance corporations and pension funds								
Financial net worth	..	..	..	..	..	-77 726	..	..
Financial assets	..	..	..	..	..	53 389	96 721	121 046
Currency and deposits	..	..	..	..	..	21 967	24 537	42 285
Debt securities	..	..	..	..	..	17 273	38 900	47 782
Loans	..	..	..	..	..	334	..	..
Equity and investment fund shares	..	..	..	..	..	2 751	12 706	10 653
Equity	..	..	..	..	..	2 035	..	..
Investment fund shares	..	..	..	..	..	716	..	..
Money market fund shares	..	..	..	..	..	..	..	..
Non-Money market fund shares	..	..	..	..	..	..	..	..
Insurance pension and standardised guarantees	..	..	..	..	..	0	..	..
Financial derivatives and employee stock options	..	..	..	..	..	0	..	..
Other accounts receivable	..	..	..	..	..	11 065	20 404	20 130
Financial liabilities	..	..	..	..	..	131 116	..	..
Debt securities	..	..	..	..	..	0	..	..
Short-term debt securities	..	..	..	..	..	..	..	..
Long-term debt securities	..	..	..	..	..	..	..	..
Loans	..	..	..	..	..	471	..	..
Short-term loans	..	..	..	..	..	471	..	..
Long-term loans	..	..	..	..	..	1	..	..
Equity and investment fund shares	..	..	..	..	..	17 264	..	..
Insurance pension and standardised guarantees	..	..	..	..	..	109 642	..	..
Financial derivatives and employee stock options	..	..	..	..	..	0	..	..
Other accounts payable	..	..	..	..	..	3 738	..	..
Non-financial assets	..	..	..	..	..	77 726	..	..
Insurance corporations								
Financial net worth	..	..	..	..	..	-38 781	-49 467	-61 434
Financial assets	..	..	..	..	..	42 239	49 141	60 578
Currency and deposits	..	..	..	..	..	17 277	20 572	27 458
Debt securities	..	..	..	..	..	12 058	12 843	15 087
Loans	..	..	..	..	..	166	175	195
Equity and investment fund shares	..	..	..	..	..	2 376	3 162	3 488
Equity	..	..	..	..	..	1 792	2 516	2 552
Investment fund shares	..	..	..	..	..	584	646	936
Money market fund shares	..	..	..	..	..	0	0	0
Non-Money market fund shares	..	..	..	..	..	0	0	0
Insurance pension and standardised guarantees	..	..	..	..	..	0	0	0
Financial derivatives and employee stock options	..	..	..	..	..	0	0	0
Other accounts receivable	..	..	..	..	..	10 362	12 388	14 349
Financial liabilities	..	..	..	..	..	81 019	98 608	122 012
Debt securities	..	..	..	..	..	0	0	0
Short-term debt securities	..	..	..	..	..	0	0	0
Long-term debt securities	..	..	..	..	..	0	0	0
Loans	..	..	..	..	..	352	993	742
Short-term loans	..	..	..	..	..	351	993	742
Long-term loans	..	..	..	..	..	1	0	0
Equity and investment fund shares	..	..	..	..	..	13 187	13 281	15 375
Insurance pension and standardised guarantees	..	..	..	..	..	64 015	79 702	100 376
Financial derivatives and employee stock options	..	..	..	..	..	0	0	0
Other accounts payable	..	..	..	..	..	3 465	4 632	5 519
Non-financial assets	..	..	..	..	..	38 780	49 286	61 434
Pension funds								
Financial net worth	..	..	..	..	..	-38 946	..	..
Financial assets	..	..	..	..	..	11 151	47 581	60 467
Currency and deposits	..	..	..	..	..	4 690	3 965	14 827
Debt securities	..	..	..	..	..	5 215	26 057	32 695
Loans	..	..	..	..	..	168	..	..
Equity and investment fund shares	..	..	..	..	..	374	9 544	7 165
Equity	..	..	..	..	..	243	..	..
Investment fund shares	..	..	..	..	..	132	..	..
Money market fund shares	..	..	..	..	..	..	..	..
Non-Money market fund shares	..	..	..	..	..	..	..	..
Insurance pension and standardised guarantees	..	..	..	..	..	0	..	..
Financial derivatives and employee stock options	..	..	..	..	..	0	..	..
Other accounts receivable	..	..	..	..	..	704	8 015	5 781
Financial liabilities	..	..	..	..	..	50 097	..	..
Debt securities	..	..	..	..	..	0	..	..
Short-term debt securities	..	..	..	..	..	..	..	..
Long-term debt securities	..	..	..	..	..	..	..	..
Loans	..	..	..	..	..	120	..	..
Short-term loans	..	..	..	..	..	120	..	..
Long-term loans	..	..	..	..	..	0	..	..
Equity and investment fund shares	..	..	..	..	..	4 077	..	..
Insurance pension and standardised guarantees	..	..	..	..	..	45 627	..	..
Financial derivatives and employee stock options	..	..	..	..	..	0	..	..
Other accounts payable	..	..	..	..	..	273	..	..
Non-financial assets	..	..	..	..	..	38 946	..	..

Note: Detailed metadata at: http://metalinks.oecd.org/instinv/20170920/75e8

Table 4. Portfolio composition by type of investor

As percentage of financial assets and of financial liabilities

Per cent

	2009	2010	2011	2012	2013	2014	2015	2016
Investment funds								
Financial assets	..	..	..	..	..	100.0	100.0	100.0
Currency and deposits	..	..	..	..	..	50.8	28.6	28.2
Debt securities	..	..	..	..	..	44.0	63.0	63.6
Loans	..	..	..	..	..	0.0	0.0	0.0
Equity and investment fund shares	..	..	..	..	..	5.2	8.4	8.2
Insurance pension and standardised guarantee schemes	..	..	..	..	..	0.0	0.0	0.0
Financial derivatives and employee stock options	..	..	..	..	..	0.0	0.0	0.0
Other accounts receivable	..	..	..	..	..	0.0	0.0	0.0
Financial liabilities	..	..	..	..	..	..	..	..
Currency and deposits	..	..	..	..	..	..	..	..
Debt securities	..	..	..	..	..	..	..	..
Loans	..	..	..	..	..	..	..	..
Equity and investment fund shares	..	..	..	..	..	..	..	..
Insurance pension and standardised guarantee schemes	..	..	..	..	..	..	..	..
Financial derivatives and employee stock options	..	..	..	..	..	..	..	..
Other accounts receivable	..	..	..	..	..	..	..	..
Insurance corporations								
Financial assets	..	..	..	..	..	100.0	100.0	100.0
Currency and deposits	..	..	..	..	..	40.9	41.9	45.3
Debt securities	..	..	..	..	..	28.5	26.1	24.9
Loans	..	..	..	..	..	0.4	0.4	0.3
Equity and investment fund shares	..	..	..	..	..	5.6	6.4	5.8
Insurance pension and standardised guarantee schemes	..	..	..	..	..	0.0	0.0	0.0
Financial derivatives and employee stock options	..	..	..	..	..	0.0	0.0	0.0
Other accounts receivable	..	..	..	..	..	24.5	25.2	23.7
Financial liabilities	..	..	..	..	..	100.0	100.0	100.0
Currency and deposits	..	..	..	..	..	0.0	0.0	0.0
Debt securities	..	..	..	..	..	0.0	0.0	0.0
Loans	..	..	..	..	..	0.4	1.0	0.6
Equity and investment fund shares	..	..	..	..	..	16.3	13.5	12.6
Insurance pension and standardised guarantee schemes	..	..	..	..	..	79.0	80.8	82.3
Financial derivatives and employee stock options	..	..	..	..	..	0.0	0.0	0.0
Other accounts receivable	..	..	..	..	..	4.3	4.7	4.5
Pension funds								
Financial assets	..	..	..	..	..	100.0	100.0	100.0
Currency and deposits	..	..	..	..	..	42.1	8.3	24.5
Debt securities	..	..	..	..	..	46.8	54.8	54.1
Loans	..	..	..	..	..	1.5	0.0	0.0
Equity and investment fund shares	..	..	..	..	..	3.4	20.1	11.9
Insurance pension and standardised guarantee schemes	..	..	..	..	..	0.0	0.0	0.0
Financial derivatives and employee stock options	..	..	..	..	..	0.0	0.0	0.0
Other accounts receivable	..	..	..	..	..	6.3	16.8	9.6
Financial liabilities	..	..	..	..	..	100.0	..	..
Currency and deposits	..	..	..	..	..	0.0	..	..
Debt securities	..	..	..	..	..	0.0	..	..
Loans	..	..	..	..	..	0.2	..	..
Equity and investment fund shares	..	..	..	..	..	8.1	..	..
Insurance pension and standardised guarantee schemes	..	..	..	..	..	91.1	..	..
Financial derivatives and employee stock options	..	..	..	..	..	0.0	..	..
Other accounts receivable	..	..	..	..	..	0.5	..	..

Note: Detailed metadata at: http://metalinks.oecd.org/instinv/20170920/a49a

UNITED KINGDOM

Table 1. Financial assets and liabilities of institutional investors, 2016

Million GBP

	Investment funds				
		Non-money market funds			Money market funds
	Total	Total	Open-end non-money market funds	Closed-end non-money market funds	Total
Financial assets	..	..	..	..	..
Currency and deposits	..	..	..	..	..
Debt securities	..	..	..	..	..
Debt securities, short term	..	..	..	..	..
Debt securities, long term	..	..	..	..	..
Debt securities issued by residents	..	..	..	..	..
Debt securities issued by non-residents	..	..	..	..	..
Loans	..	..	..	..	..
Loans, short-term	..	..	..	..	..
Loans, long-term	..	..	..	..	..
Loans granted to residents	..	..	..	..	..
Loans granted to non-residents	..	..	..	..	..
Equity and investment fund shares/units	..	..	..	..	..
Equity and investment fund shares issued/units by residents	..	..	..	..	..
Equity and investment fund shares/units issued by non residents	..	..	..	..	..
Other accounts receivable	..	..	..	..	..

	Investment funds				
		Non-money market funds			Money market funds
	Total	Total	Open-end non-money market funds	Closed-end non-money market funds	Total
Financial liabilities	..	..	..	..	..
Currency and deposits	..	..	..	..	..
Debt securities	..	..	..	..	..
Debt securities, short term	..	..	..	..	..
Debt securities, long term	..	..	..	..	..
Loans	..	..	..	..	..
Loans, short-term	..	..	..	..	..
Loans, long-term	..	..	..	..	..
Equity and investment fund shares/units	..	..	..	..	..
Insurance pension and standardised guaratees	..	..	..	..	..
Financial derivatives and employee stock options	..	..	..	..	..
Other accounts payable	..	..	..	..	..

	Insurance corporations and pension funds				
		Insurance corporations			Pension funds
	Total	Total	Life insurance corporations	Non-life insurance corporations	Total
Financial assets	4 748 003	..	..	..	..
Currency and deposits	178 662	..	..	..	..
Debt securities	1 232 409	..	..	..	..
Debt securities, short-term	18 202	..	..	..	..
Debt securities, long term	1 214 207	..	..	..	..
Debt securities issued by residents	856 423	..	..	..	..
Debt securities issued by non-residents	375 986	..	..	..	..
Loans	186 006	..	..	..	..
Loans, short-term	..	..	..	..	..
Loans, long-term	..	..	..	..	..
Loans granted to residents	..	..	..	..	..
Loans granted to non-residents	..	..	..	..	..
Equity and investment fund shares/units	1 768 855	..	..	..	..
Equity and investment fund shares/units issued by residents	980 337	..	..	..	..
Equity and investment fund shares/units issued by non residents	788 518	..	..	..	..
Other accounts receivable	40 691	..	..	..	..

	Insurance corporations and pension funds				
		Insurance corporations			Pension funds
	Total	Total	Life insurance corporations	Non-life insurance corporations	Total
Financial liabilities	4 475 325	..	..	..	..
Currency and deposits	..	..	..	..	..
Debt securities	30 170	..	..	..	..
Debt securities, short term	..	..	..	..	..
Debt securities, long term	..	..	..	..	..
Loans	94 680	..	..	..	..
Loans, short-term	76 908	..	..	..	..
Loans, long-term	17 772	..	..	..	..
Equity and investment fund shares/units	125 053	..	..	..	..
Insurance pension and standardised guarantees	4 005 131	..	..	..	..
Financial derivatives and employee stock options	132 635	..	..	..	..
Other accounts payable	87 656	..	..	..	..

Note: Detailed metadata at: http://metalinks.oecd.org/instinv/20170920/75e8

UNITED KINGDOM

Table 3. Financial assets and liabilities of insurance corporations and pension funds

Million GBP

	2009	2010	2011	2012	2013	2014	2015	2016
Insurance corporations and pension funds								
Financial net worth	184 790	181 428	135 828	160 010	136 790	143 467	184 567	272 678
Financial assets	2 951 455	3 092 101	3 498 198	3 693 798	3 680 454	4 342 756	4 212 347	4 748 003
Currency and deposits	126 488	121 646	132 249	133 141	148 751	149 574	144 147	178 662
Debt securities	781 222	820 621	913 525	969 101	969 521	1 073 515	1 075 301	1 232 409
Loans	86 489	128 072	144 811	176 481	205 884	168 102	173 835	186 006
Equity and investment fund shares	1 187 705	1 287 062	1 218 545	1 371 315	1 427 865	1 469 498	1 572 022	1 768 855
Equity	682 551	670 114	577 998	607 181	615 396	631 210	616 362	700 652
Investment fund shares	505 154	616 948	640 547	764 134	812 469	838 288	955 660	1 068 203
Money market fund shares	..	..	..	..	..	..	..	..
Non-Money market fund shares	..	..	..	..	..	..	..	..
Insurance pension and standardised guarantees	622 890	602 550	916 977	886 210	767 983	1 296 356	1 115 396	1 206 729
Financial derivatives and employee stock options	96 580	95 112	141 106	126 284	126 134	151 268	100 552	134 651
Other accounts receivable	50 081	37 038	30 985	31 266	34 316	34 443	31 094	40 691
Financial liabilities	2 766 665	2 910 673	3 362 370	3 533 788	3 543 664	4 199 289	4 027 780	4 475 325
Debt securities	26 113	24 120	24 065	26 222	23 878	27 997	24 740	30 170
Short-term debt securities	..	..	..	..	..	..	..	..
Long-term debt securities	..	..	..	..	..	..	..	..
Loans	39 732	35 655	43 764	66 165	72 834	61 493	60 284	94 680
Short-term loans	30 570	27 561	37 687	41 227	47 256	42 127	41 915	76 908
Long-term loans	9 162	8 094	6 077	24 938	25 578	19 366	18 369	17 772
Equity and investment fund shares	58 532	64 639	55 474	74 313	95 947	114 139	124 170	125 053
Insurance pension and standardised guarantees	2 475 831	2 624 580	3 030 431	3 162 075	3 143 797	3 749 493	3 638 043	4 005 131
Financial derivatives and employee stock options	93 633	92 064	135 695	124 780	124 802	148 331	98 871	132 635
Other accounts payable	72 824	69 615	72 941	80 233	82 406	97 836	81 672	87 656
Non-financial assets	..	..	..	..	..	..	..	..
Insurance corporations								
Financial net worth	..	..	..	..	..	..	..	..
Financial assets	..	..	..	..	..	..	..	..
Currency and deposits	..	..	..	..	..	..	..	..
Debt securities	..	..	..	..	..	..	..	..
Loans	..	..	..	..	..	..	..	..
Equity and investment fund shares	..	..	..	..	..	..	..	..
Equity	..	..	..	..	..	..	..	..
Investment fund shares	..	..	..	..	..	..	..	..
Money market fund shares	..	..	..	..	..	..	..	..
Non-Money market fund shares	..	..	..	..	..	..	..	..
Insurance pension and standardised guarantees	..	..	..	..	..	..	..	..
Financial derivatives and employee stock options	..	..	..	..	..	..	..	..
Other accounts receivable	..	..	..	..	..	..	..	..
Financial liabilities	..	..	..	..	..	..	..	..
Debt securities	..	..	..	..	..	..	..	..
Short-term debt securities	..	..	..	..	..	..	..	..
Long-term debt securities	..	..	..	..	..	..	..	..
Loans	..	..	..	..	..	..	..	..
Short-term loans	..	..	..	..	..	..	..	..
Long-term loans	..	..	..	..	..	..	..	..
Equity and investment fund shares	..	..	..	..	..	..	..	..
Insurance pension and standardised guarantees	..	..	..	..	..	..	..	..
Financial derivatives and employee stock options	..	..	..	..	..	..	..	..
Other accounts payable	..	..	..	..	..	..	..	..
Non-financial assets	..	..	..	..	..	..	..	..
Pension funds								
Financial net worth	..	..	..	..	..	..	..	..
Financial assets	..	..	..	..	..	..	..	..
Currency and deposits	..	..	..	..	..	..	..	..
Debt securities	..	..	..	..	..	..	..	..
Loans	..	..	..	..	..	..	..	..
Equity and investment fund shares	..	..	..	..	..	..	..	..
Equity	..	..	..	..	..	..	..	..
Investment fund shares	..	..	..	..	..	..	..	..
Money market fund shares	..	..	..	..	..	..	..	..
Non-Money market fund shares	..	..	..	..	..	..	..	..
Insurance pension and standardised guarantees	..	..	..	..	..	..	..	..
Financial derivatives and employee stock options	..	..	..	..	..	..	..	..
Other accounts receivable	..	..	..	..	..	..	..	..
Financial liabilities	..	..	..	..	..	..	..	..
Debt securities	..	..	..	..	..	..	..	..
Short-term debt securities	..	..	..	..	..	..	..	..
Long-term debt securities	..	..	..	..	..	..	..	..
Loans	..	..	..	..	..	..	..	..
Short-term loans	..	..	..	..	..	..	..	..
Long-term loans	..	..	..	..	..	..	..	..
Equity and investment fund shares	..	..	..	..	..	..	..	..
Insurance pension and standardised guarantees	..	..	..	..	..	..	..	..
Financial derivatives and employee stock options	..	..	..	..	..	..	..	..
Other accounts payable	..	..	..	..	..	..	..	..
Non-financial assets	..	..	..	..	..	..	..	..

Note: Detailed metadata at: http://metalinks.oecd.org/instinv/20170920/75e8

UNITED STATES

Table 1. Financial assets and liabilities of institutional investors, 2016

Billion USD

	Investment funds				
	Total	Non-money market funds			Money market funds
		Total	Open-end non-money market funds	Closed-end non-money market funds	Total
Financial assets	19 798	17 070	16 140	930	2 728
Currency and deposits	215	36	..	36	178
Debt securities	6 662	4 916	4 506	410	1 746
Debt securities, short term	650	131	131	..	519
Debt securities, long term	6 013	4 785	4 375	410	1 227
Debt securities issued by residents	..	..	..	..	..
Debt securities issued by non-residents	..	..	..	..	..
Loans	1 266	466	242	224	800
Loans, short-term	1 042	242	242	..	800
Loans, long-term	224	224	..	224	..
Loans granted to residents	..	..	..	..	..
Loans granted to non-residents	..	..	..	..	..
Equity and investment fund shares/units	11 205	11 205	11 103	102	..
Equity and investment fund shares issued/units by residents	..	..	..	..	..
Equity and investment fund shares/units issued by non residents	..	..	..	..	..
Other accounts receivable	450	447	290	157	4

	Investment funds				
	Total	Non-money market funds			Money market funds
		Total	Open-end non-money market funds	Closed-end non-money market funds	Total
Financial liabilities	20 126	17 398	16 140	1 258	2 728
Currency and deposits	..	..	..	..	..
Debt securities	416	416	..	416	..
Debt securities, short term	0	0	..	0	..
Debt securities, long term	416	416	..	416	..
Loans	484	484	..	484	..
Loans, short-term	256	256	..	256	..
Loans, long-term	228	228	..	228	..
Equity and investment fund shares/units	19 130	16 402	16 140	262	2 728
Insurance pension and standardised guaratees	..	..	..	..	..
Financial derivatives and employee stock options	..	..	..	..	..
Other accounts payable	96	96	..	96	..

	Insurance corporations and pension funds				
	Total	Insurance corporations			Pension funds
		Total	Life insurance corporations	Non-life insurance corporations	Total
Financial assets	27 406	8 672	6 764	1 908	18 734
Currency and deposits	202	96	69	27	106
Debt securities	8 414	4 435	3 408	1 027	3 979
Debt securities, short-term	205	109	58	51	96
Debt securities, long term	8 209	4 326	3 350	976	3 883
Debt securities issued by residents	..	..	..	..	..
Debt securities issued by non-residents	..	..	..	..	..
Loans	682	644	628	16	38
Loans, short-term	176	168	167	1	8
Loans, long-term	506	476	461	15	30
Loans granted to residents	..	..	..	..	..
Loans granted to non-residents	..	..	..	..	..
Equity and investment fund shares/units	11 532	2 598	2 109	490	8 933
Equity and investment fund shares/units issued by residents	..	..	..	..	..
Equity and investment fund shares/units issued by non residents	..	..	..	..	..
Other accounts receivable	1 747	867	520	348	879

	Insurance corporations and pension funds				
	Total	Insurance corporations			Pension funds
		Total	Life insurance corporations	Non-life insurance corporations	Total
Financial liabilities	26 742	7 833	6 388	1 445	18 909
Currency and deposits	71	71	71	..	..
Debt securities	..	..	..	..	..
Debt securities, short term	..	..	..	..	..
Debt securities, long term	..	..	..	..	..
Loans	93	93	90	3	..
Loans, short-term	93	93	90	3	..
Loans, long-term	..	..	..	..	..
Equity and investment fund shares/units	759	759	344	415	..
Insurance pension and standardised guarantees	25 279	6 370	5 511	859	18 909
Financial derivatives and employee stock options	..	..	..	..	..
Other accounts payable	540	540	372	168	..

Note: Detailed metadata at: http://metalinks.oecd.org/instinv/20170920/75e8

UNITED STATES

Table 2. Financial assets and liabilities of investment funds

Billion USD

	2009	2010	2011	2012	2013	2014	2015	2016
Investment funds								
Financial net worth	-227	-222	-221	-224	-264	-297	-337	-328
Financial assets	12 375	13 366	13 356	15 252	17 667	18 864	18 672	19 798
Currency and deposits	726	616	503	540	585	582	499	215
Debt securities	4 907	5 062	5 456	6 147	5 980	6 124	6 186	6 662
Loans	654	649	706	787	946	1 150	1 138	1 266
Equity and investment fund shares	5 777	6 722	6 360	7 372	9 706	10 539	10 436	11 205
Equity	5 777	6 722	6 360	7 372	9 706	10 539	10 436	11 205
Investment fund shares	..	..	..	..	..	..	..	..
Money market fund shares	..	..	..	..	..	..	..	..
Non-Money market fund shares	..	..	..	..	..	..	..	..
Insurance pension and standardised guarantees	..	..	..	..	..	..	..	..
Financial derivatives and employee stock options	..	..	..	..	..	..	..	..
Other accounts receivable	311	316	331	407	451	469	413	450
Financial liabilities	12 603	13 587	13 577	15 475	17 931	19 160	19 009	20 126
Debt securities	144	145	153	179	355	403	396	416
Short-term debt securities	0	0	0	0	0	0	0	0
Long-term debt securities	144	145	153	179	355	403	396	416
Loans	286	315	431	542	497	536	520	484
Short-term loans	111	139	241	348	282	304	284	256
Long-term loans	175	176	190	194	214	231	235	228
Equity and investment fund shares	12 113	13 063	12 923	14 657	17 005	18 139	18 013	19 130
Insurance pension and standardised guarantees	..	..	..	..	..	..	..	..
Financial derivatives and employee stock options	..	..	..	..	..	..	..	..
Other accounts payable	60	64	71	96	74	82	80	96
Non-financial assets	227	222	221	224	264	297	337	328
Money market funds								
Financial net worth	..	..	..	..	..	..	..	..
Financial assets	3 316	2 804	2 691	2 693	2 718	2 725	2 755	2 728
Currency and deposits	695	591	475	504	551	544	464	178
Debt securities	2 103	1 700	1 692	1 605	1 634	1 510	1 582	1 746
Loans	490	489	501	555	502	654	699	800
Equity and investment fund shares	..	..	..	..	..	..	..	..
Equity	..	..	..	..	..	..	..	..
Investment fund shares	..	..	..	..	..	..	..	..
Money market fund shares	..	..	..	..	..	..	..	..
Non-Money market fund shares	..	..	..	..	..	..	..	..
Insurance pension and standardised guarantees	..	..	..	..	..	..	..	..
Financial derivatives and employee stock options	..	..	..	..	..	..	..	..
Other accounts receivable	27	24	23	29	32	17	10	4
Financial liabilities	3 316	2 804	2 691	2 693	2 718	2 725	2 755	2 728
Debt securities	..	..	..	..	..	..	..	..
Short-term debt securities	..	..	..	..	..	..	..	..
Long-term debt securities	..	..	..	..	..	..	..	..
Loans	..	..	..	..	..	..	..	..
Short-term loans	..	..	..	..	..	..	..	..
Long-term loans	..	..	..	..	..	..	..	..
Equity and investment fund shares	3 316	2 804	2 691	2 693	2 718	2 725	2 755	2 728
Insurance pension and standardised guarantees	..	..	..	..	..	..	..	..
Financial derivatives and employee stock options	..	..	..	..	..	..	..	..
Other accounts payable	..	..	..	..	..	..	..	..
Non-financial assets	..	..	..	..	..	..	..	..
Non-money market funds								
Financial net worth	-227	-222	-221	-224	-264	-297	-337	-328
Financial assets	9 060	10 562	10 665	12 558	14 950	16 139	15 917	17 070
Currency and deposits	31	25	28	35	34	39	36	36
Debt securities	2 804	3 362	3 764	4 542	4 346	4 614	4 604	4 916
Loans	165	160	205	232	444	496	438	466
Equity and investment fund shares	5 777	6 722	6 360	7 372	9 706	10 539	10 436	11 205
Equity	5 777	6 722	6 360	7 372	9 706	10 539	10 436	11 205
Investment fund shares	..	..	..	..	..	..	..	..
Money market fund shares	..	..	..	..	..	..	..	..
Non-Money market fund shares	..	..	..	..	..	..	..	..
Insurance pension and standardised guarantees	..	..	..	..	..	..	..	..
Financial derivatives and employee stock options	..	..	..	..	..	..	..	..
Other accounts receivable	284	293	308	378	419	452	403	447
Financial liabilities	9 287	10 784	10 886	12 782	15 213	16 436	16 254	17 398
Debt securities	144	145	153	179	355	403	396	416
Short-term debt securities	0	0	0	0	0	0	0	0
Long-term debt securities	144	145	153	179	355	403	396	416
Loans	286	315	431	542	497	536	520	484
Short-term loans	111	139	241	348	282	304	284	256
Long-term loans	175	176	190	194	214	231	235	228
Equity and investment fund shares	8 797	10 260	10 232	11 964	14 287	15 414	15 259	16 402
Insurance pension and standardised guarantees	..	..	..	..	..	..	..	..
Financial derivatives and employee stock options	..	..	..	..	..	..	..	..
Other accounts payable	60	64	71	96	74	82	80	96
Non-financial assets	227	222	221	224	264	297	337	328
Open-end non-money market funds								
Financial net worth	..	..	..	..	..	..	..	..
Financial assets	8 574	10 022	9 990	11 701	14 008	15 125	14 998	16 140

UNITED STATES

Table 2. Financial assets and liabilities of investment funds *(cont.)*

Billion USD

	2009	2010	2011	2012	2013	2014	2015	2016
Currency and deposits	..	..	..	..	..	..	..	..
Debt securities	2 547	3 054	3 342	3 985	3 877	4 132	4 176	4 506
Loans	119	115	149	168	229	249	221	242
Equity and investment fund shares	5 689	6 626	6 265	7 271	9 592	10 419	10 335	11 103
Equity	5 689	6 626	6 265	7 271	9 592	10 419	10 335	11 103
Investment fund shares	..	..	..	..	..	..	..	..
Money market fund shares	..	..	..	..	..	..	..	..
Non-Money market fund shares	..	..	..	..	..	..	..	..
Insurance pension and standardised guarantees	..	..	..	..	..	..	..	..
Financial derivatives and employee stock options	..	..	..	..	..	..	..	..
Other accounts receivable	219	227	234	277	310	325	266	290
Financial liabilities	8 574	10 022	9 990	11 701	14 008	15 125	14 998	16 140
Debt securities	..	..	..	..	..	..	..	..
Short-term debt securities	..	..	..	..	..	..	..	..
Long-term debt securities	..	..	..	..	..	..	..	..
Loans	..	..	..	..	..	..	..	..
Short-term loans	..	..	..	..	..	..	..	..
Long-term loans	..	..	..	..	..	..	..	..
Equity and investment fund shares	8 574	10 022	9 990	11 701	14 008	15 125	14 998	16 140
Insurance pension and standardised guarantees	..	..	..	..	..	..	..	..
Financial derivatives and employee stock options	..	..	..	..	..	..	..	..
Other accounts payable	..	..	..	..	..	..	..	..
Non-financial assets	..	..	..	..	..	..	..	..
Open-end investment funds								
Financial net worth	..	..	..	..	..	..	..	..
Financial assets	11 890	12 825	12 680	14 394	16 725	17 850	17 753	18 868
Currency and deposits	695	591	475	504	551	544	464	178
Debt securities	4 650	4 755	5 034	5 590	5 510	5 642	5 758	6 252
Loans	608	604	650	722	731	903	920	1 042
Equity and investment fund shares	5 689	6 626	6 265	7 271	9 592	10 419	10 335	11 103
Equity	5 689	6 626	6 265	7 271	9 592	10 419	10 335	11 103
Investment fund shares	..	..	..	..	..	..	..	..
Money market fund shares	..	..	..	..	..	..	..	..
Non-Money market fund shares	..	..	..	..	..	..	..	..
Insurance pension and standardised guarantees	..	..	..	..	..	..	..	..
Financial derivatives and employee stock options	..	..	..	..	..	..	..	..
Other accounts receivable	246	250	256	306	342	342	276	293
Financial liabilities	11 890	12 825	12 680	14 394	16 725	17 850	17 753	18 868
Debt securities	..	..	..	..	..	..	..	..
Short-term debt securities	..	..	..	..	..	..	..	..
Long-term debt securities	..	..	..	..	..	..	..	..
Loans	..	..	..	..	..	..	..	..
Short-term loans	..	..	..	..	..	..	..	..
Long-term loans	..	..	..	..	..	..	..	..
Equity and investment fund shares	11 890	12 825	12 680	14 394	16 725	17 850	17 753	18 868
Insurance pension and standardised guarantees	..	..	..	..	..	..	..	..
Financial derivatives and employee stock options	..	..	..	..	..	..	..	..
Other accounts payable	..	..	..	..	..	..	..	..
Non-financial assets	..	..	..	..	..	..	..	..

Note: Detailed metadata at: http://metalinks.oecd.org/instinv/20170920/75e8

Table 3. Financial assets and liabilities of insurance corporations and pension funds

Billion USD

	2009	2010	2011	2012	2013	2014	2015	2016
Insurance corporations and pension funds								
Financial net worth	412	556	778	821	590	725	637	664
Financial assets	19 629	21 495	22 211	23 433	24 910	25 964	26 225	27 406
Currency and deposits	146	153	161	175	170	188	193	202
Debt securities	6 173	6 657	7 077	7 475	7 518	8 042	8 010	8 414
Loans	528	522	536	550	566	601	642	682
Equity and investment fund shares	7 560	8 486	8 266	9 208	10 876	11 263	11 011	11 532
Equity	3 767	4 235	4 157	4 687	5 505	5 657	5 530	5 931
Investment fund shares	3 793	4 250	4 108	4 521	5 371	5 606	5 480	5 601
Money market fund shares	314	279	296	277	282	283	287	280
Non-Money market fund shares	3 479	3 971	3 812	4 244	5 088	5 323	5 194	5 321
Insurance pension and standardised guarantees	3 986	4 375	4 750	4 555	4 267	4 258	4 753	4 830
Financial derivatives and employee stock options	..	..	..	..	..	..	..	..
Other accounts receivable	1 236	1 303	1 421	1 468	1 514	1 613	1 617	1 747
Financial liabilities	19 217	20 939	21 433	22 612	24 321	25 239	25 588	26 742
Debt securities	..	..	..	..	..	..	..	..
Short-term debt securities	..	..	..	..	..	..	..	..
Long-term debt securities	..	..	..	..	..	..	..	..
Loans	61	56	61	66	75	77	83	93
Short-term loans	61	56	61	66	75	77	83	93
Long-term loans	..	..	..	..	..	..	..	..
Equity and investment fund shares	570	639	587	584	646	691	663	759
Insurance pension and standardised guarantees	18 137	19 811	20 367	21 435	23 026	23 855	24 247	25 279
Financial derivatives and employee stock options	..	..	..	..	..	..	..	..
Other accounts payable	369	363	356	465	521	554	531	540
Non-financial assets	248	243	247	249	257	262	272	282
Insurance corporations								
Financial net worth	553	699	925	982	772	917	814	839
Financial assets	6 448	6 941	7 284	7 667	7 935	8 365	8 294	8 672
Currency and deposits	78	84	85	98	83	94	100	96
Debt securities	3 459	3 730	4 007	4 128	4 040	4 278	4 219	4 435
Loans	487	478	495	511	530	562	605	644
Equity and investment fund shares	1 801	1 986	1 976	2 198	2 533	2 618	2 540	2 598
Equity	567	589	607	685	795	847	835	983
Investment fund shares	1 233	1 397	1 369	1 513	1 738	1 771	1 705	1 616
Money market fund shares	109	85	88	84	70	72	78	59
Non-Money market fund shares	1 124	1 313	1 281	1 429	1 668	1 699	1 627	1 557
Insurance pension and standardised guarantees	23	25	25	26	29	30	32	31
Financial derivatives and employee stock options	..	..	..	..	..	..	..	..
Other accounts receivable	601	637	696	708	720	785	798	867
Financial liabilities	5 895	6 242	6 359	6 685	7 163	7 449	7 479	7 833
Debt securities	..	..	..	..	..	..	..	..
Short-term debt securities	..	..	..	..	..	..	..	..
Long-term debt securities	..	..	..	..	..	..	..	..
Loans	61	56	61	66	75	77	83	93
Short-term loans	61	56	61	66	75	77	83	93
Long-term loans	..	..	..	..	..	..	..	..
Equity and investment fund shares	570	639	587	584	646	691	663	759
Insurance pension and standardised guarantees	4 815	5 114	5 294	5 509	5 868	6 064	6 138	6 370
Financial derivatives and employee stock options	..	..	..	..	..	..	..	..
Other accounts payable	369	363	356	465	521	554	531	540
Non-financial assets	242	237	240	243	251	256	265	275
Pension funds								
Financial net worth	-141	-143	-147	-161	-182	-192	-178	-175
Financial assets	13 181	14 554	14 927	15 765	16 976	17 598	17 931	18 734
Currency and deposits	68	68	76	77	87	94	93	106
Debt securities	2 714	2 927	3 070	3 348	3 478	3 764	3 791	3 979
Loans	41	44	41	40	36	39	37	38
Equity and investment fund shares	5 759	6 500	6 290	7 011	8 342	8 645	8 470	8 933
Equity	3 199	3 646	3 550	4 002	4 710	4 810	4 695	4 948
Investment fund shares	2 560	2 853	2 740	3 008	3 633	3 834	3 775	3 985
Money market fund shares	205	195	208	194	212	211	208	222
Non-Money market fund shares	2 355	2 659	2 532	2 815	3 420	3 624	3 567	3 764
Insurance pension and standardised guarantees	3 963	4 349	4 725	4 529	4 238	4 228	4 721	4 799
Financial derivatives and employee stock options	..	..	..	..	..	..	..	..
Other accounts receivable	636	665	725	760	794	828	819	879
Financial liabilities	13 322	14 697	15 074	15 926	17 158	17 791	18 109	18 909
Debt securities	..	..	..	..	..	..	..	..
Short-term debt securities	..	..	..	..	..	..	..	..
Long-term debt securities	..	..	..	..	..	..	..	..
Loans	..	..	..	..	..	..	..	..
Short-term loans	..	..	..	..	..	..	..	..
Long-term loans	..	..	..	..	..	..	..	..
Equity and investment fund shares	..	..	..	..	..	..	..	..
Insurance pension and standardised guarantees	13 322	14 697	15 074	15 926	17 158	17 791	18 109	18 909
Financial derivatives and employee stock options	..	..	..	..	..	..	..	..
Other accounts payable	..	..	..	..	..	..	..	..
Non-financial assets	6	6	6	7	7	7	7	7

Note: Detailed metadata at: http://metalinks.oecd.org/instinv/20170920/75e8

Table 4. Portfolio composition by type of investor

As percentage of financial assets and of financial liabilities

Per cent

	2009	2010	2011	2012	2013	2014	2015	2016
Investment funds								
Financial assets	100.0	100.0	100.0	100.0	100.0	100.0	100.0	100.0
Currency and deposits	5.9	4.6	3.8	3.5	3.3	3.1	2.7	1.1
Debt securities	39.7	37.9	40.9	40.3	33.8	32.5	33.1	33.7
Loans	5.3	4.9	5.3	5.2	5.4	6.1	6.1	6.4
Equity and investment fund shares	46.7	50.3	47.6	48.3	54.9	55.9	55.9	56.6
Insurance pension and standardised guarantee schemes	0.0	0.0	0.0	0.0	0.0	0.0	0.0	0.0
Financial derivatives and employee stock options	0.0	0.0	0.0	0.0	0.0	0.0	0.0	0.0
Other accounts receivable	2.5	2.4	2.5	2.7	2.6	2.5	2.2	2.3
Financial liabilities	100.0	100.0	100.0	100.0	100.0	100.0	100.0	100.0
Currency and deposits	0.0	0.0	0.0	0.0	0.0	0.0	0.0	0.0
Debt securities	1.1	1.1	1.1	1.2	2.0	2.1	2.1	2.1
Loans	2.3	2.3	3.2	3.5	2.8	2.8	2.7	2.4
Equity and investment fund shares	96.1	96.1	95.2	94.7	94.8	94.7	94.8	95.1
Insurance pension and standardised guarantee schemes	0.0	0.0	0.0	0.0	0.0	0.0	0.0	0.0
Financial derivatives and employee stock options	0.0	0.0	0.0	0.0	0.0	0.0	0.0	0.0
Other accounts receivable	0.5	0.5	0.5	0.6	0.4	0.4	0.4	0.5
Insurance corporations								
Financial assets	100.0	100.0	100.0	100.0	100.0	100.0	100.0	100.0
Currency and deposits	1.2	1.2	1.2	1.3	1.0	1.1	1.2	1.1
Debt securities	53.6	53.7	55.0	53.8	50.9	51.1	50.9	51.1
Loans	7.5	6.9	6.8	6.7	6.7	6.7	7.3	7.4
Equity and investment fund shares	27.9	28.6	27.1	28.7	31.9	31.3	30.6	30.0
Insurance pension and standardised guarantee schemes	0.4	0.4	0.3	0.3	0.4	0.4	0.4	0.4
Financial derivatives and employee stock options	0.0	0.0	0.0	0.0	0.0	0.0	0.0	0.0
Other accounts receivable	9.3	9.2	9.6	9.2	9.1	9.4	9.6	10.0
Financial liabilities	100.0	100.0	100.0	100.0	100.0	100.0	100.0	100.0
Currency and deposits	1.4	1.1	1.0	0.9	0.7	0.8	0.9	0.9
Debt securities	0.0	0.0	0.0	0.0	0.0	0.0	0.0	0.0
Loans	1.0	0.9	1.0	1.0	1.0	1.0	1.1	1.2
Equity and investment fund shares	9.7	10.2	9.2	8.7	9.0	9.3	8.9	9.7
Insurance pension and standardised guarantee schemes	81.7	81.9	83.2	82.4	81.9	81.4	82.1	81.3
Financial derivatives and employee stock options	0.0	0.0	0.0	0.0	0.0	0.0	0.0	0.0
Other accounts receivable	6.3	5.8	5.6	7.0	7.3	7.4	7.1	6.9
Pension funds								
Financial assets	100.0	100.0	100.0	100.0	100.0	100.0	100.0	100.0
Currency and deposits	0.5	0.5	0.5	0.5	0.5	0.5	0.5	0.6
Debt securities	20.6	20.1	20.6	21.2	20.5	21.4	21.1	21.2
Loans	0.3	0.3	0.3	0.3	0.2	0.2	0.2	0.2
Equity and investment fund shares	43.7	44.7	42.1	44.5	49.1	49.1	47.2	47.7
Insurance pension and standardised guarantee schemes	30.1	29.9	31.7	28.7	25.0	24.0	26.3	25.6
Financial derivatives and employee stock options	0.0	0.0	0.0	0.0	0.0	0.0	0.0	0.0
Other accounts receivable	4.8	4.6	4.9	4.8	4.7	4.7	4.6	4.7
Financial liabilities	100.0	100.0	100.0	100.0	100.0	100.0	100.0	100.0
Currency and deposits	0.0	0.0	0.0	0.0	0.0	0.0	0.0	0.0
Debt securities	0.0	0.0	0.0	0.0	0.0	0.0	0.0	0.0
Loans	0.0	0.0	0.0	0.0	0.0	0.0	0.0	0.0
Equity and investment fund shares	0.0	0.0	0.0	0.0	0.0	0.0	0.0	0.0
Insurance pension and standardised guarantee schemes	100.0	100.0	100.0	100.0	100.0	100.0	100.0	100.0
Financial derivatives and employee stock options	0.0	0.0	0.0	0.0	0.0	0.0	0.0	0.0
Other accounts receivable	0.0	0.0	0.0	0.0	0.0	0.0	0.0	0.0

Note: Detailed metadata at: http://metalinks.oecd.org/instinv/20170920/a49a

LITHUANIA

Table 1. Financial assets and liabilities of institutional investors, 2016

Million EUR (2015)

	Investment funds				
	Total	Non-money market funds			Money market funds
		Total	Open-end non-money market funds	Closed-end non-money market funds	Total
Financial assets	506	506	170	336	0
Currency and deposits	81	81	34	47	0
Debt securities	158	158	34	124	0
Debt securities, short term	10	10	2	8	0
Debt securities, long term	149	149	32	117	0
Debt securities issued by residents	119	119	26	93	0
Debt securities issued by non-residents	40	40	9	31	0
Loans	11	11	0	11	0
Loans, short-term	1	1	0	1	0
Loans, long-term	10	10	0	10	0
Loans granted to residents	8	8	0	8	0
Loans granted to non-residents	4	4	0	4	0
Equity and investment fund shares/units	225	225	96	129	0
Equity and investment fund shares issued/units by residents	129	129	55	74	0
Equity and investment fund shares/units issued by non residents	96	96	41	55	0
Other accounts receivable	29	29	5	24	0

	Investment funds				
	Total	Non-money market funds			Money market funds
		Total	Open-end non-money market funds	Closed-end non-money market funds	Total
Financial liabilities	672	672	169	503	0
Currency and deposits	0	0	..	..	0
Debt securities	2	2	0	2	0
Debt securities, short term	0	0	..	..	0
Debt securities, long term	2	2	..	..	0
Loans	97	97	0	97	0
Loans, short-term	28	28	0	28	0
Loans, long-term	69	69	0	69	0
Equity and investment fund shares/units	543	543	164	379	0
Insurance pension and standardised guaratees	0	0	..	..	0
Financial derivatives and employee stock options	1	1	1	0	0
Other accounts payable	28	28	4	24	0

	Insurance corporations and pension funds				
	Total	Insurance corporations			Pension funds
		Total	Life insurance corporations	Non-life insurance corporations	Total
Financial assets	3 811	1 203	..	..	2 607
Currency and deposits	325	92	..	..	233
Debt securities	1 504	521	..	..	983
Debt securities, short-term	0	0	..	..	0
Debt securities, long term	1 504	521	..	..	983
Debt securities issued by residents	734	333	..	..	401
Debt securities issued by non-residents	770	188	..	..	582
Loans	7	7	..	..	0
Loans, short-term	0	0	..	..	0
Loans, long-term	7	7	..	..	0
Loans granted to residents	7	7	..	..	0
Loans granted to non-residents	0	0	..	..	0
Equity and investment fund shares/units	1 815	432	..	..	1 384
Equity and investment fund shares/units issued by residents	33	7	..	..	26
Equity and investment fund shares/units issued by non residents	1 782	424	..	..	1 358
Other accounts receivable	143	135	..	..	8

	Insurance corporations and pension funds				
	Total	Insurance corporations			Pension funds
		Total	Life insurance corporations	Non-life insurance corporations	Total
Financial liabilities	4 347	1 739	..	..	2 607
Currency and deposits	0	0	..	..	0
Debt securities	0	0	..	..	0
Debt securities, short term	0	0	..	..	0
Debt securities, long term	0	0	..	..	0
Loans	88	88	..	..	0
Loans, short-term	20	20	..	..	0
Loans, long-term	68	68	..	..	0
Equity and investment fund shares/units	280	280	..	..	0
Insurance pension and standardised guarantees	3 876	1 301	..	..	2 575
Financial derivatives and employee stock options	5	2	..	..	3
Other accounts payable	97	68	..	..	29

Note: Detailed metadata at: http://metalinks.oecd.org/instinv/20170920/f3c4

Table 2. Financial assets and liabilities of investment funds

Million EUR

	2009	2010	2011	2012	2013	2014	2015	2016
Investment funds								
Financial net worth	0	0	0	-4	-4	-16	-47	-166
Financial assets	133	181	151	182	240	292	354	506
Currency and deposits	20	13	10	11	27	36	44	81
Debt securities	21	36	34	42	81	99	113	158
Loans	0	0	0	1	4	11	11	11
Equity and investment fund shares	92	132	106	126	129	143	178	225
Equity	33	50	36	47	52	61	86	196
Investment fund shares	60	83	70	80	77	82	92	29
Money market fund shares	0	2	0	0	0	0	0	0
Non-Money market fund shares	59	81	70	80	77	82	92	29
Insurance pension and standardised guarantees	0	0	0	0	0	0	0	0
Financial derivatives and employee stock options	0	0	0	0	0	0	1	1
Other accounts receivable	0	0	0	1	0	4	6	29
Financial liabilities	133	181	151	186	244	309	401	672
Debt securities	0	0	0	0	0	0	0	2
Short-term debt securities	0	0	0	0	0	0	0	0
Long-term debt securities	0	0	0	0	0	0	0	2
Loans	0	3	2	1	5	17	5	97
Short-term loans	0	3	1	0	5	0	0	28
Long-term loans	0	0	1	0	0	16	5	69
Equity and investment fund shares	133	177	148	184	237	285	390	543
Insurance pension and standardised guarantees	0	0	0	0	0	0	0	0
Financial derivatives and employee stock options	0	0	0	0	0	0	0	1
Other accounts payable	0	1	0	2	2	7	5	28
Non-financial assets	..	..	..	..	4	19	47	210
Money market funds								
Financial net worth	0	0	0	0	0	0	0	0
Financial assets	18	23	15	12	0	0	0	0
Currency and deposits	5	3	4	4	0	0	0	0
Debt securities	12	20	11	7	0	0	0	0
Loans	0	0	0	0	0	0	0	0
Equity and investment fund shares	0	0	0	0	0	0	0	0
Equity	0	0	0	0	0	0	0	0
Investment fund shares	0	0	0	0	0	0	0	0
Money market fund shares	0	0	0	0	0	0	0	0
Non-Money market fund shares	0	0	0	0	0	0	0	0
Insurance pension and standardised guarantees	0	0	0	0	0	0	0	0
Financial derivatives and employee stock options	0	0	0	0	0	0	0	0
Other accounts receivable	0	0	0	0	0	0	0	0
Financial liabilities	18	23	15	12	0	0	0	0
Debt securities	0	0	0	0	0	0	0	0
Short-term debt securities	0	0	0	0	0	0	0	0
Long-term debt securities	0	0	0	0	0	0	0	0
Loans	0	0	0	0	0	0	0	0
Short-term loans	0	0	0	0	0	0	0	0
Long-term loans	0	0	0	0	0	0	0	0
Equity and investment fund shares	18	23	15	12	0	0	0	0
Insurance pension and standardised guarantees	0	0	0	0	0	0	0	0
Financial derivatives and employee stock options	0	0	0	0	0	0	0	0
Other accounts payable	0	0	0	0	0	0	0	0
Non-financial assets	..	..	..	..	..	..	..	..
Non-money market funds								
Financial net worth	0	0	0	-4	-4	-16	-47	-166
Financial assets	116	158	136	170	240	292	354	506
Currency and deposits	15	10	6	7	27	36	44	81
Debt securities	8	16	24	35	81	99	113	158
Loans	0	0	0	1	4	11	11	11
Equity and investment fund shares	92	132	106	126	129	143	178	225
Equity	33	50	36	47	52	61	86	196
Investment fund shares	59	82	70	80	77	82	92	29
Money market fund shares	0	2	0	0	0	0	0	0
Non-Money market fund shares	59	80	70	80	77	82	92	29
Insurance pension and standardised guarantees	0	0	0	0	0	0	0	0
Financial derivatives and employee stock options	0	0	0	0	0	0	1	1
Other accounts receivable	0	0	0	1	0	4	6	29
Financial liabilities	116	158	136	174	244	309	401	672
Debt securities	0	0	0	0	0	0	0	2
Short-term debt securities	0	0	0	0	0	0	0	0
Long-term debt securities	0	0	0	0	0	0	0	2
Loans	0	3	2	1	5	17	5	97
Short-term loans	0	3	1	0	5	0	0	28
Long-term loans	0	0	1	0	0	16	5	69
Equity and investment fund shares	115	154	133	172	237	285	390	543
Insurance pension and standardised guarantees	0	0	0	0	0	0	0	0
Financial derivatives and employee stock options	0	0	0	0	0	0	0	1
Other accounts payable	0	1	0	2	2	7	5	28
Non-financial assets	0	0	0	4	4	19	47	210
Open-end non-money market funds								
Financial net worth	..	..	..	0	0	0	-3	1
Financial assets	..	..	..	128	155	158	180	170

Table 2. Financial assets and liabilities of investment funds *(cont.)*

Million EUR

	2009	2010	2011	2012	2013	2014	2015	2016
Currency and deposits	..	..	..	4	22	24	31	34
Debt securities	..	..	..	16	24	24	21	34
Loans	..	..	..	0	0	0	0	0
Equity and investment fund shares	..	..	..	107	109	110	126	96
Equity	..	..	..	40	44	47	61	84
Investment fund shares	..	..	..	68	65	63	65	13
Money market fund shares	..	..	..	0	0	0	0	0
Non-Money market fund shares	..	..	..	68	65	63	65	13
Insurance pension and standardised guarantees	..	..	..	..	..	..	..	..
Financial derivatives and employee stock options	..	..	..	0	0	0	0	0
Other accounts receivable	..	..	..	0	0	1	1	5
Financial liabilities	..	..	..	128	155	159	183	169
Debt securities	..	..	..	0	0	0	0	0
Short-term debt securities	..	..	..	..	..	..	..	..
Long-term debt securities	..	..	..	..	..	..	..	..
Loans	..	..	..	0	0	0	0	0
Short-term loans	..	..	..	0	0	0	0	0
Long-term loans	..	..	..	0	0	0	0	0
Equity and investment fund shares	..	..	..	126	154	158	181	164
Insurance pension and standardised guarantees	..	..	..	..	..	..	..	..
Financial derivatives and employee stock options	..	..	..	0	0	0	0	1
Other accounts payable	..	..	..	2	1	0	2	4
Non-financial assets	..	..	..	0	0	0	3	5
Open-end investment funds								
Financial net worth	0	0	0	..	0	0	-3	1
Financial assets	124	161	129	..	155	158	180	170
Currency and deposits	20	9	10	..	22	24	31	34
Debt securities	17	29	24	..	24	24	21	34
Loans	0	0	0	..	0	0	0	0
Equity and investment fund shares	87	122	95	..	109	110	126	96
Equity	31	46	32	..	44	47	61	84
Investment fund shares	56	76	63	..	65	63	65	13
Money market fund shares	0	2	0	..	0	0	0	0
Non-Money market fund shares	56	74	63	..	65	63	65	13
Insurance pension and standardised guarantees	..	..	..	..	..	..	..	..
Financial derivatives and employee stock options	0	0	0	..	0	0	0	0
Other accounts receivable	0	0	0	..	0	1	1	5
Financial liabilities	124	161	129	..	155	159	183	169
Debt securities	0	0	0	..	0	0	0	0
Short-term debt securities	..	..	..	..	..	..	..	..
Long-term debt securities	..	..	..	..	..	..	..	..
Loans	0	3	2	..	0	0	0	0
Short-term loans	0	3	1	..	0	0	0	0
Long-term loans	0	0	1	..	0	0	0	0
Equity and investment fund shares	124	157	126	..	154	158	181	164
Insurance pension and standardised guarantees	..	..	..	..	..	..	..	..
Financial derivatives and employee stock options	0	0	0	..	0	0	0	1
Other accounts payable	0	1	0	..	1	0	2	4
Non-financial assets	0	0	0	..	0	0	3	5

Note: Detailed metadata at: http://metalinks.oecd.org/instinv/20170920/f3c4

Table 3. Financial assets and liabilities of insurance corporations and pension funds

Million EUR

	2009	2010	2011	2012	2013	2014	2015	2016
Insurance corporations and pension funds								
Financial net worth	-3	18	-152	-63	-149	-349	-437	-536
Financial assets	1 960	2 017	2 093	2 482	2 576	2 909	3 252	3 811
Currency and deposits	177	139	123	139	107	205	275	325
Debt securities	1 035	882	937	1 109	1 131	1 188	1 342	1 504
Loans	4	3	1	2	3	4	1	7
Equity and investment fund shares	633	879	915	1 113	1 219	1 387	1 497	1 815
Equity	19	30	22	19	27	27	32	25
Investment fund shares	614	849	893	1 094	1 193	1 359	1 464	1 791
Money market fund shares	1	4	5	2	1	5	1	2
Non-Money market fund shares	612	845	888	1 092	1 191	1 354	1 463	1 789
Insurance pension and standardised guarantees	16	15	15	16	16	16	18	16
Financial derivatives and employee stock options	1	0	0	0	0	0	0	0
Other accounts receivable	95	98	101	103	98	109	120	143
Financial liabilities	1 964	1 999	2 245	2 545	2 724	3 258	3 690	4 347
Debt securities	0	0	0	0	0	0	0	0
Short-term debt securities	0	0	0	0	0	0	0	0
Long-term debt securities	0	0	0	0	0	0	0	0
Loans	5	15	7	9	14	62	83	88
Short-term loans	0	12	0	0	0	0	13	20
Long-term loans	4	3	7	9	14	62	70	68
Equity and investment fund shares	216	185	184	192	175	209	197	280
Insurance pension and standardised guarantees	1 672	1 709	1 994	2 285	2 468	2 914	3 324	3 876
Financial derivatives and employee stock options	0	0	1	0	0	1	1	5
Other accounts payable	71	91	59	58	67	71	85	97
Non-financial assets	..	..	..	..	..	..	..	..
Insurance corporations								
Financial net worth	-3	18	-152	-63	-149	-349	-437	-536
Financial assets	992	862	883	1 058	958	991	1 066	1 203
Currency and deposits	62	76	44	85	56	87	71	92
Debt securities	589	458	484	556	491	458	463	521
Loans	4	3	1	2	3	4	1	7
Equity and investment fund shares	225	212	238	297	296	320	395	432
Equity	7	9	9	7	9	12	18	13
Investment fund shares	218	203	229	290	287	308	377	419
Money market fund shares	1	3	5	2	1	1	1	2
Non-Money market fund shares	217	199	224	289	286	307	376	417
Insurance pension and standardised guarantees	16	15	15	16	16	16	18	16
Financial derivatives and employee stock options	1	0	0	0	0	0	0	0
Other accounts receivable	95	98	101	101	96	105	119	135
Financial liabilities	995	844	1 035	1 121	1 107	1 339	1 504	1 739
Debt securities	0	0	0	0	0	0	0	0
Short-term debt securities	0	0	0	0	0	0	0	0
Long-term debt securities	0	0	0	0	0	0	0	0
Loans	5	15	7	9	14	62	83	88
Short-term loans	0	12	0	0	0	0	13	20
Long-term loans	4	3	7	9	14	62	70	68
Equity and investment fund shares	216	185	184	192	175	209	197	280
Insurance pension and standardised guarantees	705	564	787	862	859	1 000	1 145	1 301
Financial derivatives and employee stock options	0	0	1	0	0	1	1	2
Other accounts payable	69	81	57	56	60	67	78	68
Non-financial assets	..	..	..	..	..	..	..	..
Pension funds								
Financial net worth	0	0	0	0	0	0	0	0
Financial assets	969	1 155	1 210	1 424	1 617	1 918	2 186	2 607
Currency and deposits	115	64	79	55	51	118	204	233
Debt securities	446	424	453	552	641	730	879	983
Loans	0	0	0	0	0	0	0	0
Equity and investment fund shares	407	667	677	816	923	1 066	1 101	1 384
Equity	12	21	13	12	17	15	14	12
Investment fund shares	396	646	664	804	906	1 051	1 087	1 372
Money market fund shares	0	0	0	0	0	4	0	0
Non-Money market fund shares	396	646	664	804	906	1 047	1 087	1 372
Insurance pension and standardised guarantees	0	0	0	0	0	0	0	0
Financial derivatives and employee stock options	0	0	0	0	0	0	0	0
Other accounts receivable	0	0	0	1	2	4	2	8
Financial liabilities	969	1 155	1 210	1 424	1 617	1 918	2 186	2 607
Debt securities	0	0	0	0	0	0	0	0
Short-term debt securities	0	0	0	0	0	0	0	0
Long-term debt securities	0	0	0	0	0	0	0	0
Loans	0	0	0	0	0	0	0	0
Short-term loans	0	0	0	0	0	0	0	0
Long-term loans	0	0	0	0	0	0	0	0
Equity and investment fund shares	0	0	0	0	0	0	0	0
Insurance pension and standardised guarantees	967	1 145	1 207	1 422	1 609	1 914	2 179	2 575
Financial derivatives and employee stock options	0	0	0	0	0	1	0	3
Other accounts payable	2	10	2	2	8	3	6	29
Non-financial assets	..	..	..	..	..	..	..	..

Note: Detailed metadata at: http://metalinks.oecd.org/instinv/20170920/f3c4

Table 4. Portfolio composition by type of investor

As percentage of financial assets and of financial liabilities

Per cent

	2009	2010	2011	2012	2013	2014	2015	2016
Investment funds								
Financial assets	100.0	100.0	100.0	100.0	100.0	100.0	100.0	100.0
Currency and deposits	15.0	7.1	6.7	6.1	11.1	12.2	12.5	16.1
Debt securities	15.4	19.7	22.7	23.3	33.5	33.8	32.0	31.3
Loans	0.2	0.1	0.2	0.7	1.7	3.7	3.2	2.2
Equity and investment fund shares	69.2	72.9	70.2	69.4	53.5	48.9	50.3	44.5
Insurance pension and standardised guarantee schemes	0.0	0.0	0.0	0.0	0.0	0.0	0.0	0.0
Financial derivatives and employee stock options	0.0	0.1	0.1	0.1	0.1	0.0	0.3	0.2
Other accounts receivable	0.2	0.0	0.1	0.3	0.1	1.5	1.7	5.7
Financial liabilities	100.0	100.0	100.0	100.0	100.0	100.0	100.0	100.0
Currency and deposits	0.0	0.0	0.0	0.0	0.0	0.0	0.0	0.0
Debt securities	0.0	0.0	0.0	0.0	0.0	0.0	0.0	0.3
Loans	0.1	1.7	1.2	0.3	2.0	5.4	1.3	14.4
Equity and investment fund shares	99.6	97.6	98.2	98.6	97.1	92.3	97.3	80.9
Insurance pension and standardised guarantee schemes	0.0	0.0	0.0	0.0	0.0	0.0	0.0	0.0
Financial derivatives and employee stock options	0.1	0.0	0.3	0.0	0.0	0.1	0.1	0.2
Other accounts receivable	0.2	0.6	0.3	1.1	0.9	2.2	1.2	4.2
Insurance corporations								
Financial assets	100.0	100.0	100.0	100.0	100.0	100.0	100.0	100.0
Currency and deposits	6.3	8.8	5.0	8.0	5.9	8.8	6.7	7.6
Debt securities	59.4	53.1	54.8	52.6	51.2	46.2	43.4	43.3
Loans	0.4	0.3	0.2	0.2	0.3	0.4	0.1	0.6
Equity and investment fund shares	22.7	24.6	26.9	28.1	30.9	32.3	37.1	35.9
Insurance pension and standardised guarantee schemes	1.6	1.8	1.7	1.5	1.7	1.6	1.7	1.4
Financial derivatives and employee stock options	0.1	0.0	0.0	0.0	0.0	0.0	0.0	0.0
Other accounts receivable	9.6	11.4	11.4	9.6	10.0	10.6	11.1	11.2
Financial liabilities	100.0	100.0	100.0	100.0	100.0	100.0	100.0	100.0
Currency and deposits	0.0	0.0	0.0	0.0	0.0	0.0	0.0	0.0
Debt securities	0.0	0.0	0.0	0.0	0.0	0.0	0.0	0.0
Loans	0.5	1.8	0.7	0.8	1.2	4.6	5.5	5.1
Equity and investment fund shares	21.7	21.9	17.7	17.2	15.8	15.6	13.1	16.1
Insurance pension and standardised guarantee schemes	70.8	66.8	76.0	77.0	77.6	74.7	76.1	74.8
Financial derivatives and employee stock options	0.0	0.0	0.1	0.0	0.0	0.0	0.0	0.1
Other accounts receivable	7.0	9.5	5.5	5.0	5.4	5.0	5.2	3.9
Pension funds								
Financial assets	100.0	100.0	100.0	100.0	100.0	100.0	100.0	100.0
Currency and deposits	11.9	5.5	6.5	3.8	3.2	6.2	9.3	8.9
Debt securities	46.0	36.7	37.5	38.8	39.6	38.0	40.2	37.7
Loans	0.0	0.0	0.0	0.0	0.0	0.0	0.0	0.0
Equity and investment fund shares	42.1	57.8	56.0	57.3	57.1	55.6	50.4	53.1
Insurance pension and standardised guarantee schemes	0.0	0.0	0.0	0.0	0.0	0.0	0.0	0.0
Financial derivatives and employee stock options	0.0	0.0	0.0	0.0	0.0	0.0	0.0	0.0
Other accounts receivable	0.0	0.0	0.0	0.1	0.1	0.2	0.1	0.3
Financial liabilities	100.0	100.0	100.0	100.0	100.0	100.0	100.0	100.0
Currency and deposits	0.0	0.0	0.0	0.0	0.0	0.0	0.0	0.0
Debt securities	0.0	0.0	0.0	0.0	0.0	0.0	0.0	0.0
Loans	0.0	0.0	0.0	0.0	0.0	0.0	0.0	0.0
Equity and investment fund shares	0.0	0.0	0.0	0.0	0.0	0.0	0.0	0.0
Insurance pension and standardised guarantee schemes	99.8	99.1	99.8	99.8	99.5	99.8	99.7	98.8
Financial derivatives and employee stock options	0.0	0.0	0.0	0.0	0.0	0.0	0.0	0.1
Other accounts receivable	0.2	0.9	0.2	0.2	0.5	0.2	0.3	1.1

Note: Detailed metadata at: http://metalinks.oecd.org/instinv/20170920/a49a

Table 1. Financial assets and liabilities of institutional investors, 2016

Million RUB

	Investment funds				
		Non-money market funds			Money market funds
	Total	Total	Open-end non-money market funds	Closed-end non-money market funds	Total
Financial assets	1 766 933	1 766 933	155 323	1 611 610	..
Currency and deposits	194 437	194 437	5 969	188 468	..
Debt securities	200 520	200 520	83 508	117 012	..
Debt securities, short term	..	..	..	..	..
Debt securities, long term	..	..	..	..	..
Debt securities issued by residents	171 805	171 805	62 431	109 375	..
Debt securities issued by non-residents	28 715	28 715	21 078	7 637	..
Loans	215 754	215 754	14	215 740	..
Loans, short-term	..	..	..	..	..
Loans, long-term	..	..	..	..	..
Loans granted to residents	..	..	..	..	..
Loans granted to non-residents	..	..	..	..	..
Equity and investment fund shares/units	999 279	999 279	60 331	938 948	..
Equity and investment fund shares issued/units by residents	927 673	927 673	42 075	885 598	..
Equity and investment fund shares/units issued by non residents	71 606	71 606	18 256	53 351	..
Other accounts receivable	156 943	156 943	5 501	151 442	..

	Investment funds				
		Non-money market funds			Money market funds
	Total	Total	Open-end non-money market funds	Closed-end non-money market funds	Total
Financial liabilities	2 839 758	2 839 758	155 323	2 684 435	..
Currency and deposits	..	..	..	..	..
Debt securities	..	..	..	..	..
Debt securities, short term	..	..	..	..	..
Debt securities, long term	..	..	..	..	..
Loans	..	..	..	..	..
Loans, short-term	..	..	..	..	..
Loans, long-term	..	..	..	..	..
Equity and investment fund shares/units	2 584 387	2 584 387	153 431	2 430 956	..
Insurance pension and standardised guaratees	..	..	..	..	..
Financial derivatives and employee stock options	..	..	..	..	..
Other accounts payable	255 371	255 371	1 892	253 479	..

	Insurance corporations and pension funds				
		Insurance corporations			Pension funds
	Total	Total	Life insurance corporations	Non-life insurance corporations	Total
Financial assets	5 186 580	1 772 300	-	..	3 414 280
Currency and deposits	1 177 055	603 586	-	..	573 469
Debt securities	2 396 130	497 670	-	..	1 898 460
Debt securities, short-term	..	..	-	..	..
Debt securities, long term	..	..	-	..	..
Debt securities issued by residents	2 238 463	377 089	-	..	1 861 374
Debt securities issued by non-residents	157 668	120 581	-	..	37 086
Loans	15 166	15 154	-	..	12
Loans, short-term	..	..	-	..	..
Loans, long-term	..	..	..	..	..
Loans granted to residents	13 474	13 462	..	..	12
Loans granted to non-residents	1 692	1 692	..	..	0
Equity and investment fund shares/units	1 077 174	149 964	..	..	927 210
Equity and investment fund shares/units issued by residents	1 063 183	143 163	..	..	920 020
Equity and investment fund shares/units issued by non residents	13 991	6 801	..	..	7 190
Other accounts receivable	370 208	355 080	..	..	15 128

	Insurance corporations and pension funds				
		Insurance corporations			Pension funds
	Total	Total	Life insurance corporations	Non-life insurance corporations	Total
Financial liabilities	5 354 385	1 936 139	..	..	3 418 246
Currency and deposits	..	..	..	..	..
Debt securities	12 999	12 999	..	..	0
Debt securities, short term	..	..	..	..	..
Debt securities, long term	..	..	..	..	..
Loans	10 622	10 587	..	..	35
Loans, short-term	..	..	..	..	..
Loans, long-term	..	..	..	..	..
Equity and investment fund shares/units	872 819	688 635	..	..	184 184
Insurance pension and standardised guarantees	4 289 594	1 082 139	..	..	3 207 455
Financial derivatives and employee stock options	0	0	..	..	0
Other accounts payable	168 352	141 780	..	..	26 572

Note: Detailed metadata at: http://metalinks.oecd.org/instinv/20170920/75e8

RUSSIAN FEDERATION

Table 2. Financial assets and liabilities of investment funds

Million RUB

	2009	2010	2011	2012	2013	2014	2015	2016
Investment funds								
Financial net worth	-321 423	-453 212	-555 940	-599 116	-927 518	-1 067 975	-1 133 161	-1 072 824
Financial assets	717 293	764 464	845 167	1 011 243	1 187 664	1 359 209	1 547 779	1 766 933
Currency and deposits	90 793	96 173	105 313	153 160	233 794	194 966	234 968	194 437
Debt securities	44 528	44 118	61 175	84 965	106 406	144 442	163 010	200 520
Loans	1 743	6 297	6 518	4 485	5 573	5 048	6 302	215 754
Equity and investment fund shares	493 938	488 490	507 649	582 323	568 263	676 092	743 265	999 279
Equity	484 892	482 268	499 573	571 058	553 341	651 281	709 459	981 172
Investment fund shares	9 047	6 223	8 076	11 264	14 922	24 810	33 806	18 107
Money market fund shares	..	..	..	..	..	..	..	..
Non-Money market fund shares	9 047	6 223	8 076	11 264	14 922	24 810	33 806	18 107
Insurance pension and standardised guarantees	..	..	..	..	..	..	..	..
Financial derivatives and employee stock options	..	..	..	..	..	..	..	..
Other accounts receivable	86 291	129 386	164 511	186 310	273 629	338 662	400 234	156 943
Financial liabilities	1 038 715	1 217 676	1 401 107	1 610 359	2 115 182	2 427 184	2 680 939	2 839 758
Debt securities	..	..	..	..	..	..	..	..
Short-term debt securities	..	..	..	..	..	..	..	..
Long-term debt securities	..	..	..	..	..	..	..	..
Loans	..	..	..	..	..	..	..	..
Short-term loans	..	..	..	..	..	..	..	..
Long-term loans	..	..	..	..	..	..	..	..
Equity and investment fund shares	946 495	1 130 038	1 294 249	1 456 131	1 870 555	2 141 000	2 387 732	2 584 387
Insurance pension and standardised guarantees	..	..	..	..	..	..	..	..
Financial derivatives and employee stock options	..	..	..	..	..	..	..	..
Other accounts payable	92 220	87 638	106 857	154 229	244 627	286 184	293 207	255 371
Non-financial assets	321 423	453 212	562 096	747 099	928 734	1 057 455	1 133 161	1 072 824
Money market funds								
Financial net worth	..	..	..	..	..	..	..	..
Financial assets	..	..	..	..	..	..	..	..
Currency and deposits	..	..	..	..	..	..	..	..
Debt securities	..	..	..	..	..	..	..	..
Loans	..	..	..	..	..	..	..	..
Equity and investment fund shares	..	..	..	..	..	..	..	..
Equity	..	..	..	..	..	..	..	..
Investment fund shares	..	..	..	..	..	..	..	..
Money market fund shares	..	..	..	..	..	..	..	..
Non-Money market fund shares	..	..	..	..	..	..	..	..
Insurance pension and standardised guarantees	..	..	..	..	..	..	..	..
Financial derivatives and employee stock options	..	..	..	..	..	..	..	..
Other accounts receivable	..	..	..	..	..	..	..	..
Financial liabilities	..	..	..	..	..	..	..	..
Debt securities	..	..	..	..	..	..	..	..
Short-term debt securities	..	..	..	..	..	..	..	..
Long-term debt securities	..	..	..	..	..	..	..	..
Loans	..	..	..	..	..	..	..	..
Short-term loans	..	..	..	..	..	..	..	..
Long-term loans	..	..	..	..	..	..	..	..
Equity and investment fund shares	..	..	..	..	..	..	..	..
Insurance pension and standardised guarantees	..	..	..	..	..	..	..	..
Financial derivatives and employee stock options	..	..	..	..	..	..	..	..
Other accounts payable	..	..	..	..	..	..	..	..
Non-financial assets	..	..	..	..	..	..	..	..
Non-money market funds								
Financial net worth	-321 423	-453 212	-555 940	-599 116	-927 518	-1 067 975	-1 133 161	-1 072 824
Financial assets	717 293	764 464	845 167	1 011 243	1 187 664	1 359 209	1 547 779	1 766 933
Currency and deposits	90 793	96 173	105 313	153 160	233 794	194 966	234 968	194 437
Debt securities	44 528	44 118	61 175	84 965	106 406	144 442	163 010	200 520
Loans	1 743	6 297	6 518	4 485	5 573	5 048	6 302	215 754
Equity and investment fund shares	493 938	488 490	507 649	582 323	568 263	676 092	743 265	999 279
Equity	484 892	482 268	499 573	571 058	553 341	651 281	709 459	981 172
Investment fund shares	9 047	6 223	8 076	11 264	14 922	24 810	33 806	18 107
Money market fund shares	..	..	..	..	..	..	..	..
Non-Money market fund shares	9 047	6 223	8 076	11 264	14 922	24 810	33 806	18 107
Insurance pension and standardised guarantees	..	..	..	..	..	..	..	..
Financial derivatives and employee stock options	..	..	..	..	..	..	..	..
Other accounts receivable	86 291	129 386	164 511	186 310	273 629	338 662	400 234	156 943
Financial liabilities	1 038 715	1 217 676	1 401 107	1 610 359	2 115 182	2 427 184	2 680 939	2 839 758
Debt securities	..	..	..	..	..	..	..	..
Short-term debt securities	..	..	..	..	..	..	..	..
Long-term debt securities	..	..	..	..	..	..	..	..
Loans	..	..	..	..	..	..	..	..
Short-term loans	..	..	..	..	..	..	..	..
Long-term loans	..	..	..	..	..	..	..	..
Equity and investment fund shares	946 495	1 130 038	1 294 249	1 456 131	1 870 555	2 141 000	2 387 732	2 584 387
Insurance pension and standardised guarantees	..	..	..	..	..	..	..	..
Financial derivatives and employee stock options	..	..	..	..	..	..	..	..
Other accounts payable	92 220	87 638	106 857	154 229	244 627	286 184	293 207	255 371
Non-financial assets	321 423	453 212	562 096	747 099	928 734	1 057 455	1 133 161	1 072 824
Open-end non-money market funds								
Financial net worth	-2 084	-2 238	-2 388	-2 528	-2 526	-2 400	-2 920	0
Financial assets	101 912	128 527	107 837	112 154	137 703	111 968	137 979	155 323

Table 2. Financial assets and liabilities of investment funds *(cont.)*

Million RUB

	2009	2010	2011	2012	2013	2014	2015	2016
Currency and deposits	4 259	4 599	3 991	7 149	15 862	10 863	9 497	5 969
Debt securities	18 361	23 081	28 488	40 247	64 521	38 613	57 923	83 508
Loans	0	0	0	0	0	0	0	14
Equity and investment fund shares	72 406	92 371	66 530	57 055	47 940	55 217	65 307	60 331
Equity	71 633	89 715	62 069	49 831	38 593	36 877	39 934	47 567
Investment fund shares	774	2 656	4 461	7 224	9 347	18 340	25 373	12 764
Money market fund shares	..	..	..	..	..	..	..	..
Non-Money market fund shares	774	2 656	4 461	7 224	9 347	18 340	25 373	12 764
Insurance pension and standardised guarantees	..	..	..	..	..	..	..	..
Financial derivatives and employee stock options	..	..	..	..	..	..	..	..
Other accounts receivable	6 886	8 477	8 828	7 703	9 381	7 275	5 252	5 501
Financial liabilities	103 997	130 766	110 224	114 682	140 229	114 368	140 898	155 323
Debt securities	..	..	..	..	..	..	..	..
Short-term debt securities	..	..	..	..	..	..	..	..
Long-term debt securities	..	..	..	..	..	..	..	..
Loans	..	..	..	..	..	..	..	..
Short-term loans	..	..	..	..	..	..	..	..
Long-term loans	..	..	..	..	..	..	..	..
Equity and investment fund shares	102 409	128 626	108 600	113 360	138 551	111 901	139 000	153 431
Insurance pension and standardised guarantees	..	..	..	..	..	..	..	..
Financial derivatives and employee stock options	..	..	..	..	..	..	..	..
Other accounts payable	1 587	2 140	1 625	1 323	1 678	2 466	1 899	1 892
Non-financial assets	2 084	2 238	2 388	2 528	2 526	2 400	2 920	0
Open-end investment funds								
Financial net worth	-2 084	-2 238	-2 388	-2 528	-2 526	-2 400	-2 920	0
Financial assets	101 912	128 527	107 837	112 154	137 703	111 968	137 979	155 323
Currency and deposits	4 259	4 599	3 991	7 149	15 862	10 863	9 497	5 969
Debt securities	18 361	23 081	28 488	40 247	64 521	38 613	57 923	83 508
Loans	0	0	0	0	0	0	0	14
Equity and investment fund shares	72 406	92 371	66 530	57 055	47 940	55 217	65 307	60 331
Equity	71 633	89 715	62 069	49 831	38 593	36 877	39 934	47 567
Investment fund shares	774	2 656	4 461	7 224	9 347	18 340	25 373	12 764
Money market fund shares	..	..	..	..	..	..	..	..
Non-Money market fund shares	774	2 656	4 461	7 224	9 347	18 340	25 373	12 764
Insurance pension and standardised guarantees	..	..	..	..	..	..	..	..
Financial derivatives and employee stock options	..	..	..	..	..	..	..	..
Other accounts receivable	6 886	8 477	8 828	7 703	9 381	7 275	5 252	5 501
Financial liabilities	103 997	130 766	110 224	114 682	140 229	114 368	140 898	155 323
Debt securities	..	..	..	..	..	..	..	..
Short-term debt securities	..	..	..	..	..	..	..	..
Long-term debt securities	..	..	..	..	..	..	..	..
Loans	..	..	..	..	..	..	..	..
Short-term loans	..	..	..	..	..	..	..	..
Long-term loans	..	..	..	..	..	..	..	..
Equity and investment fund shares	102 409	128 626	108 600	113 360	138 551	111 901	139 000	153 431
Insurance pension and standardised guarantees	..	..	..	..	..	..	..	..
Financial derivatives and employee stock options	..	..	..	..	..	..	..	..
Other accounts payable	1 587	2 140	1 625	1 323	1 678	2 466	1 899	1 892
Non-financial assets	2 084	2 238	2 388	2 528	2 526	2 400	2 920	0

Note: Detailed metadata at: http://metalinks.oecd.org/instinv/20170920/75e8

Table 3. Financial assets and liabilities of insurance corporations and pension funds

Million RUB

	2009	2010	2011	2012	2013	2014	2015	2016
Insurance corporations and pension funds								
Financial net worth	-53 422	-77 451	-59 743	-36 437	-174 679	-195 800	-189 916	-167 805
Financial assets	1 569 827	1 754 805	2 138 367	2 623 687	3 285 681	3 621 747	4 383 131	5 186 580
Currency and deposits	426 888	459 955	575 393	782 878	884 194	1 009 962	1 124 722	1 177 055
Debt securities	446 486	456 295	634 828	766 267	1 118 204	1 246 384	1 815 796	2 396 130
Loans	15 060	9 145	15 342	10 643	14 830	21 854	12 441	15 166
Equity and investment fund shares	406 619	541 295	571 913	637 540	707 154	740 973	909 213	1 077 174
Equity	269 389	379 740	408 386	409 928	471 794	512 665	638 755	850 250
Investment fund shares	137 229	161 555	163 527	227 612	235 360	228 308	270 458	226 924
Money market fund shares	..	..	..	..	..	..	..	..
Non-Money market fund shares	137 229	161 555	163 527	227 612	235 360	228 308	270 458	226 924
Insurance pension and standardised guarantees	65 297	70 267	71 588	90 002	108 240	158 480	130 128	150 781
Financial derivatives and employee stock options	..	..	..	..	..	..	31	65
Other accounts receivable	209 478	217 847	269 302	336 293	453 059	444 094	390 799	370 208
Financial liabilities	1 623 249	1 832 256	2 198 110	2 660 124	3 460 360	3 817 547	4 573 047	5 354 385
Debt securities	4 458	18 331	9 823	13 764	16 456	11 227	10 662	12 999
Short-term debt securities	..	..	..	..	..	..	..	..
Long-term debt securities	..	..	..	..	..	..	..	..
Loans	24 960	26 388	27 716	22 965	22 629	18 545	11 657	10 622
Short-term loans	..	..	..	..	..	..	..	..
Long-term loans	..	..	..	..	..	..	..	..
Equity and investment fund shares	349 563	360 561	391 464	470 831	642 559	710 356	765 520	872 819
Insurance pension and standardised guarantees	1 068 896	1 257 975	1 640 176	2 006 075	2 602 244	2 874 440	3 622 879	4 289 594
Financial derivatives and employee stock options	..	..	..	..	..	..	0	0
Other accounts payable	175 372	169 001	128 931	146 489	176 472	202 979	162 329	168 352
Non-financial assets	53 422	77 451	90 315	95 194	91 047	97 464	95 451	95 341
Insurance corporations								
Financial net worth	-45 558	-69 469	-54 416	-34 113	-164 872	-188 535	-182 588	-163 839
Financial assets	836 355	857 179	944 406	1 076 411	1 233 629	1 443 045	1 507 129	1 772 300
Currency and deposits	253 326	258 372	325 448	353 259	375 724	439 713	521 204	603 586
Debt securities	205 332	200 130	231 397	255 781	307 279	330 003	368 514	497 670
Loans	13 482	8 162	13 191	9 163	14 648	21 710	12 334	15 154
Equity and investment fund shares	110 866	116 887	100 438	126 166	138 441	157 677	147 278	149 964
Equity	103 319	106 278	91 407	117 211	129 721	149 017	133 406	141 959
Investment fund shares	7 546	10 609	9 032	8 955	8 720	8 660	13 872	8 005
Money market fund shares	..	..	..	..	..	..	..	..
Non-Money market fund shares	7 546	10 609	9 032	8 955	8 720	8 660	13 872	8 005
Insurance pension and standardised guarantees	65 297	70 267	71 588	90 002	108 240	158 480	130 128	150 781
Financial derivatives and employee stock options	..	..	..	..	..	..	31	65
Other accounts receivable	188 052	203 361	202 343	241 975	289 297	335 462	327 638	355 080
Financial liabilities	881 913	926 648	998 822	1 110 524	1 398 501	1 631 580	1 689 717	1 936 139
Debt securities	4 458	18 331	9 823	13 764	16 456	11 227	10 662	12 999
Short-term debt securities	..	..	..	..	..	..	..	..
Long-term debt securities	..	..	..	..	..	..	..	..
Loans	24 669	26 232	26 319	20 669	21 452	17 086	11 488	10 587
Short-term loans	..	..	..	..	..	..	..	..
Long-term loans	..	..	..	..	..	..	..	..
Equity and investment fund shares	254 710	259 219	293 839	362 679	517 612	567 245	600 911	688 635
Insurance pension and standardised guarantees	429 818	462 226	545 931	579 072	684 034	845 958	928 531	1 082 139
Financial derivatives and employee stock options	..	..	..	..	..	..	0	0
Other accounts payable	168 258	160 640	122 910	134 340	158 947	190 064	138 125	141 780
Non-financial assets	45 558	69 469	82 419	89 494	85 687	92 936	91 487	91 044
Pension funds								
Financial net worth	-7 864	-7 982	-5 327	-2 324	-9 806	-7 265	-7 328	-3 966
Financial assets	733 472	897 626	1 193 961	1 547 276	2 052 053	2 178 702	2 876 002	3 414 280
Currency and deposits	173 562	201 583	249 945	429 619	508 470	570 249	603 518	573 469
Debt securities	241 154	256 165	403 431	510 486	810 925	916 381	1 447 282	1 898 460
Loans	1 577	983	2 151	1 480	182	144	107	12
Equity and investment fund shares	295 753	424 409	471 475	511 374	568 714	583 296	761 935	927 210
Equity	166 070	273 463	316 979	292 717	342 074	363 648	505 349	708 290
Investment fund shares	129 683	150 946	154 496	218 657	226 640	219 648	256 586	218 920
Money market fund shares	..	..	..	..	..	..	..	..
Non-Money market fund shares	129 683	150 946	154 496	218 657	226 640	219 648	256 586	218 920
Insurance pension and standardised guarantees	..	..	..	..	..	..	..	..
Financial derivatives and employee stock options	..	..	..	..	..	..	0	0
Other accounts receivable	21 426	14 486	66 959	94 318	163 762	108 632	63 161	15 128
Financial liabilities	741 336	905 608	1 199 288	1 549 600	2 061 859	2 185 967	2 883 330	3 418 246
Debt securities	0	0	0	0	0	0	0	0
Short-term debt securities	..	..	..	..	..	..	..	..
Long-term debt securities	..	..	..	..	..	..	..	..
Loans	291	155	1 397	2 296	1 177	1 459	169	35
Short-term loans	..	..	..	..	..	..	..	..
Long-term loans	..	..	..	..	..	..	..	..
Equity and investment fund shares	94 853	101 342	97 625	108 152	124 947	143 111	164 609	184 184
Insurance pension and standardised guarantees	639 078	795 749	1 094 245	1 427 003	1 918 210	2 028 482	2 694 348	3 207 455
Financial derivatives and employee stock options	..	..	..	..	..	..	0	0
Other accounts payable	7 114	8 361	6 021	12 149	17 525	12 915	24 204	26 572
Non-financial assets	7 864	7 982	7 896	5 700	5 360	4 528	3 963	4 298

Note: Detailed metadata at: http://metalinks.oecd.org/instinv/20170920/75e8

Table 4. Portfolio composition by type of investor

As percentage of financial assets and of financial liabilities

Per cent

	2009	2010	2011	2012	2013	2014	2015	2016
Investment funds								
Financial assets	100.0	100.0	100.0	100.0	100.0	100.0	100.0	100.0
Currency and deposits	12.7	12.6	12.5	15.1	19.7	14.3	15.2	11.0
Debt securities	6.2	5.8	7.2	8.4	9.0	10.6	10.5	11.3
Loans	0.2	0.8	0.8	0.4	0.5	0.4	0.4	12.2
Equity and investment fund shares	68.9	63.9	60.1	57.6	47.8	49.7	48.0	56.6
Insurance pension and standardised guarantee schemes	0.0	0.0	0.0	0.0	0.0	0.0	0.0	0.0
Financial derivatives and employee stock options	0.0	0.0	0.0	0.0	0.0	0.0	0.0	0.0
Other accounts receivable	12.0	16.9	19.5	18.4	23.0	24.9	25.9	8.9
Financial liabilities	100.0	100.0	100.0	100.0	100.0	100.0	100.0	100.0
Currency and deposits	0.0	0.0	0.0	0.0	0.0	0.0	0.0	0.0
Debt securities	0.0	0.0	0.0	0.0	0.0	0.0	0.0	0.0
Loans	0.0	0.0	0.0	0.0	0.0	0.0	0.0	0.0
Equity and investment fund shares	91.1	92.8	92.4	90.4	88.4	88.2	89.1	91.0
Insurance pension and standardised guarantee schemes	0.0	0.0	0.0	0.0	0.0	0.0	0.0	0.0
Financial derivatives and employee stock options	0.0	0.0	0.0	0.0	0.0	0.0	0.0	0.0
Other accounts receivable	8.9	7.2	7.6	9.6	11.6	11.8	10.9	9.0
Insurance corporations								
Financial assets	100.0	100.0	100.0	100.0	100.0	100.0	100.0	100.0
Currency and deposits	30.3	30.1	34.5	32.8	30.5	30.5	34.6	34.1
Debt securities	24.6	23.3	24.5	23.8	24.9	22.9	24.5	28.1
Loans	1.6	1.0	1.4	0.9	1.2	1.5	0.8	0.9
Equity and investment fund shares	13.3	13.6	10.6	11.7	11.2	10.9	9.8	8.5
Insurance pension and standardised guarantee schemes	7.8	8.2	7.6	8.4	8.8	11.0	8.6	8.5
Financial derivatives and employee stock options	0.0	0.0	0.0	0.0	0.0	0.0	0.0	0.0
Other accounts receivable	22.5	23.7	21.4	22.5	23.5	23.2	21.7	20.0
Financial liabilities	100.0	100.0	100.0	100.0	100.0	100.0	100.0	100.0
Currency and deposits	0.0	0.0	0.0	0.0	0.0	0.0	0.0	0.0
Debt securities	0.5	2.0	1.0	1.2	1.2	0.7	0.6	0.7
Loans	2.8	2.8	2.6	1.9	1.5	1.0	0.7	0.5
Equity and investment fund shares	28.9	28.0	29.4	32.7	37.0	34.8	35.6	35.6
Insurance pension and standardised guarantee schemes	48.7	49.9	54.7	52.1	48.9	51.8	55.0	55.9
Financial derivatives and employee stock options	0.0	0.0	0.0	0.0	0.0	0.0	0.0	0.0
Other accounts receivable	19.1	17.3	12.3	12.1	11.4	11.6	8.2	7.3
Pension funds								
Financial assets	100.0	100.0	100.0	100.0	100.0	100.0	100.0	100.0
Currency and deposits	23.7	22.5	20.9	27.8	24.8	26.2	21.0	16.8
Debt securities	32.9	28.5	33.8	33.0	39.5	42.1	50.3	55.6
Loans	0.2	0.1	0.2	0.1	0.0	0.0	0.0	0.0
Equity and investment fund shares	40.3	47.3	39.5	33.0	27.7	26.8	26.5	27.2
Insurance pension and standardised guarantee schemes	0.0	0.0	0.0	0.0	0.0	0.0	0.0	0.0
Financial derivatives and employee stock options	0.0	0.0	0.0	0.0	0.0	0.0	0.0	0.0
Other accounts receivable	2.9	1.6	5.6	6.1	8.0	5.0	2.2	0.4
Financial liabilities	100.0	100.0	100.0	100.0	100.0	100.0	100.0	100.0
Currency and deposits	0.0	0.0	0.0	0.0	0.0	0.0	0.0	0.0
Debt securities	0.0	0.0	0.0	0.0	0.0	0.0	0.0	0.0
Loans	0.0	0.0	0.1	0.1	0.1	0.1	0.0	0.0
Equity and investment fund shares	12.8	11.2	8.1	7.0	6.1	6.5	5.7	5.4
Insurance pension and standardised guarantee schemes	86.2	87.9	91.2	92.1	93.0	92.8	93.4	93.8
Financial derivatives and employee stock options	0.0	0.0	0.0	0.0	0.0	0.0	0.0	0.0
Other accounts receivable	1.0	0.9	0.5	0.8	0.8	0.6	0.8	0.8

Note: Detailed metadata at: http://metalinks.oecd.org/instinv/20170920/a49a

ORGANISATION FOR ECONOMIC CO-OPERATION AND DEVELOPMENT

The OECD is a unique forum where governments work together to address the economic, social and environmental challenges of globalisation. The OECD is also at the forefront of efforts to understand and to help governments respond to new developments and concerns, such as corporate governance, the information economy and the challenges of an ageing population. The Organisation provides a setting where governments can compare policy experiences, seek answers to common problems, identify good practice and work to co-ordinate domestic and international policies.

The OECD member countries are: Australia, Austria, Belgium, Canada, Chile, the Czech Republic, Denmark, Estonia, Finland, France, Germany, Greece, Hungary, Iceland, Ireland, Israel, Italy, Japan, Korea, Latvia, Luxembourg, Mexico, the Netherlands, New Zealand, Norway, Poland, Portugal, the Slovak Republic, Slovenia, Spain, Sweden, Switzerland, Turkey, the United Kingdom and the United States. The European Union takes part in the work of the OECD.

OECD Publishing disseminates widely the results of the Organisation's statistics gathering and research on economic, social and environmental issues, as well as the conventions, guidelines and standards agreed by its members.

OECD PUBLISHING, 2, rue André-Pascal, 75775 PARIS CEDEX 16
(01 2017 17 1 P) ISBN 978-92-64-28227-8 – 2017

www.ingramcontent.com/pod-product-compliance
Lightning Source LLC
Chambersburg PA
CBHW061213240926
51846CB00006B/1205